To Buddy Schulberg

Best wishes

Buddie

Follow your dad!

Marion Davies

Adolph Menjou

Sept. 8/26

To Buddy

"never forget —

you're a Schulberg"

Ricardo Cortez

aug. 23/26

To Buddy

From just a bum off

Old Ironsides

Wallace Beery

MOVING PICTURES

BUDD

MOVING

Memories of

SCHULBERG

PICTURES

a *Hollywood* *Prince*

STEIN AND DAY/Publishers/New York

Except for the stills, all the photographs in this book are from the private collections of Sonya, Budd, and Ad Schulberg.

First published in 1981
Copyright © 1981 by Budd Schulberg
All rights reserved
Designed by Louis A. Ditizio
Printed in the United States of America
STEIN AND DAY / *Publishers*
Scarborough House
Briarcliff Manor, N.Y. 10510

Library of Congress Cataloging in Publication Data

Schulberg, Budd
    Moving pictures, memories of a Hollywood prince.

    Includes index.
    1. Schulberg, Budd—Biography. 2. Authors, American—
20th century—Biography. 3. Moving-pictures—United States—
Biography. I Title.
PS3537.C7114Z52   818'.5209 [B]   80-9055
ISBN 0-8128-2817-8   AACR2

*For Ad and B.P., my parents—
motion-picture pioneers—
and for Sonya and Stuart,
with love*

OTHER WORKS BY BUDD SCHULBERG

ACKNOWLEDGMENTS

Background material for this work, particularly in the early chapters, has been drawn from B. P. Schulberg's unpublished manuscript, *Thirty-Odd Years.*

In the course of writing this book, the author has received invaluable editorial suggestions, at first from his late wife, Geraldine Brooks, and later from Jeanne Bernkopf, Maurice Rapf, Betsy Langman Schulberg, Alyss Dorese, and Sol Stein.

Over the years, Stan Silverman unselfishly has read and reread the manuscript with both friendly heart and critical eye, a combination that has aided and greatly encouraged its progress. The writer is also grateful to Mabel Nowark, whose magic fingers typed and retyped the manuscript around the clock, oblivious of weekends. To all the above, and to others who helped along the way—as we say in Mexico—"a thousand thank-you's."

—Brookside, February 1981

CONTENTS

Follows page 55

Ad Schulberg, and B. P. Schulberg, *circa* 1928

Edwin S. Porter, the director of *The Great Train Robbery,* with an early version of the film projector

Pat Powers, Adolf Zukor, Mrs. Zukor, Al Kaufman, and B. P. Schulberg, in front of the *Santa Fe Chief*

Ad, B.P., and Joe Roche

Jerry Mayer and B. P. Schulberg patting the head of a lion badly in need of a hairdresser

The Schulberg library

Jackie Coogan's birthday party, with Marjorie Lesser, Julian "Buddy" Lesser, Budd Schulberg, and Sonya Schulberg

B. P. Schulberg, Ad, and baby Budd

Leon Errol, Al Kaufman, Buddy Rogers, Jack Okie, Jessie Lasky, B. P. Schulberg, Clive Brook, Ruth Chatterton, a mystery couple, Eddie Goulding, Harry Green, and Mike Levee

The Mayer–Schulberg studio north of downtown Los Angeles

B. P. Schulberg and Ad, *circa* 1927, on a trip through the Panama Canal

I

GENESIS

1

ETWEEN ME AND my childhood is a wall. I struggle with some half-remembered incident, and it is like a loose stone in the wall. The loose stone may be a chance word or a dimly remembered face, the faintest fragment of a memory. I work at that fragment with the fingers of my mind, until I am able to pull it out and hold it in my hands. Now it is a little easier to loosen another stone, and another, until I have made a hole large enough to crawl through. On one side of the wall is a man in his sixties who has seen almost everything— marvelous days when life cries out *Yes Yes Yes*! with Molly Bloom, and days so dark that I begin to question Faulkner's Nobel confidence that man will endure. On the other side of the wall is the infant who has seen almost nothing except fingers and toes and the dim boundaries of an airless room.

To tell my story from the point of view of the infant who becomes the child, the youth, and the adult is to employ a familiar literary device but one that has never seemed altogether scrupulous to me. But to write it from the hindsight, the so-called wisdom which is really that of the navigator making corrections for errors, is equally unsatisfactory. The one-year-old lives on in the man of sixty-odd and the sixty-odd was there in the frightened one-year-old who didn't know where he was or why he was; the mind is the same one, merely battered, challenged, and improved. This is not the complete story, the accurate replay, this is only what the one-year-old, and all the progressive years that inhabited the body identified as *budd schulberg,* have been able to piece together. I am my own team of archeologists digging down in time, and the memories are scattered shards, a haphazard collection until they are assembled. If sometimes the four-year-old thinks or talks like a man of sixty, or the sexagenarian sounds more like a child of four, you may charge that to the inevitable failures in the methods of personal archeology. Or to the failure of this sort of dichotomous collaboration.

So I invite you to follow me through the wall. Peer into the door of the splendid New York apartment house on 120th Street, facing Mt. Morris Park, where I opened my eyes for the first time. I was in a small, Victorian-cluttered bedroom of a three-room apartment off Fifth Avenue in a comfortable middle-class section of upper Manhattan called Harlem. The young Jewish doctor who lived in the building handed me to my mother, Adeline. Barely out of her teens, weighing only ninety pounds, she was frail, sensitive, and pretty in that wistful Mary Pickford-Lillian Gish way that was the style before the flappers displaced them in the Twenties. Young Adeline had been carried across the ocean in her mother's arms, the Jaffe family on the run from the Cossacks who terrorized their native Dvinsk, the lowly village-sister of Minsk and Pinsk that was in Poland or Sweden or Germany or Russia as the tides of history changed the flags but not the bottom-dog status of the Jews in the ghetto near the river Dvina. Practically all Adeline could recall from that brief period was a trip to St. Petersburg with her mother Hannah, escorted by her uncle, a diamond-cutter to the Czar, one of the few Jews allowed to enter that hallowed Russian Orthodox capital. There Grandmother Hannah woke in terror. In a nightmare she had seen a plague settle over Dvinsk, killing her children. When she took the next train back she found that her dream had been a subconscious flash of reality. An epidemic had swept through the ghetto and the three children next in age to baby Adeline were dead. Hannah's best friend who lived in the adjoining cottage had lost all her children and had drowned herself in the well.

The tragedy triggered Hannah's decision to join her husband in America. Grandpa Max had gone on ahead to try and plant a few seeds of security on which the Jaffe family could depend if they were able to reach that mysterious new world. Now Hannah's Brother-the-Diamond-cutter used his money to bribe the border guards. An underground railroad said to be financed by the Rothschilds moved the Jaffe family, Hannah, the two older sons Joseph and David, and the infant Adeline, into Germany, Amsterdam, Liverpool . . . where somehow they found their way into one of those overcrowded steerage holds where they rocked and pitched, threw up and prayed, wondered and wearily waited in pursuit of a dream they had not yet learned to call American, a dream that took them to the cluttered narrow streets and the dark and crowded tenements of the Lower East Side.

Adeline's father, Max, was one of the tens of thousands of lost souls transplanted from Russian ghettos to their American equivalent. At least on Madison Street there were no Cossacks to come charging into their village and burn their huts. And no pogroms. Only a harsh and hostile metropolis that dared them to struggle to survive. Grandpa Max ran a humble luggage store, the poor selling to the poor, and lived in a dream world of pious poverty. He was one of the nondescript army of Jews without money, who lived for their Sabbath ceremonies and the protective socializing of the synagogue.

My paternal grandfather, Simon, had only one thing in common with Grandpa Max: poverty. For some mysterious reason, Grandpa Simon emigrated to Bridgeport, Connecticut (where my father was born), then found his way to Manhattan's Lower East Side. While Max spent every moment he could spare from his home or the luggage shop *davening* in the synagogue, Simon never went to *shul*. Instead, to the horror of my paternal grandmother, Sarah, he took to drink. He would spend his days and nights in the riverfront saloons with the Irish bums, loafers, sailors, and petty hoodlums.

This singular grandfather, it seemed, had also adopted the splendid belligerence of the Irish. Because he had a round, ruddy face and refused to wear a beard, the barflies did not hesitate to speak their minds on the subject of "the dirty Jews" infesting the neighborhood. This was just what Grandpa Simon was waiting for. "I'm a Jew meself!" he'd announce with an ethnic pride the Irishers considered their own special province. Then he'd challenge them to come outside. Adeline remembers Grandpa Simon returning home, staggering from booze and punches, but proud of the walloping he had given "them anti-Semits."

As I grew a little older I always knew what Grandpa Max was doing because I could see him doing it, languishing sadly in his rundown luggage store, or presiding proudly in the synagogue. But Grandpa Simon's life was a mystery. For years, as I became interested in our little stump of a family tree, the more I asked "What did my grandfather do?", the less satisfactory was the answer. "Oh he . . . he was a . . . he did all sorts of things, he . . ."

"But what did my grandfather *do?*" I would beg of my mother, my father, and other relatives. One day, years later, Father finally broke down and told me: "Buddy, your grandfather—well, I suppose you'd have to call him a bum. He never held a regular job. He'd pick up a dollar a day as a sandwich man—a fellow who walks the street with a sandwich-board slung around his neck—'Eat at Joe's'—a human billboard. That's all I can tell you." Apparently Grandpa's life-style was to take that hard-earned buck, slap it down on the bar of the corner saloon, and nurse his five-cent beer while waiting for the next anti-Semitic remark.

Between Grandpa Simon bending his elbow in the saloon and Grandpa Max rocking back and forth in his beloved synagogue, there was very little money coming in to either the Schulberg or the Jaffe family. But, as with so many second-generation ghetto children, there seemed to be some special spark burning in Ben Schulberg and Adeline, who became childhood sweethearts. Ben enjoyed school and was soon bewitched by the sound of the English language. The brightest boy in his class, he was singled out to go to Townsend Harris, then the model high school in Manhattan. There he won a prize for the best short story by a schoolboy in the city of New York. Adeline also loved books and dreamed of becoming a librarian. Ben went on to City College, and began reading through the English classics. But with Grandpa Simon unable to provide anything but his daily beers, help was needed to put food on the table and Ben had to go to work. Luck brought him a job as a copyboy for Franklin Pierce Adams, the eminent "F.P.A.," conductor of "The Conning Tower" column in *The New York Mail,* which was to be read even more widely when Adams moved on to *The World.*

Bitten by the newspaper bug, Ben was promoted to cub reporter on the *Mail.* One of his jobs, "the lowest on the paper," he said, was to review the one-reel movies that were mushrooming in the nickelodeons of the Bowery and along 14th Street. His reviews led to a job as associate editor of one of the earliest trade journals, *Film Reports,* where he was paid a then-comfortable salary of twenty-five dollars a week and a percentage of the ads he could bring in. This meant open sesame to all the film production then flourishing in New York.

Movies were called "flicks" in those days because they really flickered. The Edison Company that controlled the patent and hence the industry was convinced that a one-reel, ten-minute show was the ultimate for the medium. Still, the motion picture was such a novelty that tens of thousands of nickels flowed into the makeshift "movie houses" every week. Young Schulberg, already signing himself "B. P. Schulberg" to make his byline belie his age, found himself on the ground floor of the infant industry.

The slender, pink-faced 22-year-old who stared down at the infant me looked neither old enough to be a father nor mature enough to be a veteran writer of the photoplay, as it was then called. But already he had cranked out hundreds of one-reel photoplays, at the rate of two a week, and as a sign of his veteran's status, had been invited to write the preface to A. W. Thomas's *How to Write a Photoplay.*

Thomas's byline on the title page is followed by five lines of identification:

> President Photoplaywright Association of America, Editor Photoplay Magazine, Editor Photoplay Scenario, Author of Photoplay Helps and Hints and the Photoplay "Punch"; Member of the Photoplay Authors' League, Screen and Ed-Au Club.

Perhaps this long-forgotten photoplaywright felt a need to write this advertisement for himself because, from 1905 onward, the screenwriter has always been low-man on the cinematic totem pole. The most ardent movie buff will remember the entire cast of a given picture, and tick off the names of the director and the producer. Ask him the name of the scribe who conceived the plot, the characters, the theme, and who wrote the words his favorites speak with such conviction, and a vague cloud floats across his eyes. Books on Hollywood and the history of motion pictures spawn like minnows in the spring, but the genesis and development of the photoplaywright (now simplified to *screenwriter*) remain virtually unrecorded. Even the writers themselves have not regarded their profession with sufficient seriousness to trace its history. Still, my boyish-faced papa was one of the originals, and so I came into the world hearing not the strains of "Rock-a-bye, Baby" or "Just a Song at Twilight," but the clicking of typewriter keys.

The films that were being cranked out in the year of my birth held enough promise for Vachel Lindsay, the populist poet, to write a book titled *The Art of the Moving Pictures,* in which he trumpeted the movies as the most revolutionary civilizing force since the invention of the printing press. My father prized that book because he was as much in love with words as he was with the play without words that had become his passion and his livelihood. The catchy tom-tom rhythms of Vachel

Lindsay, sounding social warnings, contributed to the background music of my early years, along with the clicking of that old Underwood and the cranking of the now-obsolete boxlike movie camera.

For, by the time I appeared in 1914, my father was working for one of the first film tycoons, the diminutive, untiring immigrant fur worker, Adolph Zukor, whose Famous Players Company was still a fledgling. For writing scenarios and publicity, B.P. had now achieved the lordly salary of fifty dollars a week. And he was moonlighting: writing a series of four one-reel documentaries on Sylvia Pankhurst, the English suffragist leader, who had come to America to promote the cause, and who had been dragged off to jail from the meeting my mother had attended. It was through Adeline's connections with the movement that B.P. had gotten the assignment, at fifty dollars per reel. So my birth had been financed in true collaboration: my father's screenwriting skills married to my mother's interest in the feminist pioneers. This was a first for all three of us: my first moments on earth, my father's first documentary film, and my mother's first efforts as a writer's agent.

My delivery, my baby clothes, and all the luxuries that would be lavished on my infancy were supplied by the latest and liveliest of the arts. My first carriage was presented to me by the Adolph Zukors, and from their farm outside the city they sent fresh milk and eggs to help little Buddy, as I was called, grow strong. The Zukors' son-in-law, Al Kaufman, an executive in the young company and a crony of B.P.'s, presented me with a sailor suit. Mary Pickford, at twenty-one the most famous of the Famous Players, sent Buddy a woolly blanket. B.P. had just written one of her current movies (and long one of her favorites), *Tess of the Storm Country,* and had coined the phrase that practically became part of her name, "America's Sweetheart." The business that people had scoffed at as an overnight fad when my father first drifted into it was going through its first great transition. Mary Pickford (nee Gladys Smith), who had earned five dollars a day as an anonymous extra in 1909, was earning an astronomical four thousand dollars a week in 1914. The American public, tired of stale vaudeville jokes and third-rate touring companies, had discovered its favorite form of entertainment. Mary Pickford, Charlie Chaplin and Theda Bara, the Keystone Kops and the Bathing Beauties were the angels flying round my crib. But Hollywood was still a primitive barn in open western country where a failed theater director named Cecil B. DeMille was making his first movie, *The Squaw Man,* for an odd couple of film pioneers, Jesse Lasky, a congenial trumpet-player-vaudevillian, and his single-minded, irascible, ex-glove salesman brother-in-law, Sam Goldfish.

Back in Harlem, I was overdressed and pampered by a young mother so ambitious for my intellectual progress that while she was carrying me she had spent as much time as she could in libraries, taking poetry courses at Columbia and reading Tennyson, Milton, and Shelley, determined that I should become, at the very least, Stephen Crane and John Galsworthy combined.

Maybe it was the lack of a family tree. We sprang like Minervas from the ghetto brow, barely knowing our grandparents, our great-grandparents lost in the great Russian miasma. Like African slaves in America, our births, marriages, and deaths in Czarist Russia had gone unrecorded. Who were my great-grandfathers, my great-grandmothers? Did they earn a living, did they love each other, were they killed in pogroms? No one has ever been able to tell me. I read Nabokov and I marvel at the rich tapestry: What a parade of predecessors! There is Grandfather the Minister of Justice. There is Grandmother the Baroness. There is the great-great-grandfather the General, in command of "The Nabokov Regiment." "*Eppis,*" my mother would have said.

Over the centuries Nabokov ranges, like an elegant but greedy unicorn, until the history of the Nabokovs becomes the history of Mother Russia herself, complete with loyal Ministers of State who are intimates of the Czar and rebellious Decembrists on their way to the scaffold. What a proliferation of Nabokovs, all the way back—Nabokov points out modestly—to a Russianized Tatar Prince Nabok Murza, in 1380. Six hundred years of Nabokovism! I want to cry out, "Vladimir, we came from your country, too, but while you were living on great estates and making history, we were huddled in our little synagogues, and in our village huts, hiding from history. Even the serfs looked down on us. We held no titles, never raced in luxurious sleighs through the forests of our dachas, we had no French, English, and German tutors, our ancestors did not distinguish themselves in celebrated duels and affairs of state. We were just poor Russian or Latvian Jews who lived out our unrecorded existences."

Oh, but wait, we did have one claim to fame. My mother never tired of boasting about him when we were young: Pinsker, her mother's brother, our "diamond-cutter to the Czar," who had special permission to live—beyond the Pale—in that vast expanse of European Russia forbidden to ordinary Jews. I had visions of this legendary ancestor in his fur-lined jacket and handsome fur cap, enshrined in his diamond-cutting workshop in a corner of the Winter Palace, cutting exquisite, gleaming spheres for the pleasure of the Czarina. The Pinskers carried this high calling to the New World. While the Jaffes were sweltering in cramped railroad flats on the Lower East Side, the Pinskers were operating jewelry shops in Middletown, Connecticut, where their sons attended Wesleyan University, and where Adeline would be invited to escape the heat, the noise, and the smell of the ghetto summers. Middletown opened a window to what life could be like in America.

2

IF WE HAD no family tree, yet ours was another kind of family, stretching horizontally, composed of motion-picture pioneers with whom my father the writer soon found himself involved. Before he was twenty, he had gone to work for the now-forgotten pioneer, Edwin S. Porter, truly the father of the American motion picture. It has become the convention to accord that role to D. W. Griffith, and to think of Griffith, DeMille, and Chaplin, along with the novice entrepreneurs Zukor, Lasky, Laemmle, and Goldwyn, as the creators of the first American films. But way back in 1903, years before these other pioneers had shot or presented their first reel, Porter had made the seminal narrative film, *The Life of an American Fireman*. This jumpy eight-minute flick, primitive and childish as it may look today, was a first step in the long march of the American film. In the period into which I was born, B.P. was working with Porter, fascinated with his technical inventions and his creative discoveries. Having heard these stories of Porter's achievements firsthand, I accept them as part of my birthright. He is my Grand Duke.

In the days of Thomas Edison's domination of the infant film industry at the turn of the century, Edwin S. Porter served as one of his mechanics and cameramen. An irony of Edison's life is that, though he is credited with inventing the motion picture, his true love was the phonograph. He *was* interested in the coordination of sound and picture, but his young English assistant and co-inventor, William Kennedy Laurie Dickson, was far more enthusiastic than Edison about the possibility of projecting motion pictures on a large screen. Edison favored the peep-box in the penny arcade, and even after the motion-picture screen emerged from its historic but unprepossessing Room Five in East Orange, New Jersey, he had no faith in the commercial future of the movies. Still, the nickelodeons were catching on, and so Edison reluctantly gave the audience what it seemed to want, twenty or thirty feet of moving pictures depicting *New York in a Blizzard,* or scenes of our sailors landing in Cuba, grandiosely titled *Our Flag Is Here to Stay.* Or, for the wicked, some enticing flashes of *Fatima's Coochee-Coochee Dance.*

Basically a mechanic-inventor rather than an artist-director, Ed Porter happened to see one of the supernatural films that the French magician Georges Méliès had made in Paris. These Méliès films were the very first not to rely on actual photographed events but on staged theatrical scenes that told a story. With his mechanical mind—so my father would tell me when I was young—Porter examined these innovative movies frame by frame. Méliès was able to transfer his sleight of hand to the screen, able to change a pumpkin into a royal coach. He anticipated Walt Disney by 35 years, and his *A Trip to the Moon,* caricaturing the scientific daydreams of the 1900s, foreshadowed the optic miracles that the motion-picture camera was about to achieve. Méliès' movies, Porter told my father, were "the fastest moving pictures" he had ever seen. After a few tentative imitations of Méliès' magic films, he was ready to make his landmark "story picture." The pragmatic tinkerer would choose a subject eminently down to earth: a fire. A mother and child trapped in a flaming house. Horse-drawn fire engines racing to the rescue. Precious lives saved in the nick of time!

Because Porter knew that Edison's mind was closed to the artistic possibilities of his mechanical invention, he conspired to shoot his innovative story-film in secret. Without Edison's knowledge (according to my father), Porter worked out his pioneer scenario. First, a shot of the house catching fire. Then a historic close shot (antedating Griffith's more sophisticated use of this device) of the frantic mother gesticulating at the window. Cut back to the firehouse. The mustachioed firemen are lounging around until galvanized into action by the sound of the alarm. Then came the first American use of intercutting, the technique that was to become the spine of cinematic storytelling. Back again to the fire, the flames licking higher. Then cut to the fire wagon, drawn by powerful horses galloping down the street. Finally, a breathtaking climax, the last-minute rescue of the mother and child, with the house collapsing in flames behind them as they are carried to safety.

There it was, an American *first,* a creation that was to have as great an impact on the country as the invention of the telephone, the telegraph, and the electric light. The theater, the opera, the dance, and the concert had been the luxuries of the wealthy and the middle class. Porter's *The Life of an American Fireman* opened the door to the art form of the poor, the art form soon to be enjoyed by millions of people all over the world.

But that door was not opened without a struggle from The Wizard, as Edison was known for his inventions of the incandescent light and the phonograph. A full generation before the advent of sound, he had worked to synchronize dialogue and music with moving pictures. But Porter knew the old man's mentality, and he was in a cold sweat when he ushered Edison into the small projection room at the New Jersey laboratory. If you brought a mechanical development to Edison he would always take time to examine it. But he seemed strangely impatient with this latest brainchild. Edison fidgeted through the first four or five minutes of this historic film and then turned on his employee: "Porter, you must be crazy. I keep telling you people will never sit still for a whole reel. Eight minutes on a single story! It won't sell. People want variety. At least four or five subjects on every reel."

"But Mr. Edison, if they read dime novels, why can't they follow a single story on the screen?" So Porter described the classic confrontation to my father. "Once we show them they can *see* a story, as well as read it, they'll never go back to 'The Destruction of the Standard Oil Plant at Bayonne,' or the vaudeville juggling acts we've been giving them." When Edison refused to believe it, Porter boldly offered to pay for the negative himself if *Fireman* proved to be a failure.

"Porter, all this celluloid must be going to your brain," Edison argued. "I understand this picture cost eight hundred dollars. If I take you up on your offer you'll be dead broke."

Porter stuck to his guns. Or his fire hoses. The picture went out to the nickelodeons and the little storefront theaters that were beginning to pop up around the country, and the effect was electric: what Griffith's *The Birth of a Nation* would be to the next decade, and *Gone With the Wind* to the 1940s.

With this success behind him, Porter was permitted to make an even more ambitious picture, what my father called "the Man o'War of American movies" because it sired an endless list of winning offspring all the way down to *Butch Cassidy and the Sundance Kid*. There had been those who thought that *The Life of an American Fireman* was a fluke, its success based on its novelty. But *The Great Train Robbery* proved that the American story film was here to stay. Again, it was full of innovations that have been attributed to Porter's successor, D. W. Griffith: the close-up, the dissolve, direct cuts from scene to scene without even a dissolve or a subtitle to clue the audience, letting the forward thrust of the story carry the viewers with it. Two lines of simultaneous action were juxtaposed, the train robbers escaping while the telegraph operator, bound and gagged, was discovered by his daughter in the station office. The action intercut between the posse formed to apprehend the robbers and the robbers themselves riding across western country to make their escape. At times Porter's camera panned with his pursuing horsemen. At times he tilted his camera downward to follow the robbers scrambling down a wooded hillside. For the first time in history, the camera was moving with its subjects. Finally there was a sensational trick ending, a close-up of the face and hand of a besieged bandit firing his gun directly at the audience. The Edison handbill informed exhibitors that they had the choice of using this spectacular close-up either at the beginning of the picture as a "teaser," or at the climax. When the shot was fired at the audience the effect was so startling that people actually jumped up from their seats and ran out of the theaters. So most of the pioneer showmen chose to use it at the end. The financial success of *The Great Train Robbery* finally convinced even the doubting Thomas Edison that the one-reel story film was a popular art form. The work of Edwin S. Porter was now studied—in New York and Chicago, in London, Paris, and Rome—his imitators taking their cameras out of doors, releasing them from their fixed positions, and making "chase" movies that were soon rivaling the originator's.

When Porter left Edison in 1912 to form his own firm, Defender Films, my father approached the famous director on the set of his primitive studio in The Bronx and asked him to take out an ad in *Film Reports*. He would, he told my father, if the young man could write one that pleased him.

My father hurried back to his small office on Broadway to grapple with the problem. At the end of the day he was back on Porter's set with his brainstorm: "Defend Your House [i.e., the movie theater] With

Defender Films." Porter not only bought the ad, he felt he had stumbled upon a fresh writing talent that he could put to use in his studio. When he invited B.P. to write a scenario, Father admitted that although he was associate editor of *Film Reports* at that time, he had never actually seen a photoplay. Porter promptly handed him the scenario of a current production, *The School Marm's Ride for Life.*

"That script was exactly a page and a half long," Father told me, "with a couple of crude sentences describing each of the eighteen scenes. 'This is a scenario?' I asked Mr. Porter. The great director, who had just introduced D. W. Griffith to motion pictures as an actor in *Rescued from an Eagle's Nest,* assured me that this was a shooting script. 'Well, if this is a scenario, then I am a scenario writer,' I told him." That same day, during his lunch hour, B.P. dashed off his first scenario. Porter was so pleased with it that he appointed him his regular scenario writer.

"It was great fun, really easy and exciting," B.P. liked to reminisce. "I'd think up a plot and write it on Monday. Porter would cast it, paint his sets, and pick out locations on Tuesday. He would shoot the picture on Wednesday, by which time I'd be ready with the next one, which he'd cast, plan, and shoot by Friday. On Saturday our two one-reelers were shipped off to the distributors. That was our routine, week in and week out, over the two years before you were born.

"Actually I had started out with hopes of becoming a short-story writer, maybe even a novelist. And when F.P.A. accepted a few of my contributions for his 'Conning Tower' I had dreams of becoming another Jack London. But when I got married and your mother became pregnant with almost indecent haste, I knew that the life of a freelance writer would put us back in the ghetto. So I welcomed a chance to write those scenarios, even though I had no illusions that they were anything but dime novels flashed on a screen. By the time I met Porter, though he was the preeminent man in his field, he had really gone as far as he could go as a filmmaker. He had tried a few flights of imagination, inspired by Méliès, like *The Dream of a Rarebit Fiend,* and he had also tried his hand at social consciousness with a film called *The Kleptomaniac* about a wealthy lady who gets slapped on the wrist for shoplifting, while a poor mother goes to jail for stealing a loaf of bread for her hungry children. But mostly his preference was for the sentimental and melodramatic, and in those early years, happy to get my thirty dollars a week for the two scenarios plus bonuses for the extra work I did, I ground out a mess of footage. But the moving-picture show was still such a novelty that audiences all over the country flocked to see our insipid offerings. You had to be really stupid and totally incompetent *not* to make money."

My father remembered his very first scenario. With an eye to the approaching holiday season, he opened it with a kind-hearted cop who finds a lost child on Christmas Eve and takes her home to his wife and his own two children. The child explains, in a subtitle written by B.P., that she has run away from home because her mother has remarried and her stepfather is cruel to her. The big twist in the story was the wife's discovery that the little girl is her own sister's child! The cop and his wife decide to adopt the little girl, and since they don't know her name they call her their Christmas *Carol.* The picture fades out on the cop's equally kindhearted children sharing their Christmas presents with their new "sister."

"We can laugh at it now," B.P. told me, "but *A Cop's Christmas Carol* cleaned up. There were actually lines at the little glass box offices. And all the ladies were sniffling into their handkerchiefs. Mr. Porter not only gave me an extra bonus that Christmas, he promoted me to Scenario Editor!"

While I was still in the fetal stage, the scenarios that my father was coping with were in a similar phase of primal development. At first they were jotted down on scraps of paper and the backs of envelopes by the producers themselves, and by their directors, the actors, bookkeepers— even the elevator men in those drafty lofts that passed for studios. But the hunger for the new entertainment was so insatiable that soon the producers—or manufacturers, as they were first called—actually began advertising for movie stories. "Earn one hundred dollars a month by writing photoplays!" was the siren song in popular magazines. The headline was a teaser, for the smaller print explained that the price for each accepted photoplay would be ten dollars. So all you had to do to earn your C-note was to write ten acceptable photoplays a month.

"They came pouring in, mostly in illegible scrawls," B.P. would tell me, "written on everything from postcards to butcher paper. Everybody who paid his nickel to see one of our shows thought it was easy money to dash off a movie. Most of them were illiterate. Nearly all of them were godawful. I sat there with the lofty title of Scenario Editor for Rex Films (the successor to Defender), reading literally thousands of pages of handwritten drivel, with titles like 'A Counterfeiter's Regret,' or 'Never Darken My Door Again,' in which the entire plot was told in the title. One in five hundred was acceptable. I told Mr. Porter that my job was cruel and unusual punishment. I would rather write all the scripts myself than plow through moronic mush like 'A Widow's Revenge' and 'The Black Sheep Reforms.'"

But Porter was not only making his own films now, he was training new directors to work under him. The motion-picture audience and my mother's middle were growing proportionately. My infancy, the infancy of Edison's Kinetoscope, and Porter's callow moving-picture shows are intertwined.

Self-proclaimed experts and "scenario schools" offered courses in photoplay writing for fees ranging from one dollar to twenty-five. The fakers who had dealt in patent medicines simply moved on to the new opportunity. They would offer to read, criticize, and correct scenarios for fees as low as fifty cents to a dollar. "Those fourflushers who had never been inside a film studio—such as they were—or had never seen a scenario were posing as old masters and pocketing fifty or sixty dollars a week, real money in those days," my father told me. "I would have to read these 'corrected' scenarios and often they were worse than the originals."

At the ripe old age of twenty, B. P. felt qualified to write that preface to *How to Write a Photoplay*. Giving up on the illiterate amateurs whose scenarios overflowed his desk, he suggested to Porter that they buy from or build up a staff of professional writers. Among these pioneer screenwriters was Frances Marion, who started at fifteen dollars for one scenario or twenty-five for two, and who worked her salary up over the next twenty years to two thousand dollars a week, with screen credit on such MGM powerhouses as *Stella Dallas, Anna Christie, The Champ,* and *Dinner at Eight.* Anita Loos sold her first scenario for fifteen dollars to D. W. Griffith when she was fifteen, launching the author of *Gentlemen Prefer Blondes* on her marathon filmwriting career. Women's Lib has no cause for complaint on the subject of pioneer screenwriters. For there was also Jeanie MacPherson, the silent actress later identified with nearly all the Cecil B. DeMille spectaculars; Clara Beranger, who married Cecil's brother, William DeMille; and Ouida Bergere, who married Basil Rathbone and graduated from scripting silents to staging Hollywood's most stylish parties. And there was also Louella O. Parsons, who later ruled over Hollywood as the gossip columnist of the Hearst Syndicate.

If B. P. sounds like the only boy writer of his day, I should add that there were others in that Middle Stone Age of the cinema. Bannister

Merwin wrote the very first serial, *What Happened to Mary,* named for Mary Fuller, one of the Edison Company's earliest stars. Harold McGrath wrote another of those early serials, *The Adventures of Kathlyn,* starring Kathlyn Williams, who worked for Colonel William N. Selig, a fabled film prospector in the early days of the Gold Rush, a man who was to loom large in my Hollywood childhood. Another filmwriting pioneer was Hal Reid, whose son Wallace was soon to become one of the screen's first matinee idols, along with Mary Pickford's flamboyant brother Jack and the irrepressible Marshall (Mickey) Neilan.

Father in the year of my birth was ready to soar from a salary of two hundred dollars a week to a luxurious five hundred dollars. A writer with a facile, retentive mind, a flair for showmanship, and a sense of his own worth as a literate diamond in the murky field of illiteracy, he had come to the right business at the right moment, when it was growing out of its funky nickelodeon phase.

There was a stampede to "get into the movie game," and if you couldn't get a job in front of the camera as a featured player or as a five-dollar-a-day extra, or behind it as a director, cameraman, or technician, you could always try your hand at scribbling. When my father and mother wheeled my fancy carriage through Mt. Morris Park, they would be intercepted by passersby who had heard that young Schulberg was Edwin S. Porter's Scenario Editor and would press on him their latest inspirations for Mary Pickford. Scenario writing became such a national madness that books on how to grind out these newfangled concoctions became bestsellers. While I was being pushed through that park, or being induced to eat with games like "Here we go down into the subway!" with my mouth encouraged to open to provide the subway entrance, associates of B.P. were writing books like *The Reel Thing* and *The A.B.C. of Motion Pictures.* In *The Motion Picture Story,* B.P.'s friend William Lord Wright advises,

> the trend of the motion picture is now upward, not downward, and the
> more refined one makes his stories the more will he contribute to the
> general uplift of cinematography.... Write of what you know; you have no
> business knowing anything about the seamy side of life. If you do know it,
> keep it to yourself.

As an example of an effective "heart-interest story," Wright recommended *Three Children,* written by James Dayton and produced by Harry A. Pollard for the Universal Film Manufacturing Company. Here is the original synopsis:

> Billy and Grandfather are 'pals.' One is not happy without the other. However, Billy's mother is frequently annoyed by Grandfather's old-fashioned ways and influences her husband to send Grandfather to the Old Folks' Home. Grandfather realizes his son's position and does not object. Billy misses Grandfather greatly. He visits him occasionally at the Old Folks' Home. Grandfather tells Billy that he has no teeth, no hair, and can't walk very well, and that Billy's Pa and Ma cannot afford to have him around. A new baby comes to Billy's home. Billy doesn't think much of the new arrival, he would rather have his Grandfather. He notices the new baby has no teeth, no hair, and cannot walk so he resolves to trade it to the Old Folks' Home for Grandpa. Grandfather brings Billy and the new baby home safely and Billy's mother decides that all three children are indispensable to her happiness.

The book includes a 14-page shooting script, building to this climax:

> SCENE 56. INTERIOR OF LIVING ROOM.
> The husband and the wife both ashamed, uncomfortable— Billy brings grandfather in—asks his mother whether grandfather can't stay and live with them—his mother smiles at her husband and goes to grandfather—shakes hands with him and asks him to stay –everyone happy—mother places the baby in grandfather's arms—all fuss over the baby.
>
> SUB-TITLE 16 _____ THREE CHILDREN
> CLOSE UP. Tint for firelight effect of the grandfather, Billy, and the baby lying on the couch asleep—
>
> FADE OUT

That, says Mr. Wright, "is a good example of a heart-interest photoplay as written by a staff writer."

These fustian little how-to books passed on to me by my father represent the missals of the new church of motion pictures into which I was born, and in which I was to be reared as an acolyte dedicated to the gospels of Porter and Griffith.

When the Screen Club presented its first Annual Ball in 1913, on the eve of my birth, it was celebrating "the first social and fraternal organization to be formed for the folk of the motion picture art." The first president of the Club was King Baggott, with the classic profile and slicked black hair of the Broadway matinee idol he had been before "photo playing." In his film debut for Carl Laemmle's IMP Studio (forerunner of Universal) he had played opposite Florence Lawrence, the first true star of the "moving picture show," known as "The Girl of a Thousand Faces," who had been signed "for life" at a spectacular fifteen thousand dollars a year. The Screen Club testimonial to King Baggott packs a lot of film history into a few quaint lines: "The result of his work in his first effort was so gratifying that a most tempting offer was made to Mr. Baggott, which caused his forsaking of the drama for pictures. Since his first appearance in pictures in 1909, he has played in no less than one picture every week. He has written and played in more than fifty of his own pictures in a year."

The First Vice-President of The Screen Club was John Bunny, the first of the movies' fat-man comedians, who had played everything from circuses to Shakespeare before coming to the screen in 1910. Second Vice-President was a man my father knew well and loved to talk about, whose name had been Max Aronson before it was anglicized to Gilbert M. Anderson. But it was as Broncho Billy, the first cowboy star (after his movie debut in *The Great Train Robbery*), that Gilbert né Max was known to the growing film audience that was making the American western its favorite subject.

Bronco Billy always claimed that he had been born in Arkansas and had been a cowpuncher before going into vaudeville, the path that led him to Edwin S. Porter's office at the Edison Studio. Porter told my father than an authentic cowboy was just what he needed for his chase scene at the end of the picture. The chase was to be filmed in the wilds of New Jersey, not far from the Edison Studio. Broncho Billy was told to meet them at the location on horseback. When he failed to show up, Porter had to double for him himself. When the company got back to the livery stable where the tired nags had been rented, Porter asked if anyone had seen the missing Anderson. "Oh yeah," the liveryman reported. "He rented a horse—but he didn't seem to know the head from the tail. Bessie here threw him off before he got to the end of the driveway. He was afraid to get on again, so he took the next train back to New York." Eventually Broncho Billy climbed on again, and scored in one-reelers to become the father of the cowboy stars.

Billy was also the first actor to go into business for himself, in tandem with George K. Spoor, one of the Chicago pioneers. Spoor and Anderson's Essanay Film Manufacturing Company was one of the early "majors," with the enterprising Anderson shooting his Broncho Billy series at the rate of one a week on location in California. Because he and Spoor ran their own company, Broncho Billy was the first star to get his name on the screen, at a time when the "manufacturers" were opposed to screen credit because it would give the players an exaggerated sense of their own worth.

A young English comedian touring with the Karno mime company— Charlie Chaplin—was lured from the stage by Mack Sennett to bring his cane, derby, and baggy pants to the screen at a salary of one hundred and fifty dollars a week. Chaplin's name wasn't even attached to these riotous one-reelers, but audiences didn't need a name. They just wanted to see more comedies with the funny little fellow in the baggy pants. Broncho Billy, working in California in his own unending cowboy series, went to see Charlie and—even though Spoor had literally never heard the name of Charlie Chaplin—talked his partner into offering him one thousand dollars a week. The shrewd Charlie bargained this salary to twelve hundred and fifty dollars a week, and the Chaplin comedies began making millions for Essanay. While I was still crawling around my playpen, Chaplin's salary was to leap from $75,000 to a world-shaking $670,000 a year, when Mutual outbid Essanay's half-a-million.

At that first ball of The Screen Club, two hundred of the movie game's overnight elite celebrated in the Terrace Garden of the old Hotel Astor until dawn. While Father stayed on after midnight to drink with his cronies, Mother had to leave to get up early the next morning for her job with the Jewish Consumptive Relief Society. She was also working for the Educational Alliance. A child of the ghetto who still looked like a child, this little package was deceptive, for she was determined to rise above that ghetto background. She was already a bear for culture, for self-improvement, hungry for books, ideas, causes. She wanted something fine, "the better things," not just the material success that Ben was beginning to enjoy through his lofty position with Edwin S. Porter, but Knowledge, Art, a Meaning to Life. She wanted to associate with intellectuals, like the young socialists on the Lower East Side who talked so eloquently of the need to overthrow the Czar, to free not only the Jews but the toiling masses of the world. . . .

Ad fancied herself a socialist, as well as a suffragist, a champion of unwed mothers and the sweatshop workers in the dingy garment lofts grateful for their 14-hour-a-day jobs at five dollars a week. Nor was her young husband insensitive to the plight of the poor on the narrow streets of lower Manhattan. He had written a feature story for the *Mail* about the ragged Irish and Italian children who send Santa the list of toys they most desire, only to wake up to empty stockings. Why couldn't metropolitan "Santas" read their appeals in the dead-letter section of the Post Office and surprise the kids with at least one of the things they asked for? Father's suggestion touched a nerve, setting off a spontaneous campaign to bring toys to the city's poor.

But the sons of defeated fathers, if they had the talent and the "go," were rapidly becoming Americanized. The spirit of Horatio Alger was a heady brew. Look at the little orphan who lived on their block, Eddie Cantor, determined to become a comedian, even though the act he performed at one of B.P.'s Townsend Harris highschool debates, combining a Yiddish accent with blackface, convinced Ben, Ad, and all his other young friends that he must give up this silly dream and find an honest job. And there were Benny Leonard and the other clever Jewish boxers literally fighting their way out of the ghetto. And the teenage Jews who were scornful of their pious, passive fathers, and who were hustling, scheming, studying, and clawing their way into the mainstream. B.P. wasn't going to climb up on a horse like Broncho Billy Aronson/Anderson and there was no way he was going to change his name (although he did hide his provocative middle name Percival under the initials he used all his life), but he was a kind of intellectual Broncho Billy galloping out of Rivington Street through the *New York Mail* and "The Conning Tower" and *Film Reports* to the parvenu but self-important Screen Club.

A prodigy in all departments, B.P. had already learned to mix pleasure with business. He liked to sit through the night playing poker and drinking with his pals Al Lichtman and Al Kaufman, and with an Irish crony of whom Ad spoke all her life with fury and indignation: Joe Roche, an Irish writer of sorts, a happy-go-lucky good-time Joey who, she was convinced, had been placed upon this earth to lead B.P. from the straight and narrow. Joe used to come home with B.P. at dawn and sleep it off on the couch while Ben went back to his desk as scenario editor. B.P. had great energy, a gourmand's appetite for life, an ability to burn his candle at both ends and still manage to last the night.

Mr. Porter was impressed with Ben's creative vitality and his conscientiousness. As films rapidly improved in quality—leading Porter, the mechanic, into a world of mass entertainment he had helped to create and yet was not adequately prepared for—he found the young man with the facile typewriter and the quick turn of phrase the ideal right hand for his growing production company. Porter had graduated to more complicated films like *Alice in Wonderland* that needed a somewhat more literate touch, although a few years later my father would laugh at the "literacy" of those naive subtitles.

Our next step upward geographically and socially was to an apartment at the corner of Fifth Avenue and 110th Street overlooking Central Park. Not only outside but inside as well, my three-year-old eyes perceived a haze of green, from the leather chairs to the drapes and carpeting—a testimony to the Irish persuasiveness of Father's sidekick. Although I failed to appreciate the improvement in my station, the Schulbergs were moving up in the world. We now had an Irish maid, apparently just off the boat from County Somewhere, who *Yes Mum*'d my mother, who was uneasy about this new relationship because she had not yet learned to give orders. But by the time I was old enough to remember these things she would be ordering servants around like a Nabokov Baroness. Imagine the Jews of Pinsk and Dvinsk and Minsk with *goyische* maids! This was part of the Americanization that our first generation was taking to with such ease. Our maid was called Jemmy and she was paid at the going rate of five dollars a week. She was to be the first of a long line of nurses, Fräuleins, and mademoiselles who would serve as mother-replacements in the days of our opulence.

3

DID NOT know why we had moved to a grander apartment. I do remember more space to explore and a larger park to play in and marvelous packages on Christmas with a large bell symbolizing the wonders of F. A. O. Schwarz. I was unaware that this largesse stemmed from an important merger between Edwin S. Porter and Adolph Zukor, one of the original moguls. Like Porter, Zukor became surrogate grandfather to take the place of my *nebbish* Grandpa Max and my reprobate Grandpa Simon. That's why I find, while I know virtually nothing about Simon and remember only dimly Max's gray, unsuccessful life, I seemed to know, from an early age, everything about "Uncle" Adolph.

If the wave of Jewish immigration in the Eighties and Nineties could be divided into *nebbish* and *mensch,* little Adolph was a giant *mensch.* This small, quiet man who spoke simple English with a pronounced Hungarian accent, and who continued to keep me supplied with milk and eggs from his country estate, was one of the very few in the rough-and-tumble world of pioneer moviemaking who never lost B.P.'s respect. Toward most of the tycoons, first to last, from Thomas Edison and his hatchetman Jeremiah J. Kennedy, boss of the powerful Film Trust, to later moguls like L. B. Mayer and Harry Cohn, B.P. was to bear bitter grudges, cultivated with a devotion born of a thin skin and an erratic temperament better suited to the arts than to business. But when it came to Adolph Zukor, from my father's first day on the job to his traumatic release from Paramount some twenty years later, I never heard a word of criticism or even the hint of rancor.

It was my father who told me the true-life fable of the 15-year-old Jewish orphan from Eastern Europe who had come to America in the late 1880s, his baggage consisting largely of intelligence, determination, an appetite for hard work, and an instinct for the main chance. An undersized urchin with forty dollars sewn into the lining of his second-hand vest, little Adolph found a job at two dollars a week in an upholstery sweatshop. From there he graduated to four dollars a week as an errand boy for a furrier. Adolph tipped the scales as a miniflyweight and he learned to box so he could protect himself from the bigger boys in the loft.

In his days as a teenage fur-worker, Adolph Zukor happened to work alongside a bigger, slightly older boy who had come over from Hungary a year earlier: Maxie Schosberg—my father remembered the name because it was so similar to our own. With a year's headstart on Adolph, Maxie was already bursting with the go-getting American spirit. Why work for a boss who turned the sweat of your labor into profit for himself? The main chance lay in business for yourself. And the way to begin was literally waiting for them on the floor around their work bench. A natural salesman, Maxie saw the birth of a new fad: fur scarfs. They could take the fur trimmings on the floor and sew them into scarfs. They worked at this after hours in the shop and in their separate tenement rooms. Adolph did most of the hand work; Maxie sold the scarfs in the street. They made them fast and he sold them cheap and soon they had a handful of capital to buy their own pelts. Adolph began depositing the modest (but for him impressive) profits in the Dry Dock Savings Bank. The restless Maxie moved on to Chicago where the fur business was thriving. Soon after, Adolph withdrew his savings, now several hundred dollars, and caught a cut-rate train to Chicago where he quickly found work as a fur cutter at twelve dollars a week. But the seed of going into business for himself had taken root, and soon he was in touch again with Maxie Schosberg. They pooled their meager savings to form the Novelty Fur Company.

The company facilities consisted of a single room on LaSalle Street and a rented sewing machine. Adolph did the sewing, Maxie the selling, and at the end of their first season each of them banked one thousand dollars above expenses. At the end of the first year the Novelty Fur Company had expanded, with a flourishing branch in Peoria and twenty-five employees. Adolph's bank book showed a balance of more than eight thousand dollars.

Still, there seemed no logic in giving up a modestly profitable fur business in Chicago to try his hand at the newfangled moving-picture show. "Mr. Zukor backed into the movie game more or less by accident," B.P. told me. He had loaned a relative three thousand dollars to invest in a penny arcade on 14th Street in lower Manhattan. Penny arcades were becoming the new low-life entertainment. A nickel in a slot brought coochee-coochee dancers and other delights on Edison's Kinetoscope, or Sousa's Band on his Graphophone. There were rifles to fire at moving ducks, and bags to test punching power against the recorded impact of the reigning prizefighters of the day. Passersby had nickels jingling in their pockets; a restlessness for new forms of entertainment was in the air. But somehow the penny arcade in which Zukor had entrusted his three thousand dollars was being mismanaged, and so the young furrier decided to move back to New York and look into the business himself. Fade out Zukor the furrier, fade in Zukor the motion-picture pioneer. Fascinated with the potential of the new entertainment, he joined forces with Marcus Loew, another ex-furrier, and decided to expand the operation with branches in other cities. Then young Zukor met Bill Brady, the big, out-going, energetic, openhanded Broadway man-about-town.

Brady told Zukor of a brand-new form of entertainment he had just seen in Chicago. It was called "Hales Tours" and "Scenes of the World" and was the brainstorm of the Fire Chief of Kansas City. Chief Hales had created a simulated railroad car which customers could board from the observation platform. Once settled in their seats, there were sounds of steam and a loud railroad bell. The uniformed ticket-taker would shout "All aboard!" and then the car would lurch into simulated movement, rattling and swaying, while the passengers would face a screen fixed to the end of the observation platform on which they could watch a moving-picture travel adventure: ascending the Alps, peering into the depths of the Grand Canyon, or crossing the Rockies. It was as if Edison and Disney had combined their talents. Brady and Zukor pooled their resources to obtain the franchise from Hales for New York City and other Eastern centers. Customers flocked onto the novel contraption by the thousands. Bill Brady was noisily elated and Adolph Zukor, always more self-contained, was quietly pleased. They were enjoying a healthy return on their sizeable investment.

But once customers had enjoyed the Hales Tour experience, they seemed to feel no great desire to return. They had come for the novelty and now sought other forms of entertainment. So Zukor decided on an experiment. A few years earlier he had been impressed by Porter's *The Great Train Robbery*. In ten minutes it had told a gripping story, without the use of a single word or a single subtitle. Zukor had gone back to see the "play without words" again and again. Now he suggested to Brady that they try a parlay—first the now-familiar Hales Tour with the railroad car swaying and the moving scenery taking their customers on a vicarious trip. Then bring the car to a halt and, on the stationary Pullman, show *The Great Train Robbery,* followed by any other story films they could rent. In other words, turn their simulated railroad car into a movie theater!

The experiment worked so well that Zukor was convinced that what the people were truly hungry for was movies, not theatrical travelogues. In fact he had made it his business to ask departing customers which they had most enjoyed, the travelogue stunt or the Porter movie. The response was overwhelming. Nine out of ten customers wanted to see the movie again. Whereupon the decisive, increasingly Americanized Hungarian Jew told his exuberant Irish partner that they should junk Hales' railroad cars—even though each car, with its elaborate equipment to make it rattle and sway, had cost about $8,000. They would be junking $180,000 worth of equipment.

Deciding to be a silent partner in whatever scheme his young associate chose to get them off the hook, Brady went back to his first love, the Broadway stage. Zukor opened a small movie house, the Comedy Theater, on 14th Street next door to his penny arcade. Over the next two years he brought to Brady's office the returns from his movie exhibition. At the end of that time they were not only out of debt on the costly Hales Tours investment, they were in the black. The nickelodeon was no overnight fad, as most theater and vaudeville people believed. Millions of five-cent customers were coming to the movies, and wanted to keep on coming.

Zukor's vision was my birthright. This surrogate grandfather was one of the first to realize that audiences would tire of the standard one-reel fare, those pale carbon copies of the original *Great Train Robbery* being cranked out by Porter's imitators, and that people would grow as weary of stale and repetitive ten-minute movies as they had of the Tours. Zukor had a dream. He saw the movies not for what they were at the end of their first decade, but for what they could become in the decades to follow. European filmmakers were making forty- and fifty-minute spectacles—biblical films and historical dramas. That was the direction in which the cinematic tide was moving; common sense and foresight told Zukor to move with it. He was prepared to gamble his life savings on the improvement of motion pictures, and that gamble was to bring my father to his side as one of his most valued young lieutenants. Zukor's dream was to bring the world's great plays and literature to the screen and to people them with the finest actors and actresses who could be lured from the legitimate stage. It was time to move up from nickelodeon owner to motion-picture manufacturer.

An Italian-made four-reel version of *Quo Vadis?* had been booked into the Astor Theater, at an admission price of one dollar. The Motion Picture Patents Company—comprising the Edison Company and eight other associated companies that forbade outsiders to use their equipment—was unable to bar *Quo Vadis?* or any other foreign-made film, because Edison had not bothered to establish European patents. (He had told Porter, back in 1900, that it wasn't worth the two hundred and fifty dollars it would cost to establish his trademark in Europe.) So there was a great leak in the Patents Company dam. Zukor stood outside the Astor and watched the line of hungry filmgoers willing to pay a whole whopping dollar to see *Quo Vadis?* Other multiple-reel films, as they were then called, the Italian *Cabiria* and the French *Les Misérables,* were also drawing lines to the box office. Even though the self-satisfied officers of the Patents Company were determined to lock the movies within their old one-reel formula, he knew the motion picture was ready to take a giant step, from nickels to dollars, from one reel to four, from a penny-arcade business to the only art to become an industry and the only industry to become an art.

The diminutive Adolph supplied his theaters with moving pictures of higher quality by forming his own film-producing company, Famous Players, furthering his concept in employing theater marquee names instead of the unknown silent performers. Still thinking like a furrier, Zukor knew he would need "a good inside man" and "a good outside man"—someone to make the product and someone to front for it and sell it. For the inside man, his number-one choice was the leading American director of that day, B.P.'s boss, Edwin S. Porter. His offer to Porter was that he become Director-General of Famous Players.

Porter and Zukor got along *famously,* as my incorrigible punster-father insisted, and the deal was made on a handshake, with B.P. brought along as scenario editor and publicity director. An ardent

29

sloganeer, B.P. dreamed one up for the new company: "Famous Players in Famous Plays." Porter had told Zukor that "Young Ben Schulberg is a crackerjack with words." Zukor told my father that a new film company fighting against the all-powerful Patents Company trust would need a barrage of publicity to put itself on the map. The challenge excited my father. He was also excited by the prospect of making more money, to support his new marriage and its soon-to-appear firstborn. Zukor said this would have to be a gamble for all of them: There would be a heavy investment before any returns were in. But all three men were convinced that the little minds of the big Trust were dead wrong, and that the Zukor-Porter-Schulberg vision—unless blocked by Patent Company thugs and legal harassment—would carry the day.

It was like a war, this conflict between the imagination of the Independents and the tight-minded obstinacy of the Trust. B.P. felt as if he were engaged in a cultural revolution. Ever practical, Mr. Zukor told B.P. he would have to be satisfied with the five hundred dollars a week that Porter had been paying, plus two hundred shares of stock in the new company. If the company prospered they would all share in its growth.

To get "famous players" to work for a lowly nickelodeon owner, Zukor had to find a way to make movies seem respectable. If he were to try on his own to lure to the silent screen such towering stage figures as James O'Neill, James K. Hackett, John Barrymore, Mrs. Minnie Maddern Fiske, Pauline Frederick, and Marguerite Clark, he would probably not even be admitted to their dressing rooms. The gulf between the theater and the movies seemed unbridgeable. (Film stars were to assume the same attitude toward television in the early years of the little box.)

So Zukor found a calling card in Daniel Frohman. The Frohman brothers, Daniel and Charles, were, with David Belasco, the Big Three of the Broadway theater. But for the past few seasons, Daniel Frohman had had a series of flops. So when he was invited to become managing director of Famous Players, he accepted—and famous players at last became accessible to Famous Players.

In public and in private, Frohman spoke highly of the future of the motion picture, and my father found himself writing heady press releases. James O'Neill (now better known, sadly, as the prototype of the father in his son Eugene's *Long Day's Journey into Night*) was signed to launch Famous Players' new program of four-reel pictures with a film version of his great stage success *The Count of Monte Cristo,* under the direction of Edwin S. Porter. And James K. Hackett was signed to appear in *The Prisoner of Zenda* (based on another of Frohman's Broadway hits), again with Porter directing and with subtitles by B.P.

Along with my father, Porter brought with him to the Zukor organization another now-forgotten but once greatly influential figure, J. Searle Dawley. Porter had recruited Dawley from the stage, where he had been a successful stock player. Where Porter excelled in scenes of action and as an innovative film editor, Dawley's interest as a director was in performances. He made perhaps the first effort to tone down the bravura acting of the stage actors, trying to guide them toward the more subtle pantomime suited to plays without words. He also served as a casting director for Porter, roaming Broadway in search of out-of-work actors who might be effective in their films.

My father the phrasemaker hung a neat identification collar on Dawley: "The man who made Famous Players famous." And it was true that in my highchair days, long before Father's work had any meaning for me, Dawley was directing such famous stage stars as Mrs. Fiske, House Peters, Cissy Loftus, John Barrymore, and Mary Pickford. Some names were never to lose their luster while others were to drop into the dustbin like J. Searle Dawley's.

Father received pats on the back for his glowing announcement of the signing of O'Neill and Hackett. "Whenever I did something that particularly pleased Mr. Zukor, he would take me to Sulka's and buy me a tie," he told me. "Finally one day I balked. 'Mr. Zukor,' I said, 'I appreciate your generosity, but I now have so many ties I don't have room for them on my rack.' 'So what would you suggest instead?' asked the imperturbable Mr. Zukor. 'A r-r-raise,'" my father stammered. (Ever-facile when there were words to write, B.P. frequently stammered when trying to speak them.) Zukor, always firm but rarely unreasonable, accepted his young writer's suggestion and B.P. moved up from fifty to one hundred to two hundred dollars a week in the period immediately preceding my arrival.

Then the forward progress of the new company hit its first detour. While Famous Players was boasting that it was on its way to cornering the market in theatrical stars, news came from overseas that a French film company, Eclipse, had just completed a four-reel film starring Sarah Bernhardt in her own stage triumph, *Queen Elizabeth.*

"Mr. Zukor was shaken," my father told me. "Facing the daily crises of a newborn film company, he was usually stoic. But this time he showed signs of panic. How could they base a new company on the concept of corralling the most famous players when the single most famous player in the world, the Divine Sarah, had already made her first film for a rival company? Eclipse. Was there more than coincidence in the company's name? Could this signify the eclipse of Famous Players?"

"I wonder if they have an American outlet?" asked Al Lichtman, the energetic salesman for the company. Word came back that the American rights were still for sale. Zukor tried to buy the film for fifteen thousand dollars, a handsome advance in those days, but the French company held out. Determined to have Sarah Bernhardt on his roster at any cost, he finally settled for eighteen thousand dollars down, with a second eighteen thousand to be paid from box-office returns.

It was an unprecedented sum. People up and down Broadway pointed to their temples and told my father his boss must be crazy. Thirty-six thousand dollars represented nearly three-quarters of a million nickels! That is what Famous Players would have to repay before the company earned the first dollar on its investment.

"There was talk that our small ship would sink before it even left the harbor," my father remembered. "The Zukors let their maid go and moved to a smaller apartment where Lottie Zukor did all the work. But Mr. Zukor never lost his composure. He had an inborn dignity. Innate class."

Zukor realized that the enormous advance to which he had committed the company could never be covered by the nickelodeons. For "Famous Players Presents Sarah Bernhardt in *Queen Elizabeth*" he would charge a roadshow admission price of one dollar. And instead of showing the picture at his little Comedy Theater on 14th Street, he would, through the good graces of Daniel Frohman, lease the Frohmans' grandiose legitimate theater, the Lyceum. If Porter's *The Great Train Robbery* was a milestone in its day, Zukor would make *Queen Elizabeth* a milestone in terms of ultrarespectable, luxury-house exhibition that would attract the carriage trade, a breakthrough to a new audience that had scorned the flickers and had considered only the opera or legitimate theater worthy of its patronage.

But before *Queen Elizabeth* could be brought to the rococo Lyceum, several major obstacles had to be overcome. First, the Eclipse Company had to be—in the words of my father—literally eclipsed. So, in the great tradition of press agentry, B.P. sat down and banged out a glowing account of Zukor's determination to win for Famous Players the services of the greatest living international star. Adolph Zukor, in my father's dream story, had traveled to Paris to convince *La Sarah divine* that she should appear in a film version of her foremost stage success. At first she had resisted the entreaties of this great American producer, B.P.'s story went on, but Zukor argued that when the last members of her live audience died her art would die with them. However, if she would repeat her performance before a motion-picture camera, it would be preserved for all time. "Madame Bernhardt, you owe it to posterity to make this film," my father had his employer saying to the aging French star. Finally she had consented, and at last when the great Bernhardt saw herself on the screen for the first time she had embraced her producer, crying, "M'sieu Zukor, you have put the best of me in pickle for all time!"

B.P.'s touching scene caught the eye of the press, not only in New York where it was featured, but all over the world, including Paris where Mme. Bernhardt had completed the film before ever having heard of Adolph Zukor and his still-obscure Famous Players. Zukor was entranced with the story. He read it over and over again until he could recite it by heart. Five years later when Famous Players was celebrating its first half-decade, a testimonial banquet was held at the Hotel Astor, presided over by Mayor John Purroy Mitchel. After the Mayor's eloquent eulogy to Zukor, he called on the president of the company to tell the distinguished guests, all two thousand of them, what had been the single greatest experience of his career. Zukor took a deep breath and told the story of his ocean voyage to Europe to seek out Sarah Bernhardt and talk her into appearing in her first motion picture. Zukor didn't leave out a word in his imaginary meeting, even to her throwing her arms around him with those immortal words, "You have put the best of me in pickle for all time!"

But there was still the ever-pressing problem with the Trust. Adolph Zukor had to go hat in hand to the powerful J. J. Kennedy and beg for a license from the Patents Company. For three hours the deceptively meek Zukor was kept waiting. When Kennedy finally heard the little man's request, he hesitated. He saw no reason to encourage an upstart member of the Independents. These "illegal" outfits, the Laemmle IMP company, the Lasky-Goldfish-DeMille Company, William Fox—not to mention the now-forgotten David Horsley, Edwin Thanhouser, and Mark Dintenfass—were like a band of Indians encircling the wagon train of the establishment who held fast to their monopoly of the almighty Patent, and who used the license as a club to fight off these new, aggressive, and far more imatginative competitors.

A council of war was held in Daniel Frohman's spacious office above the Lyceum Theater (the Famous Players offices in the Times Building were too modest for such a meeting) and it was decided to go ahead with the Grand Opening, to which public officials, Broadway celebrities, members of the literati, and wealthy patrons of the arts had been invited. My father worked around the clock to bombard the newspapers with releases, to send out personal invitations to important personages, and to prepare the souvenir program.

But at five o'clock on the afternoon of the opening, the official permission still had not arrived from the Patents Company—a tense moment. If the film was screened without the precious license it would undoubtedly be subject to an injunction, possibly even a police raid. What to do? Zukor was a determined but cautious man. My father thought they should defy the Trust and run the picture for its prestigious audience. It would become a cause célèbre, a front-page story, and put further pressure on the Trust. There was always the streak of the rebel in my father: a desire to shock mingled with a bent to crusade. He would have enjoyed—indeed later did enjoy—taking on the Trust in editorial confrontation.

But in this case the silky, behind-the-scenes maneuvering of Daniel Frohman proved more effective. This was no ordinary Independent film that the Patents Company was rejecting. This would be the first time the renowned Sarah Bernhardt had ever exhibited her art on the American screen. It would be a black eye for the established film industry if they were to bar the image of the Divine Sarah from the Lyceum. Furthermore, Frohman argued—since his distinguished brother Charles, who had never before relented in his opposition to motion pictures, was allowing this one to be shown in their own legitimate theater—the Trust would put itself in the position of being anti-art and anti-culture if it did not go along with Charles's largesse. Frohman's prestige and his eloquence carried the day. Shortly before the historic screening, Zukor received a telegram from Kennedy declaring that due to the international eminence of Madame Bernhardt a license was being issued for this particular film. Famous Players had won its battle for *Queen Elizabeth*. But the war against independent production and exhibition went on.

Next day there was a news story, prompted by B.P.'s energetic releases, on the enthusiastic response of the scores of literary, artistic, and dramatic figures who showed up at the Lyceum, who had sat entranced throughout the four reels, and who had applauded at the end as though Madame Bernhardt were there in person to take a bow. But the officials of the Trust who attended out of curiosity remained unconvinced. The exclusive audience was impressed, they argued, only because they were seeing Sarah Bernhardt. Try the same four-reel experiment with your ordinary actor and this overly ambitious form would fall flat on its face.

While I was teething, this Motion Picture War of Independence was seething. General Kennedy employed an army of spies to infiltrate the independent productions. Spying was easy because filmmaking was still so informal. When extras were needed they were usually recruited from the curious onlookers attracted to the open sets. There were no unions or guilds to bar the way to instant employment. And the young moviemakers were ever on the lookout for fresh talent, from bit players to technicians. Just as my father had walked in on Edwin S. Porter at his studio in The Bronx and immediately become a photoplay writer because he obviously knew how to put words together, so anyone who had ever tinkered with a camera and knew how to thread one with raw stock might find himself hired on the spot as a cameraman.

Kennedy's spies were paid not only to report back to him, but to sabotage independent production. James Cruze, later to become famous as the director of *The Covered Wagon* in the heyday of the silents, told my young father of a typical Trust-war incident: He was acting in a western on the plains of Mamaroneck, with the good guys shooting it out with the bad guys, their blank cartridges giving off the sound of a miniwar, when suddenly a live bullet went crashing through the unlicensed or "pirated" camera, ending in every sense the shooting for that day and very nearly the life of the cameraman as well. One of the good guys, now revealed as a Kennedy goon disguised as a cowboy, spurred his bronco to make his getaway from Jim Cruze and the Thanhouser Company extras whom this sabotage had transformed into a genuine posse.

Goons were sent out from the Trust to destroy Independent equipment, expose their film, and burn their sets. An "extra" would suddenly turn out to be a process server, with orders for the police to confiscate equipment. The dragons in my fairy tales were Kennedy and his goons.

Despite the financial and political power of the Trust, month by month the Independents were winning. And they were winning for the same reason that rebel leaders often win—they had the people with them. Zukor, with Porter and B.P. and the rest of his advance guard, was right: Once audiences saw lengthier films with better stories and finer actors they quickly turned away from the stale old one-reelers that the Trust companies went on cranking out at so much a foot. Once they saw someone on the screen to whom they responded emotionally they demanded to know his name, or hers. When Mary Pickford was appearing in one-reelers for Biograph, one of the most influential companies in the Trust, she began to receive a stream of letters—the first fan mail. Instead of embracing this great new audience, Biograph gave it the back of its hand. Thousands of letters, my father remembered, were simply dumped into the trash can. People begging to know the name of "that cute little girl with the beautiful curls" were not to be told that she was Mary Pickford. For if Little Mary, as her fans began to call her, began to realize her importance, she would want more money. Mary had been on the stage since she was five years old, touring with her mother Charlotte; at fifteen she had a sense of the dollar and of her impending value at the box office. Give her and her tough old mama an inch and they would take a mile, J. J. Kennedy argued.

"They actually thought they could keep her anonymous," my father told me. "She was making one picture a week, and with every release she was becoming more of a national idol. Talk about not being able to see the handwriting on the wall, they literally couldn't see the close-up on their own screen. So Mary Pickford came to us, to Famous Players, and first we paid her twenty thousand a year and then one thousand dollars a week, then two thousand, and finally four thousand—but she and her mother were never satisfied—especially when they heard that her chief rival in popularity, Charlie Chaplin, had just signed a new contract for six hundred and seventy thousand dollars a year. Suddenly four thousand a week—even back in '16, the good old days before taxes—looked like chicken feed. She wanted a thousand dollars a day."

Charlotte and Mary were perhaps the first star bargainers in the history of this tough bargaining business to employ the now familiar blackmail against which the best written contract is helpless: "Little Mary is so unhappy at hearing how much more Charlie Chaplin is making that the poor child is positively sick. She might become too upset to come to work. And if she does show up at the studio, how can she do her best work when her mind is distracted by her financial problems?"

"What a crisis that was for Mr. Zukor, for all of us," Father said. Zukor used to walk the streets all night trying to solve problems like that. If he signed her, it would be at a staggering sum for twenty pictures a year; they would have to raise prices at all the movie theaters springing up around the country. He paid and prayed.

"She was not just the first screen idol, she had become a national institution," my father explained. "The symbol of rags to riches, of the good little girl overcoming evil. The titles of the pictures we made with her say a lot about what she meant to America: *Cinderella, Poor Little Rich Girl, Pollyanna, Rebecca of Sunnybrook Farm, A Dawn of Tomorrow.* . . . . She was poised delicately between childhood and adolescence. Even when she was twenty years old, married to Owen Moore, and able to play young romantic leads, America still wanted to see her with her long golden curls and her puckered little-girl lips. They wanted to keep her a perennial child. I really think she was the perfect symbol of our own wide-eyed innocence, before the War and the new generation of sheiks and flappers changed our morality.

"Calling Mary 'America's Sweetheart' was not exactly a stroke of genius. I was simply putting down in two words what everybody in America seemed to be feeling about her. I was standing in front of a theater one day watching people buy tickets to see Mary in one of the early movies I wrote for her when a middle-aged couple stopped in front of a display of stills from the picture. 'There she is,' the husband said. 'My little sweetheart.' Remember, people really talked a lot more sentimentally in those days. 'She's not just your little sweetheart, she's everybody's sweetheart,' his wife said. It rang a bell. That's exactly what she was— *America's Sweetheart!* I went back and tried it first on Al Kaufman, and then on Mr. Zukor himself, and they loved it. I wrote it into our next ad and she's been 'America's Sweetheart' ever since."

By the time I was three years old, the businesslike Mary and her shrewd mother-manager Charlotte Smith were raising the ante to ten thousand a week, and half the profits. They insisted that her pictures— now limited to ten a year—not be sold in a block with all the other Famous Players product but released through a subsidiary to be called the Mary Pickford Famous Players Company. In four incredible years, unlike any in the history of entertainment from Aesop to Zukor, Little

Mary had gone from an uncredited fifty-dollar-a-week moving-picture-show performer to a star whose earning power for a single year had rocketed to a cool million. It was a price that not even Zukor was prepared to pay, even though, in that same dynamic period, he had gone from an obscure nickelodeon owner to president of a twenty-five-million-dollar company that was growing every day.

Although I had adopted Ed Porter and Adolph Zukor as my simulated uncles, I never thought of Mary Pickford as a vicariously glamorous aunt. Maybe I inherited from B.P. a sense of her ingratitude for his services. I had only the dimmest memory of her, unlike my lasting impressions of Mr. Zukor, and my trips to the Zukor farm in New York City—where I saw my first cow. (In our apartment overlooking the park I had been drinking the fresh milk delivered by the Zukor chauffeur without appreciating the source of this cool white liquid.) My "bad" grandfather Simon had disappeared, mysteriously, and my "good" grandfather Max wasn't much fun, drinking tea from a saucer and rocking back and forth muttering prayers in a strange language. But "Uncle" Adolph was young and spry, a neat, energetic, kindly figure as he showed off his horses and cows.

Influenced by the European-made biblical spectacles, D. W. Griffith, while still working for Biograph, went out to California to make his ambitious four-reel *Judith of Bethulia.* One of the reasons he took that long trip across the continent was to get out from under the grip of the Trust. Independents were going to "the coast," as it was called then and has been known ever since, not so much for the perpetual sun that would light roofless interiors (winter sunshine was more accessible in Florida) as to escape the goons and the process servers of the Trust. It was this game of cat-and-mouse that really started Hollywood on its way to becoming the film capital of the world.

Even when Griffith brought his four-reel film east, hoping its impact would soften the hearts or strengthen the minds of the Patents Company executives, they insisted on clinging to their antique ways. *Judith of Bethulia* was released one reel at a time, like a serial. They could not recognize the genius of the filmmaker who was on the threshold of making the film that is the second great landmark in the history of American cinema: *The Birth of a Nation.* He had to leave Biograph and the Trust, and form his own independent company to make that film on a scale—*twelve* reels—that horrified and outraged the Trust mentality.

Half a dozen times during the making of that unprecedented film,

Griffith ran out of money. He begged and borrowed to keep it going. Its final cost was unthinkable for its day: one hundred thousand dollars. But when it finally opened, in 1915, its reception was so overwhelming that controversy over the "multiple film" became academic.

The picture was screened at the White House for President Wilson, a symbolic first. There were special screenings for the Supreme Court and for the diplomatic corps. And when it opened in New York, seats were priced at an unheard-of two dollars, as high as for a Broadway play. Blacks, then called Negroes, protested the blatant bigotry of the film, adapted as it was from a popular novel, *The Clansman,* extolling the virtues of the K.K.K. The film was a cultural schizoid, as backward politically and racially as it was advanced cinematically. But in vain did Booker T. Washington, Jane Addams, Dr. Charles Eliot of Harvard, and Oswald Garrison Villard protest "the humiliation of ten million American citizens." Blacks and liberals were swept aside as the public lined up across the country to see "the greatest motion picture ever made." The gross reached fifteen million dollars, more than ten times what this supposedly spendthrift picture had cost. Once an audience had experienced *The Birth of a Nation,* how could they ever again be satisfied with the stilted one-reelers of the Trust?

The lawsuit of the Independents against the Trust was being fought all the way up to the Supreme Court. The fact that the motion picture, through the work of Griffith and the vision of men like Zukor and Porter, had established itself as an art form that could hold an audience spellbound for an hour and a half or even two hours—that fact undoubtedly affected the judgment of the Hughes Court. Its decision: that the patents of the Trust were invalid, and that the motion-picture camera and projection machine could not be dominated by one small group. "That was the first Declaration of Freedom of the Screen," my father told me. "None of us who fought that antitrust action against the Patents Company will ever forget it." For Zukor and Griffith, for Porter and Schulberg, for Carl Laemmle, Jesse Lasky, Sam Goldwyn, and all the rest of the rebels, this was their Yorktown. The Trust that had held on like a bulldog, threatening Zukor, inhibiting Griffith, blasting opponents for daring to make longer and better pictures, was forced to retire from the field.

The decision came in 1916, when I was two. Porter was now at work in Rome on a spectacle, *The Eternal City,* starring one of the great actresses of the day, Pauline Frederick. Porter had never attempted a film on such a scale, costing as it did more than a hundred thousand dollars, and he found it difficult to stage this lavish production in a foreign country. When he came back from Rome he sat down and talked over his problem with my father. He had been a poor boy with little education, though with a strong social conscience in the tradition of his contemporaries, novelists like Frank Norris, Stephen Crane, and Jack London. His mechanical inventiveness and sense of social realism had enabled him to make his ground-breaking films. But now he felt that the art form he had originated was passing him by. His cinematic inventions looked crude alongside D. W. Griffith's, J. Stuart Blackton's, Allan Dwan's. . . .

Though he was only middle-aged, and could have remained as Director-General of Famous Players, Porter told my father that he thought it was time for him to quit. He did not feel equipped to direct talented actors in the subtleties of the craft. In another few years, he predicted, other Griffiths would come along who would put his efforts to shame. Porter was proud of his position as the father of the American story-film. In a single decade he had seen the American "moving picture show" develop from the primitive *Life of an American Fireman* to the complexity of *The Birth of a Nation,* followed by an even more ambitious Griffith project, *Intolerance,* telling the story of man's intolerance to man on four different historical levels, from Rome to modern times, with sets as grandiose as the ones which would soon become synonymous with the prototypical megaphone-wielder C. B. DeMille. "I know when I'm licked," Porter told my father. "I can't compete with these new fellers D.W. and C.B. I've had my day."

Whereupon Mr. Porter sold all of his stock back to Famous Players, and returned to his first love, tinkering with machines. Joining the Precision Machine Company, he continued to perfect cameras and projection machines. He was a wealthy man, although he would have been considerably wealthier if he had grown with Famous Players as it expanded in partnership with the Jesse Lasky Film Company, which in time would become Paramount Pictures.

B.P. never saw him again—was never able to track him down. Mysteriously, he dropped completely out of sight. None of the notables he had worked with, Zukor, Pickford, or Griffith, ever heard from him. The only rumor was that he prospered until the crash of 1929, when he lost the savings of a lifetime. When he died in 1941 he was working as an obscure mechanic, still tinkering, totally forgotten by the industry he had virtually created.

Fifty years later I happened to mention Porter's name to one of this country's most famous directors. "Edwin S. Porter?" he said. "I never heard of him." "Pal," I said, "if there hadn't been an Edwin S. Porter, there might never have been a you." One of these days the motion-picture industry, which never has had much respect for its history, failing to set up a museum, burning historic negatives, and neglecting its founders, will suddenly have an attack of conscience and offer a post-humous award to the first American filmmaker. But until that moment, this tribute from the son of his scenario editor: To the Granddaddy of us all.

4

ONCE THE TRUST wars were behind us and Zukor's policy of big stars in big pictures had put the old giants of the one-reel days out of business, the growth of Famous Players was reflected in the personal geography of the Schulbergs. Starting from 120th Street and Mt. Morris Park and moving to the larger apartment on 110th Street overlooking Central Park, we advanced to an even grander apartment near Zukor's and Pickford's on Riverside Drive, with a balcony where I could play and watch the ships go up and down the Hudson.

My memories of those New York days before the move to Hollywood are haphazard and piecemeal, the chance groupings and color patterns a child sees in his kaleidoscope. I remember that balcony on the river, remember making paper airplanes that would spiral down toward the toylike trees and the little cars far below. I remember collecting tinfoil, rolling it into balls and giving them to my mother for "our boys over there." I didn't know what war was, but it was fun to see how much foil I could gather and press together into a silvery ball. While we were singing cheery war songs like "Pack Up Your Troubles in Your Old Kit Bag," and while millions of young men were dying in the war to end wars, the movies did their bit by cranking out propaganda films like *To Hell with the Kaiser* and *The Woman the Germans Shot* and sending such glorified patriots as Mary Pickford and Doug Fairbanks across the country selling Liberty Bonds.

More important to me was that the Irish immigrant maid was

replaced by a beautiful and soothing woman called Wilma, who was slightly darker than the rest of us, like my cocoa after she had poured a little warm milk into it. I loved my mother and my father, but I don't remember them in those years as vividly as I do Wilma. One of my earliest senses of pleasure was of her *color,* as she would lean over my crib and over the small yellow bed with the elaborately carved head-board into which I was graduated when my sister Sonya arrived. I was four years old then, and in that short period from 1914 to 1918 it had become bad taste for babies to be born at home. Home births were for immigrants and peasants, for the poor. I remember my mother returning to Riverside Drive from the hospital with Sonya, and Wilma paying a great deal of attention to the little intruder, and my worrying that I was going to lose her to the homely little thing in the cradle that everyone thought was so cute.

Wilma must have handled this well, for Sonya remembers her lovingly, while I also felt reassured that Wilma had not deserted me. Mostly I remember her gentleness. I remember my mother and father telling me they were going off on a trip—I think it was to Atlantic City to a motion-picture exhibitors' convention—and my asking, "Is Wilma going, too?" And when I was assured that Wilma would stay right here with us, I said something like, "Then I don't care when you come back." I remember Wilma's face, gently disapproving, and my mother's tears.

One day when Sonya was nearly two, Wilma set her on the park bench and began to chat with some other nurses. I was busy feeding a squirrel. Suddenly Wilma ran up to me: "Isn't little Sonya with you?" When I shook my head, Wilma raced around looking around bushes and begging the other nurses to join the search. She was crying and that made me want to cry, too. We searched for half an hour, with Wilma becoming more and more hysterical.

When we hurried back to the Riverside Drive apartment to break the news, Mother screamed at her, then phoned B.P. at the studio to call the police.

"How could you let our little girl out of your sight?" Mother was accusing Wilma. And Wilma was sobbing, "If they don't find her I'll kill myself! I swear I'll kill myself!"

A few minutes later Father came rushing in. Movie people were looked on as overnight millionaires, and he was terrified that Sonya had been kidnapped. The cops questioned Wilma and me but we were very little help. Sonya simply had vanished into thin air. I pressed my head against Wilma's heaving breast and sobbed, "I'll never see that little face again!" It sounded like a subtitle from one of Father's photoplays. But what I was really crying about was the fear of losing Wilma. For Father was angrier than I had ever seen him before, and the more he shouted at her the more she cried out that it was all her fault and she wanted to die.

If Wilma died, who would take care of me? I wanted to die too.

Then one of the policemen looked up from the phone. "One of our boys just found her—at the edge of the park!" My parents rushed out. There at the 125th Street police station was little Sonya, perched on the sergeant's desk, quietly licking an ice cream cone.

At home the distraught Wilma rocked Sonya in her arms and bathed her with grateful tears. Father went back to his studio, and Mom went back to her meetings. And I had Wilma back again.

Mother loved us, and expressed that love through her determination to improve us, but she was *busy*. The winds of social change blowing through the middle Teens bestirred her wavy blonde hair. A suffragist since before I was born, an active member of the Godmothers' League for unwed mothers, she continued to support the socialism-tinged Educational Alliance. When Emile Coué, the French psychotherapist, was all the rage, we had to recite at bedtime, "Every day in every way I'm getting better and better. . . ." Night after night I slipped off to sleep drugged in self-improvement. No doubt about it, Adeline Jaffe Schulberg, our frail little flower of the East Side ghetto, the would-be librarian, was reaching up for every intellectual branch she could close her little hands around. She attended lectures the way the masses who were gradually making us rich lined up for their moving-picture shows.

With Wilma as our full-time nurse and companion, we naturally came to depend on her emotionally. Mothers and fathers were for getting presents from and saying goodnight to. It was through Wilma that I learned, inadvertently, that there was something difficult in having a dark skin in a white world.

I saw very little of my father—as publicity director of Famous Players he was out most nights, dining and drinking with movie stars and directors and visiting firemen—and I suppose I was trying to ingratiate myself with him so he would take more notice of me. I asked him if I could pour the cream into his morning coffee. He had been out late with his company cronies, Al Lichtman, Al Kaufman, and Frank Meyer, the studio manager—they called themselves "The Four Hoarsemen" because in their cramped offices at the studio on 26th Street they had to shout their business to each other over the din of the Model T's and the heavy clop-clopping of the horses pulling delivery wagons. Anyway, B.P. had been a little late in rising and he was in a hurry to get to the day's work. Picturemaking was a passion with him, and Mary Pickford was finishing one of the films he had written. I wasn't interested in Mary Pickford, nor was I aware that her phenomenal success was helping him to pay for this airy apartment. My personal star was Wilma, and as I poured the cream into his coffee, I said, "L-l-look, D-Daddy, I'm m-making a Wilma c-color."

My father glanced nervously at Wilma, who was beginning to clear the table. He had exceptionally pale skin, almost porcelain in quality, his fine features and his sandy hair and his high white collar all seeming to blend together. I thought of my mother as pale pink, with faint roses glowing from her cheeks and a pretty mouth that was much redder than the rest of her. Wilma was the only person I had ever seen who looked like rich cream stirred into black coffee. My father turned back from Wilma and his voice was scolding. "Buddy, I want you to remember this. You must never, *never* mention Wilma's color again. We are all very fond of Wilma. She's become like a member of the family. It isn't nice to talk about people's color." This was half a century before "Black Is Beautiful." It was back in the know-nothing days of "Black Is Invisible," or "Black Is Unmentionable."

In a few minutes Dad was rushing off to the studio. To another big, exciting day, another hit movie for "America's Sweetheart," whose curls were as yellow as butter and whose skin was as white as snow. All the movie stars were snow-whites. The Pickford sisters and the Gish sisters, and Florence Lawrence, "The Girl of a Thousand Faces," every one of them white.

I went out on the balcony and stared at the river. Why was it bad to mention Wilma's color? Especially when it seemed a prettier color than pale white or pink. It seemed exactly the right color for skin to be. Hadn't we spent the summer in Far Rockaway where my own very white skin had finally tanned and my mother had announced happily, "Look at little Buddy—he's brown as a berry!" Why was it nice for me to be brown as a berry, but not nice for me to mention Wilma's coffee-and-cream color?

When my mother saw me brooding on the balcony, not playing with my tin soldiers (I had a big set of American doughboys and they were always destroying the rival set of dirty Huns), she asked me what was the matter, and when I told her, she did her best to explain, in the limited vocabulary of 1918. She said it might offend Wilma because white people considered Negro people their inferiors. They had come over from Africa as slaves and did not have the advantages of education or the cultural background that we enjoyed. Of course Wilma was something of an exception. Her father had been a minister or a teacher or something and she seemed to be far better educated than "most of them." We were very lucky to have someone like Wilma to take care of Sonya and me, Mother said. And this whole color thing—I was much too young to worry about it. My mother knew a great deal about psychology from books (I think she was then in her Behaviorism period, a disciple of Watson), and for her age and time she was unusually well-read in this field, but I don't think even Ad could comprehend the deep impression that Wilma and her color and the "problem" of her color were having on me.

I finally went to the source that day, to Wilma herself. When I asked her what I had said that was wrong, she took me up on her lap and kissed my cheek and I held her smooth coffee-colored earlobe. "Buddy, you're awfully little to understand this. But maybe some people can understand things at four that other people can't understand when they're a hundred-and-four. There's nothing wrong with saying what color a person is. I don't mind my color. I think it's a nice color, just like you said. The reason why your daddy said it isn't nice to mention it is because most people are glad that they're white and most of the colored people know it would be a lot easier for them if they were white. But there's nothing wrong with being my color, or chocolate brown or coal black. The only thing wrong is the way some people feel about it."

"But w-why do they f-feel that way about it.?"

Wilma hugged me. "Maybe the time will come when people will all be just *people* and won't pay no mind as to whether they're white or brown or peppermint stripe."

That made me laugh. Peppermint stripe would be fun.

Wilma kissed me again. "Children just seem to start out knowing all the things that big people forget."

A fire in the middle of the night! My father and mother jumped up and threw their clothes on. I heard frantic cries: "My god! We'll be ruined! We'll lose everything!" I can still remember the fear, the sense of a terrible threat to our existence. No, the fire was not in our Riverside

Drive apartment, but at the studio: the old Famous Players studio, a four-story building on 26th Street and Eighth Avenue where all my father's hopes and dreams, current activities and professional future lay. While B.P.'s salary was still a relatively modest two hundred dollars a week, the shrewd and benevolent Mr. Zukor also paid his key young employees one share of stock per week, so that we had an equity in the company. An equity that was literally going up in flames.

The Famous Players Film Company had not been using the entire building, only the top two floors, and the roof where sets had also been constructed. It was a rundown neighborhood with a junk shop and a Chinese laundry across the way. Twenty-sixth Street was very narrow, and cumbersome horse-drawn wagons parked along the curb made access by the huge firetrucks extremely difficult.

Father and Mother stayed there until dawn, inside the police barricade, while the firemen fought a losing battle against the flames. Actually the building was a firetrap, a jerry-built renovation of an old armory. As the disaster was reconstructed, it had started in a braid or rope factory on the second floor and had raged upward through the Famous Players offices on the third floor and the flimsy sets and cutting room on the top floor. Film companies were uninsurable because of the flammability of their product. So the entire assets of Famous Players were seemingly being consumed in that flaming inferno of a "studio." However, since insurance was not available, Frank Meyer, the studio manager, had installed a fireproof vault on the third floor; in it, seventeen completed but still unreleased features had been deposited.

The night of the fire all of the Famous Players "family," my father included, had gone to a lightweight boxing match between two great Irish fighters, Packy McFarland and Mike Gibbons. (Irish fighters were then the dominant performers, with the East Side Jews getting ready to battle them for supremacy. There were some marvelous Negroes—Jack Johnson, Sam Langford, Joe Gans—but the great Black tide was still to come.) All the Famous Players crowd were ardent fight fans, maybe because their leader, Mr. Zukor, had implemented his meager earnings as a fur worker with five-dollar purses as a flyweight. The entire staff had gone to the big fight that night, with one exception: Frank Meyer. He had decided to pass up the event to finish cutting the latest Mary Pickford film. Apparently he was trapped up there in the cutting room and my parents, along with the rest of the "family," were terrified that he would be burned alive in his cubbyhole. But suddenly he appeared. It was a scene as melodramatic as anything he had been working on. He had been trapped on a fire escape but had finally managed to jump across to an adjoining roof. To keep the fire from spreading, firemen had been pouring powerful streams of water onto that roof and instead of burning to death, Frank had almost been drowned. He was soaked to the skin and shivering, but quite alive.

To my parents and their friends waiting outside, it was miraculous to see him emerge from a building now totally ablaze. But they were movie people and after being reassured of Frank's safety, their first question was: Did the Pickford film burn? And what about the cans of film on shelves in the cutting room? Frank said he had fought through the smoke to throw as much footage as possible into the cylinder vault. This was heroic but only partly reassuring. If the walls fell in as they threatened to, it was doubtful that the precious vault would survive. And even if it did, the intensity of the fire might be so great that enough heat would be generated inside the cylinder to melt their completed films. They had been trying to turn out fifty feature films a year, or one a week, to satisfy the aroused appetite of the American public—with a new Mary Pickford picture promised every month—and the loss of their product plus the loss of a huge investment in equipment could mean the end of Famous Players.

While watching his first studio engulfed in flames, Adolph Zukor remained incredibly cool, according to my father. He never lost control of himself, never cried out, but simply waited for the smoke to clear. "I never admired him as much as I did during those hours when we were waiting to see if the roof was—literally—going to fall in on us," my father told me. "The rest of us were hysterical, but Mr. Zukor, who had the most to lose, stood there like a general watching his army go into a crucial battle. If the fire resulted in total loss, I'm sure he had no idea how he would meet his next payroll. But he assured us that come what may we would all be paid at the end of the week."

By morning the building had been reduced to smoking rubble. The fireproof vault had come loose from the wall but was found in the wreckage, too hot to open. For three days, B.P. paced with Zukor and the rest of the staff, waiting to know whether or not they were still in business. On the third day a safecracker was employed to open the vault: The lock had melted or jammed in the intense heat. Not only were those seventeen film negatives intact, but the Pickford film and the other cans of material that Frank Meyer had frantically tossed into the fireproof container could be sent out to the theaters waiting for them across the country. Famous Players was saved.

Zukor wasted no time renting an abandoned riding academy across town, on East 56th Street. There a new studio was quickly set up and the hectic pace of turning out what were then super films with Zukor's illustrious company of star names continued. But every one of Zukor's famous stars of the stage—John Barrymore, James K. Hackett, Minnie Maddern Fiske—had to play second fiddle to the movies' first Cinderella girl, Mary Pickford. Little Mary's movies were grossing more than all the others put together.

The midtown livery stable was my first studio. Four years old, a towheaded kid dressed up for the occasion in a new sailor suit, I held tightly to my father's hand as we entered that strange, enormous room, dark in the back and very bright in the front, with strong lights shining into the faces of the actors. What struck me most was that there were so many people standing around in the dark watching so few people in the light. A young man seemed to be in charge because he was busy telling everybody what to do. He would say "Action!" and the people in the bright lights would begin acting funny. A young girl with long yellow hair suddenly began to cry. "W-w-why is she c-crying, Daddy?" My father raised to his lips a long tapering index finger. "Shhh," he whispered. "They're shooting." Then he bent over and put his mouth to my ear. "That's Mary Pickford. She's not crying. She's just *acting* that she's crying."

I was confused and frightened. "But w-why?"

The director looked around, pained. "B.P., please! This is a tough scene."

Another man standing alongside him called out loud as if he was talking to everybody but stared sharply at me, "Quiet, everybody!" Again the director said "Action!" and again the young girl in the white dress and white stockings said a few words and then began to cry. She kept on crying until the man in charge said "Cut," and then she stopped, just as suddenly as she had started, and asked in a businesslike voice, "How was that?" "Better," said the young man with the megaphone. Then she started crying again and everybody watching her seemed very pleased, and then they turned off the big bright lights. It was very dark in there, and a bunch of men started taking the furniture away and moving the walls around. Two men could lift them like cardboard. My father led me toward the young girl in white who was now sitting in a chair while a woman fixed the long yellow curls that hung down almost to her waist. A man was dabbing some white stuff on her face with a powder puff. The young man with the megaphone, with a handsome ruddy face and wavy hair, was kneeling in front of her.

"Mary," my father said, "I'd like you to meet my little boy Buddy."

The people working to make her pretty stood back a moment while she drew me toward her and kissed me on the forehead. "Buddy," she said, "I hope you'll always be a buddy to me."

I don't actually remember blushing when Mary kissed me, but I remember the embarrassment caused by all the fuss that was made about it. The man with the megaphone, whom I was later to know as Mickey Neilan, a matinee idol before he succeeded D. W. Griffith as Mary's film director, this ruddy-faced stranger shouted at me, "Hey! Cut that out, Buddy boy. Don't you know I'm jealous?" Everybody laughed and my face felt very hot because I didn't know what they were laughing at. Then he picked me up and affectionately bounced me up and down. "No hard feelings, Buddy. You're a good-looking kid. A helluva lot better-looking than your old man. How'd ya like to be in my next movie?"

"N-n-*no!*" I said. And everybody laughed again.

D. W. Griffith and C. B. DeMille may have been greater directors, but when you seek a prototype of the carefree movie days of the Teens and Twenties, Mickey Neilan was the man. Think of the Twenties and you think of Valentino, Greta Garbo, Mae Murray, Chaplin, Keaton, and Lloyd, of Irving Thalberg, Ernst Lubitsch, Von Stroheim, John Ford. . . . Those were the gold-dust days, and in his prime nobody had more gold dust in his hair or in his laughing eyes than the Mickey Neilan who lifted me up on the set of *Amerilly of Clothes Line Alley.*

5

AT FOUR YEARS of age I would seem to have been in kiddie's heaven, with prosperous parents who doted on me, a nurse who loved me—a child who had been kissed by America's Sweetheart, who could go with his father to the studio whenever he wished to see movies being made, and who had been assured by his studious and well-meaning mother that he could do anything he really wanted to do. When epidemics hit the city—influenza and infantile paralysis—I was quickly motored upstate to the safety of Schroon Lake. My mother read me the best children's literature available to develop my mind. I learned to read before I went to kindergarten. The famous friends of my parents kept telling them how precociously intelligent I was. In other words, it would have seemed to the objective observer that the little Schulberg boy, whose papa was getting to be such a big shot at Famous Players while still in his mid-twenties, had the whole big world for his toy balloon.

I could run, I could jump, I could read, I was well coordinated, I could remember every detail of the stories that were read to me, I loved my mother and father, even was surprisingly fond of my baby sister, I was a friendly little tyke, gentle with animals. Yes, I seemed to have been favored by the gods all right. They had lavished everything on me. Except for one slight oversight. The gift of speech.

Another child would ask me my name and I'd try to say, "B-b-b-b . . . . ," then run home sobbing, "I c-c-can't t-t-talk . . ." When I opened my mouth to speak I stammered and stuttered and lisped. To say a word, I would squeeze my eyes together until tears leaked from the corners.

My frantic mother took me to the doctor to see if there was anything wrong with my oral equipment. The doctor put a stick on my tongue and I even stammered my "A-a-ahs . . ." Nothing wrong that Dr. Jellyhouse (what a deliciously unforgettable name for a pediatrician) could see, but he passed us on to a specialist. The specialist could locate no physical disability.

So Ad tried a psychologist, a friend of hers, one of the early practitioners in that virgin field, explaining that I had been a nervous child. Colic. Crying all night. When she had taken me to Schroon Lake with Lottie Zukor and son Eugene and others of the Zukor clan, they had complained because the walls of the old resort hotel were anything but soundproof and my wailing kept them up all night. Ad and the mind doctor discussed my affliction in terms of my father. B.P. also stammered. Not all the time but when he was under stress. One theory is that your mind is working too fast and the tongue can't keep up with it. Another is that stammering or stuttering is an attention-getting mechanism although it seems to me that little Buddy was being smothered in attention.

Then Mother took me back to her favorite hunting ground, Columbia University. If I had not come along so soon (nine and a *half* months after their marriage, she always delicately insisted), she would have liked to try for a degree there. At Columbia we entered a speech therapy class for afflicted children and their parents. A group of us would walk around in a large circle, like performing seals, first *singing* lines that the therapist would give us, then repeating them in a singsong voice. Ludicrous as it may sound, there was more method than madness in the system. The most extreme stammerer can sing the lyrics of a song without difficulty. Even if you try to stammer a song, you can't. It has to do with breathing. Stammerers and stutterers do not have enough air in their lungs when they begin to talk. Inhaling deeply, as when preparing to open one's mouth in song, allows the words to flow out smoothly. Marion Davies, W. R. Hearst's gift to Hollywood, was a chronic stutterer. When she became hopelessly stuck in the middle of a sentence, the golden-haired pixie would break into song.

This cure for stammering worked beautifully—in the therapy sessions. Within the halls of Columbia my stammer-stutter magically disappeared. But as soon as I was on my way home again, I would try a

sentence and hear myself saying, "M-m-mommy, c-c-can I-I-I . . ."
Sometimes she would cry in frustration. What had she done wrong?
What was the matter with me? Was I imitating my father? What was I
frightened of? I stammered my way from therapist to therapist and in
and out of special schools. The most expensive advice proved unavail-
ing. I didn't even learn to sing. Of course there were compensations.
From childhood on I loved to listen to people talk. Becoming a good
listener was a natural development. Years later when I found myself
having to speak in public, with the old stammer still reflected in prolonged hesitations, I enjoyed an extra flow of adrenalin when I finished
my talk, a sense of having faced up to a maddening defect and overcoming it.

My stammering also had a productive side effect for my mother.
Already intrigued by Freud and the early stirrings of psychoanalysis, she
continued to search the reason for my speech defect in the works of Brill
and Jung and other disciples who were beginning to spread and develop
their own theories. But the stammering little light of her life went right on
stammering.

B.P. Schulberg, patriarch.

Ad Schulberg, matriarch.

There wasn't room for both. *Circa* 1928

Edwin S. Porter, the director of *The Great Train Robbery,* gave B.P. Schulberg his first film job. Porter is seen here with an early version of the film projector.

Ad and B.P. and an old
crony of his, Joe Roche.

▲ The crown princes of Hollywood were not beyond a bit of
fun. Here we see Jerry Mayer (brother of L.B. Mayer) and
B.P. Schulberg patting the head of a lion badly in need of a
hairdresser. The picture was taken c. 1922 at the old
Mayer-Schulberg studio, which was attached to the Selig
Zoo. This picture, in fact, was the genesis of the idea for an
MGM lion.

◀ In front of the Santa Fe Chief (c. 1925). At the far left is
Pat Powers, an early motion picture boss; stepping just a
bit forward to be noticed is mogul Adolf Zukor; next to
him, a bit back of course, Mrs. Zukor; and Al Kaufman,
Zukor's son-in-law, who along with B.P. Schulberg was offered $500 a week for life in 1914, when money was
money. At the far right is B.P.

The moguls of early Hollywood lived well, but few pictures exist of the interiors of their homes. This is the Schulberg library which was catalogued and its volumes numbered by a professional librarian. Ad's first career was as a librarian. B.P. was extremely fond of rare books, and on Sundays he would read to his family from the classics.

Jackie Coogan's tenth birthday party (1924). Coogan is in front at the center. At his left and right are Marjorie Lesser and Julian "Buddy" Lesser, whose father, Sol Lesser, made a fortune on Tarzan pictures. Budd Schulberg is in military academy uniform on the first step at the extreme right. To his left is his sister, Sonya.

B.P. Schulberg, Ad, and baby Budd

In the back row: Leon Errol, comedian; an unidentified person; Al Kaufman; Buddy Rogers; and just below him, Jack Oakie. In the front row: Jesse Lasky of Famous-Players-Lasky, one of the early moguls; B.P. Schulberg in a characteristic stance; actor Clive Brook; Ruth Chatterton; a mystery couple (possibly visiting Romanian nobility or a bogus Bulgarian prince); director Eddie Goulding; comedian Harry Green; and Mike Levee, studio executive and later one of the leading agents.

▲ The Mayer-Schulberg studio, which was carved out of the old Selig Studio and Zoo north of downtown Los Angeles. It was then a rural neighborhood that featured an alligator and ostrich farm. The building is typical of the flamboyant stucco architecture of the day. The operating partnership was ruptured when Mayer became head of MGM in 1924.

B.P. Schulberg (again in his characteristic stance) and Ad, *circa* 1927, on a family trip through the Panama Canal

6

OWN AT THE Famous Players studio B.P. was doing a bit of stammering too, but it had no effect on his increasing importance as one of Zukor's fair-haired boys. Things were going so well that one day their shrewd, self-contained boss called into his office the Three Musketeers—Al Kaufman the son-in-law studio manager, Al Lichtman the film salesman, and my father. For a conservative man, Zukor made them a most unusual proposition. He was prepared to raise their salaries from two hundred dollars a week to five hundred dollars a week—for life. In the Wilson era, five hundred a week was a fortune. And for life!

My father looked at his two pals and muttered something about wanting to go off with the two Al's and think it over. The three of them, up-and-coming film tycoons, all of them still in the pink of youth, ordered a round at the saloon across the street from the studio, and discussed this unexpected offer. From the conservative point of view, Al Kaufman suggested, five hundred a week plus increasing stock in the company would set them up for life. At the age of 25 they would never have another financial care as long as they lived.

The three young men discussed it excitedly over a second round of drinks, and then a third. They were feeling on top of the world. "Let's go in and grab it before Uncle Adolph changes his mind," Al Kaufman said. But halfway through his third highball my father was having second thoughts. "Wait a minute, Al. Five hundred looks awfully big this year. And probably will next year. And maybe even the year after. But we've seen Mary Pickford go from a hundred dollars a week to ten thousand a week in the short time we've been working with her—well, we aren't America's Sweetheart but in a couple of years we might be worth a thousand a week. Or two thousand. We're on the ground floor of a business growing bigger every day. Five years from now we may feel that Mr. Zukor has got us caught in his trap at five hundred a week."

Al Lichtman agreed. He and Ben were born gamblers, at cards, at the crap tables, and with their lives. "I'm with B.P. Let's ask for five hundred for the next two years. During that time we work like hell, make ourselves indispensable. Then we go in and ask for more."

Flushed both with alcohol and their own daring, the three young men trooped back to Mr. Zukor's office. Before they could deliver their decision, he could read it on their faces. "Gentlemen," he said, beating them to the punch, "I've thought it over and I withdraw the offer."

So B.P. was back to his salary of two hundred a week. But he told my mother he felt sure he had made the right decision. He knew he had hitched his wagon to a star, or rather two stars, Zukor and Pickford, and soon they would be strengthened through amalgamation with the Jesse Lasky-Sam Goldfish company, whose young, still inexperienced, but already self-confident director was Cecil B. DeMille.

Lasky, Goldfish, and DeMille were such a strange grouping that they might be thought of as The Odd Triple. Goldfish, later to become Goldwyn, had been a twelve-year-old Jewish refugee from Poland who managed to work his way to America in steerage, wangle a job as an apprentice in a glove factory in Gloversville, New York, and, although his grasp of the English language was rudimentary, become a glove salesman. In his late twenties he came to Manhattan to open his own glove agency.

There he met an altogether different kind of Jew, Jesse Lasky, second generation from California, who had knocked around as a reporter on *The San Francisco Post,* as a luckless miner in the Alaska gold rush, and had finally drifted to Honolulu as a cornetist, the only white man in the Royal Hawaiian Band. Apparently this was not distinction enough and soon Jesse was back in San Francisco, talking his sister Blanche, also a cornetist, into forming a vaudeville team, The Musical Laskys. With their mother along to take care of them, The Musical Laskys toured the backwaters of the vaudeville circuit, lucky to earn fifty a week for the act. Then Lasky happened to hear one of the better cornetists of the day, B.

A. Rolfe, and suggested they go into business together. Lasky would be his manager. The partnership generated musical acts up and down the East Coast, until finally the tall, gentle, pince-nezed Jesse felt he was ready for something even more ambitious: launching the Folies Bergère as New York's first cabaret.

It was a dismal failure and Lasky was now desperate to find some other toehold in the entertainment business. He had an idea for a one-act comic opera and tried to sign William DeMille, a successful playwright, as the librettist. But with a hit play on Broadway, he considered such an offer below his standards. So Mama DeMille, who managed William and his younger brother Cecil, decided her number-two son could do the job. In his early thirties Cecil had had only moderate success as an actor in touring companies and was now trying his hand at playwriting. When Cecil wrote the comic opera quickly and acceptably, Lasky signed him to write other one-act sketches at the rate of twenty-five dollars a week.

While Lasky and DeMille were making something less than vaudeville history, Sam Goldfish was losing interest in his glove business because he was finding a new outlet for his restless nature—moving pictures. Jesse's sister Blanche had married the enterprising Sam, in part because she was weary of the one-night stands and insecurities of show business, and ready to settle down to economic security. But Sam had first been attracted to the adventure films of Broncho Billy Anderson, and then to the longer, classier films of Famous Players, and now he proposed to his brother-in-law that they take a flyer in the movie business. At first Lasky was cool to the idea. At least he knew something about vaudeville, about music. And yet, he had to admit at a pessimistic dinner with Cecil, he was still beating the bushes of failure: "I'm 32 and all I'm doing is comic operas." Said DeMille, "And I'm writing twenty-five-dollar-a-week vaudeville turns."

After dinner they strolled over to the Lambs Club. There, drinking champagne in the taproom, was Dustin Farnum, who had just starred on Broadway in *The Squaw Man,* one of the stage hits of the year. Lasky and DeMille looked at each other and a bell sounded simultaneously in both heads. Here was their first star and their first movie! They approached him, introduced themselves, and asked him if he would like to be in their first motion picture. Farnum had appeared in a foreign film, and was intrigued with the new medium.

Next day the Lasky Feature Play Company was capitalized at $25,000, with Lasky and DeMille subscribing $5,000 each, mostly borrowed from relatives, and the aggressive Sam Goldfish offering to underwrite the rest. Farnum was offered $5,000 worth of stock for his services but he preferred hard cash. A few years later that stock would have been worth more than a million dollars.

The rights to *The Squaw Man* were acquired for $5,000 in cash and $5,000 in notes. There was $15,000 left for DeMille and Farnum to go to the Southwest (the setting for the picture), set up a studio, buy the equipment, and hire technicians and a cast. While DeMille and Farnum were making this pioneer journey—a journey that was to have a direct effect on my life and that of my family—Goldfish and Lasky worked feverishly to sell their nonexistent picture to independent exchanges for cash, or for notes which they could discount at the bank. The little company was hanging by a thread, a company that had never produced a picture and that was entrusting its entire capital to a twenty-five-dollar-a-week sketch-writer who had never directed a film.

The rest is Hollywood history at its most quixotic. Near the intersection of rural Sunset Boulevard and Vine Street, then a picturesque country lane flavored with the scent of orange blossoms and lined with pepper trees, DeMille found an old barn which he rented for one hundred dollars a week. The actors were bounced to work in a second-hand truck from a dilapidated boardinghouse a mile away.

DeMille, who had never really found himself on Broadway, knew he had found his medium now. In three weeks *The Squaw Man* was in the can and he was ready for the five-day railroad journey east to show the first production of the Jesse Lasky Feature Play Company to its backers. After some technical difficulties with projection which threatened to wipe out the entire assets of the company, *The Squaw Man* was exhibited successfully, and earned back twice its investment. This money was immediately invested in a second DeMille feature, *Brewster's Millions,* which enjoyed even greater success. *The Squaw Man* had been thrown into theaters like a quickie, without any fanfare, because the small company had no money for publicity and they needed as quick a return as possible. But for their second picture, they borrowed from B.P.'s sense of promotional ballyhoo. They rented a legitimate theater and coaxed and begged every stage star and Manhattan celebrity to be on hand for the gala opening. Mr. Zukor accepted the invitation, went to the showing with my father, and was impressed with what these newcomers had been able to achieve.

Instead of treating the upstart Jesse Lasky as a rival, Zukor welcomed him into the fraternity of serious filmmakers. He invited him to lunch at Delmonico's and discussed with B.P. and the other young partners the advantages of bringing the Lasky Company into the fold. Zukor now owned movie theaters as well as producing facilities, those theaters were changing their bills twice a week, and Famous Players was unable to keep up with this appetite for celluloid. Lasky, Goldfish, and DeMille struck him as enterprising young men, ready to enlarge their Hollywood barn into a full-time movie studio.

Soon B.P. was announcing the merger. It was now Famous Players-Lasky, with the gentlemanly, ebullient Jesse Lasky operating from the little studio among the orange groves while Adolph Zukor continued to preside over his growing empire from his studio in New York.

Since Sam Goldfish also remained in New York, this brought him head to head with Zukor and it was obvious that each was too strong-willed for the other. Goldfish withdrew, to go into partnership with the Selwyn brothers. But Sam was a congenital loner, daring and dynamic and emotionally designed for one-man operations. Soon he was shearing off from the Selwyns to form his own company: the Samuel Gold-*wyn* Company. "Sam not only walked away with half their company but half their good name," said Father.

Another lone wolf whom Adolph Zukor tried to corral and tame was that wild man of the early independents, Lewis J. Zeleznick, who had shortened his name to Selznick. He belongs to the Schulberg saga partly because my father had to cope with his outrageous publicity techniques, but also because there seems to have been a dramatic inevitability about the way Selznick's son David kept getting involved with Schulbergs, father and son. David would get his training as a producer through assisting B.P. in the glory days when my father was a four-star mogul. The time would come when I would be signed by David to one of those seven-year contracts in what David hoped would be a Schulberg-Selznick relationship in reverse. "You know, Buddy," David said to me when he was hiring me right out of college, "it's really as if the Selznicks and the Schulbergs are so intertwined that it's all one big story."

All one big story. At least all one beginning and all one pattern. Like Sam Goldfish in Poland and Adolph Zukor in Hungary, like my father's family and Mother's in Latvia, L.J. escaped from Russia and its pogroms and its lack of opportunity for Jews. He was twelve years old when he fled the Cossacks, somehow making his way to England, and then on to America. He became a jeweler in Pittsburgh, opened a bigger jewelry store in New York City. It went broke. Other immigrants might have been crushed, but L.J. was as little discouraged by this failure as is a crapshooter who lets all his winnings ride on the next roll and comes up with snake-eyes. What do you do, shoot yourself? Hell no, you find another sucker to borrow from and you roll again. That was L.J. Made to order for those gold-rush days. If you hit, you hit big. If you crapped out you found yourself another stake and strode back to the table.

I wasn't there, of course. I was still in that speech therapy class at Columbia walking around the large room holding the hand of my mother on one side and the hand of the mother of a fellow-stammerer on the other, singsonging, "I can speak like this without stammering if I really want to. . . ." *I can do anything I really want to. . . .*

L. J. Selznick may not have been aware of Dr. Coué, but the grand-pappy of the Power of Positive Thinking was his man, too. If at first you don't succeed, try, try again. These weren't bromides: In the days of my childhood, when the silent movies were growing out of short pants, these were daily challenges. After auctioning off his failed jewelry store, pocketing a few diamonds for a rainy day, L.J. renewed his acquaintance with a man he had befriended in Pittsburgh, Mark Dintenfass, a herring salesman turned moviemaker. Every one of the early moguls stumbled, tripped, or backed into the movies, but Selznick's meeting with Dinten-fass marked—if you will excuse another B.P.ism—perhaps the most bizarre entry into motion pictures in the history of our bizarre business.

L.J. learned from Dintenfass that Universal, one of Famous Players' early rivals, was torn in two by a bitter struggle for control between "Uncle" Carl Laemmle and Pat Powers. Dintenfass's stock in the company could tip the scale either way.

Uncle Carl, as he came to be called because he hired so many relatives from his native Germany that a small army of employees could literally call him uncle, had operated a chain of nickelodeons before he merged his independent company with that of Pat Powers. But this oddly matched pair turned out to be in agreement on only one issue, their hatred of the Trust. By the time L. J. Selznick heard about their feud they were engaged in bitter civil war. The Universal offices at 1600 Broadway were an armed camp. This battleground provided the ideal stage for the impulsive and daring L. J. Selznick. He told his friend Dintenfass that he would sell the ex-herring salesman's stock to either Powers or Laemmle, thereby giving one or the other control of the divided company. He approached Powers first, but Powers said he didn't need the Dintenfass stock. An ex-blacksmith who towered over the diminutive Laemmle, he could whip Laemmle's ass without the formality of stock majorities. So Selznick made a similar approach to Uncle Carl. Laemmle was more amenable. He bought the Dintenfass stock.

Pat Powers's methods continued to be muscular. Confronted with a showdown meeting of bank examiners and accountants to decide which faction owned what, he ordered his minions to toss the company records out the window. While Uncle Carl was shooting a picture at their jointly owned studio, Powers had his troops drive a van up to the set and begin to remove the props and equipment. Uncle Carl called the police. But Pat so charmed the boys in blue with his Irish brogue that they actually helped dismantle the Laemmle set.

On such chaos did L.J., the wild man of those pioneers, feed. He noticed an empty office, set up shop in it, and although he had absolutely nothing to do with the company other than having served as intermediary for the Dintenfass stock, he appointed himself general manager of Universal, complete with a door plate and stationery. There was such a total breakdown between the two sides that each assumed he was working for the other. From the moment he sat down at the desk he had appropriated, L.J. knew that he had found his calling. He had always said that jewelry was strictly for suckers. And he had thought he was safe with that business because God had made so many of them. But the movie business was completely crazy. Anybody could get in—all you need is the gall to walk in and hang up your shingle. You look around and you see what the successful people are doing and you beat them at their own game.

Selznick's first act of derring-do was to use the Universal office to launch his own company, and to woo the beautiful Clara Kimball Young away from Vitagraph, the veteran company that had built her into one of the first bright stars of the day. Her abandonment of Vitagraph for this reckless interloper sent shock waves through the young industry. Why, this ex-"general manager" of Universal didn't even have the money to pay Clara's salary. But money was always the least of L.J.'s worries. He simply announced his new star in *The Common Law,* sold the picture in advance to exhibitors across the country, hustled some backing from Wall Street for his explosive new company, and, with the glamorous Mrs. Young as the shining star atop his rapidly erected Christmas tree, soon had it adorned with such marquee names as Lew Fields, Alice

Brady, Lillian Russell, and Lionel Barrymore. A fearless collector of other people's ideas, he was soon advertising "Features with Well Known Players in Well Known Plays." Quickly mastering the art of adding insult to injury, he put this sign advertising his productions in lights larger and brighter than my father's "Famous Players in Famous Plays."

Soon there were no fewer than ten signs on Broadway brashly proclaiming *Lewis Selznick Presents*: Elsie Janis, who wowed the doughboys over there; exotic Russian star Nazimova in a smash film-adaptation of her stage hit, *War Brides*; the handsome leading man, Owen Moore, soon to win the hand of Mary Pickford; the Talmadge sisters, Norma and Constance; and the young Ziegfeld beauty, Olive Thomas. Selznick the bankrupt jeweler had transformed himself into Selznick the star maker, with a stable of box-office attractions outshining the roster of Famous Players-Lasky.

Not only had Selznick eclipsed the Famous Players' electric-light signs on Broadway, stealing their cherished slogan in the bargain, he had actually sent a cable to the fallen Czar Nicholas II:

WHEN I WAS A BOY IN RUSSIA YOUR POLICE TREATED MY PEOPLE VERY BAD. HOWEVER NO HARD FEELINGS. HEAR YOU ARE NOW OUT OF WORK. IF YOU WILL COME TO NEW YORK CAN GIVE YOU FINE POSITION ACTING IN PICTURES. SALARY NO OBJECT. REPLY MY EXPENSE. REGARDS YOU AND FAMILY.

SELZNICK

It happened that at that moment L.J.'s next film was to be *The Fall of the Romanoffs*.

Lewis Selznick was the first of the original moguls to live like a mogul. It was said that his number-one star was also his number-one paramour. And that the long, thickly carpeted corridor to his private office was lined with uniformed guards. It was said that hopeful young actresses nicknamed him C.O.D. because the passions of his leading ladies were invariably tested on his red-velvet casting couch. His richly furnished 22-room apartment on Park Avenue, his staff of liveried servants, his collection of Ming vases from China, his four Rolls-Royces, his thousand-dollar-a-week allowances to his teenage sons, David and Myron, and his offering them as many starlets as they could handle, his taste for the finest of French wines and the largest of Havana cigars, his reckless gambling: The life style of this scandalous instant millionaire set the stereotype for motion-picture tycoons that a score of quiet, thoughtful, withdrawn Irving Thalbergs would never live down. Indeed, the L. J. Selznick appetite for life was to leave its stamp on his sons as it did on my father and L. B. Mayer, Darryl Zanuck, Jack Warner, Harry Cohn, and the other great studio kings who were to reign over Hollywood's imperial days.

The quiet, undemonstrative Zukor, exasperated with L.J.'s "showmanship," his excessive living habits, and most of all with his penchant for stealing Famous Players' ideas, summoned my father to discuss what to do about it. In behalf of Famous Players, my father had staged the first celebrated openings, with the stars of other companies and the leading celebrities of the city invited to attend. But L.J. was making those openings seem tame by staging his with military bands, ragtime music, dancing girls, and the atmosphere of an incipient orgy.

"From the beginning I've fought for good taste," Mr. Zukor said solemnly, looking at the Selznick billboards from his office window. "But this man cheapens everything he touches. He's a disgrace to our business. We've got to get rid of him!"

"Maybe we can talk him into going back to Russia to present his offer to the Czar in person," my father suggested. "The Red Guards will take one look at that cigar-smoking capitalist and throw him into the same cell with Nicholas."

Zukor wasn't amused. He was a man of total concentration and now his mind was fixed on running this unpredictable rival out of motion pictures. "He's *meshugah* for those Chink vases," Zukor said. "Tell him I'll meet him at the Astor. I'll offer him five thousand a month to live in China. He can fill a palace with his dancing girls and those crazy vases of his."

The story sounds apocryphal but since both my father and L.J.'s son David told it to me in almost identical steps twenty years apart, I believe it. In fact the entire saga of Lewis J. Selznick has the ring of apocrypha, for L.J. was always larger than life. But the tales my father taught me are authentic.

When Adolph Zukor had his meeting with Lewis Selznick at the Hotel Astor and made his desperate proposition to this thorn in the heel of the young film company, L.J. laughed in his face. "Hell no, Adolph! You can't send me to China!" he roared. "I'm having too much fun!"

So Zukor conceived a less direct, more insidious idea. He would make Selznick a partner! He would offer L.J. one million dollars to give up his own company and form a new one, a subsidiary of Famous Players to be called Select, in which Selznick and Zukor would each own 50 percent of the stock. L.J. could still produce his own pictures with his own stars, but they would be made at the steadily expanding Famous Players-Lasky studio in Hollywood, under the aegis of the parent organization.

"Even if it wasn't a brilliant business move," my father told me, "it was worth a million dollars to Zukor to remove the name of Selznick from the billboards of Broadway. L.J. would still make a lot of money but there would be no more L.J. SELZNICK PRESENTS. L.J. would prosper, but under the thumb of Zukor, in anonymity."

The plan worked, but only for a while. The original creator of Advertisements For Myself sulked in his opulent tent of anonymity; he now had a million dollars and no fun. And he had always taught his sons that money was only worth making as a means of gaining fame, power, and a hell of a good time. Broke and out of work only a few years before, now he could lose a hundred thousand dollars in a jumbo pot at a poker game, laugh off his outrageous bluff of a hand, light up a dollar Havana, and be eager for the next deal. "Mr. Zukor despised him," Father told me later, "but I always had a sneaking admiration for him. He wasn't a good gambler because he liked to bluff all the time, in business and at cards, but at least he did it in a big way. And he always laughed when he lost."

B.P., as I was to observe him in the years ahead, wasn't a bluff in his profession. He had a real gift for writing and later making and promoting pictures. But he was the same kind of gambler Selznick was. My mother tells me that L.J. and B.P. at the same poker table were an impossible pair. Both of them liked to go all out on every hand regardless of how poor it was. To throw their cards down and watch the other players vie for the pot was to be out of action, to miss the excitement. In self-defense, Adeline, shy and still naive in her early twenties, learned to play poker and was soon playing it more knowledgeably than Ben; Florence Selznick too learned to hold her own in those wild games with big-league gamblers like Joe Schenck, Bill Brady, the "Zukor boys" Kaufman and Lichtman, and the cigar-smoking happy loser, B.P.

For my parents' fifth wedding anniversary, L.J. presented them with an expensive poker table, large enough to seat eight players. There were brass indentations for chips in the felt beside the place of each player, and the large circular table had an outer rim also trimmed in felt into which a winning player could sweep his chips. It was to become a family heirloom, accompanying us to Hollywood and holding an important place in half-a-dozen homes from Los Angeles to Malibu and back again as our fortunes rose and ebbed. I was to watch B.P. throwing his money away on that table through a thousand and one nights. On that same anniversary, the expansive L. J. Selznick gave me a toy card table: in the hope that I would develop into the same reckless plunger he had encouraged his sons to be? But my father's profligacy at that table and at countless tables in private homes and casinos around the world forever cured me of the gaming itch.

B.P.'s gambling, like L.J. Selznick's, was of Dostoevskian proportions. Instant psychoanalysis tells us that they were suffering from guilt at the size of their weekly paychecks and were determined to rid themselves of the filthy stuff to which, deep down, they did not feel rightly entitled. In both L.J. and B.P. there were wild streaks, but as this father's son sees it, L.J. would cross the line into an area of questionable principles where the equally reckless but somewhat more scrupulous Schulberg hesitated to follow.

For example (while I was still four), Mr. Zukor glanced out of his office window one morning and let out the nearest thing to a scream my father had ever heard from that quiet man. What had triggered this outburst was a large sign, again dwarfing one of Famous Players', proclaiming SELZNICK PRESENTS . . . OLIVE THOMAS.

Olive Thomas was a 1918 forerunner of Clara Bow, Jean Harlow, and Marilyn Monroe. Born Oliveretta Duffy in a grimy Pennsylvania mining town, unhappily married to a drunken miner in her middle teens, escaping those depressing surroundings by fleeing to New York, she won the Christy Girl competition to find a new model, caught the eye of Florenz Ziegfeld and became a Ziegfeld Girl—with a new name and a new fame as the most glorified of the Follies beauties. Rich men filled her dressing room with American Beauty roses and tucked pearl necklaces and diamond rings into the bouquets. Olive Thomas was the toast of Broadway, but Triangle Pictures hoped to make her the toast of America. When its contract ran out, every company in town was after her, but she signed with L.J.'s precocious seventeen-year-old son Myron.

Young Myron had never produced a picture, but L.J. had filled him full of that Selznick super-confidence. More important, L.J. could use his son to get around his contract with Famous Players, calling for the removal of his name from the posters, the billboards, and the screen. But

Myron's name was also Selznick, and there was nothing in L.J.'s contract to prevent his son's using his own name over his own pictures.

But were they his own pictures? The Selznicks' Olive Thomas ploy led to another of those bitter internecine motion-picture wars. It did not require the service of the Pinkertons to discover that Myron was working out of L.J.'s Select Pictures office at 729 Broadway, and that it was full of posters featuring Olive Thomas and plans for further Myron Selznick productions. Obviously L.J. had pocketed the million dollars that Zukor had given him as a payoff and then had outfoxed him by backing his son's production company.

Famous Players fought back. Zukor had my father write an open letter under Zukor's signature in the trade papers denouncing Selznick's underhanded tactics. He engaged lawyers to hale Selznick into court and to force him out of the presidency of Select Pictures. But L.J., counterattacking, finally managed to buy out Zukor and revert to the ballyhoo of LEWIS J. SELZNICK PRESENTS. . . .

"L.J.'s gall couldn't be divided into three parts like Caesar's," said my father. "That gall was as big and as durable as Gibraltar. The sharpest knives in the industry, including my own, couldn't make a dent in it."

The happy pirate of other companies' slogans, picture ideas, and stars had paraphrased the Mutual slogan, "Mutual Movies Make Time Fly," with typically Selznickian variation, "Selznick Pictures Make Happy Hours." In a characteristic gesture of that gall which both offended and fascinated my father, L.J. had presented a gold watch to Al Lichtman, sales manager for Famous Players-Lasky, with an inscription on the back illuminated in diamonds. In small letters it said, TO AL LICHTMAN. Then, in letters more than twice that size:

From
LEWIS J. SELZNICK
In grateful appreciation of
SELZNICK PICTURES
MAKE HAPPY HOURS

The expensive gift was such a conversation piece that Lichtman could not resist showing it wherever he went, and since he was in charge of selling a hundred Famous Players-Lasky pictures a year, he was constantly on the move. So the infuriating L.J. had succeeded in hanging a widely circulated ad for Selznick Pictures on the wrist of the head salesman of his most hated competitor.

But time or fate was to do to L. J. Selznick what his most determined rivals had been unable to accomplish. The nude body of Olive Thomas was discovered sprawled across a king-size bed at the luxurious Hotel Crillon in Paris. Only 20 years old and at the height of her fame, married to Mary's madcap brother Jack Pickford (also doomed to die young from an excess of living), the beautiful Selznick star was found with an empty bottle of mercury tablets in her hand. The press of the day played up the angle of drug abuse, and so the Selznick company not only lost its most promising attraction but came under attack for foisting dissolute stars upon a trusting public. With his customary ingenuity, L.J. fought back, conceiving of Will Hays, Harding's Postmaster-General, as an official overseer of public morals to take the heat off the industry.

But there was more to come. In Adolph Zukor he had made a dangerous enemy who worked quietly behind the scenes and enticed L.J.'s first big star, Clara Kimball Young, away from him. Soon there were other raids on his crumbling empire. David and Myron would always believe that the industry ganged up to drive their old man out of the business and they may have been right. The Zukors, the Laemmles, the Goldwyns, and the Laskys all feared Selznick the buccaneer, and, as they had proved to the once almighty Trust, they could be a dangerous wolf pack when they ran together.

So the fast-moving L.J. was finally run to earth. The man who could have sold out for millions of dollars only a few years after walking uninvited into Universal was now discovering that Wall Street and the banks had lost faith in him. Companies like Famous Players-Lasky and Universal were obviously more stable and better organized. One by one he had to sacrific his Rolls-Royces. One by one Florence sold her diamonds and rubies. From the extravagant 22-room apartment on Park Avenue, the Selznicks were forced to retreat to three rooms cluttered with mementos, Ming vases, and other trophies of his short-lived glory. His main assets were his sons Myron and David, who would wreak their vengeance on what they considered an ungrateful industry with triumphs even more spectacular and longer-lasting than his own.

7

A s the picture business flourished through the war years, its economic structure became increasingly complicated. Film salesmen like Al Lichtman had been selling their companies' products state by state to exchanges or middlemen who then turned around and leased the movies to the individual theaters.

One of the pioneer theater-owners was W. W. Hodkinson, who started with one small theater in Ogden, Utah, ran it into a chain, then became interested in the distribution of films to theaters, and was soon general manager of the Western operation for the Trust. When the Trust collapsed, Hodkinson formed his own exchange or distribution company, Paramount, absorbing many smaller exchanges in the process.

Although Zukor distrusted Hodkinson as a hard-driving businessman who did not have the best interest of the production companies at heart, they pooled their interests in Paramount, which would now distribute the Zukor-Lasky pictures, with 35 percent to the producers. Hodkinson became president and general manager. Regrettably, in controlling all of the Paramount exchanges across the country, he thereby became the boss of Paramount-Famous Players-Lasky. He could tell them how many comedies he wanted, how many dramas, how to budget them, and whom to hire and fire on the basis of the box-office returns. As Father said when I first became aware of this tug-of-war between business and art, "It was not only a case of the tail wagging the dog, Hodkinson was trying to take over our bark."

At the annual Paramount meetings, Hodkinson was re-elected president by acclamation year after year. But then came the unexpected moment when a New England exhibitor rose and said, "I nominate Hiram Abrams." "That name dropped on the meeting like a bombshell," Father recalled. "Before the s.o.b. Hodkinson knew what hit him, there was a vote of hands and he was out of office. He was a silent, unfriendly man, cold and abrupt in his dealings with all of us, even Mr. Zukor. When he saw his control of Paramount, and therefore of Famous Players, disappear like *that*, he didn't say a word. He simply reached for his hat and walked out."

That week B.P. made the front pages of the New York papers with his story of the purchase of Paramount by Famous Players for $25,000,000. "Now the bark was back where we in the studio felt it belonged, in the head of the dog. Or, to vary the metaphor, the Jonah of film production had somehow managed to swallow the whale of distribution."

It seemed like something of a miracle at the time, but actually it was a nice example of the quiet way Adolph Zukor worked behind the scenes. For months he had been having secret meetings at his Riverside Drive apartment with Hiram Abrams of Boston and his partner Walter Green, who together controlled all of the distribution in New England. At those meetings, Abrams and Green agreed to vote their Paramount stock on Zukor's side. In return Abrams would become president of the newly constituted Paramount.

The Zukor strategy worked to perfection. The next step was to buy Paramount outright. Zukor and his company now controlled motion pictures from their inception to the theaters. By acquiring a chain of motion-picture palaces, Famous Players in half a dozen years was well on its way to replacing the Trust. Paramount, the first national distribution chain, could now supply two Famous Players-Lasky pictures a week to theaters from Bangor to San Diego.

Outgrowing its improvised Manhattan studio, Famous Players had built an imposing new studio in Astoria. On the West Coast, the barn that Jesse Lasky and C. B. DeMille had rented was not only enlarged into a full-size studio stage but was now surrounded by other stages. Instead of bedding down in a primitive boardinghouse in the wilds of Hollywood, stars like Geraldine Farrar, lured to the new movie capital from the Metropolitan Opera by the engaging Lasky, arrived in private railroad cars and enjoyed what was then considered luxurious surroundings at the Hollywood Hotel, the only hotel in that rural village.

I saw this expansion through the eyes of my father, who had been assigned by Zukor to assist Hiram Abrams in the important job of running Paramount. The Abramses, moving down from Boston after the Zukor coup, took over a large apartment at 110th Street and Central Park West. My first memory of being attracted to a young woman other than Wilma is associated with the Abrams household. She was the Abrams daughter, who had reached the advanced age of thirteen. She would play with me and take care of me while our parents played their incessant card games, talked shop, or gossiped about who was sleeping with whom. The choicest morsel of the day was that while America's Sweetheart still looked sweet fifteen in her Pollyanna roles, Little Mary had been cheating on husband Owen Moore with dashing Doug Fairbanks, her companion on the Liberty Bond tours. But I was more interested in the Abrams girl. Although she cannot be romanticized into a first love—alas, I cannot even call back her first name—I remember her as a tantalizing influence on my four- and five-year-old life.

While I was gazing into his daughter's eyes, Hiram Abrams was apparently resisting and resenting the position of figurehead in which Adolph Zukor placed him. Zukor's time was increasingly devoted to the complex financial activities of running a multi-million-dollar nationwide film company. B.P. was no longer his immediate right hand, as he had been since the merger with Porter. Now my father was spending his working hours and more and more of his social hours (they have a tendency to overlap in the movie business) with Hiram Abrams. When tension between Zukor and Abrams approached the breaking point, B.P. found himself so intimately associated with his immediate superior that he began to take his side against Zukor's.

There were intense business discussions between my father and my mother. Adeline had begun to appreciate their stake in this growing industry. B.P.'s salary of five hundred dollars a week was the least of it. There was that Famous Players stock, which was already worth some $200,000. As a young film executive, B.P. was initiative, ingenious, creative; but already my mother was beginning to call him a *schnook* when it came to business.

The bad blood between Zukor and Abrams continued until the head of Famous Players made up his mind that there was no longer any room in the company for the newcomer. Whereupon B.P., without telling Mother—who would have cautioned him against such a precipitate move—marched in and told his old boss that if Abrams went he would have to go with him. Zukor was in a bad mood. The influenza epidemic that past summer had caused the first box-office depression. And now he had just heard his biggest star, Mary Pickford, after all the concessions he had made to her, was deserting him for a million-dollar-a-year contract at First National, a new rival formed by theater owners who had decided to make their own pictures, much as Zukor had done half a dozen years earlier.

In addition to her unprecedented million, the hard-driving Mary had also wangled $50,000 a year for Mama Charlotte and four pictures a year for brother Jack at $50,000 each. A million and a quarter for the Pickford family had broken Zukor's paternalistic hold on the star he (and B.P., Mickey Neilan, and others) had created.

Now an embattled Zukor urged B.P. not to follow Abrams out of Paramount-Famous Players-Lasky. Abrams, he warned, was head-strong and untrustworthy: B.P., who was then 26 years old, should stay with the company he had helped to build. In fact Mr. Zukor would even consider giving him Abrams's job, since he felt that B.P. had the potential while Abrams lacked the stature of a big-league motion-picture executive. But B.P., now grown fiercely loyal to Abrams, stuck to his guns.

Going out of his way to smother this unexpected rebellion, Zukor asked B.P. to come to his apartment after dinner that evening.

My father came home from the office visibly upset, drank a series of scotch highballs in lieu of dinner, and told my mother he was going over to see Zukor on important business (but was afraid to tell her just how crucial it was). He walked the few blocks down Riverside Drive trying to make up his mind: Which was it to be, Zukor and the company which had been B.P.'s family from his late boyhood, the expanding company which could make him a millionaire before he was thirty? Or Hiram Abrams, whom I was now calling Uncle Hiram, a man with whom B.P. would have to plot a whole new course through the high seas of increasingly rough competition?

Late into the night Adolph Zukor argued with his young but valued employee. There was no one in Famous Players with B.P.'s education, literacy, story sense, and promotional ability. Schulberg had worshipped Zukor from the day Edwin S. Porter had brought him into Famous Players as scenario editor. How could he now transfer his allegiance to a man he had met through Zukor only a few years before?

My father could not entirely explain it, even to himself. Ad (as Adeline had come to be called) knew that Ben was comfortable with Hiram, both professionally and socially, in a way he could never really be with Zukor. As he insisted, he was a one-man dog. First attached to Porter, then to Zukor—and now to Abrams. So at midnight he was still saying, "If Hiram goes, I go with him."

Uncle Adolph's anger had a very long fuse, but B.P.'s inexplicable devotion to our new Uncle Hiram brought him to the end of it. "All right, Ben," he said coldly, "I think you're being a damn fool, and I know you'll regret it. But I've said my last word about this. Come to the studio in the morning and clean out your office." He stood up and with an icy calm walked B.P. to the door. "Some day you'll want to come back without Abrams," he challenged him at the threshold.

"Adolph," my father said, calling his employer by his first name for the first time since he had met him in the old Famous Players Film Company days of 1912, "I'll only come back when you send for me!"

B.P.—as he told me when I was old enough to understand it—hurried home and briefed Ad. She had not forgotten the hungry days on the Lower East Side. She may have been a theoretical socialist but she was a practical capitalist. Her reverence for the Pankhursts and the Emma Goldmans in no way diminished her reverence for the almighty dollar. Less trusting than Ben, she examined people with a more calculating or perhaps more realistic eye.

The night of the break Ben talked excitedly of his future plans. He confessed to Ad that if he had told her of his decision to follow Uncle Hiram out of Paramount-Famous Players he knew she would have tried to talk him out of it. She reminded him that at the studio he had the respect of Zukor and a firm niche in the structure of a company so powerful that even the loss of a number-one money-maker like Mary Pickford could no longer slow its forward progress. Now he was throwing all that away for an unknown quantity, a company yet to be formed.

"But," B.P. pointed out, "the stock we've accumulated since 1912 is now worth two hundred and eighty thousand dollars. And since I'm the best press agent in the business I shouldn't have too much trouble blowing my own horn. Don't worry, Ad. Hiram and I will do something exciting."

Too exhilarated to sleep, B.P. phoned Abrams, told him of the confrontation with Zukor, and suggested they get together right then—one o'clock in the morning—to start planning their future.

So my impulsive 26-year-old father raced across from Riverside Drive to Central Park West for what was to be an historic emergency meeting.

This was soon after the Armistice, when the blessings of peace and postwar prosperity were being expressed in the building of more and more ornate movie theaters, with marble, gold leaf, crystal chandeliers, and rich carpeting giving them the look of cinematic Taj Mahals.

Nineteen-nineteen was only weeks away. This was a time for new approaches to distribution, a time for innovation. Why—my father paced up and down, pouring all this out to Abrams—should the Big Five of the industry, Pickford, Chaplin, Fairbanks, Griffith, and William S. Hart, only receive salaries, even if they ran to ten or twenty thousand a week? If these artists formed their own company they could eliminate the producing fees, take over the large profits made from distribution, and have a controlling interest in a company from which they could reap dividends even after they retired from the screen. If the Big Five could be sold on the idea of uniting, B.P. and Uncle Hiram could control their futures, in fact virtually control the industry.

Thus was United Artists born. Schulberg and Abrams talked excitedly through the night and by sunup had begun to formalize their plans. B.P. would immediately start writing a prospectus for the new company, which was to become a manifesto of artistic independence entitled "Eighty-nine Reasons for United Artists." While B.P. was banging out this presentation, Uncle Hiram would be using his prestige as the former president of Paramount to study the contractual relations between Pickford and Chaplin, now at First National, and Fairbanks and Griffith at Famous Players-Lasky. Once they knew when these four key figures, and the earnest horse-faced Western star Hart, would be free of their present obligations, my father and Uncle Hiram could approach them with this unprecedented idea of becoming not only the highest-priced stars in the world but their own bosses as well.

Abrams and Schulberg again swore each other to secrecy. It was one of those ideas so daring and yet so simple that it could be "borrowed" by the first person who got wind of it—even the stars in question, who might then proceed without the participation of my father and Abrams. Charlotte and Mary Pickford were veteran operators who had proved they could negotiate with and outmaneuver the canniest minds in the business. And Charlie Chaplin gave almost as brilliant a performance in a business meeting as he did in his comedies. Like my mother, Charlie was another of those idealists who talked socialism and practiced capitalism. Uncle Hiram and my father plotted their strategy carefully. The secret plans for the organizing and launching of United Artists went on in both households, with B.P. banging out his "Eighty-nine Reasons" on his old Underwood, while Ad patiently did the clean retyping.

The frenzy of United Artists activity I dimly remember, but the period— the end of World War I—is placed clearly in my mind, for the Armistice Day parade or riot or mass hysteria is one of those experiences caught and forever held in the memory of a child. All of a sudden (or so it seemed to the small boy who heard the news) the war was over! What it meant to me mainly was no more of those silvery tinfoil balls to roll. In some way I never comprehended, they had "helped" to win the war.

My mother took me in a touring car across town to Fifth Avenue, to a grandstand reserved for important personages. Apparently we qualified because Father had been writing Liberty Bond speeches for Pickford, Fairbanks, Chaplin, and the other movie stars who had been trekking back and forth across the country urging the public to back up our boys in the trenches.

In all my life I had never seen so many people crowded into the streets. They were all around our car, screaming and laughing, crying and kissing. As we neared Fifth Avenue we had to get out and walk because the street was jammed with people dancing, singing, and hugging each other. Nice people made room for us in the grandstand and we spent hours there watching the parade go by. I guess the entire city was either marching in that parade or shouting and clapping their hands at it as it moved up the Avenue.

After a while I got very tired and had to go to the bathroom and since Mother (obviously) couldn't get me there, I began to wet my pants and cry. A soldier, a real doughboy in a khaki uniform with ribbons on his chest and several pretty girls hanging onto him, picked me up and said, "What's the matter, buddy?"—it was always strange how everybody seemed to know my name—"You shouldn't be crying today! This is the happiest day in the history of the world!" And everybody around him started to yell, "The war is over!" "Hang the Kaiser!"; and I got so nervous and scared that I wet the front of the hero's uniform. Then I really got scared that this soldier would get mad at me but instead everybody was laughing, even the hero, and when he handed me back rather gingerly to my mother he said to his crowd of admirers, "Well, it could be worse. It was a helluva lot wetter in the trenches!"

I knew the trenches were wet, in fact were full of water like a bathtub, because I had just seen my first movie. It was *Shoulder Arms* with

Charlie Chaplin. My parents had taken me to see it one weekend in Atlantic City. Everything I knew about the war I had learned from *Shoulder Arms,* which made it look awfully dirty and sloppy and uncomfortable for "our boys in the trenches." I have never seen the movie since, even in the Chaplin retrospectives, but over the years I've been able to describe one scene that fastened itself inside my head like a barnacle:

Charlie, the most miserable of doughboys, is getting ready to go to bed in his watery trench. He stretches and yawns and acts like a man about to climb into a clean double bed in a luxury hotel. He reaches down beneath the surface of the water, pulls up a soggy pillow, pats it and fluffs it up as if it were warm and dry, and then places it at the bottom of the trench under water again. Then Charlie puts his two hands against his cheek, lies down on his side, sighs blissfully as if he could not have been cozier or more comfortable, and disappears into the muddy water.

I remember how hard I laughed and how sad I felt. That was the measure of his genius.

By the end of 1918 my father had polished his "Eighty-nine Reasons for United Artists" until they glittered like the stars around the Paramount mountain. And he and Uncle Hiram were supremely confident that their new concept of a company would soon outshine Paramount-Famous Players-Lasky.

Now I was beginning to hear about Hollywood for the first time. We were going to take a long, long train ride all the way across the country to a beautiful place on the opposite side. There it was warm with sunshine even in the winter time and all kinds of tropical fruit grew in abundance, oranges and grapefruit and figs and dates. It was a place where the air was clear and the climate so healthy that thousands of people traveled there every year just to enjoy the sun, the pastoral landscape, and the rejuvenating breezes. Little Sonya would stay home with Wilma while I accompanied my parents on the four-and-a-half-day Pullman journey. It was to be a great adventure for all of us, since my father, despite his high position at Famous Players, had never been farther west than Chicago, and Ad's travels had been restricted to Middletown, Atlantic City, and Far Rockaway.

Castles-in-the-sky for the have-nots from the ghettos of Eastern Europe were floating down to rest on that distant shore of the blue Pacific. It had to be blue. Just as surely as the sands had to be golden and the skies sunny and cloudless. For so it was writ in the Book of Celluloid Dreams that beckoned us westward.

"All . . . aaaaaaboard!" My father handed me up the steps of the platform onto the crack *20th Century Limited* and into the waiting arms of a man in a white jacket with a big black face and a lot of smiling teeth. "Welcome aboard, young man. Are you goin 'tuh Chicago?"

"N-n-no, I'm going to H-h-h-h . . ." I wasn't trying to give Hollywood the old ha-ha. It simply came out that way. Still smiling, the porter led us and the Abramses down the long windowed corridor to our drawing rooms.

A few minutes later we heard the sound of the Pullman doors slamming shut, the engine whistle calling us to attention, and then with a gentle lurch we were rolling forward through the dark tunnel to an unknown place called Chicago.

To the Motion Picture
An Appreciation

By B. P. SCHULBERG

MARVEL of science, mirror of art, product of the ingenuity of man and the inventive power of his mind—we speak to you, the Motion Picture!

Not with the sword, not with the oppression and persecution of cruel might, but with more human sobs and smiles, you have conquered the world!

You are the struggle and the victory! You are Aspiration and Achievement—Hope and Realization!

You are King in the Land of Mechanical Wonders, supreme in the domain of daring dreams!

Your silence speaks of the genius of man, the strength of his purpose, the courage of his endeavors, and the wealth and worth of his labors. You are the mute voice of progress, the echo of creative potency, the symbol of constructive force.

You are the soul of skill and the spirit of Service, the essence of energy, and the germ of enterprise. You thrill with the common sympathy of the universe, and throb with the throes and thralls of united humanity.

You translate the world's sorrows, and delineate life's joys. You bear the burden of the earth, the load of care and misery and evil, the pathetic definition of futility and fatality; yet you catch the gleam of a sunbeam, the lilt of a song—and we laugh!

YOU TEACH! You distribute knowledge, diffuse the secrets of science and the glories of art; you spread civilization. You bring light where is darkness, and life where is only existence. You banish ignorance; you cheer and comfort.

YOU PREACH! Your pulpit is the hearts of the world, your creed faith and sympathy.

Motion Picture, you are great. You are the agent of the age, the messenger of futurity!

You are great—and we are grateful!

From the program for the First Annual Ball of the Screen Club, April 19, 1913. B.P. Schulberg, then all of 21, had already been a film publicist and a screenwriter and was now a Famous-Players-Lasky executive. Here, a sample of public relations writing *circa* 1913.

8

E N ROUTE TO Chicago on the *20th Century Limited,* the Schulbergs and the Abramses had three drawing rooms—one for my parents, one for Uncle Hiram and his wife, and a third for their tall thirteen-year-old daughter and me.

After dinner in the dining car, where courteous Negro waiters balanced their trays like circus performers, Uncle Hiram and B.P. went back to one of the drawing rooms, and in a cloud of cigar smoke began figuring out how much they would offer the Big Five they were going to collar in Los Angeles, and how much they would try to keep for themselves. Of course the first step was to convince Chaplin, Pickford, Fairbanks, Griffith, and Hart. They decided to make Chaplin target number one because he was the best combination of artist and money man; riding high now at First National, he wanted to be his own producer and director. Surely he would be attracted to the concept of complete artistic freedom for his future work, along with a healthy chunk of the profits of distribution and exhibition.

It was already past my bedtime, and the adults suggested that Miss Abrams put me to bed in the upper slung down from the ceiling. The tracks were making a lot of noise—for some reason they had suddenly become much louder—and there was no window up there through which I could look out, so after a while I called down to Miss Abrams in the lower berth. She was stretched out in a nightgown, reading a fan magazine. *Photoplay* and *Screenland* were getting popular then. And it wasn't only Chaplin, Pickford, Fairbanks, and Hart that the movie fans of the late Teens wanted to read about. They wanted to know all their newfound heroes and heroines: Wally Reid, Norman Kerry (patriotically changed from *Kaiser* because of the war), the Gish sisters, Pearl White, the Talmadge girls, Theda Bara, Tom Mix, Geraldine Farrar, William Desmond Taylor, Gloria Swanson, Katherine MacDonald, Fatty Arbuckle, Buster Keaton, Lila Lee, Lon Chaney, Billie Burke, Bebe Daniels, Blanche Sweet. . . . The sky spreading across the country from our *20th Century Limited* twinkled with a thousand stars. It was a world of vamps and virgins, tough guys, shieks, and funnymen.

When I leaned over the side of my upper to tell Miss Abrams that I wanted to come and join her, she invited me to climb down and tuck in. Then she read a little while longer and turned out the light. I felt much safer with her large and comforting warmth to curl up against.

Sleep was interrupted when the train suddenly came to a stop with a screeching of wheels and the cars bumping together. I didn't know where we were. . . . I only remember Miss Abrams raising the wide green window shade, and our peering out with heads close together. On the other side of a big city railroad platform was another train that had just pulled in from the opposite direction. An Army train, full of doughboys. It was early in the morning, maybe one or two A.M., but all those soldier boys were up and dressed in their uniforms and leaning out the open windows. They were in a holiday mood, almost as crazy with joy as the day they had been yelling "Hooray for the Yanks!" and "Hang the Kaiser!" on Fifth Avenue. Only now they were shouting things like, "Hey kid, you oughta be ashamed of ya'self!" "Hey, kiddo, how about givin' us a chance?" "Hey, girlie, you're wastin' ya time—how about me?"

The banter from the Army car went on for a few minutes and then a whistle blew—that lovely, prolonged, repeated steam-engine sound—and our train began to lurch slowly forward, the doughboys leaning out of their cars shouting affectionately obscene farewells.

Miss Abrams lowered the blind but the night lights of the city we were passing through flickered around the edges of the window shade into our darkened, cozy drawing room.

What were all those soldier boys laughing about, I wanted to know? What were all those things they were shouting at us?

"You see, boys and girls are different. It doesn't matter now when you're so small and I'm so much older than you. But in about ten years it won't seem right for us to be sleeping together in the same bed like this."

"Mommy and Daddy sleep in the same bed. And so does your Mommy and Daddy."

"That's different. They're married."

But the doughboys who were laughing and shouting about coming over and getting into bed with her, they weren't married to her? Sometimes people do it when they aren't married, Miss Abrams said. They aren't supposed to, but they do. She knew all about it from an older girl who had explained it to her. Soldiers who came back from the war seemed to like to do it a lot. And vamps in the movies like Theda Bara and Alla Nazimova could make men want to do it so bad that it drove them out of their minds.

After that, whenever I crawled into the lower to join Uncle Hiram's daughter, as I did every night of our long trip to California, it was with a new sense of excitement. She never went beyond that first lesson in *la différence* but the risqué invitations shouted across the station platform were to be planted forever in my mind as the first tentative opening of that mysterious door through which we all must pass on our way from the cloying innocence of Mary Pickford to the forthright carnality of Mae West.

Chicago was cold, hurried, and confusing. The *20th Century Limited* had come to the end of its line and all our luggage—great steamer trunks along with a van full of suitcases—had to be removed from drawing rooms and baggage car and transported through a chill, noisy city to another station where we were to board a second train, the *Santa Fe Chief,* which would carry us the rest of the way to Los Angeles.

Another great train to explore, this one even grander than the first. Now the Schulbergs and the Abramses were really traveling in style, for in addition to our three drawing rooms we had an extra compartment, with doors that could open into the adjoining drawing room, so that during the day the adults had a fair-sized living room in which to play their card games, plan their strategy, and even eat and drink. Sometimes my roommate and I would have our meals in the dining car while our parents had theirs served in their rooms. How important I felt being allowed to dine alone with Miss Abrams in that restaurant on wheels!

After we left the East, the landscape changed dramatically. From the splendid balcony large enough for two rows of seats at the rear of the observation car, Miss Abrams and I could watch midwestern America streaming backward as the great *Chief* sped determinedly westward. Then on to the hot, dry, unexpected Southwest, as exciting to my parents as it was to me.

A man was racing his horse alongside the train. A man with a big hat and a rope wound round the saddle: a cowboy, an honest-to-God cowboy, not Max Aronson pretending to be Broncho Billy but a cowhand who looked after cows and steers and bulls and didn't aim his gun at you, didn't go around looking for the bad guys in the black hats, but was just out there in the dust and the grime working the range for a living. A true-to-life cowboy such as Daddy's movies and Uncle Hiram's movies and C. B. DeMille's movies would never show, because all work and no gunplay doesn't make jack, as my father would have said.

I watched my first real cowboy disappear into the dust of the sagebrush and the cactus. We were in rugged Western country now, crossing New Mexico. It was so hot and dusty that we could no longer sit on the observation platform, 110 in the shade, with no shade in sight for what looked like five hundred miles. We fought off the heat of the Southwest by pulling sheets from the berths, wetting them with what passed for cool water in the pull-down sink, and then draping them across the drawing-room windows: air conditioning, vintage 1918. . . . Who would travel today, in an unairconditioned train through heat that blistered the land? Unthinkable. We lived the unthinkable, just as the pioneers who preceded us loaded their families and their spare worldly goods into covered wagons, crossed a continent without roads, climbed and descended hostile mountains, ran out of food and water, starved and drank a handful of sand for their final toast to whatever god drove them westward. . . .

Those were pioneers, and so were we, the Schulbergs and the Abramses, even though we traveled strictly first class.

And although the *Santa Fe Chief* was proud of its cuisine, the confident B.P. in all his 26-year-old affluence had made arrangements with the dining-car captain to take on special supplies at each great terminal where its local product was prized: choice beef in Kansas City and freshly caught brook trout in Colorado. . . . With what marvelous ease did the son of the dollar-a-day sandwich man take to his newfound luxury. With the grace of a Jay Gatz he identified himself to the captain as soon as we were comfortably installed in our drawing rooms, but not in the brash, money-flashing, grammar-smashing way of the immigrant moguls among whom he moved. No, the young man from Rivington Street who had already forgotten the sound of Yiddish, having exchanged it for the language of Dickens, Galsworthy, and Shaw, knew to the manner born how to express his desires subtly to the traveling maitre d', how to suggest the handsome bribe that would be forthcoming for extra favors without so much as a whisper of that vulgar commodity called money. "It's all arranged," he said to my mother, "we'll have brook trout for dinner at seven o'clock." And at seven, there we were in the gleaming dining car, the adult Schulbergs and Abramses at their elegant table for four, Miss Abrams and I seated across the aisle at our own table for two, dining on fresh-caught trout cooked to perfection.

In the movies, you always knew when William S. Hart was headin' into Injun country because suddenly, as the wagon train went by down in the valley, there would be a close shot of feathered headgear rising menacingly from behind a rock on the mountainside. Then a fierce bronze face (a painted Caucasian) would signal to a group of fellow-savages waiting behind him, their deadly bows and arrows at their sides. On *our* wagon train, the *Santa Fe,* the arrival of the Redskins was also announced by bows and arrows, but they were not weapons but souvenirs, hung along the window rails of our Pullman car, along with a generous spread of Indian blankets and silver necklaces. They had been put on at some mysterious stop before we were awake, the work of Hopis, Zunis, and Navajos, subdued long ago. Now they were working for Fred Harvey, who held the restaurant concession for the *Santa Fe* and also had a corner on the souvenir market.

It was because of Fred Harvey, we learned, that our train lingered an extra half hour in Albuquerque. It was there in the awful but somehow exciting heat of the New Mexican depot and trading post that I saw my first Indians. My small blue eyes were looking into their large brown ones because I was on my feet and they were squatting on the ground, leaning against the outside walls of the station facing the tracks. Silently they held up their wooden souvenirs, feeble miniatures of the weapons with which they had hoped to fight off the white man's guns a few generations earlier. The Indian wars were over now, though some of the older men squatting with the women and the doe-eyed children must have remembered the last of the lost battles. Now they were here on their ragged posteriors at Fred Harvey's Albuquerqueland, hoping to sell a few limp trinkets to the palefaces whose pocket-money jingled louder than Navajo drums and Hopi tambourines.

Then we heard the train whistle—another "A-aaal aaaa-board!"—

and we were rolling westward again. We sped through desert country, sand and cactus and sagebrush stretching to the horizon and little towns so hot that, at the water stops, the adults debated whether it was better to swelter inside or outside the train. I walked importantly up and down the blistered platform with my Miss Abrams, getting used to the heat now, the sun beating down on us, one or two sullen Indians still trying to peddle their little bows and arrows and some modest brown pottery.

Gallup was even hotter than Albuquerque. I heard "Mohave Desert" and was told people died out there from the heat and lack of water. My mother pointed to the skulls of oxen bleached white, and to a forest that in some mysterious process over millions of years had been turned into stone. A large stone with the beautiful grain of wood was pressed into my hand, the beginning of my rock collection.

The Colorado was not the welcome blue-green of a fresh flowing river but a disappointing muddy brown. Brown was the color of everything in New Mexico and Arizona and Nevada. The people were brown and the water was brown and the sunbaked adobe houses were brown. The mountains were brown and the bushes were brown. Once in a while we saw a strange little animal scurrying over the desert and it too was brown . . . the whole Southwest seemed to be a blur of brown as we raced on to California. But the cactus was green, and the sky overhead, clear as a movie-studio backdrop, was an endless reach of blue.

From her guidebook, Mother pointed out the sights; I still remember those early geography, history, and geology lessons. Mother wanting to be sure her little genius squeezed every possible ounce of knowledge from this maiden journey. Always trying a little too hard and yet somehow succeeding in planting seeds, ideas, questions, bits of fact, observations, theories that would penetrate the skull of her five-year-old and cling there like burrs.

Late that night in the drawing room, Ad's conversation with Ben grew heated as they prepared for bed. He and Uncle Hiram were now only one day from Los Angeles. B.P. had rehearsed his Eighty-nine Reasons for United Artists until he could recite them in his sleep. But, she demanded, what did he have on paper? Shouldn't he have a contract with Hiram Abrams? At the very least, a letter of agreement? After all, Abrams would be approaching the Big Five with the prestige of his recent presidency of Paramount. B.P. would be there simply as Abrams's young assistant, even though he had masterminded the plan. Uncle Hiram looked like an important motion-picture executive. B.P., after eight years as a scenario writer, editor, and publicist, still looked as if he had strayed from the campus of C.C.N.Y.

Voices grew in volume and intensity. B.P. felt challenged because Ad was always questioning his business judgment. She thought he was too easily taken in by people, too impulsive, too ready to accept their word on good faith: a creative mind, but lacking common sense. Gullible. So anxious for people to like him that he never wanted to question their motives. A *schnook*. He was on the threshold of sparking the formation of a new company that could make motion-picture history. But, she repeated until Father began to lose his temper, what did he have on paper? What proof did he have that this was *his* idea, and that he would be an equal partner with Hiram Abrams?

"My God, Ad," Ben said, "these aren't strangers you're talking about. You can't go through life being suspicious of everybody. This is Hiram. My closest friend. We shook hands on the agreement. He appreciates the fact that I took his side against Zukor. We're in this together. When we talk Chaplin, Pickford, and Fairbanks into this, when we're ready to draw up the papers to found United Artists, then we'll spell out our duties and our share of the business."

"Ben, I'm warning you," Mother said again. "I don't care how close you and Hiram are. If I were you, I'd get it on paper—before we get to Los Angeles."

My father told my mother to mind her own business. What did she think she was, a theatrical attorney without a diploma?

9

THE LAST MORNING, the fourth day out from New York City, began with a sense of exhilaration. Any minute now we'd be crossing the border into California. In 1918 the name still had a magical ring.

Finally leaving the desert behind, we entered the land of the orange groves. More orange trees than any Easterner had ever seen, miles and more miles of them, each one decorated like a Christmas tree with great orange bulbs. From the observation car Miss Abrams and I could smell them and almost taste them. Indeed for lunch we did taste them: oranges sliced thinly, scalloped, sprinkled with powdered sugar and decorated with a maraschino cherry, served as a special dish.

San Bernardino. We were in the land of Spanish names that spoke to us of a time when California was a country of Spanish land grants that stretched for twenty miles from fence to fence, and of Spanish missions, San Juan Capistrano, San Diego, and Santa Barbara. The Yankee gold-rushers had moved in on the Spanish and the Mexicans, and had taken over the city we would soon be reaching, Los Angeles, the city of the angels. The orange trees were behind us at last, but we were passing vineyards, passing a dried-up creek that was grandly described as the Los Angeles River, and then we all had our noses to the windows as we approached the low-lying nondescript skyline of northeast Los Angeles, rolling to a stop at an odd-looking red-brick Moorish-style station. With a grand flourish the smiling porter brushed us off in what was not so much a cleansing as a ceremony of arrival. The sun was beating down, not as intensely as in Needles near the Arizona border but hot enough to inform us that we had come to a lush and exotic land.

Our luggage piled onto baggage trucks, we were driven through a small Far Western city of undistinguished four- and five-story buildings. We passed the Spanish Plaza: Olivera Street, all that was left of the original village of the *conquistadores* and their Indian peons. A real Mexican church. And then just as suddenly as we had come upon it we left it behind. We were crossing Main Street, not the derelict alley for winos it would be half a century later but the main thoroughfare of downtown L.A., narrow, crowded with autos and people and streetcars clanging.

Our proud procession of Schulbergs and Abramses drove to the grandest hotel in town, the Alexandria. Standing there in all its glory at Fifth and Spring Streets (today a rundown relic in the slums), it was named for the great Mediterranean port founded by Alexander the Great. Many miles to the west was our Venice, with canals that were said to rival Italy's own, and, halfway between, a Greek theater, open to the starlit skies and scooped out of a Santa Monica mountainside to suggest a theater in Athens, though the dramas performed were more apt to be pious morality plays than the works of Euripides and Aristophanes.

Into the lobby of the Alexandria we marched. How vast and grand it seemed, with marble pillars, and its fabulous million-dollar rug, so named not for its cost, though it seemed opulently Persian to our Eastern feet, but because it was there that Mack Sennett and Charlie Chaplin, Louie-come-lately Mayer and his star Anita Stewart, Joe Schenck with his stars the Talmadge sisters, Mabel Normand, D. W. Griffith, William Desmond Taylor—geniuses, con men, cloak-and-suiters become overnight movie moguls—cooked up their million-dollar deals. From that crowded, overly ornate lobby sprang the new spirit of the new industry being born before our eyes.

The lobby was also full of unknown girls showing off their faces and their figures in hopes of being discovered. And in those simpler, silent days, girls with striking faces *could* be discovered on the spot. Along with Geraldine Farrar and Mary Garden from grand opera there were a host of hopefuls from all the little towns across the country, waiting for Mack Sennett to put them into fetching one-piece bathing suits. The doors of the Alexandria lobby were not marked Ladies and Gentlemen but Obscurity and Fame.

And along with all those names and would-be names, there were the sightseers, the rubes, the hicks, the marks rubbernecking around the lobby to catch sight of a famous face— "Hey, ain't that Wally Reid?" "You'll never guess who I just saw getting out of her motor car—hot damn!—Beverly Bayne!"

For the country boys and even the mashers from Council Bluffs there was a new little racket called the Alexandria Game. A sharper would slyly elbow up to someone at the bar and ask what famous movie star he had seen in the lobby. "Well, I just saw Phyllis Haver," the country boy would say. "Boy, she slays me! I'll tell you one thing, she c'n put her shoes under my bed any old time!"

"Phyl Haver," the sharper answered. "Listen, kiddo, I just happen to be her assistant director. And you know what she is, she's a goddam nymphomaniac. I mean she hasn't got the morals of a loose goose. After she finishes a picture all she likes to do is stay upstairs in her room and get laid by strangers about ten times a day."

The mark gulped his drink and ordered one for his new friend. "Say, mister, I'm just passin' through town, you don't think—hah!—you don't think you could take me up and give me a knockdown to Phyllis Haver? Boy, wait 'til I get home and tell that one around the barbershop!"

For a consideration, like twenty dollars, the self-appointed assistant director offered to bring the visitor upstairs to his liaison with Miss Haver. And upstairs in Room 422 lounging around in a negligee was Phyllis Haver, or a reasonable facsimile thereof. . . . The little butter-and-egg man was too excited to tell the difference. Con men used to make themselves fifty to a hundred smackers a day escorting suckers up to rooms of "Gloria Swanson," "Norma Talmadge," and "Katherine MacDonald."

The Alexandria! Until the business moved uptown to the larger and grander Hotel Ambassador in the early Twenties, it was the capital of filmania. The whole damned industry was there together in one big hotel. You could get laid, you could become a star, you could start a new movie company, and you could go broke, all in that same place the same afternoon.

A generation later there was to be a famous bordello in Hollywood that offered a variation of the Alexandria Game. There you could find look-alikes for Carole Lombard, Jean Harlow, Claudette Colbert, and Nancy Carroll. But the later clientele was indulging in fantasies while the greenhorns in the throbbing lobby of the Alexandria, living in simpler times, really believed they were achieving an immortal roll in the hay with Bebe Daniels or Alice Joyce.

I'm not sure whether it was because of these nefarious goings-on in the lobby and the bar and the upper floors of the Alexandria, or because it started to rain, that my mother decided to remove me from its hectic atmosphere. I remember that the rain bucketed down; the land of eternal sunshine began to look like a Griffith production of the Great Flood. I sat by the window staring at the sheet of water and crying. I had been promised a trip to the mountains. But here I was in downtown Los Angeles, with no park to play in, not even a balcony, surrounded by a lot of noisy, frantic, laughing people. Their names meant nothing to me. "I w-w-want to s-see the m-m-mountings," I cried. "Mom, you and D-d-daddy promised me I could see the sun sh-sh-shine on the mountings."

One reason Ad had made up her mind to take me away from the lurid Alexandria, away to something finer, was that she was hating Los Angeles herself, the phonies and the fourflushers who passed themselves off as producers and directors, the little whores ("hoors," she called them) who knew only one way to become actresses. The phonies and the fourflushers and the wheeler-dealers are there to this very day, in their Cardin suits, their dark locks looped over their foreheads, their eyes roving and their minds spinning. But in those days it was a little easier because everything was new and everyone was an overnight wonder. Who knew Triangle Pictures from Quadrangle Pictures, or World from World-Wide? Who knew if you were talking to the junkman who hadn't even sold his broken-down wagon, or to the mastermind of the next big merger between Metro and Goldwyn (the Goldwyn Company that the peripatetic loner Sam had already abandoned to form a still-newer Samuel Goldwyn Company)?

Everything was in flux the day we walked into the Alexandria lobby, the old standbys like Essanay and Vitagraph on their way down, fly-by-nights like Peralta and Jewel just passing through, the big independents like Famous Players-Lasky and Universal very much holding their own, and a whole new cluster of companies signing one or two stars and one or two top directors and beginning to claw their way up.

I wish I'd been old enough to understand more of what I saw, but I heard it all in due time, from my parents and their friends who were dealing in the lobby in the late Teens. So I feel as if I was there for the famous fisticuffs—one of filmdom's many such unscheduled events—between Charlie Chaplin, the Little Tramp with a penchant for Lolitas, and Louie Mayer, the ex-junkman and not yet the polished rajah, super-showman, super-hypocrite, arch-conservative of my highschool days. Chaplin had just suffered a tempestuous divorce from Mildred Harris, the wife he had taken (under rather hurried circumstances) when she was sixteen, and was feuding with L.B., who was just getting his first movie company together. Needing every star name he could attract, Mayer was billing Mildred as "Mrs. Charlie Chaplin," which sent Charlie into a fury.

Encountering Chaplin in the Alexandria dining room, the pugnacious L.B. challenged him to step outside onto that million-dollar rug, and is said by my mother and father, who happened to have ringside seats, to have flattened the highest-paid actor in the world. L.B. must have felt he had no choice. Anita Stewart was his only star. Marshall Neilan was his name director, but Mickey often would not even tolerate the eager boss's presence on his set. If L.B. was going to survive he needed every break he could get, and if they weren't coming his way he simply had to make them himself, and damn the consequences, damn Charlie Chaplin, screw the world! The Alexandria days were desperate times. Those were the days from hunger, when what you lacked in credentials and assets you made up in bluff and *chutzpah.*

Eager to expose me to the tropical countryside of southern California, Ad hired a car and driver and we went what seemed a very great distance, from Sunset Boulevard as it wound through small-town Los Angeles on its way west, through sparsely settled Hollywood with its little movie studios, white bungalows, and stucco bungalow courts. We paused at Sunset and Vine, and stared at the spreading Famous Players-Lasky studio, where DeMille was remaking *The Squaw Man,* which had established him as a director five years before. Even though they'd lost Mary Pickford, the studio was still going full blast. They had Gloria Swanson, whom C.B. was transforming from a background bathing beauty to a foreground sophisticated siren in naughty pictures like *Don't Change Your Husband* and *Male and Female.* The former one-barn studio was now devouring all the open country around it.

But of course we couldn't stop in to visit, not with B.P. on the outs with Zukor and ready to start a rival company. No, we kept right on driving into Beverly Hills, way out in the country then, a lone house here and there on the flatlands, and back up on the hillocks at the foot of the Santa Monica Mountains a few mansions of the stars, modeled on Spanish haciendas, surrounded by acres of terraced gardens and groves.

The landmark on Sunset Boulevard in Beverly Hills, toward which we were slowly motoring, was the enormous pink stucco Beverly Hills Hotel. It's still there today, its architecture essentially unchanged but its reason for being entirely transformed. Today its Polo Lounge has taken over from the Alexandria lobby. Basically the same sort of people, only in different clothes, different hairdos, different vocabularies, are still wheeling and dealing. But when we first came to the Beverly Hills Hotel, it was an isolated resort hotel filled with wealthy old couples from the East, the white gentile aristocracy wintering in the sun of the Far West as now they winter in Palm Beach or the Bahamas. White-haired ladies rocked on the front portico. Oriental servants in uniform performed their duties with quiet bows. Everything was hushed and genteel. The gardens outside the hotel offered an exotic zoo, with plume birds from Florida and South America, and many different kinds of monkeys.

No talk of movies here. Chances are my mother and I would never have been admitted to this elite clientele if they had known my father's calling. For although the Great War had broken down some of the resistance to the movie people, "No movies" was still a sign to be found in many a boardinghouse window on the quiet streets of Hollywood. The gentle old ladies who came to the Beverly Hills Hotel to escape the bitter Eastern winters and to enjoy the purest of air and the clearest of skies would have turned up their noses at the sight of Fanny Ward or Lila Lee. They might stare at a face so perfectly formed that it could be blown up to the full size of a silver screen and still betray no blemish, but there would still be that turn-away voice of disdain, "She's a movie!"

10

M Y FATHER AND Uncle Hiram had an appointment with the elusive Charlie Chaplin, who was sometimes at the Alexandria, sometimes at the Athletic Club which he used as a sort of hideout from the mobs, sometimes at a large house he had rented far to the west of downtown Los Angeles—a genius in the studio, a troubled recluse away from his work, drawn both to intellectuals and empty-headed nymphets. B.P. and Uncle Hiram had sounded out his cronies and felt they were approaching him at the opportune moment when he was quarreling with First National and looking for new outlets for maturing work like *The Kid.*

Father and his partner spent a full evening with Charlie Chaplin, and Hollywood's first authentic genius-performer was intrigued. He would have complete artistic freedom, he would make even more money from distributing his films through his own company than he was earning at First National, and he would have a sizable interest in the future of the company as a whole. Years after he retired, although he was then only 29, he would continue to be a major stockholder in United Artists.

He liked the idea well enough, Charlie said, to recommend it to his friends Mary Pickford and Doug Fairbanks. Meanwhile, B.P. enlisted the support of D. W. Griffith. Griffith's temperament was artistic and the idea of artists joining together to form their own company, make their own pictures, and distribute them through their own organization appealed to his desire for independence from the "money men." If the other members of the Big Five came in, he was ready to be a United Artist.

Only the western hero William S. Hart had second thoughts. The plan was for each picture to be sold on its individual merits, with the star enjoying the producer's profits, except for what Uncle Hiram and my father would charge for their services. Hart would have the same stock interest as his fellow-artists but his immediate profit would come from the release of his own pictures. He gave a tentative yes but then called my father to say he had thought it over and had changed his mind, deciding to form his own company. Over the years as my father refought his battles for, with, and against United Artists—sorties, skirmishes, and frontal actions that took on the drama and the significance of a Borodino or a Balaklava—I listened to his theories of William S.'s lack of heart for this project:

Bill Hart was still a national idol. Ten-year-old kids all over the country were saying, "Let's play cowboys and Indians—I'll be Bill Hart—bang, bang, you're dead!" But the lean, unsmiling Hart had come from the stage to the movies when he was already over 40. He was now closing in on 50 and although he would go on making his *Wagon Tracks* and *Wild Bill Hickok*s for another half-dozen years, riding Pinto Ben, the horse as famous as he, Hart sensed that his star was on the wane and that he'd be overwhelmed in the company of Chaplin, Pickford, and Fairbanks. A victim of that unique American phenomenon, success in America, Bill Hart's career had reached late autumn and was beginning to feel the first chill of oncoming winter.

Only slightly daunted by the defection of the old cowboy star, Uncle Hiram and my father went on to their key meeting with Chaplin, Griffith, Pickford, and Fairbanks at Doug's new castle in Beverly Hills. It was, B.P. reported, a long and lively evening, with the four commanding figures of Hollywood's rapidly expanding industry endorsing the Abrams-Schulberg concept. With their own company to produce and distribute their own pictures, they would become overnight the dominant factor in that industry. Neither Famous Players nor First National, let alone Fox, Metro, or Universal, would be able to compete with them. Hiram Abrams, who had backed into the business less than ten years earlier selling sing-along slides to nickelodeons, and who was now an acknowledged theater veteran, would handle the distribution, while B.P. with his creative experience under Porter and Zukor would supervise the studio operation.

It turned out to be one of those nights when a battle is won but the seeds are planted for a long and losing campaign. In the course of his extensive Liberty Bond tours and his access to the White House, Doug Fairbanks had become friendly with William Gibbs McAdoo, President Wilson's son-in-law and Secretary of the Treasury until his appointment to the key wartime role of Director-General of the railroads. McAdoo was on his way to Los Angeles in his special Pullman car for a much-needed rest, and Fairbanks was planning an elaborate reception for him. With due respect to Hiram Abrams and young Schulberg, Fairbanks said, he felt that such an array of stars as Mary, Charlie, D.W., and himself should have as president of their new company a figure of national prominence, a man of the calibre of Director-General McAdoo.

"How could we say 'no' to one of the most powerful men in America, who was at that very moment tasting the fruits of victory of what we were still calling the Great War?" my father said in defense of his and Uncle Hiram's acquiescence. So a second meeting was scheduled in the luxurious bungalow that McAdoo and the President's daughter had rented for the winter in Santa Barbara, where he planned to map out his political and economic strategy for the years of leadership awaiting him. There was considerable speculation that McAdoo might be the Democratic nominee to succeed his father-in-law in the 1920 presidential race. But at this moment Doug Fairbanks had put McAdoo's name in nomination as president of United Artists, thereby threatening Uncle Hiram's ambition, and my father's as well.

At that meeting in McAdoo's spacious bungalow, the former Director-General of the railroads declined Doug's nomination. Instead he deferred to his press secretary, Oscar Price, suggesting that Price occupy the presidency, with McAdoo serving the new company as general counsel. And where would the originators of the concept, Abrams and Schulberg, fit into this new organization? Well, McAdoo strongly objected to the twenty percent for Abrams and Schulberg that had been part of the original plan. He thought two percent was more like it, with Abrams to receive that amount as general manager. Since Price had had no previous motion-picture experience, they would need Abrams's know-how to keep the distribution and exhibition wheels turning. And where did that leave my old man, on the eve of his twenty-seventh birthday? Without a single percentage point in the company he had dreamt up so enthusiastically with "Uncle Hiram." And since he was damned if he'd be a hireling, B.P. was out of a job.

After the Defeat of Santa Barbara, as my father would look back on it like a battle-scarred Napoleon, his efforts to launch United Artists were doomed to wind up as a footnote to the history of motion pictures. Indeed, a description of his role as the true father of United Artists is to be found in authoritative histories of American film. But as Samuel Goldwyn is said to have remarked, a verbal agreement isn't worth the paper it's written on. B.P.'s verbal agreement with the man for whom he had forsaken his favorable position with Adolph Zukor turned out to be the most elastic of rubber checks.

On that unhappy drive back to Los Angeles there were the inevitable recriminations. B.P. accused Hiram of selling him out. Abrams protested that Doug Fairbanks had sold them both out by turning to McAdoo and Price instead of accepting the two of them as the deal had been presented originally. (This was all the more ironic, B.P. would remember, because in a crucial earlier meeting at the Alexandria Hotel, between an alarmed Adolph Zukor and an intimidated Doug Fairbanks—a meeting called to head off Doug's rumored defection from Famous Players—Fairbanks had hurried off to study B.P.'s manifesto, "Eighty-nine Reasons for United Artists," to reinforce his stand.) It was Ben's educated guess that there had been meetings between Abrams and the McAdoo group behind his back, and that a compromise had already been worked out in which Abrams would receive a liberal salary as general manager, and a token two percent in return for not opposing the McAdoo-Price-Fairbanks ploy.

Abrams denied the accusation, but when my father urged him not to go along with McAdoo and Price and instead to stand up and fight for their rights and take the usurpers to court, Abrams demurred. They might have a chance against a Richard Rowland (then head of Metro), a lone eagle like Sam Goldwyn, or even a determined organization man like Zukor. But this was William Gibbs McAdoo, the man to whom most Democrats looked as the successor to Wilson's national leadership. What legal weapons could they muster against such artillery? They had simply been outsmarted and outmaneuvered, and Hiram Abrams argued he had no choice now but to accept the crumbs from the McAdoo table. Father stared at him and then turned to look out at the ocean as they drove on in silence.

Soon we were back on the *Santa Fe Chief* again, heading east. But the Schulbergs and the Abramses were no longer traveling together. In fact they weren't even speaking to one another. No longer could I have Miss

Abrams to turn to if I grew lonely or frightened in my upper berth. No longer would there be a guiding hand to steady me as I made my way down the lurching aisles on the long walk back to the observation car. Nor do I remember ever seeing Uncle Hiram again. Or even thinking of him as my lost uncle.

The loss of an honorary uncle was to become a familiar casualty in the motion-picture wars. It came to me at a tender age that the world of the motion picture, depending as it does on personalities and those quick-silver moments of fame and power, is particularly vulnerable to opportunism. Love knots quickly become hate knots, and oaths of personal loyalty, with rare exceptions, are made to be broken and rationalized.

Of course I claim no omniscience at the age of five. Even without Miss Abrams to sit with me out there on that wonderful observation car as I watched the sagebrush and cactus country of Arizona and New Mexico fall away, I was still having fun waving to a lone cowhand or to a few dusty travelers waiting at the little stations where the engine paused to catch its smoky breath. I didn't know that our long journey had succeeded only in surrendering an original and profitable idea to McAdoo and the screen's Top Four.

I heard but was not fully cognizant of the lectures being delivered by my mother to my father on the subject of his guilelessness in a world of cutthroats. Escaping "I told you so"s, I was now well enough acquainted with the *Santa Fe* to be able to wander from car to car alone. I would come back to find my parents playing casino, Father with a big cigar jutting from his rather delicate face, Mother frequently returning to the same sore subject. Never trust anybody in this business. It was still too volatile and crawling with phonies. The only protection was to get something on paper. When would B.P. learn not to be so trusting? How many times had she warned him not to place such blind faith in Hiram Abrams? They would all take advantage of his youth and his naivete and steal his ideas.

Over the years this would become a familiar family theme song, my increasingly suspicious and self-protective mother attacking my self-deceiving, vulnerable father for his lack of armor in the lists of business. Because Ad had an irritating tendency to be right, Father's vulnerabilities were stung to the swelling and bursting point. The *Santa Fe Chief* racing us back to the Midwest and on to Chicago arouses my first memory of bitter quarreling. Subsequent arguments were more harshly focused on Ben as a babe in the woods who would be lost without her instinct for self-preservation. Typically, the more Ad was determined to protect Ben from himself, the more he was determined to assert his independence.

In 1919, basically a happy child, with only my persistent stammering to worry about, constantly encouraged by my parents, I was pleased to be reunited with Wilma and little Sonya in the comfortable apartment on Riverside Drive. Ad was glad to be back in New York too, back to her Godmothers' League and her self-improvement courses at Columbia.

While Ad kept one eye on Freud, Jung, and Brill, and the other on my father's dreams of independent production, B.P. was preparing himself for the seminal role he would play in the 1920s. He had sued United Artists, but as ex-Uncle Hiram had predicted, his resources had proved no match for McAdoo, whose powerful firm was prepared to fight a delaying action all the way up to the Supreme Court. After a modest settlement, B.P. decided to do what so many of the first wave of movie pioneers were doing: start his own company. Too young to understand how he managed to do it, I still remember his partners, his old school-friend Jack Bachman, a serious, pipe-smoking, bookish accountant who became treasurer, and the ubiquitous Al Lichtman, "the best film sales-man in the business," also leaving Zukor and Lasky to help launch the new company. It was called Preferred Pictures, with B.P.'s slogan built into its very name, suggesting that his were the movies the public preferred.

In the style of L. J. Selznick, W. F. Fox, L. B. Mayer, and the other less-educated but equally high-flying producers, B.P. announced his new company with a flourish and opened an impressive suite of offices in the heart of the theater district on Broadway. Now he needed a star. Selznick had made his name by swiping Clara Kimball Young for World, and Fox had taken a Jewish tailor's *zaftig* daughter named Theodora Goodman and transformed her into an Arabian vampire, Theda Bara (which was Arab spelled backward); Mayer had virtually shanghaied Anita Stewart from Vitagraph. B.P. in turn wooed eminently bankable Katherine MacDonald, in those days a major flutterer of masculine hearts and the envy of distaff moviegoers for her well-bred sophistica-tion flavored with just the right degree of "naughtiness" in films like *The Woman Thou Gavest Me, The Beauty Market, Passion's Playground,* and *The Notorious Miss Lisle.*

A strawberry blonde with limpid blue eyes and the sensuous but classy

100

high-bridged nose that gave character to the leading ladies of the silent screen (*vide* Constance Talmadge, Florence Vidor, and Barbara La-Marr), Katherine MacDonald had completed her contract with Famous Players, and would soon be free of First National as well. B.P. went after her with all his boyish charm, wit, and intelligence. He wined her at the Waldorf, dined her at Delmonico's, and showed her his elaborate offices, with an Italianate boardroom featuring a long cherrywood conference table and chairs which Ad considered pretentious and needlessly costly.

Katherine MacDonald must have been impressed with that Venetian boardroom, which doubled as a projection room, and my father must have been persuasive in his promises to make her more than a leading star of the day. In his young but knowing hands she would become as much of a household word as Mary Pickford. Miss MacDonald would be known from coast to coast, he promised, as "The American Beauty Rose." Like America's Sweetheart, the American Beauty Rose had a mother who seemed to know her way around a contract, and again like Mary who always saw to it that sister Lottie was also signed, there was another flower in the family, the patrician Mary MacLaren, who would also be Preferred. After extended negotiations, during which Miss MacDonald threatened to form her own company under the Famous Players banner, or to defect to Universal, Metro, Goldwyn, or Fox, a deal was finally consummated, toasted in champagne in the grandiose boardroom, with the film press of New York on hand to wish their erstwhile colleague well.

Soon Ben and Ad were reading novels and magazine stories and going to plays to find the ideal vehicles for the first jewel in the diadem of Preferred Pictures. Meanwhile the high-living, fast-talking Al Lichtman was out in the field selling the rights to "four great new Katherine MacDonald pictures" soon to be made by The Industry's youngest and brightest producer, Adolph Zukor's own protegé, B. P. Schulberg.

Those were busy days. B.P. was writing reams of publicity for his own company and working on scenarios, banging away at his typewriter. All his life he clung to his old Underwood as an aging matinee idol clings to his toupee. In 1920 that Underwood was zipping. So was the movie business. So was the country. The Golden Age was upon us.

11

WHEN MY FATHER was organizing Preferred Pictures in New York and getting ready to set up shop at the Mayer-Schulberg Studio in Los Angeles, he was a passionate fight fan. An habitué of the old Garden on Madison Square, his favorite fighter was the Jewish lightweight Benjamin Leiner who fought under the *nom-de-boxe* of Benny Leonard. On the eve of my seventh birthday, my hero was neither the new cowboy star Tom Mix nor the acrobatic Doug Fairbanks. I didn't hoard and trade face cards of the current baseball stars like the other kids on Riverside Drive. Babe Ruth could hit 54 homers that year (when no one else had ever hit more than 16 in the history of the League) and I really didn't care. The legendary Ty Cobb could break a batting record almost every time he came up to the plate, but no chill came to my skin at the mention of his name. That sensation was reserved for Benny Leonard.

He was doing with his fists what the Adolph Zukors and William Foxes, and soon the L. B. Mayers and the B. P. Schulbergs, were doing in their studios and their theaters, proving the advantage of brain over brawn, fighting the united efforts of the *goyische* establishment to keep them in their ghettos.

Jewish boys on their way to *shul* on the Sabbath had tasted the fists and felt the shoeleather of the righteous Irish and Italian children who crowded them, shouted "You killed our Christ!", and avenged their gentle Savior with blows and kicks. But sometimes the little yid surprised his racist foes by fighting back, like Adolph Zukor, or Abe Attell, who won the featherweight championship of the world at the turn of the century, or Abe Goldstein, who beat up a small army of Irish contenders on his way to the bantamweight title. But our superhero was Benny Leonard. "The Great Benny Leonard." That's how he was always referred to in our household. There was The Great Houdini. The Great Caruso. *And* The Great Benny Leonard.

My father gave me a scrapbook, with a picture of Benny in fighting stance on the cover, and I recognized his face and could spell out his name even before I was able to read. In 1920 he was only 24 years old, just four years younger than my hero-worshipping old man, but he had been undefeated lightweight champion of the world ever since he knocked out the former champion, Freddie Welsh, in the Garden.

B.P. knew Benny Leonard personally. All the up-and-coming young Jews in New York knew Benny Leonard personally. They would take time off from their lunch hour or their afternoon activities to watch him train. They bet hundreds and often thousands of dollars on him in stirring contests against Rocky Kansas, Ever Hammer, Willie Ritchie, Johnny Dundee, Pal Moran, Joe Welling. . . . He was only five foot six, and his best fighting weight was a few pounds over 130, but he was one of those picture-book fighters who come along once or twice in a generation, a master boxer with a knockout punch, a poised technician who came into the ring with his hair plastered down and combed back with a part in the middle, in the approved style of the day, and whose boast was that no matter whom he fought, "I never even get my hair mussed!" After his hand was raised in victory, he would run his hand back over his sleek black hair, and my father, and Al Kaufman, and Al Lichtman, and the rest of the triumphant Jewish rooting section would roar in delight, as Ali's fans were to raise the decibel level at the sight of the Ali Shuffle. To shake the hand of Benny Leonard was to touch greatness and to share in his invincibility. To see him climb into the ring sporting the six-pointed Jewish star on his fighting trunks was to anticipate sweet revenge for all the bloody noses, split lips, and mocking laughter at pale little Jewish boys who had run the neighborhood gauntlet.

One of my father's friends practically cornered the market on the early motion-picture insurance business. But all through his life he would be singled out as the incredible amateur boxer who had sparred with Benny Leonard and had actually knocked Great Benny down! Every time Artie Stebbins came to our house, my father prefaced his arrival by describing

104

that monumental event. Artie Stebbins had a slightly flattened nose and looked like a fighter and it was whispered that he would have gone on to a brilliant professional career except for an unfortunate accident in which his opponent had died in the ring. No matter how modestly he dismissed the legendary knockdown of Benny Leonard—"I think Benny slipped . . ." or "I just happened to tag him right"—that knockdown remained with him as a badge of honor. My father would say with a note of awe, "He might have been another Benny Leonard!"

But when I was going on seven, there was only one Benny Leonard; my scrapbook fattened on his victories. In those days fighters fought three or four fights in a single month. Benny had been an undernourished 15-year-old when he first climbed into the professional ring, getting himself knocked out by one Mickey Finnegan in two rounds. He was knocked out again by the veteran Joe Shugrue when he was only sixteen. But from the time he reached the seasoned age of eighteen, he had gone on to win more than a hundred and fifty fights, in an era in which the lightweight division was known for its class. The Great Benny Leonard had gone to the post twenty-six times in 1919 alone, and almost every one of his opponents was a name to the cognoscenti. As for me, I had only one ambition, to become a world champion like The Great Benny Leonard. Or rather, two ambitions, for the second was to see him in action.

I had asked my father if he could take me to the Joe Welling fight, but he thought I was a little young to stay up so late. Instead he had promised to tell me all about it when he came home. That night, I waited for Father to bring news of the victory. In what round had our Star of the Ghetto vanquished the dangerous Joe Welling? How I wished I were in Madison Square Garden! Old enough to smoke big cigars and go to the fights like my father!

I have no idea what time Daddy got home that night. Probably three or four in the morning. Where had he gone with his pals after the fight? The Screen Club? The Astor? Jack and Charlie's? A dozen other speakeasies? The apartment of a friendly or ambitious young extra girl who hoped to become a Preferred feature player? When my father finally gave me the blow-by-blow next evening, he admitted that our hero had underestimated Welling's appetite for punishment. Ben and the rest of the young Jewish fancy had bet that Welling would fall in ten, as Leonard had predicted. But Welling was nobody's pushover, and he had even fought the referree who finally stopped the fight. B.P. was out five hundred smackers. He and his pals had gone back to the dressing room to see the triumphant Benny, and the fistic Star of David, still proud of his hair-comb, apologized for leading his rooters astray. B.P. told Benny about my scrapbook, and The Great B.L. promised to autograph it for me. Then the boys went out on the town to celebrate Jewish Power.

When father told me about the Joe Welling fight and helped me paste the clippings into my bulging scrapbook, I begged him to take me with him to the next Great Benny Leonard fight. "When you're a little older," he promised.

In the early weeks of 1921, he brought me the news. Great Benny had just signed to defend his title against Richie Mitchell in Madison Square Garden! Now Richie Mitchell was no ordinary contender. He was a better boxer than Joe Welling, and a harder puncher. He was three inches taller than Benny Leonard, in the prime of his youth, strength, and ability at 25, and he had more than held his own against all the good ones and some of the great ones: Wolgast, Kilbane, Tendler, Dundee, Charley White, Joe Rivers. . . . Only once in his impressive nine-year career had Richie Mitchell been knocked out. Benny had turned the trick back when I was three years old. My old man had taken the train to Milwaukee to see it, and had come back flushed with victory and victory's rewards.

Now it was time for the rematch, and Richie Mitchell had come to New York confident of reversing the only loss on his record. The day of the fight I boasted to my classmates, "I'm g-g-going to M-M-Madison Square Garden tonight t-to s-see The G-G-Great B-B-Benny Leonard!" Even if they had been able to understand me, I don't think the other kids would have known what I was talking about. When it came to boxing they were illiterates. They simply had no idea that the rematch between Benny Leonard and Number One Contender Richie Mitchell was an event more earthshaking than the election of a new President, the arrival of Prohibition, or the publication of the first novel by Scott Fitzgerald.

Finally, the moment arrived. Mother had dressed me warmly for this mid-January adventure. I was wearing long white stockings and a blue velvet suit with fur-lined coat and hat. All that was lacking was one of my father's big Cuban cigars. But it didn't matter. I would smoke it vicariously as I sat snugly beside him in the front ringside seats near our idol's corner that B.P. always got from Leonard.

106

"Well, Buddy," my father said as we got out of the cab near the crowded entrance to the Garden, "I kept my promise. Your mother thought you were still too young, but I wanted you to see The Great Benny Leonard in his prime, because it's something you'll remember the rest of your life."

There were thousands and thousands of big people, a lot of them wearing derbies, a lot of them puffing on big cigars, a lot of them red-faced from winter wind and the forbidden but ever-plentiful alcohol, bellying and elbowing their way toward the ticket-takers.

As we reached the turnstile, my father urged me ahead of him and held out a pair of tickets. A giant of a guard in uniform glanced at my father, then looked in vain for the holder of the other ticket. When he saw where Father was pointing, his voice came down to me in a terrible pronouncement, like God's: "What are ya, nuts or somethin'? You can't take that little kid in here! Ya gotta be sixteen years old!"

My father argued. He bargained and bribed. But in a city known for its Tammany Hall corruption, we had come upon that rare bird, an honest guardian of the law.

By this time Father was telling me to, for Christ's sake, stop crying! He was frantic. The preliminaries had already started, and in those days before television and radio, there were no extra bouts standing by to hold the audience until the pre-announced time for the star bout. If there were early knockouts in the prelims, B.P. ran the risk of missing The Great Benny. And we were all the way down on Madison Square at East 26th Street, miles away from home on Riverside Drive near 100th Street. If traffic was heavy he might miss the event of a lifetime. But there was nothing for it but to hail a cab, tell the driver to speed across town and up the West Side, wait for him to dispose of his sobbing and expendable baggage, and race back to the Garden. Delivered to my mother, awash with tears, I stammered out my tale of injustice. I would have to wait ten long years to be admitted to the Garden and by that time our champion would be retired from the ring. Now I would never see him, I cried, never in my whole life!

Mother tried everything in her extensive repertoire of child psychology to console me. But it was too late. For me life simply had come to an end at the entrance to the turnstile of Madison Square Garden.

To ease the tragedy, I was allowed to wait up until Father came home. And this time, sensitive to the crisis, he did not linger with his cronies over highballs at a friendly speakeasy. He came directly from the Garden, his fine white skin flushed with the excitement of what had happened.

B.P. had given the taxi driver an extra five-spot to disregard the speed limits and get him back to the Garden on a magic carpet. As he rushed through the turnstile and looked for the aisle to his seat, he heard a roar from the crowd that was like the howl of a jungle full of wild beasts. Everybody was standing up and screaming, blocking his view. A frantic glance at the second clock told him it was the middle of Round Three. When he got closer to his seat and was able to see the ring, the spectacle that presented itself was the Unbelievable. There on the canvas was our champion. And not only was his hair mussed, his eyes were dimmed as he tried to shake his head back to consciousness. The count went on, "Six . . . seven . . . eight . . ." Thousands of young Jews like my father were shouting, "Get up! Get up, Benny! Get up!" And another multitude of anti-Semitic rooters for Mitchell, "You got 'im, Richie! You got that little mockie sonuvabitch!" But just before the count of ten Leonard managed to stagger to his feet.

No, I wasn't there, but my father had caught the lightning in a bottle and had brought it home for me. I sat there watching the fight as clearly as if home television had been installed thirty years ahead of time. Our Benny was on his feet but the quick brain that usually directed the series of rapid jabs and classic right crosses was full of cobwebs. Billy Mitchell was leaning through the ropes and cupping his old fighter's hands to urge his son to "Move in, move in, Richie, finish 'im!" And Richie was trying, oh how he was trying, only a split second from being Lightweight Champion of the World, one more left hook, one more punishing right hand. . . . But Benny covered up, rolled with the punches, slipped a haymaker by an instinctive fraction of an inch, and managed to survive until the bell brought Leonard's handlers into the ring with smelling salts, ice, and the other traditional restoratives.

In the next round Richie Mitchell sprang from his corner full of fight, running across the ring to keep the pressure on Leonard and land his bruising combinations while he still held the upper hand. Everybody in the Garden was on his feet. Everybody was screaming. There had never been such fight in all of Father's ringside nights, all the way back to 1912 when he had first started going to the fights with Adolph Zukor and the Famous Players crowd. Benny was retreating, boxing cautiously, gradually beginning to focus on Mitchell's combative eyes. "On his bicycle," they called it, dodging and running and slipping off the ropes, using all the defensive tactics he had learned in his street fights on the Lower East Side and in those one hundred and fifty battles inside the ropes. And as he retreated he was talking to Mitchell—shades of Ali half a century later!—"Is that the best you can do? I thought you hit harder than that. Look, I'll put my hands down, what do you wanna bet you can't hit me? Come on, if you think you've got me hurt, why don't you fight? You look awful slow to me, Richie, looks like you're getting tired. . . ."

That round had been more of a debate than a boxing match, with Benny winning the verbal battle and Richie swinging wildly and futilely as he tried to chop Benny down. At the end of the round the ferocious Richie Mitchell did look tired and a little discouraged. The drumfire of backtalk from Leonard had disconcerted him. He had let Benny get his goat, exactly what the champion wanted. Some remorseless clock in his head was telling him that he was blowing the chance of a lifetime. In the next round, Benny was The Great Benny again. His head clearing, his body weathering the storm, he was ready to take charge. Back on his toes, he was beginning to move around the slower Mitchell, keeping him off balance with jabs and rocking his head back with that straight right hand. Near the end of the round Mitchell went to his knees.

How many times Father refought Round Six for me over the years. Benny Leonard's hair was combed straight back again. There was no more talking to distract his opponent. Benny was all business. Lefts and rights found Mitchell's now-unprotected face. Both eyes were cut and blood dripped from his nose. Caught in a buzz saw of fast hard punches that seemed to tear his face apart, the brave Irish brawler went down. But took his count and rose again to face more of the same. Now it was not boxing but slaughterhouse seven and the more humane among the crowd, including the Benny Leonard fans who had bet a bundle it would be over in eight, were imploring the referee to "Stop it! Stop it!" For Mitchell was down again, and he seemed to be looking directly into his own corner, but there was so much blood running down into his eyes that he was unseeing.

"I was watching his father, Billy Mitchell," my father told me. "I could see the whole thing being fought out in Billy Mitchell's face. He was holding a bloody towel, the towel with which he had just wiped the face of his son. His own blood was on that towel. His son Richie got up again. God almighty, he was game. He would look at Benny as if to say 'You're

109

going to have to kill me to stop me.' And Benny, he told us this a lot of times, he loved to win but he doesn't like to punish them once he knows he has them licked. He was hoping the referee would stop the fight. But the ref waved him on. Maybe he was betting on Mitchell. Maybe he figured anyone with the punch of a Richie Mitchell deserved that one extra round to see if he could land a lucky or a desperate blow. Now it seemed as if the entire Garden was chanting together, 'Stop it! Stop it! For God's sake, *stop it!*' And then as the slaughter went on, as The Great Benny Leonard went on ripping Richie Mitchell's face to bloody shreds, finally Billy Mitchell, that tough Mick, couldn't stand it any longer. He raised the bloody towel and tossed it over the top rope into the ring. And then, while Richie's kid brother Pinky and another handler climbed into the ring to revive their battered contender, Pop Mitchell lowered his head into his arms on the apron of the ring and cried like a baby."

II

EXODUS

12

B.P. WAS READY to take his Preferred Pictures out to the new movie capital. On that trip west in 1922, all of our worldly belongings were with us and, when we were helped down from the Pullman platform, we were no longer Eastern visitors from Riverside Drive. We had come to take our place in the booming society of Los Angeles, where the new oil money and the new real-estate money still looked with suspicion on the new movie money. Eventually they would all settle down together to expand, and systematically destroy, the old mission town that had become the southwestern axis of the *Santa Fe*. In our four-year absence, downtown Los Angeles had spread out in all directions, determined to turn its back on the architecture of its Hispanic past. The new conquistadors were devoted to money rather than to tradition or beauty; their aim was to build as rapidly and as profitably as possible. As we drove from the station, this time in a limousine, we passed a series of streets with names that suggested a beauty denied by the low-lying blocks of dingy two- and three-story buildings: names like Spring, and Flower, and Hope.

In later years I was to say that I had been shunted from New York to Hollywood without the courtesy of being consulted. If I had been allowed the privilege of foresight, I'm not sure I would have chosen the life of a Hollywood prince. But then I accepted it as my inheritance, my destiny, and finally as my responsibility. In my childhood the studio backlots provided my playgrounds: My best friend and I climbed to the turrets of great castles from which movie heroes had been besieged, or rode our imaginary steeds into the deserted western street that awaited the arrival of still another cowboy star. In my youth the studio offices provided a workbench from which I could observe the wheels of The Industry turning from the inside. A little later I looked at big studio tycoons with an affection considerably this side of love. All my life, mine was a love-hate relationship with those tycoons—my father's associates, rivals, and enemies in the geographical and cultural crazy quilt known as Hollywood.

Our company, Preferred Pictures, had rented a house for us in what was then considered a district far to the west of downtown Los Angeles, on Gramercy Place near Western Avenue. These days no self-respecting member of The Industry would be drawn to Western Avenue: It lies miles to the east of the Sunset Strip. But in the early Twenties, Western Avenue was aptly named, a kind of western boundary for the uptown business section. Our first home in Hollywood was a roomy bungalow on a quiet residential street of modest frame houses, with neat little lawns punctuated with orange and lemon trees. Our first backyard had tropical flowers, hibiscus and oleander, and in one far corner, an exotic stand of bamboo: my hiding place, sanctuary, or childhood temple. To squeeze into the middle of it, peering out through the uniformly rounded bars of green, was to know that my life had changed dramatically, that I was never to be a New York City boy again. Now I lived in a world of date palms and klieg lights.

My first studio, as I now think of it, was a place full of endless wonder for an eight-year-old: the now almost completely forgotten Mayer-Schulberg Studio, attached to the old Selig Studio and Zoo on Mission Road, east of Main Street. Chances are, only the oldest of the oldtimers at the Motion Picture Fund Home today would know the name of that now-dilapidated and neglected street, bordered by murky factories and cemeteries for bashed-in cars. But when the Schulbergs and the Mayers arrived as part of the movie rush of the early Twenties, Mission Road was still what its name implied: a narrow, winding rural road that led from the little Spanish church in the Plaza to the mission in the open fields.

The primitive Selig-Mayer-Schulberg studio with its dirty white stucco wall and its small silent stages looked across to two adjoining wonders, the Alligator Farm and Gay's Ostrich Farm. Since the proprietors rented their giant birds and reptiles to the studios, I had free access to those exotic farms, and with fear in my throat I could ride the ancient tame 'gator, said to be a great-great-grandfather of the little 'gators in the baby pool. I was also led about the ring astride an ostrich whose head and neck were draped with reins like a horse. One day the keeper of the ostriches gave me an enormous egg so heavy I could hardly lift it. Somehow I got it home to Gramercy Place in one piece and Wilma scrambled that incredible egg, serving Sunday brunch for fifteen people.

L. B. Mayer, his warmhearted wife Margaret, and their two daughters, slightly my senior—the pretty, gentle Edith, and the handsome, tomboyish Irene—seemed almost like a part of our household in those innocent days when we alternated Sunday brunches at our modest bungalows. Ad and Margaret would drive down to Temple Street in the Jewish quarter, and bring back for our Sunday spread such East Side delicacies as lox, smoked whitefish, cream cheese, fresh bagels, and onion rolls. Those were what I would call L.B.'s Jewish days, when he was still relatively humble, when he still liked to reminisce about having courted Margaret on his junk wagon, driving her out from South Boston for picnics in the country. Louie had nothing then but the junk he was able to salvage. That and ambition, compact physical strength, and ghetto cunning. On young Louie's wedding day some sense of the grandiose impelled him to add a middle initial to his signature on the marriage license. So he became, with a flourish of the pen, Louis B. Mayer, a precursor of the godlike figure he would eventually become when the second *M* in the enormous MGM sign over the great studio in Culver City stood for him. He would rule with a draconian hand not only his own studio but in effect The Industry, all of Hollywood as we knew it in the Twenties, the Thirties, and the Forties.

The Mayers and the Schulbergs at their Sunday brunch were feasting on the American dream. Who could have guessed how success would consume L.B. in one way, B.P. in another, and that for each the lining of the dream that seemed to shine with silver would blacken to nightmare? Who could have predicted as they observed those two resourceful young movie pioneers that one would become a despot— walking as a Caesar among Caesars, striking terror into the hearts of the 30,000 employees who manned his studios—the other a desperate victim? Both men could trace their lifelines back to poverty-stricken Jewish stock in Czarist Russia. The Mayers too had somehow managed to worm their way into steerage and to live through that seemingly endless journey across the ocean.

Like my grandfathers Max Jaffe and Simon Schulberg, L.B.'s father Jacob Mayer was lost in the bustling new world into which he had wandered. From New York, where he had been unable to survive, somehow he had found his way to Saint John in the hostile land of New Brunswick in eastern Canada. It was a move L.B. seemed never able to explain, any more than my Grandpa Simon knew what had taken his straggling family to Bridgeport, Connecticut. Without roots or possessions or any immediate means of support, these were truly the wandering Jews. Grandpa Jacob, for he seemed like my grandfather too in those days when B.P. and L.B. were still close friends, had turned to the most likely occupation of the have-nothing. He simply had picked up junk, whatever he could find that the industrious citizens of Saint John had thrown into the streets or into the garbage, and he had sold it door to door—old nails, pieces of tin, rusted locks. . . . Meanwhile, with the pennies that dribbled in from the junk that Jacob managed to peddle, his spunky wife Sarah was able to buy chickens from the farmers outside of town and to hawk them house to house at a niggling profit. And soon little Louie was out on the streets picking up rags, old papers, discarded trash. In that sense, Louie Mayer grew up in the street. The Jew-baiting that was one of the year-round sports of Saint John made him tough, and rag-picking made him resourceful and opportunistic.

L.B. and B.P. were to struggle to make their way outward and upward from these restrictive centers. But for the Old World mentalities of Grandfather Max and Grandfather Jacob, material work seemed to be a kind of sideline; their real life went on inside their synagogues.

While the minds of the elders were riveted to their Torahs, the Americanized brains of L.B. and B.P. were focused just as intently on their studio. They were not partners in the actual filmmaking. They had separate companies, with separate stars and directors, chose separate stories, and turned out separate movies. But since their resources were limited—there were Saturdays when L.B. could not meet his payroll—it had seemed to both of them sound business to rent studio space from Colonel Selig together. It was, for a while, a happy, symbiotic relationship, with both men economizing by sharing a single reception office, common guards and cleanup men, and carpentry and paint shops, and even exchanging and redressing sets for their sometimes interchangeable plots.

A sixty- or eighty-thousand-dollar picture could enjoy a return of five or ten times its film cost *if* it could hold its own against the product of major companies with large chains of their own theaters. Famous Players, Fox, and First National had replaced the Patents Company, and were taking on all the monopolistic controls of the bygone Trust. The infighting to get hold of as many theaters as possible was as intense and bitter as the earlier struggle to set up independent exchanges and theater chains.

While my father and L.B. were struggling to make their movies cheaper and better and to squeeze them into the programs of the big theater chains, I was having the time of my eight-year-old life as an almost daily visitor to the Selig Zoo. Colonel Selig—whether this impressive military title stemmed from the Spanish-American War or his own showman's imagination I will never know—was perfectly cast for his role, a ruddy-faced hail-fellow with a Falstaffian figure. I remember him as a kind of W. C. Fields, without Fields's bibulous craftiness (on stage) or bibulous meanness (in his private life).

When my father first came to the Selig Zoo and set up with L.B. the painted half-moon sign of the Mayer-Schulberg Studio, he had told me the Colonel was one of the original film pioneers. A one-man vaudeville show, Selig had toured the West Coast as a magician and early minstrel man. Once he had seen Edison's Kinetoscope, in '96, he had begun tinkering with his own invention for screen projection, joining half a dozen others who were working independently on this logical extension of the Edison peephole. The result was the Selig Polyscope. At the same time that Edwin S. Porter was experimenting with his story films in New York, Colonel Selig was operating his innovative little studio in Chicago. When another colonel, Teddy Roosevelt, announced that he was going to go big-game hunting in Africa, Selig's nose for showmanship led him to the White House. What he proposed was a documentary innovation—that a Selig cameraman go along to record the trip for posterity: Col. Selig Presents Col. Roosevelt's Big Game Hunt In Africa! According to Selig, the ebullient Teddy had cried "Bully!" to the idea. But somehow, when the actual expedition was under way, Selig found himself double-crossed. Instead of a Selig cameraman, a Smithsonian technician was taken along on the safari. Perhaps someone had whispered in the President's ear that these movie people were something less than respectable.

Colonel Selig plunged in with his usual energy and daring. If the Selig Polyscope Company was unable to go to Africa, the Selig Company would bring Africa to Chicago. Accordingly, he acquired a lion and other beasts from a bankrupt traveling circus and built an African setting into a corner of the Selig studio. He hired an actor to impersonate the famous big-game hunter from 1600 Pennsylvania Avenue from mustache to safari outfit. A handful of Chicago Negroes who had never been closer to Africa than the Loop were pressed into loincloth service as his runners. The lion, Selig had confided to my father, was a rather tired or cowardly old fellow who had to be prodded into action. He would lie around the set and the stage hands could walk right over him. They would have to pull his tail to make him react. Once this tame cousin of the mighty king of the jungle yawned and the cameraman astutely shot a close-up of the gaping mouth and supposedly deadly teeth. When the ancient beast fell asleep, they photographed him as if he were dead, and then cut to the bogus T.R. pointing his rifle at him. When Teddy Roosevelt returned home in triumph happily displaying his trophies of the adventure, Col. Selig released his one-reel film, *Hunting Big Game in Africa.* The name of Roosevelt was never mentioned in the film; it didn't have to be. T.R. was the acknowledged inventor of the African safari, and timing the Chicago Colonel's film to the arrival of the Washington Colonel's party made an ideal box-office launching. The naive movie public of that day was fascinated by what they accepted as authentic and thrilling footage of Roosevelt's gung-ho penetration into Darkest Africa.

Now that his first African picture was such a success, Col. Selig figured he might as well continue making sequels ostensibly photographed on the Dark Continent. African adventure pictures became a Selig specialty. To the lot on Mission Road the rotund Colonel brought his menagerie, now expanded from the poor creatures who had inhabited his Chicago studio. There were a noisy assembly of monkeys, from little spiders to extroverted chimps, plume birds, a couple of elephants and camels, reindeer and bears, panthers, tigers, and lions. And that original lion, star of *Hunting Big Game in Africa,* was said to be still in residence.

I can't vouch that it was the same one who had played possum to an unknown actor's "Teddy Roosevelt," but I do remember well the old lion we called Leo, an aged, blinking precursor of the mighty beast that a few years later became the roaring trademark of almighty Metro-Goldwyn-Mayer. Leo was the most pacific of jungle beasts. Ex-jungle, one should say. His mascot and constant companion was a little black-and-white mutt that someone had mischievously named Tiger. Whenever Leo the lion was removed from his cage to take his place before the cameras in one of Col. Selig's African adventure films, Tiger had to go along. Leo would refuse to perform, indeed he would even refuse to eat if Tiger were not at his side. I loved to watch them curled up together in their cage. Sometimes Leo would be half dozing while Tiger played idly with his tail. So gentle was this old lion that I was allowed to go into the cage and stroke his head.

Bordering the far edge of my desk is a row of old photographs from those innocent days, pictures that graphically reinforce these memories. One of my favorites presents my father, standing beside Leo, with L.B.'s brother Jerry on the other side. In the background is a studio stage and just behind this oddly assorted trio are some large wooden trunks, probably for costumes, that look like a throwback to stagecoach travel. In this historic photo, three contrasting expressions create a comedic tableau. B.P. in his five-button vest and smartly tailored suit looks as poised as if he were in his office posing with a visiting celebrity. The old lion's mouth hangs open more in ennui than anger, his eyes sleepy, his body like that of a seedy, stuffed animal from the prop department. Mayer's brother, wearing a cap and a rumpled suit, has one tentative hand on the lion's head, his face betraying acute anxiety, his right foot pointed, obviously ready to run for cover the moment the camera clicks.

Proud of that picture, B.P. kept it with him on his moves from house to house during his long climb up and down the Hollywood ladder. Since Father was anything but an outdoorsman, this was one of the few photographs ever taken of him in what might be called—if you overlook the decrepitude of the sleepy lion—a heroic pose. Even when we had our own tennis court, Ben rarely appeared on it, and in the flush late Twenties when we bought a sixty-foot yacht for no other reason than that each of his prosperous friends seemed to have one, he would send me off on expeditions to Coronado and Catalina but would never go near it himself. Yes, B.P. was a dedicated indoorsman. You never saw my father with a fishing rod in his hand, or walking barefoot on the beach at Malibu. His milieu was projection rooms, fight arenas, gambling casinos, boudoirs, and book-lined dens. Proud of his fair white skin, he rarely exposed it to the sun and the elements. Rooms full of expensive cigar smoke were his natural habitat. Even in those early Twenties, when he was still only a budding tycoon, his trademark was the ever-present outsize Upmann cigar. He would smoke one when he woke up in the morning and chain-smoke several dozen more through the day and far into the night. One dollar apiece they cost, even in 1922, and every Monday a shipment of seven boxes arrived from Dunhill's in New York. In the late Twenties, with the first faint glimmer of a social conscience, I did a little arithmetic on the weekly cost of my father's Upmann habit. B.P. was smoking up one hundred and sixty-eight dollars' worth of Corona Coronas a week, I calculated, with another seven dollars thrown in for parcel post. That didn't include the ones he gave away.

But who counted? In that free-living, optimistic year of 1922, my father was a 30-year-old boy wonder starring his American Beauty Rose in a series of spicy dramas like *The Beauty Market, The Beautiful Liar, The Woman's Side,* and *Domestic Relations.* Daring stories for their day. Still a press agent at heart, B.P. had publicity releases put out in the form of four-page, eight-column newspapers, with headlines screaming across the entire front page:

KATHERINE MACDONALD—MOST BEAUTIFUL WOMAN ON THE SCREEN—
IN "THE BEAUTY MARKET," BASED ON SEX ANTAGONISM WITH
A GREAT PLOT THAT HOLDS UNTIL THE FINAL FADE-OUT!

More than a dozen of these yellowed scare sheets rest on a side table in my den and cry to me their daring tales of period sophistication that once seemed so bold but that more than a half a century later seem closer to *Godey's Lady's Book.* Across that Grand Canyon of time I hear my father's ebullient journalese in this typical subheading:

Men of Wealth Barter Gold for Wives Whose Entrance Fees of Gowns and Social Rank Are Bought with Suitors' Gifts Pawned for Cash . . . and Amelie's Hand Is Won . . . A Diamond Brooch Binds the Sale. She Pays—and Pays with a Price "The Beauty Market" Derides with Scorn and Sneers.

The ludicrous Theda Bara vampire-sex of the war years was being replaced with something closer to the real thing—refined sex, the naughtiness that lurked behind every Nice Nellie. You watched the fair and elegant Alice Terry or the seemingly proper Agnes Ayres nicely but seductively turn away from the passionate Latin glances of Valentino and you were in on the mysterious secret of sex that was creating a new approach to morality in America. It was a morality inextricably braided through the new materialism. The shop girls, the seamstresses, the maids, the small-town housewives finally emerging from their Victorian cocoons lived vicariously the lives of Gloria Swanson and Barbara LaMarr and Katherine MacDonald, and aspired to elegant clothes like their idols, with those dazzling jewels, saucy hats, and seductive hairdos. Von Stroheim was making his extravagant *Foolish Wives,* Gloria Swanson was up to her neck in rhinestones and millionaires in *The Impossible Mrs. Bellew,* and Katherine MacDonald was being wicked and even ruthless, but oh so chic and beautifully dressed, as she went about her scandalous adventures.

"Sin now, pay later" would sum up the plots of most of the successful movies in those innocently wicked early Twenties. B.P.'s *The Beauty Market* offered the same callow sophistication as the then-daring Scott Fitzgerald novel, *The Beautiful and Damned.* Both Fitzgerald and the creators of *The Beauty Market* were stricken with a double vision and a double morality, glorifying the society they were so heatedly exposing, exposing the society they could not resist glorifying.

In picture after picture, the Katherine MacDonald formula of fashionable sin built B. P. Schulberg's Preferred Pictures into one of the strongest of the new independent companies. The American public, B.P. insisted, accepted Katherine MacDonald as "the most beautiful woman in the world," in part because she was strikingly attractive with a patrician self-confidence and partly because his press agentry had fixed this hyperbolic description in its collective mind. But how did the American Beauty Rose reciprocate? She played mean little tricks on B.P. and his directors, Victor Schertzinger, Tom Forman, and Louis Gasnier, three of the top men of their day. For instance, she wore an expensive necklace (her own) in her first scene for *White Shoulders,* and once the jewelry was established as part of her wardrobe for that sequence, she refused to wear it again until Preferred Pictures rented the necklace from her at an exorbitant figure for the duration of the filming.

At those Sunday brunches, L.B. would match B.P.'s charges of Miss MacDonald's duplicity with his own tales of abuse at the hands of his star Anita Stewart. Mayer's *bête noire* was Rudy Cameron, who had been Miss Stewart's leading man before retiring from the screen to become her husband/business manager. "Mr. Stewart," as he was often called, had accused L.B. of using his romantic wiles on Anita in the New York days when Mayer was trying to woo her away from Vitagraph. In turn L.B. had accused Cameron of being a second-rate leading man who saw a more secure future as the bedmate and financial advisor of Anita Stewart. Since he paid her an annual salary, L.B. was determined to get as many pictures a year as possible from his box-office star; Cameron was equally determined to limit their number. On the day that a new Anita Stewart movie was scheduled to start shooting, Cameron would frequently appear at the studio without his celebrated wife. Miss Stewart had been so overworked due to Mayer's inhuman schedule, the wily ex-leading man would explain, her doctor had advised her to remain in bed for another week. If she were forced to appear before the cameras prematurely, L.B. would have to take the responsibility for permanent damage to her health.

Facing these professional crises, L.B. had developed a unique defense mechanism. Told, for instance, by an emissary from the bank that his credit had run out and that he could not expect another loan to meet next week's payroll, L.B. would groan, roll his eyes, clutch his heart, and crumple to the floor. His loyal secretary was so used to this phenomenon that she kept a bowl of water and a towel handy. Creditors who managed to work their way into Mayer's still-modest office would often retreat in confusion and sympathetic concern, fearing that their pressure had caused what might prove a fatal heart attack.

Whether L.B.'s pitching headlong to the carpet was an indication of devilish histrionics or of some genuine nervous or physical disorder is still a matter of speculation in our family. My mother, for instance, was inclined to believe that L.B.'s fainting fits were the real thing. "He was a very emotional man, so intense that he might be described as on the borderline of insanity. Well, maybe that's too extreme, but L.B. was always very strange. Absolutely the worst hypochondriac I ever met. He was paranoid about his health, as if the whole world was conspiring to give him a heart attack, or double pneumonia, or whatever disease was fashionable at the time. So, in a crisis, whereas B.P. would start to stutter, L.B. would faint. He was always an extremist. One moment he could be so cocksure of himself that he was positively obnoxious. But the very next moment, facing a situation for which he was not prepared, or for which he knew he did not have the resources, he could break out in a cold sweat, lose his voice and actually his ability to function."

The explanation of this neurasthenic behavior—Ad spoke from the depth of her Freudian knowledge—could be traced to L.B.'s child-hood: a father who was ineffectual; a mother who was strong. Circumstances forced the young Louie to leave home early to seek his fortune. This he did with a combination of outward courage and inner fear. When courage rode the mental saddle he could be fearless to the point of ruthlessness and tyranny. But that self-propelled courage had a way of slipping precipitately from the saddle. And when it did, the erstwhile tough-minded, two-fisted L.B. was transformed into a tower of quivering jelly. His collapse on the rug would bring his anxious secretary to his side. It was like calling into the intercom, "Send in Mother!"

One day Ad dropped in on L.B. just as he was going into one of his fits of fear. She knelt down beside him and put her hand on his perspiring forehead. "Oh, that feels so good—like the hand of my mother," whimpered the man who only a few years later would be described by one of his writers as Hollywood's Jewish Himmler.

13

OFTEN, WHEN I am asked if I was born in Hollywood, I have to pause and think because Hollywood's growing up and my own are inextricably bound together. For me, Hollywood was a way of life, indeed the only way. Except for the Armistice Parade, the day of my sister Sonya's disappearance, the Great Benny Leonard-Richie Mitchell fight, my stammering classes at Columbia, and my first visit to the Pickford-Neilan movie set, my New York days quickly receded into a vast fog of forgetfulness. For me it was Home Sweet Hollywood, a lovely place to play with lions and alligators, to ride my bike down lanes of palms and pepper trees, and to make lemonade from my own lemon tree. But by the time I was in the third grade I had learned the hard lesson that filmmaking was anything but glamorous. Not only was it hard, tedious work, with the same scene shot over and over again until a temperamental director decided it had achieved perfection, it was also a place inhabited by demoniac film producers and conniving movie stars. It was a hit-or-miss town where little film factories like Mayer-Schulberg had to grind out their dozen Katherine MacDonald movies a year, and where Anita Stewart had to be led, scolded, or dragged to her commitment of a movie a month.

Many, many years ago, I found myself trying to describe to Scott Fitzgerald the Hollywood I knew as a child. People coming to it from the East might regard it as the glamour capital, I told him, but for me the magic was stripped away when I was still struggling in the early grades at the Wilton Place public school. I saw Hollywood as a company town.

One of my father's early hits was *Rich Men's Wives,* another of those society dramas he had virtually perfected with Katherine MacDonald, only this time the fancy-dressed, high-stepping, social-butterfly wife was played by a beautiful newcomer, Claire Windsor. It was of Miss Windsor that the improbable Louella O. Parsons—our local Ogre in Charge of Hollywood Stars—repeatedly used the phrase, "She never looked lovelier." "Seen at the fabulous party so graciously hosted by Jesse and Bessie Lasky," Louella would ooze, "was that loveliest of our silent lovelies, Claire Windsor—and she never looked lovelier!" It became a standing joke: "Miss Claire Windsor was buried today at Forest Lawn—and she never looked lovelier!"

One day when I wandered into Father's office from a visit with Leo and Tiger, he said he was going to take a look at the "wild party" scene for the Claire Windsor picture he was making. I followed him onto the enormous set, the banquet hall of a millionaire's mansion. There were hundreds of pretty girls in party gowns and good-looking men in smart tuxedoes. A huge wild party was supposed to be in progress, and here is the scenario: Claire Windsor is a college flapper wooed and won by an older man, House Peters, a millionaire master of men. While he is busy making more millions, she is having one of those wickedly innocent "flings." Her husband has caught her in what looks to be a compromising position with Gaston Glass, the suave heavy. The audience knows that Claire was actually not accepting but indeed doing her darndest to repulse the insistent Gaston. In a rush to judgment, Peters turns Claire out into the cold, telling her she is not a fit mother for their baby boy.

Now comes the scene my father brought me to the stage to enjoy. Since his separation from Claire, Peters has been hitting the bootleg bottle. Meanwhile a social-climbing enchantress (Rosemary Theby) has set her little cloche for the wealthy father.

When the director, Louis Gasnier, called "Action!" the ballroom became a madhouse. Abe Lyman's Orchestra from the new Ambassador Hotel played jazz, couples danced madly, drank from silver flasks, necked ostentatiously, and in general did their Hollywood best to create the 1922 version of a Roman orgy.

In the middle of this whirling revelry was a large fountain. Fountains, as we know from our Fitzgerald, were a necessary ingredient of these jazz orgiastics. Something irresistibly drew those sheiks and flappers to wild immersions in fountains. Perhaps it was a subconscious rite of bootleg baptism.

At any rate, while I watched in eight-year-old amazement, the wicked Rosemary Theby and her flapper court, tipsied with gin, get the swell idea that the fountain needs a Cupid. Upstairs in his nursery, sleeps—if that is possible above this din of jazz and drunken laughter—little Jackie, the forgotten and neglected child of the rich man and his exiled wife. "Every fountain needs a Cupid!" Rosemary cries—in words that will later be flashed on the screen in a subtitle. Leading an impulsive charge up the stairs, Rosemary reappears with the bewildered little boy in her arms. While her supporters cheer her on, she dunks the child waist-deep in the fountain, the water from the carved bowl on top pouring out onto his blond curly head. At this moment who should suddenly appear but the prodigal mother. From her sister and the loyal nurse she has heard what is going on in her absence. Now, obsessed with mother love, she has returned to claim and save her child. No longer a Dancing Mother, she runs to the fountain, pushes aside little Jackie's tormentor, clutches the child to her heaving breast, and promises him she will never leave his side again. The drunken party is suddenly sobered. The rich poppa looks from his wife to Rosemary Theby and realizes in one of those tremulous silent moments where lie true maternity and his own love. Brought to his senses at last, he welcomes his wife back to the family hearth and drives out the heartless Other Woman and her mindless revelers. Fade Out—The End.

To me, standing there with my father watching all this, it looked frightening—and terribly real. But Monsieur Gasnier, the great French director, was not satisfied. In a heavy accent he said, "Cut! Now we do eet again. Only thees time before you put the babee in the foun-tann, hold heem up high so you do not block hees leetle face. And Claire chérie, when you feesh heem out, hold heem away from you for a mo-ment so the audience can see how wet and meeserable he ees."

I watched as the little boy, almost my size and with curly yellow hair like mine, was removed from the fountain by his father and taken to a corner of the stage where his mother and another woman dried him off, fixed his hair and put on dry pajamas— no, as I see it now he was wearing a nightshirt down to his ankles. His name, my father told me, was Baby Richard Headrick, the most famous child star in Hollywood, thanks to his recent hit, *The Child Thou Gavest Me*. And in addition to being a great little actor, he was also a noted swimmer, diver, and fencer. After the scene was over, my father promised, he would bring me over and introduce me to him.

The scene was repeated, exactly as before, it seemed to me. Again M. Gasnier called "Action!" and hundreds of men and women went into wild gyrations while Abe Lyman's jazzy orchestra blared loudly. Once again Baby Richard Headrick was thoroughly dunked in the fountain. And again my father's director had a complaint. The child must throw his arms around his movie mother after she rescues him from the fountain. He must be overjoyed—relieved—to see her. He must hug her just as he would his real mother. I thought that Mr. Gasnier was a little harsh with Baby Richie. But to my surprise, the child actor's actual father was even more so. "Now Richie, this shot is expensive! See all these people in it. This time, goddamnit, be sure and get it right, just like Mister Gasnier wants." The most famous child star in Hollywood nodded, and I thought he was going to cry, something he was supposed to do only in front of the cameras.

Now the scene was relit. Once again the hoarse command of "Action!" Once again the bouncy Abe Lyman struck up his band. One more time Baby Richard was immersed in the fountain. This time Mr. Gasnier was satisfied. "Très bien," he said. "Thees one ees a preent." I felt a sense of relief. I would not have to see Baby Richard thrown into the fountain again. But I was still innocent of the ways of moviemaking. "Now we do eet in a close shot," the director intoned. "Just the babee, his muzzer, and Rosemary . . ."

There was a break in the action as the camera crew moved their equipment closer to the fountain, the cameraman, Karl Struss, giving them instructions as to how to light the closer angle.

Meanwhile, in the corner of the set that the Headricks were using for an impromptu dressing room, another drama was going on. Baby Richie was shivering as his parents removed his soaking sleeping garment. A wardrobe lady was drying him with a big white towel while his mother held yet another dry nightshirt. They seemed to have hundreds.

"Here, now get into this," his mother said.

The child actor held himself stiffly. "I don't want to go into that fountain any more."

"You'll go into that fountain until Mister Gasnier tells us we can go home," said his father.

"But I don't want to," said the famous child actor.

His father cracked him smartly across the face. "Not too hard," said his mother. "You'll ruin his makeup."

"You'll do exactly as you're told," his father told him. Now sullenly obedient, Baby Richard Headrick allowed himself to be redressed. A makeup man dried his hair and reset the famous curls. He was ready for the close shot.

"Action—!" and this time the Abe Lyman jazz band blared forth its sound behind the camera. Several prop men lifted Baby Richard into the fountain while Rosemary Thebe shouted, "Look everybody, a little Cupid for our fountain!" Then the righteous Claire Windsor ran in and grabbed him from the water. "Cut," cried M. Gasnier in the now familiar order. "Rosemary, chérie, do not run away as soon as Claire reach-ezz zee foun-tann. Wait until she forces you away. You understan'? Now we do eet again. Thees time I will tell you when to leave—it ees a veree important mo-ment. Thees time we mus' do it right, n'est-ce pas?"

Once again the shivering child was carried soaking wet from the fountain. This time his father, who was carrying the boy, saw my father, a well-groomed authority figure on the set, and paused to make his apologies. "I'm sorry, B.P. I don't know what's wrong with the kid today. He usually gets these things on the first take. You watch, we'll get it next time." He had set the wet child down, next to me. "Right, Richie?" The father's voice was not a question but a command. The boy was shaking, and fighting back tears. At the age of six he had been in the business for several years and already sensed when he was in the presence of a producer. "Y-y-yes, D-Dad," he said, his teeth chattering. Then he looked at me. Up and down, sizing me up. "Are you an actor, too?" he asked me.

"No," I said. "I'm just watching."

"How come?"

I pointed to my well-pressed father. "He's my daddy."

"Gee, you're lucky," said Hollywood's most famous child star. "I sure wish I didn't have to be an actor."

Then he was swooped upon by his mother and the wardrobe lady, with his father taking leave of my father and following his little meal ticket back to the makeshift dressing nook. A big white towel wrapped around his soaking wet form, Baby Richard Headrick looked back over his shoulder as he allowed himself to be led away, dried again, and prepared for his next immersion. In different angles, close shots, close-ups, and reverse angles, he must have been plunged into that fountain at least a dozen more times that afternoon.

As I came to know other child stars—Jackie Coogan, his little brother Bobby, Baby Peggy, Junior Durkin, Mickey Rooney, thinking now only of those who worked for my father—I began to see a pattern: These famous little people being hugged, kissed, and praised at previews, press interviews, and gala openings were actually victims of child labor as inhuman as that of the scrawny ten-year-olds sent into the mines for ten hours a day. Like Baby Richie, they were nearly always bullied and abused by greedy and domineering parents. As they grew to teen age they invariably rebelled, turning to drink and drugs, unloving sex and care less marriages. One thinks of Judy Garland, Elizabeth Taylor, Diana Lynn. Diana was a bright and provocative actress with whom I discussed the child-star syndrome many times. She drank to excess, abusing her talent and her health, as if determined to shock her wealthy and rather self-righteous husband. "We were all a bunch of goddamned freaks," she said of herself, her childhood friend Elizabeth, and the rest of the moppet glamour group. "How could Liz be normal? How could she help hating her parents? That's how we were brought up, with fame, money, and hate. You may try to bury it in drink, or some recent sensation, but deep down you can never forgive them, and never forgive the system, for what they did to you."

Years after my shivering experience with Cupid-in-the-Fountain, I found myself on a beach in Mexico with Elizabeth and her daughter Lisa, a precious filly by Mike Todd out of Ms. Taylor. Elizabeth's sixth husband, Richard Burton, was busy on the film set nearby, emoting with Ava Gardner in *Night of the Iguana*. I told Elizabeth my Baby Richie story in exchange for some of her horror stories of childhood stardom. How genteel her parents had seemed, and what an obedient child actress she had appeared to be. She snorted as she led me and her daughter to the very end of the beach, where it was protected by an arm of coral rocks, so that the Mexican paparazzi could not get at them. "Whatever else I do for her, I will never expose Lisa to the kind of life my parents exposed me to." I glanced at the child playing in the sand. Not a replica of her mother, yet already glowing with a sultry beauty. Photogenic and irresistible. Suddenly, as Liz and I talked with our heads close together, a motor boat approached the beach. I barely glanced at it, accepting it as part of the scene. But Elizabeth had her antennae raised. She spotted the cameraman aiming his weapon at her child from the bow. The self-composed woman who had been talking to me in an undertone so as not to disturb her quietly contented little builder of castles became a banshee. "Get away! Get away! You sonofabitch! Get out of here! Stop following us! I'll break your goddamn camera!" She waded knee-deep into the surf and hurled pebbles. The transformation was frightening. I

130

was convinced that she would wade out and overturn the 24-foot boat singlehanded. The boatman must have thought so too. He began to retreat.

Still furious, Miss Taylor returned, picked up our beach towels and picnic basket and Lisa's toys, and moved further up the beach away from the water. "Goddamnit, Lisa's going to have privacy!" the voluptuous, true-grit mother cried. "Something I never had. Privacy! I'll kill those sonofabitches before I let them make a public thing of her!"

But dwelling on the ordeals to which the Baby Richie Headricks and other child stars were subjected is painting the canvas from a palette prematurely dark. For I did find joy among the alligators and ostriches and animals of the Selig Zoo, and excitement mingled with fear at watching those wild party scenes that seemed to adorn most of my father's pictures. There were memories of early filmmaking that caught my imagination. Father seemed to have developed a creative approach to moviemaking, his box-office pictures balanced by films with offbeat subjects, innovative and controversial. The winners, he would argue, should pay for an occasional experimental film, artistic but inexpensively done. And looking at it pragmatically, if one of these experiments should catch the public fancy and become a "sleeper," then a new market, a new kind of subject matter would open up.

A gambler by nature, a strange mix of drinking-wenching-studio-intellectual—and still the frustrated writer who loved to boast of the hundred-dollar gold piece he had won in the citywide highschool short story contest—B.P. read as many novels and short stories as he could cram into a crowded week. One of these, *Ching, Ching, Chinaman,* by Wilbur Daniel Steele, had won the O. Henry Prize for best story of the year. It featured Yen Sin, a lowly Chinese (a redundancy in those days of mindless white supremacy) who is washed ashore in a storm and finds himself in a smug, self-contained New England seaport town where he becomes the inevitable laundryman. Scorned as a yellow man and a heathen, Yen Sin discovers that a deacon of the church is cuckolding the minister. The accused and their supporters attempt to ridicule the charges of this Oriental pariah. Eventually the hypocrisy is exposed— and Yen Sin, who has taken the mounting abuse by turning the other check, makes the bigoted community realize that he may be closer to the ideals of true Christianity, or at least true charity, than any of the *holier-than-thou's.* . . .

131

Now, that may not be exactly an earthshaker today. But in the early Twenties the standard villains were the "Redskins," "Mexican greasers," and occasionally "a wily Chink." And black men were "coons," to be used for laughs.

To make a Chinese character the *hero* of a motion picture was just not done. But that's what B.P. proposed to do. To adapt the story he engaged two of his favorite continuity writers, Eve Unsell and Hope Loring. And assigned the direction to one of his top three, Tom Forman. For the role of Yen Sin he chose the outstanding character actor of his day, Lon Chaney, who had played scores of offbeat roles since the middle Teens but was still on the threshold of the stardom he would achieve with *The Hunchback of Notre Dame.* The ever-practical Al Lichtman warned my father that no theater was going to run the movie. And he was right. The major theater chains, Famous Players, First National, Fox, and Metro, fighting fiercely for control of first-run houses in every city, flatly refused to run *Ching, Ching, Chinaman,* even after its title was softened to *Shadows.* No self-respecting theater in New York would take the picture. B.P., riding the crest of youthful defiance, welcomed the battle.

He had taken me on the set so I could watch the unique Lon Chaney giving a sensitive and convincing performance as the gentle, hated Chinaman. In an age susceptible to overacting, Chaney was considered a model of restraint. He was to tragic mime what Chaplin was to comedic. He made every movement and every gesture count and I remember my father telling me that Chaney had learned this by communicating with his deaf-mute parents.

That movie set was a fascinating place for me to enter. There was the stooped, shuffling Lon Chaney serving tea to the errant couple, Marguerite de la Motte and Harrison Ford. Behind the camera were several dozen mysterious workers. And in the background in those days of blessed silence, a small orchestra—an organ, a violin, and a bass fiddle—played mood music, sometimes just before the scene, sometimes during the scene. Actors and actresses had special songs that would make them laugh or cry.

The picture was "sneaked" in a small town near Los Angeles—the institution of sneak previews having just begun—and to the pain of my father, the director, Lon Chaney, and the other filmmakers, it was booed. Not in the beginning, because the provincial audience clearly expected Yen Sin to belie his apparent gentleness and become an insidious Fu Manchu. But as the film went on and the good Caucasians were exposed as sinners or hypocrites and the yellow laundryman recognized as the avatar of virtue, there was audible protest from the paying customers. Half the house walked out in disgust even before it was over. Father's noble experiment seemed to be a disaster. I was proud of his response: If *Shadows* was rebuffed by the major chains, he said, he would have his distribution partner Al Lichtman try to sell it to small independent houses. When even they refused to advance money on it, B.P. told them to play it for nothing—give it a try, with Preferred Pictures gambling on a percentage of the profits, if any.

Then came good news. The National Board of Review, a welcome lever for elevating the quality of motion pictures, singled out *Shadows* for special commendation, praising its courage as a forceful lesson in religious and racial tolerance. Robert E. Sherwood lent his prestige by including it in a new annual anthology, *The Best Moving Pictures of 1922-23,* a hopeful sign that intellectuals and highbrow critics were no longer scorning the movies as pabulum for the masses. A movie could be a work of art, even carry a message, and still being entertainment to large audiences.

The year 1923 marked a long step forward in the progress of the motion picture. Sherwood described his recent conversion to the art of films: "If we can succeed in luring a larger number of intelligent people into the film theaters, we shall automatically receive more intelligent pictures." And so his companion volume to Burns Mantle's celebrated *Best Plays,* while never ignoring the sure things like Valentino's *Blood and Sand* and Fairbanks's *Robin Hood,* helped to open the doors to small, brave tries like *Shadows.*

Later that year Sherwood had kind words for another Schulberg film, *The Hero,* "that well might have proved highly unpopular with the dear old general public." Adapted by Eve Unsell from a controversial play by Gilbert Emery, it starred Gaston Glass as a war hero who in civilian life turns out to be an utterly worthless human being. Heroes were still heroes to the patriotic audiences of the early Twenties. Although the Hemingways and the Dos Passoses were beginning to question whether the War To Make The World Safe For Democracy had been cynically sold out by the international powerbrokers at Versailles, when B.P. dared to make *The Hero,* nationwide audiences still insisted that their bemedaled warriors be true blue. To evoke the sort of stir created by *The*

Hero, we would have to imagine John Wayne playing a Green Beret officer as an empty-hearted scoundrel. I was nine years old when *The Hero* was released, just barely of an age to nibble around the edges of cinematic unorthodoxy. I remember my father fighting for this film as he had fought for *Shadows.* His bread-and-butter pictures, frankly, I have to leaf through the old scrapbooks to remember. But the brave little pictures live on in my head.

Another was *Capital Punishment,* with a now totally forgotten Schulberg star, Donald Keith. A murder is committed. Donald is convicted and sentenced to the electric chair. The Governor, finally convinced that Donald is innocent, phones the warden to unstrap him from the chair. But the call is made a few seconds too late. In vain did the exhibitors, fearing for their dear old general public, plead for a last-minute reprieve, a happy ending. But young B.P. refused to bend. "If you're going to make a movie attacking capital punishment," he said, "then goddamn it, *attack it!*" Sometimes when he was aroused like that he even forgot to stammer.

B.P. never lost the touch for press agentry he had developed in his early Porter and Zukor days. Every Preferred Picture had a hardcover campaign book. No key was left untouched in B.P.'s efforts to woo the public to his Preferred Pictures. Long before "street theater" came into our language, B.P. was spelling out "street stunts" that could be set up to draw a crowd and excite them to see his picture. For instance, a woman carrying a baby accosts a man, ostensibly her estranged husband, on a public street, and begins to berate him as a cad who has deserted her. "The two actors should be Vaudeville people if possible. Impress upon them the necessity of putting *pep* in their argument as soon as the crowd collects," my father's instructions read. "They are to settle their differences and move on to the next corner to repeat the spontaneous performance. Whenever the street wife has a chance, she is to tell the crowd who pause to enjoy these matrimonial fireworks that she has just seen *The Girl Who Came Back*—and it was the movie that convinced her to give hubby another chance!"

14

I WASN'T BORN in a trunk like Judy Garland, but a silent studio was my first home. I remember it more clearly than the bungalow where we first lived on Gramercy Place, or the Wilton Place public school around the corner, where I was an ignominious figure.

I gained importance as "B.P.'s little boy" on the Mayer-Schulberg lot. So B.P.'s struggles and triumphs and street stunts were vital to me. Since he was hardly a devoted father, being preoccupied with his pictures and his extracurricular activities, the studio became my composite father. With the exception of the prize fights B.P. and I attended religiously every Friday night, the paternal ties to which I clung were the studio, its product, and my father's flair for salesmanship.

B.P.'s story conferences and projection-room "rushes" were my nursery; I went to kindergarten on his inventive promotions. A page headed SOME SNAPPY STUFF THAT'S DIFFERENT includes the following:

> Aeroplane cuts loose a girl dummy when over town. Parachute opens—dummy drops (so light, no danger). Sign on sweater—"The Girl Who Came Back." Interest in this can be worked to fever heat by inducing newspaper to print notice of girl abducted in aeroplane a thousand miles from your town, thought to be coming your way. Plant this story in outside paper first—then show to your local paper.

When the winter rainy season hit southern California, B.P. capitalized on it with the grand announcement that the extravagant outdoor garden party in *The Girl Who Came Back* would have to be reconstructed on an indoor stage, "bushes, trees, pool and all, with the oval pool in the center floating a flower-decked boat, and in whose depths splash Oriental maidens." This decision made it possible to bring into play the Schulberg Studio's new lighting paraphernalia—used for the first time on an "exterior" scene. Against that ubiquitous pool, the star Miriam Cooper, who had started the picture as an innocent country girl, had now become a bare-shouldered, sequin-gowned woman of the world swept into the arms of the bespangled and beturbaned Kenneth Harlan, a most unlikely "sheik." Hollywood had a terrible case of the Valentino vapors, and even the most Anglo-Saxon profiles in town were being pressed into service as irresistible Arabs. Indeed, "sheik" went into the language as the generic term for the playboys of the John Held, Jr., generation.

The Mayer-Schulberg Studio was not only my nursery and kindergarten. It also offered an advanced course in psychodrama, neurasthenia, and pathological insecurity. A vivid case history is that of the director Marcel DeSano, a name you will not find in any of the film histories but which lives on in our family folklore. Where DeSano came from I don't remember. He was simply one of a number of young European geniuses who materialized in early Hollywood. In silent pictures, remember, mastery of the English language was no prerequisite. In that sense motion pictures were more international than they are today. In Marcel DeSano's case, he had been around Hollywood for a year or so. He had worked for Irving Thalberg when Irving was the 20-year-old *wunderkind* of Universal. Now L.B. had brought Irving to the Mayer-Schulberg Studio as his assistant, undoubtedly the single best move Louie ever made, and the young Irving in turn had told B.P. about his problems with Marcel DeSano. DeSano talked like a genius. He had fascinating ideas. He claimed to have made brilliant short films in Europe. But Irving had never been able to sell him to the warring factions at Universal. And, Irving admitted, young Marcel was erratic. Stimulating, seemingly bursting with talent, but terribly neurotic. Irving himself wasn't yet sure enough of his position with L.B. to take on DeSano. But he thought B.P. might be interested.

Exactly the kind of challenge my father welcomed! He met with Marcel, both at the studio and at our house for dinner, and was captivated. The young director was one of a long line of European charmers who would troop through our living rooms for years to come, some of them phonies, some of them the genuine article. I see them all in a single composite, those adventurers with febrile minds and finely chiseled faces of the proper artistic intensity, kissing the hand of my mother, engaging me in flatteringly mature conversation, discussing the works of the European masters with B.P. Artists, mediocrities, poseurs—all of them HOLD-FRAME in the portrait of Marcel DeSano. Of medium height, he was delicately made, attractive in a dark, mysterious way, dapper in his dress—*dandy* is the word—a Balkan adventurer turned Parisian boulevardier. He was Jewish, but of a completely different breed from the East European and the ghetto Jews who had taken over the motion-picture business from the Edisons and the Porters. Cultivated, educated, debonair, sophisticated, he could talk brilliantly about the art of the cinema. He had seen every picture and had made a study of the techniques of the ranking directors, the incomparable Griffith, Flaherty the documentary artist, Fred Niblo, Frank Lloyd, King Vidor, Rex Ingram, James Cruze, William Desmond Taylor. . . . All he needed to join that select group, DeSano insisted, was a chance to make a picture of his own.

B.P. was intrigued. He loved to take chances on unknowns. It was like putting all his chips on a single number in a game of roulette. But there was Ad: "Ben, I'd be careful . . ." "Ben, are you sure you know enough about him? . . ." "Ben, you mustn't let him flatter you into making a hasty decision you'll regret later. . . ." And of course the more Ad reminded him of his flair for the impulsive, the more determined he was to take that plunge. Instead of entrusting his next picture, *The Girl Who Wouldn't Work,* to one of his dependable three, Gasnier, Forman, or Schertzinger, he defied Ad and his own studio associates and gave the assignment to Marcel DeSano.

In those days it was already *de rigueur* to shoot an establishing or master scene from the top to the end, and then move in for the medium close shots, the two shots (shots with two people), the close-ups. That way the film editor could assemble the scene according to what he thought was the proper rhythm—the full shot to establish the scene, the closer shots for reactions, and back to the original longer shot for the performers to make their exits. But Marcel was only half a dozen feet into his long shot when he called "Cut!" The cast and crew were astonished. In that scene the heroine was asked to slap the face of the villain. As she raised her hand, again Marcel called "Cut!" Then he shot a closer shot of the impact of the hand against the face. What DeSano was doing was cutting the picture in his head, shooting only what he had decided was necessary to the finished film. Normally it took a hundred thousand feet of raw stock edited down to get a ten-thousand-foot motion picture. Marcel was leaving himself no protection. A dangerous gamble. Willie Wyler, one of the most distinguished directors of the last forty years, shot his scenes all the way through from every possible angle. Not our Marcel DeSano.

At first the actors, the chief technicians, and my father as well were concerned with the breakneck speed with which DeSano was rushing through the picture. He had been given a three-week or eighteen-day schedule, for in those hardy years Saturday was still a working day. DeSano brought in the picture six days and $20,000 under schedule. In twelve days he had finished *The Girl Who Wouldn't Work,* and it was instantly assembled, with practically no excess footage in the film bin. The cutter couldn't believe what he was seeing and neither could my father. What was even more extraordinary, when they ran the first cut in the small projection room, it had all come together exactly as DeSano had conceived it in his mind. Everyone agreed it was one of the best pictures Preferred had ever made!

So did the sneak-preview audience. So did the general public. And so did the critics. A new European genius was welcomed to the inner circle. Hollywood was amazed. B.P.'s discovery was the talk at all the smart places where the movie crowd assembled: Montmartre and Henry's and the Coconut Grove. Thalberg wanted to borrow DeSano from B.P. for his next production. B.P. was taking bows and reminding Ad that an up-and-coming producer had to take chances and play his hunches. Discovering talent was the keystone of this burgeoning business/art. He was making a star of little Ethel Shannon, he had just signed that gum-chewing beauty contest winner from Brooklyn, Clara Bow, and now he had the overnight wonder boy, Marcel DeSano.

B.P. told Thalberg that DeSano was too precious to loan out. As soon as he had a well-deserved rest and went to New York for press interviews, he would start the sequel to *The Girl Who Wouldn't Work,* already being written by a team of lady writers. Meanwhile, B.P. dined Marcel at Victor Hugo's, took him with me to the celebrated Friday-night fights, and virtually brought him into the family. Marcel traveled with us on those hectic weekends to Catalina Island, Santa Barbara, and to the wonderfully Victorian Hotel Del Coronado near San Diego. How vividly I remember him, the natty, intense, and now famous Marcel DeSano in his smartly tailored dark suits, with expensive ties tucked into elegant vests. Marcel DeSano talking of his innovative theories of film editing. Talking of the Balzac novel he would like to do next. Talking to me on the balcony about how one day we would work together. Move over, Von Stroheim and Murnau. We have Marcel DeSano!

ACT II: Marcel went to New York in style, stayed at The Plaza, and was wined and dined by B.P.'s New York backers. He gave learned interviews to movie critics on his economical yet artistic approach to filmmaking by "editing with the camera." Serious but business-minded filmmakers like Irving Thalberg and my old man were delighted, because it was the perfect answer to the pretensions of a mad genius like Erich von Stroheim, whom Irving had had to remove from *Foolish Wives*. The headstrong Von had spent not ten days but a full three hundred and sixty-five on the picture, and not sixty thousand but over a million dollars and not twelve thousand feet but trackless miles of film that his editors claimed they were drowning in—with Von protesting that he needed still more time, more money, and more film to realize his grandiose conception.

Two weeks before the sequel to *The Girl Who Wouldn't Work* was to go into production, B.P. received a long-distance call from New York. Marcel was apologetic but he would be unable to return in time to start the picture. Mysterious pains in his chest. His physician had recommended a week in the hospital for a thorough checkup. B.P. was sympathetic. Perhaps Marcel had overworked himself in bringing the first picture in at such breakneck speed. He told his protegé to take his time—he would need all his strength for the picture ahead. They would postpone it another week or so until Marcel had recovered.

Two weeks later, Marcel called again. The specialists had been unable to discover the cause of his chest pains, and he was having difficulty in breathing. He was unable to give B.P. a starting date. At the end of the month, B.P. begged him to get back on the train and return to California. Los Angeles had its own specialists and B.P. would see to it that he had the best of care before going back to work.

When DeSano finally reappeared, Ad and Ben gave him a warm welcome. Again we drove south for a weekend together at the Del Coronado. Once again Marcel was his intense, talkative, attractive self. I remember the story conferences between him and my father: the excitement, the anticipation of the next successful picture on which they were about to embark. Week by week, Marcel's still-undiagnosed chest pains began to disappear. A combination of the California sunshine and my father's confidence in him seemed to provide the cure. A new date was set for the picture.

A week before he was to start shooting, Mrs. DeSano called with the bad news. Marcel was suffering from what was apparently a severe case of laryngitis. B.P. sent his own physician to call on him. The studio doctor reported that it was true that DeSano seemed to have lost his voice. But there did not seem to be any throat infection or inflammation that he could locate. Nor was there any problem with his chest. Ben went to see his ailing director. DeSano spoke to him in a whisper. In those days the directors talked on the set much more than they do today. Directing silent performers, they could tell them exactly what to do as the scene progressed: "Now you hear the knock on the door and you are afraid—now the door opens—and you are even more frightened by what you see. You take a few steps backward . . ." What was B.P. to do with a silent-picture genius who had lost his voice?

Upset, confused, B.P. promised to bring in another chest-and-throat specialist to make a new diagnosis the following day. But that specialist called the studio to say that he had found no one home at the DeSanos' Hollywood bungalow. For a number of days, Marcel could not be located. Then another long-distance call cleared up the mystery. Secretly, Marcel had boarded the *Santa Fe Chief* and gone back to New York. His voice sounded a little stronger but he was still suffering those severe chest pains. With his persuasive charm he apologized to B.P. for sneaking out of town, but he knew my father's own powers of persuasion and had been afraid that B.P. would talk him out of the trip. Back in New York he felt safer with his own specialists. He simply had to get to the bottom of his medical problem. Otherwise it would be impossible for him to concentrate on directing the picture.

While DeSano was in New York consulting with his own doctors, B.P.'s partner Al Lichtman called Ben to say that he had happened to be in an expensive men's store that day—and there was their elusive director having two-hundred-dollar suits made to order, discussing the sartorial details with the salesman and the tailor in what sounded like a normal and healthy voice. Growing impatient at last, B.P. phoned Marcel to ask him what was going on. Preferred Pictures had shown its continued faith in him by keeping him on salary and even absorbing the

Hollywood medical bills. He was costing the company a great deal of money, while the public was anxiously awaiting the next Marcel DeSano picture. Marcel was convincingly disingenuous. Whenever he felt depressed, he explained, as he did now when he was doing everything he possibly could to get back into shape to start the next picture—still awaiting the specialists' next report—he went out and bought himself a new suit. That was part of his therapy. As for his voice, that's what was proving so mystifying about this ailment. One morning he would wake up in full voice. The following day he would be unable to speak above a whisper. The specialists, he said, had become fascinated by his case. He seemed to have caught an absolutely original disease.

By this time, B.P. found himself pendulating between sympathy for the DeSano syndrome and exasperation at his protracted delay. Typically, they began to call Marcel DeSano "The Man Who Wouldn't Work." B.P. threatened to take Marcel off salary, and eventually, under pressure from the fellow-owners of his company, had to carry out the threat.

Marcel returned to L.A. as fast as the *Chief* could get him there. Again we weekended at the Del Coronado.

On this trip a strange thing happened to me. On the lower floor of the sprawling hotel was a bowling alley. I had never bowled before, and since I was still in knee pants, I was given the smaller ball and duckpins. Each time I rolled the ball down the alley, the pins went down. Overhead was a large slate board with the hotel records written in chalk. That day I broke the record. There was my name, Buddy Schulberg, in big white letters on the board! But when I tried to top myself, the balls refused to stay out of the gutters on either side of the alley. I bowled a miserable 58. And never again was I able to break even 75. Truth is, I was clearly a no-talent bowler. But we were constant guests at the Hotel Del Coronado throughout the Twenties and into the Thirties, and whenever I bowled I would be pointed out as the record holder. The more I bowled the lower my scores became. Finally I was too ashamed to face those challenging pins and I retired from the field. But my duckpin record lasted into the late Thirties. The god of bowling must have been guiding my hand on that record flight.

Marcel DeSano was with me when I set the record, and he seemed fascinated by my inability ever to come anywhere near that first performance. And then it struck me—without benefit of my mother's Freud, Brill, and Jung: Marcel DeSano's chest pains and throat disorders were clearly symptoms of panic after his first unexpected success. Writers face it when they approach that Second Novel, after an unanticipated first-novel success. The mysterious DeSano disease was simply Second Picture Panic. An impossible act to follow! How do I top myself? How do I go on? I've often see this agony in my creative friends, especially in neurotics who lack the emotional equipment to face the possibilities of failure that threaten every artist.

Marcel DeSano never did make that sequel to *The Girl Who Wouldn't Work.* I'm not sure he ever made another picture. Later, Irving Thalberg, still drawn to him and feeling he might succeed where B.P. had failed, gave him a chance at MGM. But once again the chest pains set in and the voice fell to a whisper.

In most cases of show-business failure, the friendship dies with it. Over and over again I have known people who thought of themselves as socially inseparable but who no longer speak to one another once their pictures flop or creative dry rot sets in. But Marcel was so ingratiating, so entertaining and stimulating at dinner and cocktail parties that he continued to fascinate both my mother and father. The Man Who Wouldn't Work went on charming the Schulberg family.

As his unemployment became chronic, as the forgetful industry no longer remembered his early (and only) success, Marcel DeSano began thinking of suicide. He would conceive a new film project and swear that if he did not manage to see it through to completion he would kill himself. One New Year's Day my father invited him to the Rose Bowl Game—California vs. Georgia Tech. It was a long drive from Hollywood east to Pasadena, especially with the elaborate morning parade of flowered floats, and Father had ordered an early start. But Marcel failed to show up at the time he had been asked. B.P. called his home. There was no answer. Father called again and again. Still no answer. When it was almost noon, B.P. said we would have to leave without him. At that moment Marcel arrived. Impeccably dressed as always, but with his face the color of ashes.

When B.P. chided him for being late, Marcel told this story: That morning he had awakened feeling particularly despondent. His wife had left him, he had no idea how he would pay his January rent, and every studio gate in Hollywood had slammed in his face. The moment to take his own life was at hand. He went out to his garage, started the motor of his car, attached a hose to the exhaust pipe, held the hose to his mouth, and lay down to await his sweet deliverance. As he lay there, cold and uncomfortable on the cement floor, he said to himself, "Marcel, if you're going to die, you might as well go in comfort." After all, he had always been a gentleman of taste and sophistication, who had developed an appreciation for luxury. So he got up from the cold stone floor and went back into his house to fetch a velvet cushion and a cashmere blanket. Thus comforted, he stretched out in the garage to resume his exhaust-pipe experience. But as he lay there inhaling the deadly vapors, he had further thoughts: "This is New Year's Day. B.P. is waiting with his car and chauffeur to take me to the Rose Bowl Game. I have a hundred-dollar bet on the Golden Bears. I might as well go to the game, see if I win my bet . . . I can always come back to the garage and get this over with later tonight."

When we heard this story—unbelievable for anyone but a Marcel DeSano—my father said, "Marcel, you've been threatening to commit suicide for years—and you're still with us. People who talk that much about suicide never do it—what you're committing is vicarious suicide. You milk all the pleasure of the contemplation of the act without the responsibility of actually having to see it through."

"Tonight, when we get back from the game, I intend to do it," Marcel insisted.

We came home from the game flushed with the excitement of one of the most bizarre games ever played in the Bowl. Roy Riegels, the towering California center, had picked up a fumble and run the wrong way, to be tackled by our little Benny Lom a few feet from his own goal line. The flustered center, fated to go down in football history as "Wrong Way Riegels," then made a bad pass from center, Benny was unable to get off his punt from behind the goal line, and Georgia Tech had scored a precious two-point "safety," winning this Lewis Carroll version of a football game 8 to 7. I had lost one dollar, Marcel had lost his hundred, and my father, betting conservatively for him, was only out one thousand. We went back to the house to replay the game over highballs, although I was still limited to sarsaparilla. Marcel stayed on to dinner, animatedly telling a film story he would like to do. He seemed to have forgotten all about his nocturnal appointment with the exhaust pipe.

FADE IN—ten years later. The scene: my mother's townhouse in London, where she was a successful theatrical agent in the late Thirties. Marcel DeSano came for dinner and stayed on for coffee and brandy— and more brandy. He was still wearing the same dark suit, although it was now shiny with age, and his expensive shirt had been to too many laundries in too many different countries. Across the years and across the continent of Europe he had been roaming in search of his tattered reputation. A cloud of mystery shadowed his survival. Still, he managed to remain dapper, attractive, intense, and creatively talkative. My mother was now a prosperous, self-assured, and beautiful woman in her early forties. As the hours grew smaller, the self-dramatizing Marcel announced to Ad that he had a confession to make: Ever since those early days in Hollywood he had been insanely in love with her. He had never revealed his persistent passion because of his loyalty to his dear old friend B.P. But now, he insisted, the moment had come for him to declare himself. Their fate, their love, their life should be forever bound together!

According to Ad, she suggested that this was only the cognac talking. With a good night's sleep he would be completely recovered. And then, since she had excellent connections with the English film companies, she would discuss with him soberly her ideas for resurrecting his career.

But Marcel was not to be put off. If she did not accept him on the spot, he vowed, he would go back to his flat and jump out the window. "Now, Marcel," Ad chided him gently, "the best thing for you to do is to go home and jump into bed and wake up with a clear head in the morning."

There had been another visitor at dinner that evening, Billy Wilkerson, publisher of *The Hollywood Reporter*. He had left before Marcel and Ad's intimate tête-à-tête. That night Ad stayed up to read a new book by Vicki Baum she was planning to sell. She had just turned out the light when the phone rang. It was Billy. Calling to tell her that Marcel DeSano had just jumped out of the window.

A footnote to the Marcel DeSano story: The night before his proposal to my mother, he had stopped at a fashionable bar where he fell into conversation with John Considine, a prominent Hollywood producer. Considine was happy to buy him a drink but would no longer trust him to direct a picture. In his cups, as was his wont (or as my father would have it, his will), John graciously ordered drinks for Marcel and himself, toasted, "To our mothers."

Marcel set his glass down on the bar. "Sorry, John, I can't drink to that. I hate my mother." A sentimental Irish Catholic, Considine was horrified. "Marcel, how can you say that? How can any son possibly hate his mother?" "Because my mother is a bitch and I hate her guts," Marcel replied. Considine exploded: "Get away from me! Anyone who says he hates his own mother doesn't deserve to live." Marcel's answer was,

"John, thank you for the suggestion. You've just convinced me not to go on living."

In the opinion of Ad, Billy Wilkerson, and other friends of John Considine, it was typical of Marcel DeSano—when he finally got around to taking the life he had been threatening to dispose of for more than a decade—that he should try to punish as many of his acquaintances as possible. They could imagine the sardonic Marcel enjoying in his last moment the guilt of the pious John Considine for contributing to a mortal sin.

Is it nostalgia that makes the directors of the Mayer-Schulberg days seem so much more theatrical than our good ones today? Maybe it's because Hollywood was then a gold-rush town with the sweet smell of carnival in the air. To watch Mickey Neilan working for Louie Mayer was to watch Peck's Bad Boy with a megaphone. Louie was still a novice in those days, hanging around the set to learn as much about picture-making as he could, and Mickey was in his prime as one of the young masters. He took delight in tormenting L.B. by going through a scene and then turning to his boss with a puckish grin: "Okay, little boy, you've had your movie lesson for the day. Now run along, back to the front office where you belong."

Mickey was a force in those days when all the front-line directors were self-appointed warlords who behaved as if the cast and crew were their private army. Major studios had not yet set up their factory systems that brought the freewheeling directors into line. By chance, Mickey had been on the *Santa Fe* with us on our second westward journey. An inexhaustible ladies' man, he never traveled or was seen in public without a beautiful doll, usually his current leading lady: Blanche Sweet, Sally O'Neill, Gloria Swanson, Joan Marsh—you name 'em and chances are, he'd had 'em. I don't remember which young actress Mickey had chosen to favor as we streamed across the continent, but I do remember an early scent of sexuality, something about that high-spirited couple sharing a drawing room that I was not supposed to know about. And I remember Mickey's antics: An inveterate practical joker, he would go down the aisle of our Pullman car giving a perfect imitation of the Negro dining-car courier calling out, "Last call for dinner!" when the first had not yet been announced, or impersonating the conductor, "Next stop, Albuquerque!" when we were still hours away.

B.P.'s street stunts for his Preferred Pictures had always walked a fine line of propriety. But when Mickey opened one of his own movies in San Francisco, while President Wilson was visiting that city in behalf of his cherished League of Nations, Mickey chose an actor known for his resemblance to the President, dressed him in presidential attire and had him driven to the entrance of the movie theater where the impersonator drew a large crowd. "I've come to your beautiful city not only to speak in favor of a lasting peace," he told hundreds of pedestrians who had begun to block traffic for a closer look at their "President," "but also to urge you to see this latest movie by my dear friend Mickey Neilan. I hear it's a corker!" The actor was booked at the nearest police station for the Neilanish caper, and Mickey himself was considered persona non grata in San Francisco until the furor died down.

As a ten-year-old I would stand on the set behind the camera, having learned exactly where to position myself so as to be out of the way of the camera crew and the sightlines of the performers, and watch in fascination as the director checked with his cameraman, usually squinting through the eyepiece for his own view of the setup, giving the actors their final instructions, and then sighing softly or shouting harshly, "All right, I guess we're ready"—sometimes adding with just the right note of jaunty sarcasm—"or as ready as we'll ever be—this is a take!" Then the assistant director would shout, "Quiet, everybody!"—though that order was not as vital as it was to be at the end of the decade when the microphone could pick up accidental sounds behind the camera—the director would give that magic command. "Action!", and another motion-picture scene was on its way to making history or clutter on the cutting-room floor.

As the actors played out their tearful dramas and the little orchestra played appropriate mood music, I realize now that I was watching an era coming to an end. After a great leap forward, the silent-movie business was sliding into one of its periodic sloughs. Two of the older companies, Metro and Goldwyn (from which Sam Goldwyn had already departed), were slipping badly. The Goldwyn Studio was an imposing plant on the uninhabited flatlands of Culver "City," but its management was chaotic. Metro had been equally badly mismanaged. The older order was passing. The now-powerful theater owner Marcus Loew, fed up with the sluggish state of the Metro studio he controlled, approached Goldwyn's successor, an early odd-ball by the name of Frank Joseph Godsol, and suggested a merger. The Metro studio would be sold, and Metro-

Goldwyn would become a single company located at the sprawling Goldwyn lot on Washington Boulevard.

Since the top executives of both Metro and Goldwyn had been fired, the Eastern stockholders, headed by Marcus Loew, were in search of new officers. At that historic moment the status of L. B. Mayer was anything but distinguished. He was no Adolph Zukor, Jesse Lasky, Samuel Goldwyn, William Fox, or even B. P. Schulberg—for during the period when Father and L.B. shared their small studio, the general range of Mayer's pictures ranged from mediocre to godawful. (His young assistant Irving Thalberg had not yet found his feet as a legitimate tycoon.) You will not find, for instance, a single Mayer picture on Robert Sherwood's list of top films for 1922-23—not even among the thirty-five additional pictures accorded Honorable Mention. No, Louis's taste was primitive and mawkish, even for those rather primitive and mawkish days. Mother-love and self-sacrifice was his cup and he encouraged it to overflow. Neither inventive, creative, nor courageous, in fact contemptuous of the virtues my father had, he possessed an altogether different kind of gift. Louie was a politician, a manipulator, and an opportunist who could have given chapter and verse to Machiavelli if only he had known how to write. Perhaps I have inherited my judgment of his character from my father. My own experiences with this Hollywood Rajah—as his gentle biographer Bosley Crowther dubbed him—will speak for themselves.

The New York attorney handling the Metro-Goldwyn merger for Marcus Loew was the astute promoter Robert Rubin. Rubin was the true mover and shaker of the organization, for, having handled Mayer's business in New York, it was he who brought together the princely Marcus Loew and the still struggling L.B. On one of his rare trips to Hollywood to reexamine his floundering Metro organization, Loew was driven out to our small Mission Road studio by Rubin. Louie was shooting one of his weepy melodramas at the moment, *Thy Name Is Woman,* with his efficient Fred Niblo directing the lovely Barbara LaMarr and "the new Valentino," Ramon Novarro. The hectic shooting schedule was interrupted for a moment while Mayer, the perfect host, introduced the Eastern mogul to his director and his exotic cast. With wonder-boy Irving Thalberg at his side, Louie was happy to explain how costs were being cut, how pictures of quality were being turned out according to the same economic plan, and their rosy plans for the future.

They had just signed a beautiful young French girl by the name of Renée Adorée, and they also had in the fold a young Canadian actress who could match looks and class with Katherine MacDonald. Her name was Norma Shearer.

Loew met them all and was impressed with Mayer's charm and expertise in the field of production and with Thalberg's quiet but clearly knowledgeable persuasion. Compared to Metro, which seemed to have run out of stars and stories and had nothing left but a few rebellious directors, Mayer's operation impressed Marcus Loew. When he and Rubin returned to New York, they convinced Joe Schenck and the other principal stockholders to place the merged companies in the hands of L. B. Mayer and his youthful lieutenant, Irving Thalberg. Considering the lowly status of L. B. Mayer Pictures at that time, the new deal was a ten-strike for Mayer, as fortuitous as any of those magic balls I had bowled at the Hotel Del Coronado. L.B.'s salary rose to fifteen hundred dollars a week for the first three years. Thalberg's weekly salary would be six hundred, with a similar figure for Rubin as the company's secretary in New York. In addition there was an inside deal, a well-kept secret from the body of stockholders, that the Mayer group (including Thalberg and Rubin) would receive 20 percent of the annual profits of the new company. Of that 20 percent, Mayer was to receive approximately 13, Rubin 5, and Thalberg 2.

But there was another great bonus in store for the on-rushing L.B. Remembering how Zukor and Famous Players had swallowed up the Selznick company and L.J.'s proud name in an earlier merger, L.B. insisted on public recognition. Marcus Loew offered him a choice: either Metro-Goldwyn Presents an L. B. Mayer Production, or Metro-Goldwyn-Mayer Presents. . . . As hungry to see his name in lights as Thalberg would prove reluctant, L.B. chose the latter.

Two old companies that had been dying on the vine and a small-time independent with a record of mediocre pictures—such were the three stars of the new triangle, three shaky little stars in the Hollywood galaxy. Who could have guessed, as the new sign went up over the old Culver City studio, that MGM would so quickly challenge and finally surpass the establishment studios of the mid-Twenties, Paramount, Fox, First National, and Universal?

I saw that historic sign rise above the vast white front-office building of

MGM. I was there at the dedication with my friend Maurice, whose father, Harry Rapf, had been brought to the new studio as an important member of the "Mayer group," as vice-president in charge of the "program" or "bread-and-butter" pictures. I sat with Maurice (staring with fascination at the "Prussian" neck of Erich von Stroheim, who sat directly in front of us) as his father stood with L.B. and Irving on the platform facing all the employees of the studio—from stars like Mae Murray, Lon Chaney, Ramon Novarro, John Gilbert, and Lillian Gish to the top directors inherited from Goldwyn, Robert Leonard, Victor Seastrom, Frank Borzage, Von Stroheim, and the irreverent Mickey Neilan, who had departed the "poverty row" Mayer-Schulberg Studio for what he thought would be the greener pastures of the Goldwyn lot.

While the movie stars, along with such visiting firemen as the admiral of the Pacific Fleet, the mayor and local civic leaders, and the drones— secretaries, painters, carpenters, mailroom boys—formed an attentive audience for this unprecedented inauguration, a giant key inscribed "Success" was handed to L.B., proudly sandwiched between his two aides, Harry Rapf and Irving Thalberg.

L.B. had a great love and genuine gift for public ceremony. There were tears in his eyes as he began his acceptance speech. Tear ducts were to Louie B. what diamonds were to Lorelei Lee. When they had first begun sharing the Selig studio, my father's nickname for his friend Louie was "The Town Crier."

"I hope that it is given to me to live up to this great trust," L.B.'s tremulous voice came down to all of us assembled there. "It has been my argument and practice that each picture should teach a lesson, should have a reason for existence. With seventeen of the great directors in the industry now calling this great institution their home, I feel that this aim will be carried out—"

At this sacred moment, there was a disturbance behind us. Mickey Neilan, in the middle of shooting the Thomas Hardy classic, *Tess of the D'Urbervilles,* noisily pushed back his folding seat and called to his crew and cast seated around him, "Okay, gang, let's get back to the set." Mickey was still a four-star general in those days and his troops carried out his orders. The entire *Tess* company followed Mickey from the dedication ceremony back to the set. There were snickers and exclamations of amazement at Neilan's audacity, and for a moment the face of the newly crowned monarch darkened in rage. But then, like a practiced political campaigner coping with a heckler, he pulled around him the mantle of dignity he had shrewdly designed for himself, and went on with his acceptance speech.

"I fully realize what a great moment this is for me," Louie intoned, and the tears fell again. "I accept this solemn trust and pledge the best that I have to give."

The entire gathering rose in a standing ovation. Von Stroheim was applauding perfunctorily. He was shooting Frank Norris's ground-breaking naturalistic novel, *McTeague* (later retitled *Greed*). Von was on his way not to a normal ten-reel picture but to an unprecedented forty-reel marathon. Far ahead of his time, he believed not in studio shooting but in taking his company to the actual locations—including Death Valley during the hottest days of the year so his actors would not have to feign their suffering from lack of water and heat prostration. He believed in giving moviegoers what *he* wanted, no matter how much it made them squirm.

Mayer's credo was exactly the opposite, to give the public what *it* wanted, right down to that lowest common denominator: the twelve-year-old mind. Family pictures. Romance. Happy endings. Movies could titillate, but in the end husband and wife, or estranged young lovers, must be reunited. That was Mayer's Law. The moral standards of middle-class America must be upheld.

Our town had just passed through a series of scandals that had rocked The Industry like our periodic earthquakes: the murder of the director William Desmond Taylor and the revelation that he had been carrying on simultaneous affairs with Mabel Normand, a victim of dope, and Mary Miles Minter, a teenage successor to Mary Pickford in roles of adolescent purity. Mabel Normand's chauffeur shot Cortland Dines in the home of Charlie Chaplin's leading lady, Edna Purviance.

And finally there was the Fatty Arbuckle case. The adorable Fatty was accused of doing something unspeakable to a young bit player during an all-night orgy in a San Francisco hotel. The actual cause of her death could not even be whispered in mixed society. After a series of trials, Fatty, one of the most famous of the silent comedians, was acquitted. But there was another court he had to face—the court of public opinion. The Hearst papers, unmindful of W.R.'s own double standard in his liaison with young Marion Davies, kept up a drumfire of abuse long after the comedian had cleared himself of legal charges. The Fatty Arbuckle story was sexy and it sold papers, and the yellow journalism on which Hearst thrived kept the case alive and juicy throughout the land. When all the hangers-on deserted Fatty, my father still befriended him. Roscoe Arbuckle, ostracized and almost forgotten only a few years after that fatal wild party, became lean, sallow, and defeated. I remember another of those weekend forays to the Hotel Del Coronado, and over the Mexican border through bawdy Tijuana to the Caliente racetrack, where no one recognized the ex-comedy star.

How much or how little of the agony of Roscoe Arbuckle I understood when I was still in knickers is difficult to recapture. I do remember the pervading sadness of the man whose now-vanished Santa Claus belly and floppy rolls of fat had made millions of people laugh all over the world. I was in high school before I heard the details of the tragic end of Virginia Rappe, but I was aware on our trip to Baja California that some terrible cloud hung over Mr. Arbuckle and that somehow the funny name Fatty had become a dirty word.

Budd thinks this is the patio of Marion Davies' bungalow on the MGM lot, and Sonya thinks it is the patio at the rear of their own home in Windsor Square. Hollywood Moorish architecture was very popular at the time. From the left: Margaret LeVino, screenwriter; Ad; Robert Z. Leonard, director of many MGM and Paramount features; Judge Ben Lindsay (author of the then scandalous book *Companionate Marriage),* who moved from Denver to the more appropriate location of Los Angeles; Marion Davies; and Harry Rapf, an MGM producer who then ranked just below L.B. Mayer and Irving Thalberg in the studio hierarchy. ▼

Ad and her three children, *circa* 1925. Budd was 11, Sonya 7, Stuart 3.

Ad on the Schulberg court— the first at Malibu—*circa* 1928

A 1928 autographed photo of Elinor Glyn, a popular novelist of the time who created "It" and dubbed Clara Bow the "It" girl. Note the "Mr." in front of B.P. Schulberg's misspelled name. Today Miss Glyn is best known for the frequent appearance of her name in crossword puzzles.

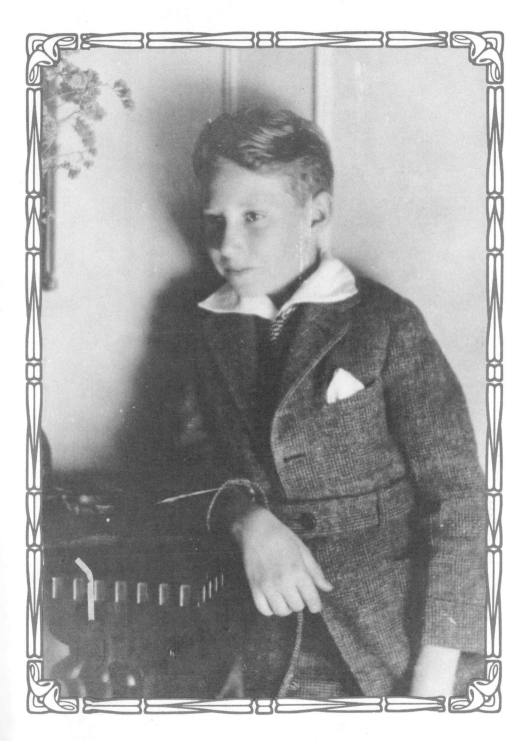

Budd Schulberg, age 8, pseudo-
contemplative, with his right arm posed
"naturally," as was the custom of the
photographers of the time.

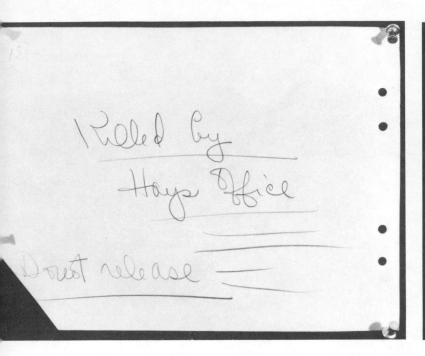

Killed by
Hays Office

Don't release

On the set of *The Spoilers*. From the right: the author; Marian Shauer; the director, John Cromwell; Mel Shauer, a Paramount Studio executive; Sonya; Stuart; B.P.; Ad; and her brother Sam Jaffe, the studio manager

In the bathtub, star William Gargan in *Living on Love,* a B.P. Schulberg production for Paramount. This production still was killed by the Hays Office for nudity. The photograph was clipped across the corner to indicate that it had been killed.

The three Schulberg children dressed up for a formal portrait, *circa* 1929. Stuart at left, Sonya at right

A rare photo of the entire Schulberg family. At left rear is Budd, and next to him his father and mother. In front are Sonya and Stuart, later the long-time producer of The Today Show. B.P. may be glowering because he has literally been dragged home by Budd from Sylvia Sidney's nearby beachhouse.

15

ETWEEN THE STRONG-MINDED ("pig-headed," the studio bosses called them) directors and the new front-office authority, the tension grew. Mickey Neilan openly defied those he despised as "the money men." With his penchant for happy endings, L.B. was soon insisting that Tess not be hanged as she is at the end of the Hardy novel, but instead receive a last-minute reprieve. Mayer's Law: Never mind the logic, send 'em home happy. Later, Mickey was to tell me, he complained to Thomas Hardy himself when he was in England shooting his next picture, and the novelist protested that his contract had promised fidelity to the book as written. But the power-minded hierarchy argued that Hardy's and Neilan's contracts had been with the old Goldwyn company that MGM had inherited. Legal or not, they insisted on ending *Tess of the D'Urbervilles* their way.

It was the beginning of a bitter struggle between the profit-oriented, conservative front office on one side, and the writers and directors on the other. But a one-sided battle it was. One by one the Neilans and Von Stroheims, and other so-called "troublemakers," were weeded out. The important directors who stayed on began to get the message. Either play the game and shoot the picture the front-office way or go their own road. Rex Ingram, riding so high with *The Four Horsemen,* chose Europe. Mickey Neilan tried to set up his own productions at First National but became one of a host of high-paid silent directors washed away in the tidal wave of sound. As for the incredible Von Stroheim, brilliant, driven, uncontrollable, Maurice Rapf and I had front-row seats watch-

ing his struggle at MGM over *Greed,* and later over *The Merry Widow.*
And when Thalberg gave up on Von Stroheim again as he had earlier at
Universal, and Von moved on to Paramount, my father took over the
front-office struggle to keep the inspired wild man from bankrupting the
studio.

While Mayer, Thalberg, and my friend's father, Harry Rapf, were
weeding out the uncontrollables and building the first great film factory,
the thorny feud between L.B. and my father was beginning to grow. Its
roots are buried in forgotten film history. I've talked with my own family
and with L.B.'s wife Margaret and his daughters Irene and Edith, and
have yet to uncover all. But I believe the breach went back to L.B.'s
secrecy about his negotiations with Rubin and Loew. The tradition of
Sunday brunch at our alternating homes, ours on Gramercy Place,
theirs on Kenmore, had brought the two pioneer producers together on a
basis of friendly exchange of professional problems. If L.B. was having
troubles with Mickey Neilan, B.P. would tell him how he thought that
burr under L.B.'s saddle could best be removed. And, in turn, L.B.
would listen sympathetically to B.P.'s tales of woe concerning the head-
strong Katherine MacDonald or his battle to get better distribution
deals from the major companies, a campaign in which these two independents had been natural allies.

But for many months, it seems, L.B. had been carrying on secret
negotiations to sell his Mayer-Schulberg Studio assets to the emerging
Metro-Goldwyn Company, along with his own services as chief executive. When Mayer pulled out, according to my father, B.P. was left
holding the bag with half a studio, half the equipment, and half the
technical pool they had been sharing. It placed B.P. and his Preferred
Pictures in a precarious financial position. Without warning, he was left
with responsibility for the entire rent of the Selig lot. When the Rubin-
Loew negotiations began, and apparently they had continued over a
long period, L.B. should have leveled with his studio partner, B.P.
reasoned. So Mayer's departure from their joint studio and his becoming
the third capital letter in MGM was preceded by a quarrel. And over the
years, that quarrel was to develop into a feud of Old Testament proportions. At least that was B.P.'s story.

Mother had a different version. L.B., in those more innocent days,
was a stickler for morality, both on and off the screen. Not only B.P.'s
movies, which had been more sophisticated than Louie's, but also

Father's private life, had begun to offend the staid Louie B. There was gossip of wild parties at the home of Ben's French director, Louis Gasnier, parties which would begin at the end of the week's shooting and would mount to a riotous climax by Monday morning. I have a faint remembrance of this, for one night after we had seen a particularly good fight at the Legion—I was still underage but could attend fights regularly now, since in Hollywood B.P. enjoyed special privileges—the chauffeur dropped Father off at Gasnier's home in Hollywood Hills.

For a moment, as B.P. approached the door, it was held open, and from the hallway came the blare of saxophones and wild laughter. A couple appeared on the stoop, still dancing to a jazzy fox-trot. The dapper casting director I recognized from the studio came out to greet my father with a tall glass in his hand. I could hear Father laughing with the others.

That moment obviously made a deep impression on my ten-year-old mind. Of course I had heard Mother complain about Louie Gasnier and his weekend parties. Gasnier, it seemed, was French and decadent, kept a number of mistresses, and his wicked ways were a temptation to my hardworking but easily distracted father. According to my mother, Gasnier maintained his position at the studio not because of the quality of his pictures but because of the merry social life he created for my father and other business associates. This morals charge Father heatedly denied. Louis Gasnier had an impressive list of silent-picture credits. It was an insult to B.P.'s intelligence to suggest there was any other reason for choosing a director.

Besides, in those years three-day binges were the weekend sport. Small-town Hollywood had to make its own entertainment. There was no television, no outdoor barbecues, no theater or opera or art, except the one they were creating in their silent studios. There was a lot of pent-up energy among those primitive talents. The whole country—if you believed Scott Fitzgerald, Samuel Hopkins Adams, and Carl Van Vechten—seemed to be going off on one prolonged toot of bathtub gin, dance crazes, and a newly liberated sense of sex. It was fun to drink because you weren't supposed to, to fornicate because Dr. Freud had now informed you that it was time to let your id take over from that puritanical superego. If the whole country was going to the party, why should Hollywood be any different? And if the Hollywood party was excessive, it was only because Hollywood had always been an excessive, speeded-up, larger-than-life reflection of the American Way. So even after the Fatty Arbuckle debacle, and the scandals the studios had learned how to hush up, the wine flowed and the sexual laughter mounted through my growing years. The effect on me and my "brother" Maurice Rapf was to inhibit rather than liberate us.

On Monday mornings the wild parties were often the talk of the little town where everybody still knew everybody. Mickey Neilan had celebrated the wrap-up of his picture by throwing a three-day party for five hundred people, with Abe Lyman's Ambassador Hotel Orchestra to welcome the daylight. We heard that scores of couples danced and drank themselves into oblivion and were still sleeping on the lawn. The police had come but the twinkle-eyed Mickey had bought them off with hundred-dollar bills. This little celebration was said to have set Neilan back $20,000. It's only money, was the Mick's philosophy, and at the rate he was earning it in those days all the party had cost him was a few weeks' salary. In those easy-come days before taxes, accountants, business managers, and tax shelters, the make-it-and-spend-it philosophy ruled the town. Americans were going to the movies by the millions. They had caught the habit. Entire families went at least twice a week. The ticket total was half the population of the United States. Mickey Neilan, as well as B.P. and the other early winners, felt secure astride their bobbing steeds on the merry-go-round.

16

ONE OF THE gold rings that my father reached out for may have looked like an extremely brassy alloy but it turned out to be eighteen karat. Her name—unknown when B.P. signed her—was Clara Bow. Every film decade seems to discover its own sex symbol: Theda Bara in the Teens, Jean Harlow in the Thirties, Jane Russell in the Forties, Marilyn Monroe in the Fifties, Raquel Welch in the Sixties, Farrah Fawcett-Majors in the Seventies, with the Earth Goddess Mae West embracing all the generations. I don't think that even B.P., who had a well-developed instinct for star power in those days, would have predicted the impact that little Clara was to have on the Twenties. In 1922 she was a red-haired, minute, effervescent flapper whose beauty-contest crown had been awarded by the cartoonist Harrison Fisher, the illustrator Neysa McMein, and Howard Chandler Christy, creator of "The Christy Girl." A bonus for Clara was a screen test, leading to a small part in *Down to the Sea in Ships*.

With his biggest star Katherine MacDonald in decline and L.B. deserting the doughty little Mayer-Schulberg ship, B.P. was on the lookout for new talent. When he saw Clara Bow in her film debut, he sent for her and promptly signed her to a long-term contract with Preferred Pictures. Clara couldn't act, and she wasn't exactly a quick study—of all the movie stars I've ever known, and I've known some famous birdbrains, Clara Bow was an easy winner of the Dumbbell Award. A lot of stars have come up so fast that they have had no chance to learn along the way. They flounder and flutter like wounded birds in

157

the blinding and confusing light of their stardom: Olive Thomas, Mabel Normand, Alma Rubens, Barbara LaMarr, Mae Murray, Harlow, Carole Landis, Hedy Lamarr, Marilyn. . . . It demands intelligence and/or strength of character to cope with the pressures of excessive celebrity. Clara Bow was definitely not a coper. She was simply an adorable, in fact irresistible, little know-nothing. It was as if Father had picked out a well-made collie puppy and trained her to become Lassie.

I remember the first time I was introduced to Clara, in my father's office at Preferred. She seemed very short, the top of her head barely reaching to his shoulder. She was wearing a tight cotton dress, and her Cupid's bow of a mouth was constantly moving in the act of chewing gum. It seemed to me that she wore both bangs and spit curls. Her cheeks were round, in fact it was a pretty moon face that she presented, with bouncy, flirty brown eyes. She was no breathtaking beauty like Claire Windsor, and her features weren't as pert and doll-like as Colleen Moore's. But she gave off sparks, vivacity, a sense of fun. Since I had become a Los Angeleno with my ear attuned to the flat Midwestern accent spoken in southern California, Miss Bow's unabashed Brooklyn-ese sounded raucous and funny. "Golly, Mr. Schulberg," she said, still on a formal basis that would soon give way to a closer relationship, "Is this your little junior? Gee, he's cute as a button!" She threw her soft little arms around me. "Where'd ya get all that pretty yellow hair?" To my embarrassment my hair was almost white, not the august white of sixty but the yellow-white of childhood.

"I had yellow hair just like that when I was his age," my father said. At thirty-three he was already turning slightly gray.

Clara Bow ran her fingers teasingly through my hair. "Mmmmm. How wouldja like ta drive up to Arrowhead this weekend, Buddy? Just the two of uz!"

"Now Clara," my father warned, as proper as Louie Mayer when his family was concerned. "He's just a little boy."

"Okay, maybe we'll hafta wait a couple years," Clara pouted. She toyed with her spit curls and seemed to be openly flirting—with both of us. I hung my head, almost physically suffering from shyness. There was something about the uninhibited affection with which actresses came at you. And except for my mother (and even she had once been offered a contract as a leading lady for Essanay), the only women I knew were actresses.

My father put a protective arm around me and ushered me toward the door. "I may not be home for dinner. I've got a story conference on *The Plastic Age* and then I've got to look at the rushes with Gasnier. But tomorrow night Jimmy McLarnin is fighting the rematch with Fidel LaBarba. Should be a great one."

"See ya, Buddy boy," Clara Bow patted my blond curly head. "C'mon 'n' see me on the set. Sincerely, I'm very glad to've meetin' yuz."

That is not funny-paper talk, but really the way the gum-chewing 19-year-old sounded as she approached the threshold of international fame as America's Number One Flapper.

When Clara started shooting her next picture for my father, I did go on the set and she ran over and kissed me and told everybody I was her secret boyfriend. Then the assistant director made sure the set quieted down because Miss Bow had a very difficult scene to play. It was a scene in which her leading man felt she had misbehaved with another man and was walking out on her. She was only flirting with the other man, the heavy, in order to make her suitor jealous enough to marry her. But the heavy had plied her with gin from his silver flask (the prop man had a trunk load of silver flasks in all shapes and sizes to accommodate the obligatory drinking scenes of Prohibition), and, unused to bootleg hooch, she had gone a little too far. But now that the man in her life had apparently abandoned her to her fate, she had to cry.

It takes a real actress to cry from the inside. The good ones reach in for a moving experience of their own, overlap it with the emotion of the scene they are playing, and cry for real. There are actresses who have to fake it: A makeup man squirts glycerine on their cheeks, then steps back behind the camera and our leading lady seems to have an eyeful of tears.

As I was to see for myself, Clara Bow's tears came a little more naturally. First the set fell silent while the director explained the scene to her. She nodded. She seemed rather nervous. Then the assistant director called for quiet, and gave the cue for the three-piece orchestra to begin. They played a soft, tender, schmaltzy rendition of "Rock-a-bye, Baby . . ." Clara, now in front of the camera, was listening intently. Not breaking the quiet mood, the director said, "Action . . ." The little behind-camera trio played on. The violin cried. The portable organ wept: "On a tree top . . . when the wind blows . . . the cradle will rock . . ."

Clara Bow, the tough little jazz baby, began to rock a little. No longer did her face look happy and full of the devil as it had at our first meeting. She was pressing her lips together and her big round eyes were blinking. "When the bough breaks . . . the cradle will fall . . ." A little shudder passed through Clara Bow. Tiny clouds of mist began to float across her eyes. "Down will come cradle . . ." Photogenic tears welled in the eyes of Clara Bow, gathered like waves in miniature and began rolling down her cheeks. "Baby, and all. . . ." Clara Bow was crying. Crying beautifully. Crying like a real actress. And when the director triumphantly cried "Cut!" Clara went on crying. The music stopped, a makeup lady powdered Clara's moist cheeks and in a few moments the mood of the tragedy subsided.

My next memory of Clara Bow is associated with my first trip to a movie location—to Pomona College, about sixty miles northeast of Los Angeles, a two-hour journey in those days—for the shooting of *The Plastic Age*. Wesley Ruggles, one of the best of his time, was directing and the cast included Clara Bow as the wild flapper, a role she was making her trademark. This time "Cynthia" comes to the college prom and breaks the heart of the pure young hero, "Hugh," played by Donald Keith, by coming on with the sophisticated college boy, "Carl," a man of the world played by a newcomer, a 20-year-old son and grandson of Mexican bullfighters from Chihuahua. The newcomer's name was Luis Antonio Damasco de Alonso. One of my father's favorite office (and dining-room) games was to choose marquee names for the young players he signed. It was he who was said to have changed Gladys Mary Smith to Mary Pickford. In the case of young Sr. Luis Antonio, at first B.P. considered Antonio Alonso. But by this time he feared that there had been too many Latin competitors—Antonio Moreno, Ramon Novarro, and some long forgotten. So he went in the other direction. It was his theory that the name chosen should already have the ring of stardom. So he wrote down the names of stars then current, and experimented with phonic amalgams. Jack Gilbert was an established star, and Ronald Colman was just coming into his own. Put those two names into a mixer, whirl them around, and what do you come up with? Gilbert Roland.

The Plastic Age is one of my most vivid early memories of silent-movie making, for many reasons. For one thing I was away from my home and family for the first time, living in a rustic hotel with the film company. Everybody went out of the way to make me feel welcome, including my gum-chewing girlfriend Clara Bow, who kept telling everybody I was her steady fella.

That location trip may have marked the beginning of my sex education, for despite the advanced Freudian theories of my mother, and my growing childhood awareness that Something was going on behind the doors of the studio offices and those Spanish stucco homes in the Hollywood hills, I was painfully naive. Girls of my own age were to be avoided whenever possible. I remember being in a rowboat at Arrowhead Lake with the child star Baby Peggy, and people teasing me about our big romance—suggesting that the pint-size actress was playing up to the boss's son so he'd talk his father into buying her a particular story. I remember trying to stay as far away as I could from Baby Peggy after that. Somehow sex and commerce, even innocent childhood attraction, were inextricably woven into the pattern of ambitious careerism. So— and Maurice Rapf's recollection overlaps with mine—instead of being thrust into a titillating pool of sexuality as might be expected of sons of Hollywood moguls, we regarded sex as something culturally corrupt. Back in those days of Jazz Babies and Dancing Mothers, sex was our own personal Watergate. We sensed the cover-up, the bald-faced lying of the front men, and the backroom payoffs.

It's true that I could feel on my skin Clara Bow's gum-chewing sex appeal. Even then I think I sensed that she communicated sexually because she had no other vocabulary. She had to flirt with me, as she did with everyone, because she simply didn't know anything else to do.

My awareness of sex on that location grew not only from my proximity to Clara Bow but from the content of the film itself. I had read *The Plastic Age;* in fact, Percy Marks's novel was the first book with an "adult" theme I had ever read. At least in those days when Victorian morality had not entirely surrendered to the new freedoms of the Twenties, it seemed like an adult theme. It was considered an ultraliberal act on the part of B.P. and Ad to expose a kid still in elementary school to a book as suggestive, downright naughty, and full of sex appeal as Marks's treatment of college life in those days when Youth was allegedly Flaming.

Partly because of my stammering, still so severe that I could not complete a single sentence, or sometimes a single word, partly because of my father's literary leanings and his hope that I'd follow in his footsteps not as a movie producer but as a writer, and partly thanks to my mother's intellectual ambition (she had begun a practice which would continue into my highschool years of paying me twenty-five cents—the rates advanced as I got into more serious literature—for every book I read and reported on to her), I had become a precocious reader. I could escape from my tormentors at the public school who imitated my

161

stammering, led the jeering laughter, and bullied me against the school-yard wall by retreating into a corner of my own room and losing myself in a book.

B.P. had read *The Plastic Age* for pleasure, because Percy Marks, a Dartmouth professor, was considered one of the better novelists of the day. His work dealt with the Prohibition generation born at the turn of the century. Father had thought I would get more out of my trip to the Pomona location if I were acquainted with the novel and able to compare it with the scenario, then with the actual shooting, and finally with the rushes and the first assembled cut: a crash course in movie-making.

There is a nervous moment in the book when our hero Hugh fears he has been caged with a roué whose self-control has lost a shameless battle to Eros. But his roommate reassures him:

"I'm a bad egg. I drink and gamble and pet. I haven't gone the limit yet—on account of my old lady—but I will."

The hottest scene, both in the book and in Father's movie, is when Hugh takes the uninhibited jazz baby Cynthia to the prom, the wettest in the history of once-staid "Sanford College":

"The musicians played as if in a frenzy, the drums pound-pounding a terrible tom-tom, the saxophones moaning and wailing, the violins singing sensuously, shrilly as if in pain, an exquisite, searing pain."

The band in the book is playing a song with which I could identify because we had it on a roll on our player piano, "Stumbling all around, stumbling all around, so funny / Stumbling here and there, stumbling everywhere—"

"Close-packed," Percy Marks wrote with knowing lubricity, "the couples moved slowly about the gymnasium, body pressed tight to body, swaying in place . . . boom, boom, boom, boom—the drums beating their primitive, blood-maddening tom-tom . . . *I fell and when I rose I felt ashamed"* / *I said I'm stumbling along, stumbling along. . ."*

The climax reeked of forbidden fruit. As the saxophones, the drum-beat, and the nearness of Hugh drive Cynthia wild, she entices him to borrow a friend's room. Fred interrupts them just in time to save them from Going All The Way. Fred is disgusted, and Hugh is so full of self-loathing that he contemplates cutting his throat with a razor blade or blowing his brains out. Next morning, Cynthia wakes up older and wiser: "I've been doing a lot of thinking. . . ." She's too fast for him, she explains. what he thought was true love was just . . . "sex attraction."

I watched the two-shot as Cynthia/Clara tells her young leading man:

> It was more my fault than yours.
> I'm a pretty bad egg, I guess; and
> the booze and your holding me was
> too much. I've spoiled the nicest
> thing that ever happened to me. . . .

It was time for that unobtrusive three-piece orchestra to slide into "Rock-a-bye, Baby" again. The script described Cynthia's lips as "trembling, her eyes full of tears." Rock-a-bye, baby . . . on the tree top . . . when the wind blows . . . the cradle will rock. . . . No more sexual saxophones moaning and tom-toms drumming. For the 20-year-old redhead with the flirty eyes, bee-stung lips, and dimpled knees, the midnight madness has given way to a mother's lullaby.

I stood behind the camera, watching the jazz baby from Brooklyn crying like the lost child she was. I didn't know it yet, but I would soon learn that Clara wasn't crying because she'd almost enticed her 20-year-old virginal leading man to "go all the way." She was crying for the little girl living in poverty in the Bay Ridge section of Brooklyn with a hard-drinking, unemployed father and a psychotic mother who beat her savagely for the slightest infraction, screamed that she would put her out of the house if Clara entered that Brooklyn movie-theater beauty contest when she was only sixteen—and, when she won the chance at a screen test, threatened to kill her if she ever went into the movies. Later, Clara explained that when she was a child she had a friend on the block whose mother would sing her to sleep to the soothing strains of "Rock-a-bye, Baby . . ." That's where her mind went whenever the screen asked her for tears. The high-kicking All-American Flapper was the little girl lost.

While Wesley Ruggles was setting up the establishing shot of Cynthia and Hugh walking down the college hill to the railroad station for their tearful farewell. I sat with Clara in the red roadster she had just bought to celebrate her raise in salary. (Acknowledging her growing popularity, B.P. had volunteered to tear up the old contract and write her a new one. That was generous of him, and there's no doubt that Father was genuinely fond of his discovery. But L.B. probably would have made a milar gesture. It was considered shrewd studio tactics to anticipate the demands of a rising star. In those days of block booking, a star's films were sold to the theaters before they were made, frequently before the producer had even decided what films he would make with his box-office attraction. Paramount would sell in advance four Swansons, four Pola Negris, three Valentinos. . . . Of course the 20-year-old Clara wasn't a temperamental superstar like the trio who were trying the well-known patience of Jesse Lasky on his Famous Players lot. Clara Bow was reckless, impulsive, naive, and vulnerable. She wasn't designing; if you wanted to be unkind you might say she was too stupid to try to manipulate the studio management. But she was also generous and trusting, and at that strategic moment in her career, my father was the closest friend she had.)

When Clara asked me how I liked school, I told her about my stammering problem; she was sympathetic and I found myself stammering a little less than I usually did—especially with people I didn't know very well. When I told her I hated school, in fact dreaded the mornings when I had to enter that enemy camp, she stroked my head—she really seemed to like my blond curly hair. And she told me again that I reminded her of what my father must have looked like when he was my age. She sympathized with me because she had hated school too: Most of the kids had been smarter than she was, better-dressed, and came from nicer homes. And, she confessed, she used to stutter, too! Oh, not a terrible stutter like Marion Davies', but enough to make it embarrassing when she had to recite in school. It was a swell piece of luck when she won that beauty contest. Even though she had really flunked her first screen test. The part she won in the beauty contest was so small and she had been so nervous doing it that when she went to see her first picture, she wasn't in it at all!

"I thought that crack about 'a face on the cutting-room floor' was just a lot of hot air," she said. "But there was little Clara all over the cutting-room floor. Then I got to play a stowaway in *Down to the Sea in Ships,* not a very big part but at least they couldn't cut me out of it, and your father sent for me and put me under contract for fifty a week. He was very polite and he made me feel better about myself. That's what I like about your father. He doesn't try to grab you right away like a lot of fellas out here. I don't read much of anything except *True Romance* and stuff like that. But he made me read this book we're shooting. He said, 'Clara dear, I think if you read it you'll understand the part of Cynthia better.' And when I did read it—well, most of it—I told Ben, I mean Mr. Schulberg, 'Heck, I ain't afraid t' play Cynthia.' I mean she's just like me—comes from New York and likes her smokes and her drinks and runs with a fast crowd. . . ."

I must have looked shocked. In those days I was as puritanical and straitlaced as Hugh Carver in *The Plastic Age*. I would try to take cigarettes out of my mother's hand, I objected to my father's taste for highballs and, like a Billy Sunday in knickers, I thought petting was for perverts. I had been relieved to read how Hugh had cast the wicked Cynthia out of his life and had promised his college adviser that never again would he (almost) give in to temptation.

Clara Bow offered me a stick of gum. "I don't know why I'm tellin' ya all this. I guess I just feel like talkin' my fool head off today. My old man and my goddamn—excuse me, my mom, they never talked to me much. All they did was yell at me and punch me around. That's why I actually prayed I'd win that beauty contest. I was only in my second year of high but if I could get into the movies I could get away from home. It wasn't a nice home like yours with parents who like ya and take care of ya. It was a dump. Your father has really been swell to me. It's like having a special teacher ya like in school. He has such nice manners and he's so smart and he never shouts at anybody. I never met anybody like him before in my whole life. You must be awful proud of him."

I said I was. Although I really didn't see that much of him. Except for Sundays . . . the Friday-night fights . . . and the sneak previews. We'd drive or we'd take the train to San Bernardino or Glendale, and the theater manager would hand out cards asking for the audience comment on the movie. The impromptu sidewalk conference outside the theater became an institution.

"Y'see, that's what I mean," Clara said. "At least he takes you with him to the sneaks. Someday you'll grow up and be a big producer becuz of all the things he's teaching ya. I know he's awful proud of ya. He's even showed me some of ya poetry."

As another outlet for the stammering, I had begun trying my hand at little rhymes that were not quite in a class with Robert Louis Stevenson's *A Child's Garden of Verses*. I was surprised to hear of Father's reaction because, while my mother had been encouraging me to write more, he had seemed rather noncommittal.

"I know yuh gonna make me awful proud of ya, too," Clara said as we sat in the roadster shoulder to shoulder and chewed gum intimately together. "Y' know I feel about ya almost like ya my little nephew. Like we're all one big happy family."

Like innocent Hugh in *The Plastic Age,* I didn't know anything about sex attraction and all that stuff. It was amazing how little I knew, considering my father's profession and my mother's early fascination with Dr. Freud and psychoanalysis. But I sensed that same Something that hung over the studio lot like incense, Something intimate in Clara Bow's relationship to our family.

Of course what I did not learn until some years later was that B.P.'s secretary, Henrietta Cohn, who had accompanied us to Hollywood, had written an anonymous letter to Ad alerting her to "the B.P.-Clara Bow situation." Henrietta was a small, intense, rather homely, extremely able and intelligent woman who spent more time with Father than Ad did, and who felt she was doing this out of loyalty both to mother and to her own boss. His career was in the ascendancy, he was considered one of the brightest and most inventive producers in the competitive town, and Henrietta was afraid a rash move might impede his otherwise inevitable climb to the top.

It seems my mother accepted this bit of intelligence from the studio philosophically. Although I didn't know it at the time, she was already resigned to his philandering. A curious mixture of old-fashioned and new-fashioned, she believed in the family with a capital F, had become disillusioned but unshaken in her love for my father, and believed he needed her steadying influence to build his career.

There must be, she was determined, no reflection of domestic turbulence within the home. The children (the third and ultimate issue, Stuart, had just arrived, our first Hollywood native son) must be raised in an atmosphere of culture and security. Furthermore, all of the producers had mistresses. If Irving Thalberg was faithful to Norma Shearer, the starlet L.B. had signed in the Mayer-Schulberg days, it may have been due as much to a weak heart as to a strong morality. Some of those back-street companions were full-fledged stars and leading ladies. Some of them were pretty bit-players carried on the company payroll at the insistence of the studio boss. "It was a terribly decadent society," my mother passed judgment. "The producers had so much more power than they do today. Anybody with a pretty face and a good figure could pass the test in silent pictures. Of course girls like Clara Bow and Colleen Moore and Blanche Sweet had some special appeal. But thousands of pretty girls were pouring into Hollywood from all over the country

166

hoping to be discovered and the men in power could really take their pick. The ones who failed to catch on in pictures became courtesans. They'd spend all of their time making themselves beautiful and glamorous for the men who kept them: sleeping late, beauty treatments, all kinds of faddist massages after bathing in perfume, milk, scented bath oils. It was like the Middle East, like sultans with their harems. They even had their eunuch yes-men who would pimp for them, front for them, appear in public with them to avoid bad publicity. I used to feel sorry for the wives of all the big producers, because most of those women had no resources with which to fight back. They just played cards with each other, or vied with each other as to who had the most expensive jewels and clothes. Nearly all of them had started out at the bottom and now that the business was becoming a billion-dollar industry, they were living in big houses surrounded by servants and seemingly everything they wanted—except a happy home life."

Ad felt superior to these luxuriously protected domestic prisoners because she had found an outlet in her studies at the local branch of the University of California, her activities in behalf of child-study and birth-control groups, and her ability to set up what was probably the first Hollywood salon, where the visiting intellectuals and artists—a Theodore Dreiser, or a Count Keyserling—would be invited to meet those members of the movie community who in Mother's rather snobbish opinion were among the less culturally retarded. She succeeded in establishing herself as an intellectual and cultural force in the Hollywood of the Twenties when those forces were sadly wanting both in supply and in demand. She was the first to bring Early American furniture, child psychology, and progressive education to Hollywood; John Dewey was more of a god to her than John Gilbert.

Her only rival was Bessie Lasky, who painted, encouraged her young son to write poetry, and drew around her an effete gathering of painters, sculptors, and aesthetic hangers-on. Ad's group seemed more oriented toward the real world and its problems.

Hollywood had been culture-conscious before. The Hollywood of the 1910s, the provincial Hollywood that had been envisioned by its pious founders as the New Jerusalem, had been determinedly cultured, though its taste ran to the precious and pretentious. The preeminent artist was Paul De Longpre, who specialized in painting beautiful flowers. The annual Pilgrimage Play was organized with the Chamber of Commerce boast, "What Oberammergau was to Europe, Hollywood is to be to all the world." There was the MacDowell Circle of Allied Arts and a natural

167

bowl in the hills became the romantic setting for classical music. There was the Easter Sunrise Service with tens of thousands climbing those brown hills to immerse themselves in the religious music. The original Hollywood of Midwestern teetotalers and God-fearing Christians liked to boast that *their* Hollywood was "The Theosophical Capital of America." Hollywood was a cultural schizophrene: the anti-movie Old Guard with their chamber music and their religious pageants fighting a losing battle against the more dynamic culture of the Ad Schulbergs who flaunted the bohemianism of Edna St. Vincent Millay and the socialism of Upton Sinclair. But there was one subject on which the staid old Hollywood establishment and the members of the new culture circle would agree: Clara Bow, no matter how great her popularity, was a low-life and a disgrace to the community.

My relationship to Clara Bow was affected neither by sexual jealousy nor by cultural superiority. As we sat there in her red roadster waiting for the assistant director to summon her for the next scene, I found her easier to be with than the girls of my own age. For all her Juicy-Fruit flamboyance, there was something wounded about her—the Rock-a-bye-Baby bit, we'd call it today—to which I could relate.

When the A.D. called over to us, "Ready for you, Miss Bow," and I followed her out of the car to watch her play the scene, a curious thing happened. It was so casual, and yet I have never forgotten it. Gilbert Roland came up to me shyly with a small folded note in his hand, pointed to Clara, and asked me if I would hand it to her. I don't know why he called on me to play Cupid. I don't even know what was in the note because I was too conscientious to read it, especially when I could feel his strong Latin eyes drilling into my back as I caught up with Clara and delivered it. She mumbled, "Oh thanks, Buddy, sweet of ya," and took a quick glance over her shoulder at the young bullfighter turned actor.

That evening they came into the local hotel dining room together, two head-turning 20-year-olds whom my father had put together from such totally different worlds—Chihuahua and Brooklyn. For the next year or so they were what Hollywood liked to call "an item." But, as a host of ardent suitors were to discover, Clara was too capricious—or too promiscuous, or vulnerable—to be ready to settle down with one.

17

THE PLASTIC AGE put Clara's saucy face on the cover of fan magazines, and in the year that followed, with Father choosing her vehicles carefully, she achieved full-fledged stardom with *Dancing Mothers* and *Mantrap.* In *Kid Boots,* he cast her opposite his and Ad's little friend from the Lower East Side, now a top Broadway song-and-dance comedian, Eddie Cantor. But what carried Clara to a peak far above silent rivals like Colleen Moore and Joan Crawford was a providential meeting that my father arranged for her with Elinor Glyn.

Elinor Glyn was the Jacqueline Susann of the Twenties, with the racy best-selling qualities of Irving Wallace and Harold Robbins thrown in. Her autographed picture on the mantle over the fireplace in my study shows a long- and strong-faced, handsome woman in her middle forties, her hair parted in the middle and looped neatly over her high forehead like a theater curtain. "William S. Hart in drag," a studio wit had described her. More sophisticated than Percy Marks, she had written novels that were considered naughty-naughty if not immoral: *Three Weeks* and *His Hour.* Now she had written *It,* a word that had its modest place in our language as an impersonal pronoun until Miss Glyn, with the showmanship of the English aristocrat she affected, dusted it off, shined it up, and upper-cased it as a more compact and suggestive word for what the Jazz Age magazines had coyly been calling S.A.

Elinor Glyn, with her arch-*grande dame* manners, her exaggerated British accent, and her sweeping conception of *it,* was as generic to the Twenties as Aimee Semple MacPherson, Peaches Browning, and—

thanks to Miss Glyn's magic wand—Clara Bow. If her work was laughed off by the highbrow critics as unadulterated junk, you would never have guessed it from Miss Glyn's hauteur. To hear her talk, she was the embodiment of all the great English lady novelists from Emily Bronte to Virginia Woolf.

When *It* was published, my father snapped it up as the ideal balloon in which to waft his red-haired protégée even higher into the Hollywood heavens. He arranged a meeting at the studio between the preeminent authoress and the preeminent Jazz Baby, and Miss Glyn placed on the head of Miss Bow the official crown: "Of all the lovely young ladies I've met in Hollywood, Clara Bow has *It*!"

Thus Clara Bow became not just a top box-office star but a national institution: The It Girl. Millions of followers wore their hair like Clara's and pouted like Clara, and danced and smoked and laughed and necked like Clara. They imitated everything but her speech because fortunately the silent screen protected them from that nasal Brooklyn accent.

Fifty-odd years ago—in the Golden Age of Babe Ruth, Jack Dempsey, Gertrude Ederle, Bobby Jones, Big Bill Tilden, and Lucky Lindy—Clara Bow reigned as the carefree princess of a carefree generation, the idol of the shopgirl and the sweetheart of the frat house. Her salary jumped like a hot tip on Wall Street from fifty to two-fifty, from five hundred to a thousand dollars a week, and then two, three, four, five thousand dollars pouring in every week! She couldn't spend it fast enough, though she found a lot of people who were happy to help her. She bought the most expensive red roadster she could find, to match her hair, and she filled it with seven chow dogs, also chosen for fur to match Clara's flaming locks. In a great blur of red she would speed down Sunset Boulevard, driving faster than the cars on the oval racetrack on the open flatlands of Beverly Hills (where the Beverly Wilshire Hotel now stands). A press agent's dream, she kept firing her chauffeurs because they were afraid to drive fast enough to please her. Her simultaneous love affairs with her leading men, her directors, and handsome hangers-on were the talk of Hollywood and the subject of spicy fan-magazine spreads.

By this time, it seems, B.P. had become more father-confessor and guidance counselor than paramour. Her own father, frankly, was a mess, though in the true Clara Bow style she remained openhearted and openhanded in her devotion. Robert Bow had followed his daughter to Hollywood, where he made awkward stabs at managing her unexpected career. Then she set him up in a dry-cleaning establishment, but even though she twisted the arm of all her studio friends to bring their business to him, the enterprise failed. Even when Clara offered to hustle the clothes from the studio to his shop on roller skates, Robert Bow failed. Undaunted, he opened a restaurant. That too went down the drain, at a cost B.P. estimated at $25,000. Everything Robert Bow touched turned to tin—or worthless paper. But in those high-kicking Twenties, it didn't really seem to matter: Clara had more than enough for everybody. Fan mail was flooding in at the rate of 3,500 letters a week. If she watched her weight and her booze—an extra few pounds on that energetic little frame could make the difference between the irresistibly curvaceous and the undeniably pudgy—there was no reason why The It Girl, still in her early twenties, could not roll along at her dizzy pace of two hundred and fifty thousand a year for at least another ten years.

While my father was working to keep Clara's star high above the world, my mother was coming to the rescue of another volatile career, Judge Ben Lindsey's. The Judge had established himself as one of the controversial figures of the period by advocating Companionate Marriage. People, according to his daring conception, should not join together in marriage without first knowing if they were sexually compatible. A period of trial marriage, in Lindsey's opinion, would avoid a great number of the divorces over which he was presiding in his Denver court. A particular case in which he voiced this opinion caused him so much notoriety that he was virtually hounded out of that straitlaced city. Ever on the prowl for intellectual innovators, Mother invited Judge and Mrs. Lindsey to come to Los Angeles as her houseguests while she tried to find a place for him in the local judicial system.

In contrast to his theories, the Judge turned out to be a mild-mannered fellow, prim in appearance, conservative in dress and manner. Somehow Ad found him a place in a Court of Domestic Relations, over which he presided with the same attack on conventional procedure he had demonstrated in Denver. He felt that a couple appearing in court for a contested divorce would have a better chance of working out their personal differences in a more relaxed atmosphere—not just in his chambers but in a private home. Sometimes Ad would be allowed to sit in on these unravelings of domestic knots, and even to put in her psychoanalytical advice. (So deep an impression did Mother's new prize make on our household that years later, when I was to be married in my father's house in Beverly Hills, I felt it only proper to track down Judge Lindsey to officiate. And preside he did, in his most unconventional style, saying "Now let me see, I forget which side you're supposed to stand on, Budd . . . I don't think I ever actually married anybody before. Mostly I helped to get them unmarried, or companionately married.")

Vanity Fair, the sparkling magazine of that era, was featuring an amusing series called Impossible Interviews, between, for example, Stalin and Rockefeller, Coolidge and Garbo. . . . One of these Impossible Interviews came to actuality in our living room when Judge Lindsey decided he would like to meet Clara Bow and asked my mother to arrange it. The apostle of unmarried sex in America wanted to interview one of its most celebrated practioners.

When Clara arrived late, as expected of sex goddesses, it was obvious she had tested her latest delivery of bootleg scotch before leaving home. Introduced by my mother, Clara said, "Hi, Judge, B.P. tells me ya believe people oughta have their fun without havin' t' get married. Ya naughty boy!" Whereupon she brought that famous Cupid's bow of a mouth close to his and gave him a fat smack on the lips. Judge Lindsey drew away—but not before a smear of lipstick was left on his face. Poor Mrs. Lindsey glanced at my mother for help. The Judge had hoped to carry on a conversation with Clara regarding her modern views on sex and marriage. Perhaps it would supply a chapter or at least some apt quotations for his next book. But Clara Bow was the original existentialist before that word was invented. She insisted that the Judge get up and dance with her, and while he tried awkwardly to oblige her, she began to play a coy game with his buttons. Beginning with his top jacket button, she said, "Rich man . . . poor man . . . beggar man . . . thief . . . ," her busy little fingers unbuttoning with each designation. By the time the childhood game had brought her to "Indian Chief," Clara Bow was undoing the top button of Judge Lindsey's fly. The ultra-liberal judge became as arch-conservative as a Salt Lake City elder. He quickly retired to the protective arm of Mrs. Lindsey, reasonably safe from Clara's ardent pursuit. In a little while the Lindseys had taken flight.

When B.P. upbraided Clara, she pouted like the child she was. "Well gee whiz, if he believes in all that modern stuff like ya say he does, how come he's such an old stick-in-the-mud?"

My father's million-dollar property had become a million-dollar headache. He used to call her Crisis-a-Day Clara. When she could not decide between two persistent lovers, Gary Cooper and the equally virile Vic Fleming, one of B.P.'s strongest directors, she had a nervous breakdown.

Her home in Beverly Hills was modest compared to Pickfair and Valentino's Falcon Lair, but it was the scene of a nonstop open house. There were all-night poker games; the back door to the kitchen was always open so that patrolling cops and other friendly passersby could drop in and help themselves to beer from the icebox; there were always jazz records playing loudly on the Victrola; Clara's bootlegger was there so often that he became one of the regular guests; and every now and then a young extra-boy or bit-player from Clara's last hit picture would threaten her with blackmail if he didn't get his love letters back.

She would bring her problems to Father's office, and he would try to bring some order to her life even if finally he was unable to provide the same service for himself. He advised her to settle down a little bit; to concentrate on a single man, if she could; to put her father on a modest salary rather than to indulge his commercial dreams at a cost of tens of thousands of dollars. He thought she should find a secretary-companion to live with her and take care of her affairs. When she followed that advice, her father promptly fell in love with the young lady and married her. So Clara had both of them to support while casting about for a new companion.

During this so-called search for stability, she wandered off to the Cal-Neva Lodge on the California-Nevada boundary at Lake Tahoe. In those days Las Vegas was not even a gleam in a Godfather's eye. But as soon as you were one inch into the state of Nevada, you could take part legally in games of chance, and the boys who operated these games were happy to make them available to the well-heeled suckers from Hollywood. So Clara Bow was introduced to the game of blackjack. A nice man in a tuxedo explained the rules to her rather quickly and gave her some pretty blue chips to play with. The trick of the game is to draw a total of 21. If you draw a card that carries your total above that amount, you lose the bet you anted. If you stop with a total under 21 and the dealer has a greater total under 21, you also lose. It's a nice game, lots of fun to play, and very nice for the boys in the tuxedoes.

Clara was already a rather proficient if reckless poker player, and this game seemed easy. The only trouble was, the dealer seemed either better at it or luckier than Clara. After twenty minutes she had lost all her pretty blue chips. But the tuxedoes could not have been more obliging.

They were happy to hand her another hundred chips. In less than an hour the dealer had raked in all her chips again. By this time she was bored with the silly little card game and thought she would try roulette. This was fine with the tuxedoes. Clara Bow didn't have to worry about credit at Cal-Neva. They would advance her anything up to one hundred thousand dollars. But meanwhile, they thrust a blank check in front of her, for her to sign for her losses at the blackjack table.

As in a scene from a movie my father was soon to produce, *Underworld,* the diminutive Miss Bow looked around at the lumbering bodyguards with wrestlers' chests stretching their starched shirt-fronts, and signed—a check for twenty thousand dollars.

What Clara thought she had lost was a mere one hundred dollars. For as she tried to explain to my father, "Y'see Ben, I thought those chips were only worth fifty cents each. It wasn' until I had to sign the check that they told me they were a hundred dollars each. I was bettin' ten 'n' twenty on every deal. How was I supposed t' know?"

My father told his tearful little sexpot that she had been duped. If they had failed to explain the value of the chips in advance, and had encouraged her to buy a second stack, she had been doubly duped. This was the morning after the infamous blackjack game and there was still time to stop payment on the check.

"Oh, what a swell idea!" she said. "They really cheated me. I shouldn't hafta pay it."

"I'll help you," my father promised, "but only on one condition, Clara. That you never go into a casino again. They're dangerous places when you don't know what the hell you're doing."

My old man was talking from firsthand experience.

"I promise. I promise. Anything to get out of this awful mess!" said the poor little rich girl.

Two days had passed when Clara called my father at midnight. She was almost too hysterical to talk. "B.P., something awful—something terrible just happened! I've got to talk to ya right away—hurry—please!"

My father put down a script he was reading late—for he worked as hard as he played—and drove out to Clara's. She was still in hysterics. Two tough customers had come from Cal-Neva to see her. Their bosses had sent them with this message: "Either you make that check good—tomorrow—or you'll get acid all over your pretty puss. Instead of the It Girl you'll be the Ain't Girl."

That may sound like dialogue left over from a Grade-B Warner

Brothers movie, but my father told me this story at least a hundred times without a single variation, until I not only memorized it but became convinced of its truth.

When Clara told him of this threat, he advised her to appear cooperative, but to ask them to pick up the check at the studio from her boss, Mr. Schulberg. She was to say that she was such a hot property that the company was prepared to pay her debt rather than risk the destruction of her face.

Early next morning my father phoned Buron Fitts, the local district attorney. This was a legitimate extortion case, but even if it hadn't been, Mr. Fitts was always ready to go out of his way to help any motion-picture executive. To put it bluntly, the studios owned Buron Fitts. This was in the post-Desmond Taylor and Arbuckle days, when scandals that might have destroyed the reputations of valuable movie stars could be hushed up by the hear-no-evil-see-no-evil approach of the D.A.'s office. This was Cover-up, Hollywood Style, in the days when the film capital was a self-sufficient oligarchy, sunny and benevolent on the surface but hard and vindictive at the core.

The Clara Bow-Cal-Neva case gave Mr. Fitts an opportunity to score a double whammy: to provide an invaluable service to a studio while throwing a net around criminal invaders from Nevada. Fitts told my father to alert his office as soon as the call came in from the Lake Tahoe boys. B.P. was to make an appointment with the goons, his tone promising payment on arrival. The call came in as expected. Fitts ordered a brace of detectives to B.P.'s office, where they staked themselves out behind the long red-gold curtains on the far wall. When the enforcers arrived, Father played out the scene he had rehearsed with the district attorney. A large checkbook was displayed conspicuously open on his desk.

"Now let me get this straight," B.P. began. "You're telling me that unless I write out this check and hand it over right now, you're going to throw acid in Miss Bow's face, so that she'll never be able to work in pictures again?"

"You heard it right, mister," one of those George Rafts rose to the bait. "And we ain't playin'. We got the juice right on us. So no more jaw-music. Gimme that check or Miss It won't be worth shit."

The visitors were enjoying their little couplet when out from behind the curtains, pistols drawn, sprang the Buron Fitts specials. Before the blackjack cowboys knew what hit them, they were in handcuffs and booked for extortion and a sheet of other crimes. For a while both my father and Clara Bow were given police protection, for fear that the Cal-Neva masterminds would retaliate. But gamblers needed the good will of the free-spending movie crowd and someone up there must have called off the dogs, for there were no further threats or efforts to get even.

There was a joke going around in the dying months of the Twenties: "She had It but she lost it at the Astor." Precisely where Clara Bow lost It was more difficult to pinpoint. The decline and fall of It and the It Girl was a downward spiral. The economic collapse near the end of 1929 had only an indirect effect on the world's most identifiable flapper. She wasn't wiped out in the market as were some of her famous co-stars. Her money had never been invested, wisely or unwisely. It was all in cash and furs and jewels and handouts and, best of all, in the contract that promised her five thousand dollars every week, come rain or come shine, come drunk or sober, come champagne happy or midnight blue, for years on end. So should Clara Bow worry?

The answer was a sobbing *yes*. The impact of sound on silence was nightmare and renaissance: literally death and life. These victims didn't jump out of windows like the Wall Street plungers. Their suicide was more gradual. Behind the locked doors of their Beverly Hills mansions, the talkie drop-outs searched for an answer to their fears and frustrations in the amber bottles their bootleggers hauled to the back door by the case.

For Clara Bow it was the beginning of a thirty-five-year death-in-life. Her first sound picture was a resounding disaster. Overnight, the Clara Bow I had listened to on my father's sets and locations, and in his office and living room, had to talk from the newly installed sound-picture screen. Millions of adoring fans heard for the first time the flat, nasal Brooklynese we who knew her had always associated with her. It was a playback to the days of Theda Bara, when the Vampire suddenly went out of style at the end of World War I. Unbelievably out of a job after having played to a million fans a week, the little Jewish girl from Cincinnati—whom William Fox promoted as an Arabian princess born at an oasis in the shadow of the Sphinx—turned to the theater. Her opening on Broadway drew a sold-out audience laced with all the reigning celebrities. The first time she opened her mouth, they laughed. *This* was the irresistible vampire against whom the Church and an organized group of outraged wives had fulminated as a threat to the established order? This was the Serpent Woman? Cleopatra and Salome incarnate? At the first sound of her childlike piping, cruel laughter ended Theodora Goodman's career.

Clara's trouble was more than vocal. In the early days of sound, photographic fluidity was surrendered to mechanical rigidity. The microphone, not yet movable from a boom, had to be hidden in a flowered plant or a centerpiece on a table. The actors had to play to it. And the camera, imprisoned in an enormous soundproof box, had lost its mobility. In those early years of primitive sound, the performers were far more circumscribed in movement than they would have been on a proscenium stage. Clara's appeal was in her movement—her impromptu Charleston, her incomparable necking. Even her moments of Rock-a-bye-Baby sadness could not be played to a stationary mike.

To add to the pressure, she was faced with the new leading men with stage experience, like Freddie March. His voice was theatrically trained and when he spoke his dialogue he did so with a confidence that conveyed a new kind of screen realism—realism in sound. And the more effective the image of this new wave from the theater, the Marches and the Ruth Chattertons, the more pathetic and ludicrous became the efforts of the great silent stars like Jack Gilbert and Clara Bow.

Life was throwing little Clara pitches she had never had to face before, sinkerballs, spitballs, and knuckleballs. Strike One was the sudden decline and fall of the flapper. In a time of breadlines, dust bowls, farm foreclosures, rent strikes, and men in frayed double-breasted suits selling apples on street corners, somehow the high-kicking, gin-swizzling, short-skirted apostles of the carefree were going out of style. Even if she had been endowed with a golden throat and the theatrical poise of an Ethel Barrymore, Clara Bow as the ultimate flapper would have been discarded in favor of new models better suited to the troubled Thirties.

Strike Two was the terrifying challenge of sound.

And Strike Three came in the form of a blonde hairdresser-turned-secretary who became Clara's constant companion. Her improbable name was Daisy DeVoe.

After Clara's first secretary became her stepmother, Daisy moved in. Thanks to her fussing over Clara's spit curls and wind-tossed bob at the Studio, Miss DeVoe had been invited to the house for one of those merry all-night poker games. Daisy stayed on until the morning, fell asleep in one of the guest rooms, and waked to find herself appointed personal secretary and live-in companion to Clara Bow. The relationship ripened into virtual sisterhood, or even closer. One never traveled anywhere without the other. At last Clara had a true protector. Daisy DeVoe stood between the beleaguered sex goddess and the outside world.

I have only fleeting memories of Miss DeVoe when she and Clara began to summer near our house at Malibu Beach. With my pal Maurice, I used to fish for tomcod off the rickety Malibu pier and sometime I'd drop off a few at Clara's. Daisy DeVoe was always the first to come to the door, knowingly separating Clara's friends from the hordes of undesirables. Clara was always effusively affectionate with me, making a fuss about the little tomcod and showing them off to her chums.

But I saw very little of Clara and Miss DeVoe because I spent most of my time on the beach or the tennis court while they seemed to spend all of their time in their little house. In fact I don't remember ever seeing them on the beach. Ever since my mother—the great innovator—had discovered Malibu as a peaceful retreat from Hollywood, and had built the first house on its crescent beach, it had quickly developed into a select, very *in* movie colony, each house that of a reigning celebrity.

Clara and Daisy simply had moved their smoke-filled nonstop party to the shores of the Pacific. They were poker people, loud-music people, night people. Although Father's liaison with Clara was by this time a burned-out case, or a case smothered in scores of subsequent cases, my mother did not like the idea of Clara's moving so close to us, and discouraged me from going over there. It wasn't jealousy on Ad's part but a lifelong contempt for the ignorant, the wastrels, the low-lifes. If I wanted adult companionship, Mother suggested, I would do much better to visit with our immediate neighbors, the Frank Capras. They were serious, productive, and moral citizens. The thoughtful Frank Capra and his loving wife Lucille went out of their way to be hospitable to the young son of a rival studio head. They were their own people and—Ad was right as usual—the ideal antidotes to Clara and her devoted Daisy.

Their first summer at Malibu, Daisy DeVoe was a time bomb ticking. It was detected by an obscure young actor who had changed his name from George F. Beldam to Rex Bell. He became a member of the Clara Bow household in that high-pressure period when Clara was suffering from mike fright. Rex Bell was the latest, most devoted, and seemingly most conscientious of Miss Bow's many suitors. He became highly suspicious of Miss DeVoe's life-style. In fact, from his favored seat at the banquet, Rex Bell was convinced that Daisy had been stealing Clara

blind. He got Clara to fire the woman with whom she had shared her house and her life for the past three years, and to file charges against her.

Rex Bell obtained a warrant to open Daisy's bank vault, and there, to no one's surprise, was an interesting collection of Clara's jewelry. There was also a parcel of Clara's missing canceled checks and, strangely enough, on each of those cancellation dates there was a transfer from the Clara Bow Special Account—over which Daisy DeVoe held complete domain—to Daisy's personal account. Apparently, for several years Daisy had been writing checks from the Clara Bow account on the basis of "one for you and one for me." And if the suspicious or perceptive Mr. Bell had not come along, the trusting Clara probably would have left her bank account and her household in her closest friend's sticky fingers until the end.

Daisy had not only heisted fistfuls of jewelry, costly gowns, and fur coats, but something she thought might be even more valuable—packets of Clara's love letters. Clara was romantic about those letters. She had a rich assortment from Gary Cooper, Vic Fleming, Harry Richman, an Ivy League football star who tried to commit suicide after Clara had kissed him so forcibly that he had begun to lose his sanity, the doctor who had performed an appendectomy on Clara and whose wife had sued Clara for alienation of affection and settled for thirty thousand dollars. . . . Clara never bothered to look over her canceled checks or to read her bank statement, but sometimes she liked to take out these letters from old beaus and enjoy a good cry. Well, now that Rex Bell had caught Daisy with her hand in the sugar bowl, the rejected companion thought those letters from lost loves offered the most promising avenue of escape.

She came to my father, and also to Clara's attorney, with a simple proposition. She would accept $125,000 in exchange for the letters; simultaneously Clara would withdraw the charges. Otherwise under cross-examination in the courtroom she would reveal all. If Daisy DeVoe was to go under, Clara Bow would go down with her.

Unfortunately, what the embattled Daisy did not realize was that although Clara had not yet gone under for the third time, she had been down twice and was now desperately treading water in a final effort to stay afloat. Clara's fans were deserting her in droves, were turning to those silent beauties able to break through the sound barrier, like Carole Lombard, or to actresses recruited from the stage, like Claudette Colbert. Putting it harshly, the reputation of Clara Bow was no longer worth

$125,000 to the studio. But even if Clara had still been the It Girl of 1928, my father probably would have followed the same course he chose: to call Hollywood's good friend, District Attorney Fitts.

With charges of extortion as an added threat, Daisy signed a thirty-page confession admitting theft of $35,000 in cash, along with all the other loot. Meanwhile, Clara was having another of the nervous breakdowns that would plague her for the rest of her tormented life. Suffering from insomnia and crying spells, she used alcohol and pills to assuage the pain.

Clara wanted to withdraw the charges against her ex-confidante, she told my father. She was afraid to face the public ordeal of the trial. Her eyes were puffy from drink and sleeplessness and anxiety, her kewpie-doll face slightly bloated, all those cute curves rounding into fleshiness. She didn't want her fans to see her this way. She was afraid of the reporters and the photographers who would hound her on her way into and out of the courtroom. And finally, she was still somewhat ambivalent toward her pal Daisy. She was convinced that Rex, who had replaced Daisy as manager of the exchequer and housemate, had been in the right and Daisy shockingly in the wrong. But Clara had given her unquestioning heart to Daisy DeVoe and she dreaded having to stand up and accuse her in court.

The migrant workers were starving in southern California and the soup kitchens in Los Angeles were doing a better business than the movie palaces, but Clara's appearance in our local court still drew thousands of curiosity seekers. The It Girl who had been the personification of the super-flapper was now subdued and withdrawn. At times she burst into tears in the courtroom as Daisy tried to fling the charges back in Clara's pretty little teeth. Daisy said she had had to write all the checks because most of the time Clara was too drunk to know what she was doing. Although it was irrelevant, she exposed Clara's exorbitant gifts to various boyfriends, from college football players to aging directors. At times the judge would have to admonish Daisy and her defense attorney: Remember, it is Daisy DeVoe who is on trial here, not Clara Bow.

But that was only for the record. In the minds of the tabloid readers and the scandalmongers it was the peccadilloes of Clara Bow that turned the trial into a drama more irresistible than *It* or *Dancing Mothers.* Clara and Daisy pointed fingers and traded tears, cries of outrage, reproachful silence, and choked-up press conferences.

When the circus was over, Daisy was convicted on only one count,

although in the opinion of the judge there was evidence to convict her on all thirty-seven. A shaken Clara appealed to the judge to be merciful in his sentencing. But he gave Daisy DeVoe eighteen months.

Although the judge had done his best to exonerate Clara, her penalties were heavier. Daisy helped to defray her defense expenses by selling a series on Clara's bedroom activities to the yellow press. It was peddled in book form as *Clara's Secret Love Life*. Clara was scheduled to start a new picture, but in an emotional session with my father she told him her nerves were shattered and she wasn't sure she could ever work again. She withdrew to a sanitarium and he signed a sexy young Irish girl, Peggy Shannon, to replace her.

Clara's contract still had several years to run, but it was canceled by mutual agreement. She was rescued from still another breakdown by Rex Bell, who married her and took her to his ranch in Nevada. It would be nice to think that they lived happily ever after. But this was no movie. Though they lived on a ranch that in Rex Bell's Midas hands grew to 350,000 acres, Clara had a weight problem, a drinking problem, a sleeping problem, and, most of all, the problem of being out of a job as the Number One Sex Goddess of the World. Washed up at 26, Clara Bow had staggered into the winter of her discontent in what should have been the summer of her youth.

It was more than half a dozen years before I saw Clara again. By that time, I was out of college and living with my father in one of those white-stucco neo-Spanish mansions in Beverly Hills. B.P. told me that Clara had just been released from a local sanitarium and had phoned to say she would like to drop in. When she arrived I saw a roly-poly woman who looked to be in her forties, although her actual age at the time was only 32. Instead of the bangs and spit curls that had given her the look of a windswept hoyden, her hair was set in a reddish-brown permanent wave. A layer of fat imprisoned the once-perfect oval face that fan magazines liked to call heart-shaped. But neither jowls nor bulges at the hips could take away from the dancing brown eyes of Clara Bow, still accentuated by their dark frame of mascara, still punctuated by eyebrows drawn with an eye for symmetry.

Father asked his butler Lloyd to bring champagne. Lloyd popped the cork and poured Moët-Chandon into three fine glasses. Clara raised the glass to her lips and peeked over the rim of it at my father with those same flashing and flirty eyes I had first seen when she was twenty and I

was ten. "Well, B.P., here we are!" she said. Behind the excess flesh, the childlike face was still there begging to be loved. I thought of the day I had sat with her in her red roadster in Pomona, with the smitten young Gilbert Roland hovering nearby. "Let's drink to all the good times we had," Clara said. "And to you, Clara dear," my father said gallantly.

Clara finished her wine, and as Lloyd refilled her glass, she looked vivacious and merry-eyed. I felt a little uncomfortable because even after all the years and all the changes they had both gone through she was being outrageously flirtatious with my father. He was only in his mid-forties at the time, but I in my intolerant early twenties felt he was far too advanced in years for these silly games.

"You know, your father and I were always very good friends," Clara said, turning those big brown saucer-eyes on me, and it was almost as if she was picking up the dialogue left over from our tête-à-tête in the roadster.

"And we still are, Clara," my father said.

"Yes, of course we still are," Clara parroted. "And we always will be—to the end of our lives." And she raised her glass to toast the promise.

"To my favorite producer," Clara said.

"And my favorite star."

"Now Ben, you're going to make me cry," Clara said. And a tiny tear slid down her round, rouged cheek. In the background I could hear the ghosts of the mood trio who used to play on her silent set: "Rock-a-bye, Baby . . . "

I felt it was their moment. And as it turned out it was, so far as I know, the last time they ever saw each other. When I rose and went over to shake her hand, she pulled me to her and kissed me on the lips. "I c'n hardly b'lieve yer so grown-up," she said, with that same Brooklyn accent. "I guess I'll always think of ya as that shy little kid who stammered so bad ya c'd hardly talk t' me. If I hadn't been in love with ya poppa, I betcha I'd've fallen in love with yuh."

I left them alone in that enormous cavern of a living room. Two of the great names of the Hollywood Twenties were like Hansel and Gretel lost in the backwoods of Beverly Hills. From the two-storied hallway, I could hear them laughing together over their champagne at some private joke from long ago.

After that farewell visit with my father, Clara Bow lived her life as a ghost of Hollywood Past, either as a prosperous rancher's wife near

Searchlight, Nevada (where the one-time actor had become a political power in the state), or in sanitariums, to which her condition increasingly restricted her. Another decade was to pass before her old friends heard of her again. In 1947 she surfaced momentarily as "Miss Hush," the mystery voice in an NBC radio contest. She murmured a mysterious jingle:

> "Two o'clock and all's well.
> Who it is I cannot tell.
> Queen has her king, it's true,
> But not her ribbons tied in blue."

Listeners phoned in to nominate the Duchess of Windsor, Alice Marble, Shirley Temple, Margaret Truman. . . . But a resourceful Midwestern housewife deciphered the hushed code: In nautical time two o'clock was four bells, and there were Clara and Rex Bell and their two sons. The anonymous *Who it is* struck echoes of the old It. *Her king* was Rex, of course. And the *ribbons tied in blue* would make a bow: a Clara Bow. For this flash of perception, the winner earned an airplane, a refrigerator, a new car, a furnace, a fur coat, and maid's service for a year. All Clara won was a few days' return to notoriety. The double prongs of the irony pressed sharply on those who had cared for her. Clara had been chosen as the target for this contest because she was so totally unknown to the new generation that was coming in as her fame was flickering out. And when she came back for her moment in the spotlight, it was through the microphone that had driven her into retirement. Instead of being seen and not heard, as in her glory years, now she was heard but unseen.

As the years rolled on, Clara became unable to speak coherently or even to recognize old friends. Every Christmas she wrote to Louella Parsons, whose column was still a king-maker and a queen-breaker in the fickle fiefdom of Hollywood. "Do you still remember me?" a shaky scrawl begged. There was another brief surfacing in 1960 when Clara wrote to Louella's rival columnist, Hedda Hopper: "I slip my old crown of It Girl not to Taylor or Bardot but to Monroe."

Unlike Marilyn, Clara Bow lingered on in living death until she was a completely forgotten sixty-year-old recluse. Her final years were spent in a small apartment in West Los Angeles, watching television. Her favorite shows were the Late-Lates. She needed lots of sleeping pills to overcome the insomnia that had set in in the days of her mike fright and the ordeal of Daisy DeVoe. Early one morning, her live-in nurse discovered, she would be able to sleep forever. Ten years of worldwide fame had been sandwiched between almost twenty years of penniless obscurity and thirty years of has-been obscurity. But for one last day little gum-chewing, g-dropping Clara was back on the front page, and not merely of the racy Los Angeles *Examiner,* but of the august *New York Times*:

CLARA BOW, THE 'IT' GIRL, DIES AT 60;
FILM ACTRESS SET VOGUE IN 1920'S.

When I stared at that story in the *Times* I thought of the vibrant Clara I had known in my youth. And although I had never met her, I thought also of Zelda Fitzgerald, who was *the* flapper of the literate international set during the same riotous period over which Clara Bow had presided. They were like opposite sides of the same shiny coin—let's call it Zelda for heads and Clara for tails—and when the coin fell dead on the dance floor both sides came up losers.

III

THE PROMISED LAND

18

WHILE L. B. MAYER was beginning to build the power base at MGM from which he would rule for the next twenty years, my father was drafted to take over as vice-president in charge of production at Paramount-Famous Players-Lasky—MGM's chief rival. Ever the cool, unexcitable pragmatist, Adolph Zukor had come to Hollywood on one of his periodic trips and decided that his West Coast studio needed reorganizing if it were to compete with the executive ability of L.B., the creative talent of Irving Thalberg, and the bread-and-butter theatrical know-how of Harry Rapf.

For Zukor, now in his early fifties, and the young writer and publicist he had considered his protegé, it was a dramatic meeting. The two men had not talked in seven years. "Well, Adolph, you sent for me." B.P. was reminding his old boss of his youthful boast that this was the only way Zukor could ever hope to get him back.

"Yes, I remember our last talk," Zukor said quietly. "But what's a little pride between friends? I've been keeping my eye on you. You've made good pictures on sensible budgets. I can see you've got an eye for talent. And *The Virginian* proves to me that you can make a big Western and not just those Clara Bow wild-party movies."

"The flapper pictures gave us the money to make *The Virginian*," my father countered.

"I don't believe in grudges," Zukor went on. "A big waste of emotion. We're still the number-one studio, but we've been slipping a little. And the Mayer-Thalberg combination, with the Loew's theaters behind

187

them, is getting stronger every day. Jesse is still my partner, there's never been a bad word between us in all these years. He's a wonderful man, but he's almost too nice. He would never hurt anybody. He's a gentleman. But as a result, I feel some of those people in our studio are taking advantage of him. We've got a lot of pigheaded stars and directors in the studio who think they can run everything to suit themselves. But we have to make fifty-five to sixty pictures a year. That needs organization and a strong hand. Jesse likes the idea of your coming back. There won't be any friction. He'll back you all the way."

They settled on financial terms that brought an overnight change to the Schulberg economy. And B.P. was allowed to bring his Preferred Pictures staff with him, including his favorite writers Buddy Leighton and Hope Loring, scenarist Eve Unsell, and the rest of the team.

So the Mayer-Schulberg era had come to an end, and with it the downtown Los Angeles studios, for the Famous-Lasky studio was truly in Hollywood, still at the site of the original Lasky-DeMille barn. Our family moved closer to the studio, across Western Avenue to a quiet street lined with palm trees, Lorraine Boulevard, in an exclusive neighborhood called Windsor Square. On Lorraine the houses were not the typical one-story wooden bungalows we had found on Gramercy Place. Lorraine was lined with spacious two-story homes that had a look of permanence.

Five-hundred-and-twenty-five Lorraine Boulevard was to be home to the Schulbergs from the middle of the booming Twenties to the depressed mid-Thirties. There were bedrooms for my parents, myself, my sister Sonya, my brother Stuart, my mother's brother Sam Jaffe (who had followed us out from New York and, true to the mores of the day, had become B.P.'s studio manager, first at Preferred, then at Paramount), plus maids' rooms for the nurse Wilma, the downstairs maid Paula, and the cook. There was also an apartment over the garage for the English chauffeur, James, who doubled as a butler for the lavish dinner parties Mother liked to give.

We felt we were living in a palace. On the main floor there was a large, ornate dining room and a sunken living room. French doors opened on a large sunroom with a cozy window seat. My mother had that sunroom extended by a dozen feet and turned it into a library of several thousand volumes, including the rare editions that both my parents had begun collecting. On the wall was an enlargement of the family bookplate featuring a poem that became the Schulberg anthem:

THOU FOOL, TO SEEK COMPANIONS IN A CROWD!
INTO THY ROOM AND THERE UPON THY KNEES,
BEFORE THY BOOKSHELVES, HUMBLY THANK THY GOD
THAT THOU HAST FRIENDS LIKE THESE!

We all caught the reading habit—but I suspect that if we hadn't caught it, it would have been drilled into us by Ad's method: She had now raised the ante to fifty cents a book to read the classics. Hardly what one would call "progressive education." It's been said that anything you are forced or bribed to do, like reading Tennyson or Shakespeare before you're ready, will leave you with a lifelong resistance to it. But Mother's system seemed to work. I began to love sitting in that library or taking a book up to my bedroom, and I learned to appreciate the simpler tales of Tolstoy, and of Melville and Dickens, when most children my age were more at home with the Bobbsey Twins and Tom Swift.

On Sundays before the elaborate midday dinner there was a family ritual that outsiders would never associate with the habits of Hollywood tycoons. Father might have been up until dawn the night before, trying to lick a particularly stubborn script with the writers, gambling away his weekly salary at the Clover Club, or carousing with his cronies. But no matter how glassy-eyed, exhausted, or hung over he might be, come Sunday morning he would preside in his monogrammed silk bathrobe over the family reading circle in the library. Grouped around him, we listened hour after hour as he read through Melville's *Omoo* and *Typee* and on to *Moby Dick*; through *David Copperfield* and *The Old Curiosity Shop*; through choice sections of *The Forsyte Saga,* and the classic Russians—Lord, how did he find time to read and we to listen to those torrents of precious words?

Father read those novels well, forgetting to stammer as he became involved in their plots and their characters, and we could close our eyes and see the scenes he was describing. Since B.P., perhaps inheriting his father's lack of Hebrew piety, never bothered with the services at Rabbi Magnin's Temple B'nai B'rith in downtown Los Angeles, and since Ad was also a liberated spirit who attended only on High Holy Days, these Sunday literary sessions were the closest we second-generation Latvian Jews came to any sort of spiritual observance.

Our family life had a split personality. Father was working furiously at the studio, working hard and well in those days. And I was fascinated with our other home—the great sets, the ancient castles, ocean liner, and Western streets. I loved to walk into the dark stages and watch the actors go through their scenes. It was fun to sit in the projection room with Father watching the rushes, or to travel with him in style to a sneak preview.

I grew up on the sidewalk conferences outside the theater that followed the previews of pictures still in the process of final editing. My father, his director, film editor, and various assistants would pass around the preview cards on which the audience had written their capsule critiques—which varied from "God bless you for making this beautiful movie!" to "Burn it—it *stinks!*"

Members of the curbstone conference would come up with flash ideas for countering unfavorable reactions: suggestions for speeding up one sequence or slowing down another, sometimes for throwing out an entire scene that seemed to stop the flow, sometimes for adding a series of intercuts without which the rhythm seemed static. Making movies for the largest possible world audience and still trying to make them well was a complicated business. At first I would look up into the thoughtful, worried face of my father and his aides without fully comprehending what they were saying. Later, as I grew up to their shoulders, I would listen more carefully, realizing that a picture could be made or destroyed in reediting and reshooting. The day would come when I would be old enough to find myself stammering out an opinion of my own.

There were no film schools in those days. But those sidewalk postmortems offered thorough lessons in practical filmmaking. Crucial decisions were made there at the curb, as the impromptu conference became an hour-long reexamination of the picture practically frame by frame. Happy endings replaced unhappies that had left the audience dissatisfied. Actors would be recalled for retakes of a scene that clearly wasn't working. Sometimes a director begged for a chance to supervise the reediting along the lines he had originally envisioned.

Sometimes of course the comments were good, and the curbstone conference became a celebration. But if half the audience had walked out, the conference became a wake, and there were angry accusations, anxious passing of the buck, and threats of resignation on the part of hotheaded directors. Most of the time the curbstone conference was a time neither for laughing nor back stabbing but simply for hard work and detailed analysis before those ten thousand precious feet of film went back to the cutting room.

Ad had brought her parents, Max and Hannah, to this bright new world of sunshine, and B.P. bought a tidy Hollywood bungalow for them. But Grandpa Max never had time to enjoy the fragrance of the citrus blossoms. He was always praying, or so it seemed to this bewildered grandchild who would stare at him across the wide, deep gulf of two generations. With the black *yarmulke* on his head, the silk *tallis* around his shoulders, the leather *tfillim* on his forearms, he would bow to the East, intoning what seemed to me an endless prayer. He would rock back and forth as he chanted in Hebrew to his demanding God. In one of our early visits to that pious bungalow I tried to interrupt him: "What are you d-doing, Gr-Grandpa?" He ignored me and went on *davening* while Grandma gently wagged her finger at me and coaxed me back to the dining-room table.

Grandfather's friends were the fathers of the other studio heads: Old Man Mayer, Old Man Warner, Old Man Cohn, and so on, all of them from the same Old World mold, all of them aged anachronisms in their dark suits and long beards, with Yiddish as their daily speech and Hebrew for their daily prayers. All of them mystified that from their loins had sprung such unlikely offsprings as a loud, wisecracking, sports-jacketed Jack Warner; a profane, irreverent, mob-oriented strongman like Harry Cohn; or a crafty, ambitious powerbroker like Louie Mayer. . . . Somehow the seed of the Old World had produced these brash, amoral, on-the-make Americans. The sons with their bankrolls and their girlfriends and their *fuck-you*'s would tolerate and humor these old men as relics of the past.

The first thing the old beards wanted in this new bungalow city baking in the sun was a *shul* where they would feel at home. (Indeed, my paternal grandmother was so attached to her *shul* in New York, directly across the narrow, teeming street from her crowded tenement flat, that she had refused to make the cross-country trek with the Jaffes and the Mayers.) In Hollywood the old men suffered culture shock: The unctuous Rabbi Magnin did not preside over a synagogue but over a Reform Temple that, like the *goyim*'s, included a Sunday school taught in English to cater to the sons and daughters of the new movie money. Temple B'nai B'rith was grand enough, modern enough, unorthodox enough to repel Grandpa, Old Man Mayer, and the rest of their bearded cronies.

So the old men got together and held a council of religious war. They wanted a real *shul* like the ones they had left behind in their cozy Eastern ghettos. For ninety dollars a month they rented a Hollywood bungalow and set about transforming the interior into something as close as they could make it to the genuine synagogue they missed. Anxious to keep the old men happy, their powerful sons sent studio carpenters and painters to bring about the transformation. The results were astonishing. From the outside, Grandpa's *shul* looked like any other little white bungalow on the street, complete with small green lawn and the obligatory miniature orange or lemon tree. But once you stepped inside you found yourself walking into an old world steeped in Jewish tradition, where Grandpa Max, and Old Man Mayer and Old Man Warner (those seemed to be their official names) and the rest of the immigrant Talmudists, finally felt at home. They sent to New York for a *real* rabbi, a little Moses who would see to it that the Laws of the Torah were upheld and the Sabbath observed as Jehovah had intended. When the rabbi arrived, a young man whose features were appropriately hidden by a bushy black beard, Grandpa and his Orthodox pals were driven down to the Santa Fe station in studio limousines as the reception committee. At last Hollywood had its own *shul* with its own rabbi who would walk to the services on the Sabbath, and who would not touch money or otherwise profane that holy day.

I remember attending the first Friday night service with my mother, to oblige Grandpa. The bungalow was now one room large enough to accommodate a congregation of perhaps a hundred. Grandpa seemed content as he swayed back and forth and repeated his Hebrew prayers. I remember the mysterious singsong chorus as the bearded fathers of the clean-shaven, worldly studio moguls demonstrated to their children and their grandchildren how to worship the relentless Lord of their universe.

Years later when Grandpa lay dying in a hospital, he prepared himself for the journey by praying, louder than I had ever heard him pray in his little Hollywood *shul*. For two days, hour after hour, he sang his Old Testament praises to his God in that mournful language I would never learn and never understand. There were no personal goodbyes or personal remembrances. He had never been close to his wife Hannah, my withered grandma, who had endured her life with a nagging sense of having married beneath her. But Grandpa Max seemed to have a direct line to Jehovah Himself. When he stopped praying at the top of his voice we knew he was dead.

While the old beards worshipped in their Hollywood *shul* and their sons worshipped at the altar of the box office, at 525 Lorraine our altar was the almighty typewriter. Sonya was to say that in the Schulberg home a typewriter held a central position corresponding to that of a piano in a less word-oriented family. It was difficult to pass it without sitting down to try out a few chords or to pick out an original little melody. With all that literature stuffed into our minds at Father's Sunday reading sessions, we Schulberg kids found the family typewriter irresistible. As a result of this literary doodling, all three of us would eventually publish works of fiction. In the Schulberg household, in the beginning was the word.

Along with the chicken pox, German measles, and scarlet fever, I came down with another childhood affliction—poetry. I no longer recall the exact moment of infection when I first began to crawl as far back as I could under the piano, to put my thoughts into rhyme. As the self-appointed, mother-encouraged poet laureate of Lorraine Boulevard, I composed couplets appropriate to various holidays. For Mother's Day I withdrew into the darkest corner under the Steinway for longer than usual: I wanted to make this my masterpiece. When I had finished it, for the third time, I waited for Mother to come home from her antique-hunting expedition in Pasadena. When I heard her drive up in her Marmon I ran to the door, my hand atremble with its sheet of literature.

"M-Mom, I just wr-wrote a p-poem!"

"Wonderful, Buddy. I'd love to read it!"

I followed my mother into the library, where she sat in one of the wing chairs and placed my poem on the circular Queen Anne table while she paused to light a cigarette. I was ashamed of her smoking because somewhere I had heard that it was not a ladylike thing to do. But that day, eager as is every writer for a first reaction to his work, I ignored Mother's Camel cigarette and kept my eyes focused on her face as she read my dozen lines, artistically divided into half a dozen couplets.

When she finished reading it, real tears, not the glycerine ones I had seen at the studio, were rolling down her smooth, pink cheeks.

"Buddy, did you really write this?"

Shyly, I admitted that I had.

"Why, I think it's beautiful! It's—a work of genius. It deserves to be published."

I glowed.

"What time will Father be home?" I asked. He had told me about having been a writer before he began making movies and running studios. I knew how much he admired writing. The only people he seemed to like having at the house were writers. Maybe when I grew up I could get to be a writer like Dad.

Mom said she thought he'd be home around seven. I spent the rest of the afternoon preparing my poem for his arrival. First I typed it out on Father's big typewriter: By going very cautiously with two fingers I finally had it on paper without a single typo. I thought it looked a little naked, so I got out my crayons and drew a gracefully waving border around it in yellow, green, and red. The frame of three colors was exactly what it needed.

At seven o'clock I placed it on my father's plate at the head of the long dining-room table. I sat at one side, Sonya on the other. The human butterball we called Baby Stuart was still up in his nursery with Wilma. At seven-fifteen Father had not arrived. I went to his plate at the head of the table and repositioned the poem at a more advantageous angle. The grandfather clock in the hall struck half-past seven. We would have to start without Father, Mother decided. I sat down and started spooning the thick pea soup, but the suspense was awful.

Although it had been nice to hear from my mother that I was a genius, I was eager for confirmation of that status from the man I'd heard proclaimed the top story mind in The Industry. I had seen how people depended on his opinions at those post-preview curbstone conferences, after the rushes in the projection room, or at the story conferences that were sometimes held in our library.

"Yes, B.P.!" "Great idea, B.P.!" "Glad you like it, B.P.!" "I think you've licked it, B.P.!" Everybody at the studio from the secretaries to the stars kept telling me how lucky I was to have such a brilliant and important father. "He's got a mind like a razor," a writer said after a heated story conference. "Cuts straight through to the heart of the problem." "He knows what he wants and never passes the buck," another said. "He doesn't shilly-shally around waiting for other people to make up his mind. He listens, carefully, and then makes his decision. And when he makes it he sticks to it, he backs up his judgment. That's unusual out here."

We had reached the dessert course, my favorite chocolate soufflé, but I could only pick at it in my anxiety. What if Father wasn't coming home at all? There could be an unexpected studio crisis: a star sick, an important picture couldn't start on schedule? Or maybe a star was feuding with her director and threatening not to report for work unless he was taken off the picture? Or what if a top writer had gone off the wagon and could not be found, his screenplay only half-completed? At the studio, crisis was an everyday occurrence.

At eight o'clock we were ready to leave the dining room. Soon I would have to go upstairs and start my homework. A few minutes after eight we heard Dad's car pulling in. Father never came home quietly. He would burst in, crying down terrible oaths on the heads of his stars, directors, the "New York office"—a Hollywood version of *Life with Father*. But his special wrath always seemed directed at the stars.

Maybe that was why I was never able to think of movie stars as the glamorous gods and goddesses worshipped in those great cathedrals, and glorified in the fan magazines. *Modern Screen, Screen Romance,* and *Photoplay* outsold all the other magazines put together. After all, they reported what time Gloria Swanson liked to get up in the morning, what her favorite breakfast foods were, what kind of bed she liked to sleep in, and of course with whom. And dealt with the burning question of whether or not Greta Garbo was truly in love with Jack Gilbert. In England the common people felt a need for a royal family with whom to identify. It seemed no accident that we called our stars of the silent screen queens and kings.

But not in the Schulberg household. Father may have sold the public on the concept of Little Mary as the perennial fifteen-year-old "America's Sweetheart," but he knew—and told us about—the tough little mind hidden beneath those golden curls, and behind all the golden smiles of the stars with whom he labored. To him, movie stars never had just two names like *Pola Negri*. Father would come bursting in shouting, "Oh-that-goddamn-bitch-how-I'd-like-to-wring-her-goddamn-neck-that-double-crossing-Pola-Negri!" I became so accustomed to hearing them addressed that way that I accepted the string of epithets as part of their names. It seemed as if all the stars in the studio, or nearly all, were engaged in a great conspiracy to try my father's patience.

But this night his mood seemed even more thunderous than usual. One of his many chores was to bring the unruly stars of the studio into line so that pictures could be put into production in an orderly manner. The only way to turn out fifty to sixty pictures a year was to start a new one every Monday. The pressures of the major-studio "dream factory" were killing. At Paramount, Father was trying to do single-handed what

195

Irving Thalberg and Harry Rapf were doing together at MGM: make a dozen to fifteen quality pictures (Thalberg) and the rest "programmers" (Rapf). The major stars were no longer permitted to choose their own stories, their directors, and their casts as they had done in the more easygoing days under Jesse Lasky. Although Lasky was now Father's official superior, he kept his promise to give him a free hand, and served as a buffer between Paramount's West Coast studio and B. P.'s rival, Walter Wanger, who was in charge of the East Coast operation. The Negris and the Swansons fought back with a vengeance, throwing the temper tantrums for which they were notorious.

This night Father came in red-faced and shouting, "God damn that stupid stubborn bitch of all bitches Pola Negri she's done it again!" As he poured out his tale of woe he made a stiff scotch-and-soda and paced around the dining-room table working off steam. It seemed that the stupid stubborn little bitch had got it into her goddamn stubborn head that she couldn't play the last scene. "So the whole company has to stand there at one thousand dollars a minute while this arrogant little bitch— who's lucky she isn't working in a sausage factory in Pinsk—locks herself in her dressing room. Now I have to drive out to Beverly and vamp her into coming back on Monday. And if she gives me any back talk I may just strangle her instead and finish the damn picture with her stand-in doing the scenes with her back to the goddamn camera. That goddamn Pola Negri thinks her picture is the only one we're making at the studio. God damn it, I could strangle her in cold blood without the slightest sense of guilt. Pola Negri thinks she's even bigger than Swanson and all she is is a pigheaded little whore!"

My father refilled his highball glass and resumed his pacing. I held my breath and waited for the storm to blow over. Why were those movie stars always trying to torture my poor father?

"Ben, why don't you sit down and start your soup? After dinner you can call Pola and try to work it out."

"I'm not ready to sit down! For Christ' sake, Ad, I just got home—give me a couple of minutes to wind down. This is the first moment's peace I've had all day. Sometimes I wish I were back on Mission Road, making one picture at a time."

"You used to yell about Katherine MacDonald then just as much as you yell about Pola Negri now," Mother reminded him.

"Katherine MacDonald was a lamb compared to this temperamental little bitch!" Father insisted.

Maybe my poem will cheer him up, I was thinking; maybe I should get up the courage to lift it from his plate and hand it to him.

Father seemed to have heard my thought because just then he glanced down at his plate and noticed the white page with my poem neatly centered in its rainbow frame.

"What the hell is this?"

"Ben, Buddy has been waiting for you for hours. A wonderful thing has happened. Buddy has written a beautiful poem. It's so—well, it's absolutely amaz—"

"Ad, if you don't mind, don't tell me what I should think of it. Let me decide that for myself."

I kept my face lowered to my plate. It could not have taken long to read that poem. It was only twelve lines. But it seemed an eternity. I was afraid to look up to see if it was bringing tears to his eyes as it had to Mother's. It was so quiet that I could hear the ice tinkling in Father's glass as he held it in one hand and my poem in the other. Then I heard him dropping the poem back on his plate again. I could not bear to look up for the verdict but in a moment I was to hear it:

"I think it's lousy."

I bent my head a little closer to my plate and tried to keep the tears inside my head.

"Ben, sometimes I don't understand you," Mother said. "This is just a little boy. You're not in your studio now. You should be pleased that he's starting to write poetry so young. What he needs is encouragement."

"I don't know why," Father held his ground. "Is there any law that says Buddy has to become a poet? Isn't there enough lousy poetry in the world already?"

I don't remember exactly how Mother fielded that one. I do remember that her voice rose and that she started saying very critical things about my father.

All through my life I have found that I remember the negatives much more clearly than the positives. A barbed line from a critical notice burrows into my skin like a chigger while an entire page of unstinted praise fades to half-forgotten generalities. And so I remember clearly my father's voice rising to meet the pitch of Mother's as he made this self-defense:

"Look, I'm paying my best writers fifteen hundred dollars a week. I've just come from a long story conference where I've been tearing their scripts apart and telling them their stuff is lousy. I only pay Buddy fifty cents a week. And you're trying to tell me I don't have a right to tear his stuff apart if I think it's lousy!"

The repetition of that hard word hit me over the heart like the fist of a Benny Leonard. I ran out of the dining room. Upstairs in my bedroom I threw myself on the bed and sobbed into my pillow. When the worst of the disappointment was drained out of me I could hear my parents still quarreling loudly across the dinner table about my beautiful/lousy poem.

Many months later when I took a second look at that controversial poem, I had to agree with my father. It was a pretty lousy poem. Maybe it was time to turn my efforts to fiction. I wrote a short story called "Ugly," influenced by Lon Chaney in *The Hunchback of Notre Dame* and *The Phantom of the Opera*. A young man is so hideous that he's ashamed to be seen in public. He travels from village to village at night and hides in the haylofts of barns so that no one will see him. In one village just before Lent, he finds a masked ball about to take place in the square. He fashions an attractive mask for himself, joins in the festivities, and enjoys the company of a woman for the first time. But when the time comes to remove the mask he runs away. In what I fancied to be the dark, Russian manner, I ended my story with the poor wretch hiding under the hay in a loft again.

When I worked up the courage to expose "Ugly" to my father, he said it was overwritten but far from hopeless. He thought I should rewrite it and simplify the prose. I was learning to rewrite. And my mother was learning that she could criticize my work without crushing me. We were all learning. I was going on thirteen, and still having a hard and unhappy time in school, learning more at home and at the studio than through any formal classes.

When I was only a few years older I stumbled into further insight one day when Sonya and I climbed up into the attic for a rainy-day exploration. Sonya did the familiar little-girl thing of flouncing around in Mother's high-heeled shoes and discarded hats. I was looking through the old magazines and papers that my father had saved. Suddenly I saw "The Man from the North," the famous (at least in our family) short story by Townsend Harris High School student Benjamin P. Schulberg that had won him the incredible prize of one hundred dollars for the best story by a New York City schoolboy. Over the years, "The Man from the North" had accumulated major literary virtue. Whenever Mother, relentlessly driving us onward and upward, wanted to invoke the family literary heritage, she would remind us that Father was not only a pioneer photoplay writer but the author of "The Man from the North." His story took on the immortality of Pushkin's "The Overcoat" or De Maupassant's "A Piece of String."

So I approached the opening line with awe. But on the second line I burst out laughing. The story was about a man lost in the frozen North, a man a New York East Side kid could never have known. The prose was Jack London in the depths of his purple. The third line, a string of adjectives, struck me as funnier than the second. By this time Sonya was at my side, wanting to know what was so funny. I started to read her the opening paragraph. She was a secret poet who never showed anything to Father because they were barely on speaking terms. Already, she knew wordiness when she heard it. We not only laughed, we became hysterical. Our legs crumpled. We rolled on the attic floor, our chests hurting. We'd try to comment on the story and go into another convulsion. We were in danger of writing our own obituaries: "Cause of death—'The Man from the North.'"

At that moment the attic door opened and Mother appeared. Our laughter had carried all the way through the large house. What had we found up here that could be that funny?

"We found D-Dad's st-st-st . . ." That was always an extremely difficult sound to make and this time, impossible. I simply handed her the manuscript.

She stared at it.

Suddenly Sonya and I had stopped laughing. We watched her, now defensively.

"*This* is what you were laughing about?"

We looked at each other and went off into another paroxysm, then stopped. Mother didn't think it was funny.

"Remember your father was only a highschool student. And after all, styles change. That was almost twenty years ago."

So Father had a beautiful/lousy literary work of his own. We nodded dutifully, but we still thought it was funny. All our lives the mere mention of the title would trigger laughter.

19

A PERSONAGE IN the eyes of my mother, catered to by Father's studio employees (including those "stupid" movie stars), made to feel important in my front-row seat at the Friday-night fights, I still suffered the miseries of a misfit at the Wilton Place Grammar School. The bullies wrestled me to the dirt of the schoolyard, threatened to beat me up, and imitated my stammering. I can still smell their clothing—a smell compounded of dirt and sweat and anti-*movie* hostility. Often I would try to avoid the yard and sneak out the front entrance of the school, longing to make it home to the security of the big house on Lorraine. Almost as often, the little cossacks of Wilton Place would scent their quarry and chase me down the block. I learned to run very fast. I didn't know it but I was already in training for the highschool runner and tennis player I would become a few years later. Often I would make it safely inside the protective door of 525 Lorraine before giving in to tears, too upset to write poetry or to play in the backyard with its swings and rings and basketball net.

But there was a punching bag on the back porch outside my bedroom. Given my mother's proclivities, it had been set up there more in the interest of child psychology than of physical culture. I was encouraged to work off my aggressions, frustrations, and hostilities by punching away at the light bag. Whether or not it was sound psychological theory I have no idea. But I became quite proficient on the light bag and have carried one with me through half a dozen different lives in Hollywood, on a Pennsylvania farm, a West Florida beach, a Beverly hill, and a Long

201

Island retreat. Working out my angers on the punching bag with a "Take this, Duke Wayne!", "And this, Dick Nixon!", and "Right in the middle of your two faces, Sam Spiegel!", it may be that I overdeveloped my capacity for absorbing emotional blows without striking back, for turning the other cheek until my head was spinning, turning instead to my punching bag with the ferocity of a Dempsey.

Although my mother was to add to her "credits" by cofounding our town's first progressive school, none of those John Dewey-like experiments were tried on me. I was flipped from the frying pan of public school into the fire of the Urban Military Academy. This was an elite concentration camp on Melrose, not far from Paramount Studio, where Major Urban, supposedly a hero of World War I, dressed us up as miniature West Point cadets and marched us up and down the parade grounds every afternoon. There is a picture of me in my smart grey uniform, complete with puttees and Sam Browne belt, my cape thrown grandly over my shoulder to display its crimson lining. But I didn't feel all that grand.

True, I wasn't chased and ridiculed for my stammering or my high position as a Hollywood prince: The Urban cadets came from well-to-do families and were much better mannered than the poorer kids in the public school. And of course the strict military discipline imposed a rigid standard of behavior in which public fighting and humiliation were sternly punished. So the cadets were civil with me, and some were even friendly because they wanted me to show them through the studio. I had the power to enter the studio, past the imposing reception booth or through the big iron gate, whenever I wanted to and with whomever I wished. Since almost everybody wanted to meet the movie stars and see movies being made, I seemed rather popular. But I came early to the feeling that it was the producer's son they were buttering up, not the stammering cadet.

I have no memories of any educational activities at Urban. What calls to me are the staccato military commands: "Fall in!" "By the right flank—march!" "Company—halt!" Those orders seemed easy to follow for everybody but me. I proved to be an incurable non-marcher. I was forever "falling in" a few seconds too late. And marching along, my mind would wander to other things—maybe the lyrics I was working on, as I added songwriting to my other accomplishments—and I would fail to hear the command and would step on the heels of the cadet directly in front of me. The drill instructor would shout "Company halt! That includes you, *Schulberg!*" When I had drained his patience he put me to the rear of the rear squad, where I comprised a squad of my own, inevitably marching out of step but no longer interfering with the rhythm and obedience of my fellow-marchers.

While I brought up the inglorious rear, our company was led by a dashing fellow on horseback, whose father was not only Mayor of Beverly Hills but probably the most famous man in America, Will Rogers. While Will, Jr., was high man on the Urban totem pole, and I the lowest, he never chewed me out like the other student officers. Junior was the sort of genial, easy-going, thoughtful fellow his old man pretended to be. Will, Jr., was a heroic figure, and I was the Good Soldier Schweik of Major Urban's Military Academy. My punishment for inept marching, below and behind the call of duty, was to have to report to Urban on Saturday mornings and march for an hour by myself.

When finally I was able to convince my parents that Urban had nothing to offer me in the way of education, a cure for my stammer, or military demeanor, I was allowed to shed my uniform and return to civilian life.

Parental love at 525 Lorraine was expressed not in terms of physical touching—embraces and kisses—but in educational and artistic prodding. Perhaps influenced by Grandpa, an austere man, and Grandma, withdrawn in unhappiness, Mother was physically undemonstrative. Cultural achievement was stressed over personal happiness. I have read somewhere that "passion for learning is for the Jews one of the ways to God." Consciously and determinedly, Mother had struggled upward and outward from the ghetto. She never forgot the teaching of one of the early leaders of immigrant Jewry, Abraham Cahan of the *Jewish Daily Forward:* "You must try to be an intellectual."

There were no pushcarts on Lorraine Boulevard, no synagogues, no frayed laundry hung out from tenement window to window. The great houses were set back from the street by spacious lawns. But the ghosts of Abe Cahan and the *Daily Forward* still breathed in our elegant Hollywood home, exhorting me to *write, learn, improve, achieve, make something of myself* that could be measured in something more valuable than money. To this day the Cahan-Ad Schulberg ethic clings to our shoulders like Grandpa's prayer shawl. If we do not write something every day we greet the darkness with an uneasy conscience. There is time off only for good behavior—if we have done enough to appease those Jewish gods or muses.

But to leave an impression of a driven child forever hiding under a piano composing poetry to please and appease his mother is to deal in half-truths. Another relationship was to dominate my youth, my friendship with Maurice Rapf. Maurice's father, as I have mentioned, was the first studio manager of Warner Brothers, then at a small lot on Sunset Boulevard. When Maurice's family bought a house on Lorraine, we began creating a busy and imaginative world of our own within the big-studio world around us.

In many ways we were conventional kids playing our games on the studio backlots or the Hollywood side streets. Instead of saying, "My pop c'n lick your pop," we literally used to say, "My father's studio c'n make better pictures than your father's." We would get into heated arguments as to which was the better movie, *The Vanishing American* with Richard Dix and Lois Wilson (mine), or *His Secretary* with Norma Shearer and Lew Cody (his). It wasn't easy to top the great *Big Parade* with Jack Gilbert and Renée Adorée (his), but I would put my best foot forward with Ralph Forbes, Neil Hamilton, Ronald Colman, and William Powell in *Beau Geste.* Maurice would say, "My father discovered Joan Crawford," and I'd say, "Well, my father discovered Clara Bow and she's even bigger than Joan Crawford." We compared comedy teams. He had Karl Dane and George K. Arthur. I had Wallace Beery and Raymond Hatton. We compared directors. I had Vic Fleming and he had King Vidor. I had Greg La Cava and he had Robert Z. Leonard.

We even compared bootblacks—the only blacks I remember on the lot in those backward days of the total flour face. I had Oscar and he had Kid Slickum. Oscar the Bootblack, as he was known to thousands of white employees on the Paramount lot, had his stand just outside the main studio gate. Part of his job was shining shoes and part was serving as a squealing, supposedly good-natured target for the passersby who would sneak up behind him and goose him outrageously. He knew the names of everybody on the lot and he'd chuckle, "Now, Mr. Sutherland" [Eddie, the comedy director]—or "Mr. Holt" [Jack, one of the stars]— "You stay 'way from me, heah? You stay 'way from me!" Sometimes they'd flip him a quarter or half a dollar just to hear his exaggerated squeals. Oscar probably earned more money every day than the average extra. And he presided over his stand rain or shine. I thought he was happy, when I was twelve. It was not until I grew into my teens that I began to think more about him and to wonder why he was the only Negro in that whole thriving studio.

In those days Windsor Square was still full of vacant lots, and the large lot on the corner of Sixth and Lorraine became a favorite playground, where Maurice and I built an elaborate underground clubhouse expertly camouflaged on the surface. Influenced by movies on the Great War— from *Shoulder Arms* to *The Big Parade*—we developed a labyrinth of hidden passageways. With Buddy Lesser, who lived around the corner and whose father Sol produced the Jackie Coogan movies, we were a little gang without a rival gang. If we were not toughened in street combat, at least we were active.

Our favorite indoor game was to take over the projection room that the Rapfs had built behind their house, invite our neighborhood friends, turn off the lights, and fight a battle royal in the dark. This was the way we celebrated all our birthdays. We would fight until we were exhausted, or until one of Maurice's parents decided we had had enough and came to turn on the lights. We were probably not nearly as physical as we thought, because with the exception of a young visitor's broken arm, I remember no serious injuries. But I do remember the surprise when a new boy came to the party, all dressed up and undoubtedly advised by his mother that he was attending a glamorous children's party at the home of an important Hollywood producer, only to be thrust into a blackout free-for-all in which his tie was yanked off, his party shirt torn, and his scruffed face pushed into the projection-room floor. Occasionally a novice would begin to cry, but most of the newcomers joined spiritedly in our battles of bloody noses and twisted elbows.

Our major obstacle to innocent laughter and bruises at the Rapf residence was Maurice's paternal grandmother. So unlike the meek, accepting ancients my grandmothers were, this fierce, proud, domineering lady from Colorado ruled the household with the absolutism of Catherine the Great. Harry Rapf's marriage to Tina—a small, very pretty woman— had been predicated on the understanding not only that Harry's mother would live with them but that she would be in charge. From the beginning it had seemed as if Tina had willingly abdicated. She lived the pampered life of a mogul's wife, enjoying her massages, her card games with the other "girls," and golf at the luxurious Hillcrest Country Club, formed by the new Jewish establishment in self-defense against the Los Angeles country clubs where Jews were blackballed—as they still are fifty years later.

Lord knows Grandma Rapf was a survivor. But it sometimes seemed that her son Harry's success as an important producer at MGM had gone to her head. She would yell at us for the slightest infraction. Her warning cry of "Moooor-eece!" would freeze us. Only a bathroom separated her room from Maurice's and if we played his radio too loudly or laughed too heartily at the jokes we were writing, her voice would come booming through the double doors, "Moooor-eece, stop that racket! I have a terrible headache! I'm going to tell your father when he gets home from the studio!"

Actually, Harry Rapf always seemed like a nice easygoing fellow who had inherited none of his mother's field-marshal authority. Writers may have sneered at his enormous nose, his malapropisms, and his lack of literary finesse, but he was bringing in the bread-and-butter pictures on schedule while Irving Thalberg was establishing himself as a perfectionist with expensive retakes. From his days as a vaudeville booker, Rapf had an eye for talent. He had signed Joan Crawford when she was still Lucille Laseur, a chorus girl at the Winter Garden in New York City. Now Harry was supervising the picture that would establish Crawford as one of Hollywood's major stars—*Our Dancing Daughters.*

But at 621 Lorraine he was still Grandma Rapf's little boy. He would scold and punish Maurice not of his own inclination but out of fear of that indomitable old tyrant.

Early on, Maurice and I developed the habit of keeping a written record of all our activities. With cyclometers on our bicycles we would clock the exact distance to Paramount Studio, the new lot on Marathon Street. We not only played Foreign Legionnaires on top of the abandoned desert fort in *Beau Geste,* we also wrote out the scenes we were enacting. We accumulated a shelfful of those primitive scenarios. One of our favorite playgrounds was the fantastic set for *Ben Hur,* a film that was to dwarf in size and cost even Griffith's colossal *The Birth of a Nation.* In fact, my father believed that *Ben Hur* added "super-colossal" to Hollywood's growing list of hyperboles. Begun by the original Goldwyn Company, *Ben Hur* had been inherited by MGM, with Mayor and Thalberg reluctantly allowing the spendthrift production to go on shooting in Italy. But production costs doubled and tripled, a new script was ordered, along with a new star (Ramon Novarro replacing George Walsh), and the multi-million-dollar production was thumbed home from Rome and the Italian seacoast to our other playground in Culver City.

Maurice's Studio, as we called it, obliged us by rebuilding the Colosseum in an open field on Venice Boulevard, a few blocks down from the MGM lot. Inside the studio, behind the huge white-stucco silent stages, realistic Roman galleys floated in battle array in an enormous tank. Of course it was fun to see this extravaganza actually being shot. We could see Ben Hur's excruciating chariot race against Messala, and we could visit young Ramon Novarro in his dressing room as he was assisted into his dashing costume as a Roman charioteer.

In those days my red-leather autograph book went with me everywhere, and there on a faded pink page is a florid inscription by the then-latest successor to Valentino. (Even studio brats raised in the shadows of the bustling front-office buildings and the towering stages were not too blasé to be autograph hounds.) Our albums were all-inclusive: With the two biggest studios in our pocket and with many of our friends' fathers at First National, Fox, and Universal, we had every star in town. Unfortunately, almost every inscription was a one-two punch to a tender ego. Although there were a few affectionate exceptions ("May you always be a Buddy to me!!—Yours forever, Clara Bow" and "To Buddy—whose buddy? Mine!—Love and Kisses, Sally O'Neill"), the principal theme running through that dog-eared little album is "Hoping you'll grow up to be as great a man as your father." In one sycophantic voice they urged me to "Follow your dad!" (Adolphe Menjou); Emil Jannings wrote exactly that sentiment in German, and Gilbert Roland in Spanish—messages clearly intended for the eyes of my father rather than for mine.

Maurice and I turned ourselves into a pair of abbreviated Ben Hurs and galloped heroically around the enormous oval of the set, managing to portray both the horses pulling the chariots and the intrepid Ramon Novarro snapping his whip over the backs of the high-spirited steeds. Although we were both desperately afraid of girls (was it despite or because of the fact that we were surrounded by starlets and would-be starlets?), we indulged our fantasies with imaginary Esthers in the stands cheering us on as we overturned the chariot of the overbearing Messala.

These phantom heroines represented our shared and secret lives. They were more real to us than the flesh-and-blood young ladies who challenged and intimidated us.

Walking toward the main entrance to Paramount, I had been approached by good-looking young girls who obviously belonged to the company of hopefuls waiting for lightning to strike. And in those far simpler times, sometimes it did. There was no Actors Guild, or Extras Guild, to serve as a go-between. A producer, director, casting director, or a self-important assistant would pick a face out of the crowd—"Just the type we're looking for!" Sometimes it was true and one of the thousands of girls in town to "break into the movie game" would get lucky and find herself a star. Sometimes the studio powers and demi-powers were merely on the make, or looking for kickbacks. It was a chancy, ever-hopeful, and corrupt little world. Outside the gates all those good-looking *have-nots,* inside so many imperious but vulnerable *haves.* Big kings and little kings who could whimsically touch you on the head with their magic wands and change your rags to cloaks of gold.

There was a kind of frenzy to the outs yearning to get in. Once two young men stopped me at the entrance to the reception area and greeted me as if we were old friends—"Hi, Buddy, how'd ya like to meet a hot little flapper who'll really knock yer eye out?" All of fourteen, I hesitated, stammering that I was going in to see some rushes with my father. This only served to incite them further. "This'll only take a minute. She lives right here in this apartment." Facing the studio was a pseudo-English apartment house full of eager beavers who watched the lot from their windows, living the moviemaking life vicariously. Carried along by their aggressive charm and never too proficient at saying "No," I found myself hurried up a flight of stairs and down a dark, uninviting hall to the door of a room overlooking the studio.

My two guides knocked happily on the door, continuing to assure me that I was going to meet someone who was really the cat's pajamas. The door opened and a wistful young redhead with bangs and spit curls, dressed flapper-style in a skirt showing off her pretty round knees, smiled at us.

"Jackie," one of the young men said, "guess who we brought to meet you. Buddy Schulberg. The boss's son!"

She smiled at me as if I already had her contract in my hand.

"What'd I tell you?" asked the other young man. "Isn't she a lulu? And who does she look like? A dead ringer. They could be twins!"

I didn't have to answer because Jackie was eager to volunteer.

"Do I really look like Clara Bow?" She fed me my lines, batting her false eyelashes at me, and going into the little vamp step identified with the It Girl. "Everytime I go out, people ask me for my autograph and call me Clara. It sure gives me a funny feeling."

The It Girl vs. the If Girl. So tantalizingly near, so desperately far. On the other side of that narrow street, somewhere over the rainbow, a pot of gold was waiting for Jackie, she thought. You didn't have to be smart, you didn't have to be an Ethel Barrymore. You just had to look cute and know your onions.

For that moment it must have seemed as if fate had served me up as Jackie's onion. Suddenly, to my extreme embarrassment, I found myself alone with her. Her friends had muttered something about having to go down to the coffee shop on the corner. Jackie sat down on the frayed couch and invited me to join her. I did but I didn't know what to say to her. She asked me if I knew Clara Bow and I said yes. She said it must be wonderful to know all the big movie stars and I said yes it was. I didn't say what my father thought of most of them and I didn't tell her what a low-down no-good common tramp my mother considered Clara Bow. She said it must be wonderful to be able to walk into the studio whenever I wanted and to be close to great people like the famous directors and my wonderful father. She edged so close to me that I could smell her perfume—or maybe her ambition. My mouth felt dry as I edged away. "You know, you're not at all the way I pictured you to be," she said. "I thought the sons of the big producers would be real shieks— real cavemen. Why," she said, puckering up and looking like Clara, "I'll bet you never even kissed a girl."

Thinking back on that entrapment, I realize that Jackie could not have been more than two or three years older than I was. But I was still a child while Jackie, physically at least, was a pocket-size adult, a sex object, an almost-It Girl on the wrong side of Marathon Street. I knew I should have invited her to accompany me into the studio. I sensed the power I had to introduce her to Vic Fleming or Eddie Sutherland—or even to the great B. P. Schulberg himself. But what I really wanted was to escape from Jackie and never see her again.

One day when I was being driven through the studio gate in the family town car to pick up my father, I glanced up through the rear window and caught a glimpse of Jackie at her second-floor lookout staring at the entrance as it stood open for the little prince whom all the sycophants accepted as Father's logical successor to the throne.

I felt a twinge of guilt about Jackie, for not having swept her into my arms and into the studio. But, like my sidekick Maurice, I was a curious mixture of emotional immaturity and professional insight. I could have told Jackie that the studio would not welcome a "dead ringer" for Clara Bow, with the same shade of red hair combed into the same bangs and spit curls, the same dimpled cutie-pie face, the same provocative Cupid's-bow mouth. Clara wouldn't welcome a double Charlestoning along in her shadow, and neither would her public. There was room for one It Girl, one ladylike Shearer, one mysterious Garbo, one saucy Mae Murray, one soulful Lillian Gish. . . . Each star was a special personality with her own inimitable identity. Each had the star quality that set her apart from a hundred imitators. There were ten thousand Jackies, luscious girls with photogenic if forgettable faces and figures perfectly proportioned if interchangeable. In time Jackie would become a carhop, an usher, a call girl, or take the bus home to North Platte and settle for marriage to an insurance salesman or the local plumber, or, if she kept her looks, a small-town politician. I could have told Jackie that Clara Bow, for all her brainlessness, was an original. She hadn't tried to be Billie Dove or Mabel Normand. And little Jackie, back on the Greyhound for the long ride home, or up at Madame Frances's luxurious bordello still passing herself off as Clara's look-alike, would never know the difference.

Meanwhile, back at the *Ben Hur* set, Maurice and I pursued our childishly elaborate fantasies. There was a current of benign sexual masochism to our scenarios. In the bowels of the Roman galley we strained at the heavy oars while an imaginary breast plated Simon Legree drove us to exhaustion with his snakelike whip. We flinched and groaned, our naked shoulders bending to the oars. We had projected ourselves so deeply into this violent hallucination that we were not even aware of intrusion until a harsh voice cut through our reverie. "Hey, you kids—what you think ye're doin' out here?"

The old watchman, who had a boring day patrolling the valuable standing sets on the backlot, obviously thought he had a couple of hot fence-jumpers on his hands. Sometimes kids would scale the walls to roam the studio. Today a studio like Universal is patrolled with Waffen-SS security measures. In those days, everything was much more relaxed.

But even then our captor was marching us off the set and threatening to turn us over to the chief of the studio police.

"You damn kids c'n be arrested for trespassing," he said. "You're comin' with me!"

I can't remember if he had us literally by the collar but that's the way it felt. And we did something slightly perverse, although it stemmed more from a severe case of modesty or insecurity than from a wish to turn the screw. We walked along silently and quietly. We let the poor old codger think he had us in his power. And then, just as we were approaching the studio police office, Maurice identified himself as the son of Mr. Rapf.

The guard stopped, turned pale, frowned, scratched his head. "You have some identification—a studio pass?"

"We don't need them. They all know us at the gate. You can ask them. Or we can go to my father's office if you don't believe me." Maurice pointed to the big white building near the gate. "It's right down there."

Our captor was becoming our captive. He could see his soft job going out the window, not because he failed to collar a pair of trespassers but because he had foolishly collared the boss's son.

"So ye're Mister Rapf's boy, huh? Great fella, your dad. You should've told me right away. Y'see, if some kids jumped over that wall 'n' drowned in the tank, their parents could hold the studio responsible and I'd lose my job. But I'll know ya from now on. Yes suh, I'll keep an eye on yuh."

Of course that is exactly what we didn't want. A number of times we were humiliated in the middle of our romantic agonies by looking up to see a studio cop or a stray carpenter staring at us as we writhed, moaned, or swore undying devotion to our invisible beloveds.

These Peeping Toms brought Maurice and me even closer together. We would retreat to another exotic standing set even further removed from the center of studio activity and commiserate with each other about the intense embarrassment we had just suffered. Undoubtedly these inadvertent voyeurs simply thought of us as a couple of crazy kids. But we felt something far more personal, a sense of guilt because our games had grown to be more than games, more than childhood imitations of our fathers' movie scenes played on the same sets where they had just been filmed. We were acting out, for our eyes and ears alone, our secret lives.

Both our ids and our muscles, our inhibited passions and the physical mischief inherent in fourteen-year-olds were expressed through the facilities of our fathers' studios. Just inside the MGM auto gate, for instance, was an enormous fig tree, a relic of the days when the whole western basin of Los Angeles was fragrant with fruit orchards. The old tree was a studio ornament now, for no one ever seemed to pick the fruit. The figs would ripen to squashy black missiles, ideal weapons for us to hurl against moving targets. Our fig tree was strategically placed facing the second-floor cutting rooms and small projection rooms which were reached by a metal staircase. Up those steps went not only cutters but directors and stars eager to see their work in progress.

Maurice and I would crouch behind the thickened trunk of the giant tree, under the dark-green protection of its heavy branches, rear back with juicy figs in our hands, and throw them with all our small but considerable might. Black fig skins and pinkish-white pulp would splatter against expensive sports jackets and famous profiles.

When our victims stopped and whirled around we would either freeze in the far reaches of the tree, or race down narrow alleys behind the projection room, through a maze of walkways and alcoves we knew as well as an Algerian sneak-thief knows the Casbah.

There was an inverse caste system to our target priorities. We didn't really want to splatter the hardworking cutters, their assistants, and the apprentices who toted the film cans. We only fell back on them for want of a bigger game. What we were really after was a John Gilbert in a dapper ascot, a chic Billy Haines, a strutting Erich von Stroheim, a swashbuckling (or swish buckling) Ramon Novarro. Nor were the glamorous ladies neglected. There was no gallantry in the heart of a studio prince. Once one's hands closed around a ripened fig, the happy-go-lucky Marion Davies could be a target. Or her pal, the bright comedienne Aileen Pringle. The fact that the ladylike Norma Shearer was known to be under the protection of Irving Thalberg provided no shield against the rotting figs that came flying mysteriously from the depths of our leafy barricade. The wicked Mae Murray offered a luscious target. And Maurice and I hold a unique place in Hollywood history. Who else can boast of scoring a direct hit with a ripe fig on the most luminous star in the Metro heavens? Greta Garbo!

Movie personnel were not our only targets. We were democratic enough to fill a brown paper bag with fig ammunition, go out the studio gate to Washington Boulevard, and let fly at the passing motorists. If they stepped on their brakes, ready to jump out of their cars and chase us, we'd race back through the gates, taking sanctuary under our friendly fig tree.

We might have continued waging our ripe-fig war if it had not been for our friend the mailboy Maurie, only a few years older than us. Passing along on his bike delivering scripts and memos, he happened to catch us unawares as we were firing our light artillery. He seemed to enjoy our assault on studio dignity. But we soon learned never to trust the mailroom boy. He would turn his own mother in to the studio cops if it meant a step up the ladder. So our mailroom Judas ratted on us, revealing us as the perpetrators of the soft-fig massacre. We were called to Harry Rapf's office and lectured severely. It was a privilege for us to have free run of the studio, and we were abusing that freedom. How could we possibly splatter Jack Gilbert and Greta Garbo with overripe figs? (Very easily, we thought to ourselves, but we hung our heads, a little frightened, if not intimidated.)

I do not say that Maurie the Mailroom Boy earned his promotion as a direct result of his betrayal of our youthful figging. It was simply a symbol of his readiness to please the stronger by turning on the weaker.

It was hardly an accident that the MGM lion was the presiding symbol of the lot. MGM was even more of a jungle than "my" studio—and a jungle is a system of survival in which the top lion intimidates the lesser lions who in turn intimidate the smaller animals, from supervisors all the way down to writers and mailroom boys.

Thus Maurie the finger-boy hustled his way up through the jungle pecking order, to become a go-fer, then a second assistant to an associate producer, and finally an associate producer himself. He may have had talent but that was a second virtue. You had to impress somebody at least one rung above you, scramble to get an *in,* and then use that in to climb up over the back of your benefactor if you could. Horatio Alger would do no less. You might call it the American way of life, to gnaw and claw your way to the top, like the Rockefellers and the Morgans and all the robber barons who aced themselves into the American aristocracy. Hollywood, after all, was only a picture of America run through the projector at triple speed.

20

Meanwhile, we continued to roam the lot with an innocence that seemed out of place in the Great-American-Dream-and-Sex Machines our studios represented. When we weren't acting out our own psychodramas on the backlot we would check the call sheets to find out what pictures were shooting and where.

The talk of MGM was the tempestuous production of *The Merry Widow,* with the gifted, manic, uncontrollable Von Stroheim directing two volatile stars, Mae Murray and John Gilbert. Mae was the original Christy Girl, one of the most coveted of the Ziegfeld Girls, who had survived into the mid-Twenties as a sexy box-office attraction. Her voluptuous dancer's body with creamy white shoulders and rounded breasts drew foul-mouthed approval from the crew. Mae had fought with Gilbert, who had walked off the set and taken refuge in his handy bottle of scotch. Now she was feuding with Von—who was intensely feudable. She had tried to get him fired from the picture because he had pronounced her dancing "rotten" in the presence of three hundred extras.

Mayer did fire Von Stroheim, substituting Monta Bell, a dependable "company man," but the extras rebelled. They belonged to what they called "Von Stroheim's Army," mostly European war veterans whose autocratic military bearing provided the ideal background for his own grandiose, foreign behavior. When Bell tried to take over the explosive production, the "Army" chanted, "We want Von Stroheim!" Ordinarily, extras got fired for that kind of insubordination. But this time they had a hole card. They had all been established in ballroom scenes, many of them clearly identifiable. It would cost thousands of dollars to replace them and reshoot those fancy-dress crowd scenes.

So L.B. decided to eat humble pie, a diet for which he had a great aversion, and rehired the rebellious Von Stroheim. Early Hollywood was so completely a world to itself that one of the local dailies carried a front-page banner that could not have been larger if President Coolidge had been assassinated:

MAE-VON SIGN PEACE!
STROHEIM WINS IN SETTLEMENT

For the public record, L.B. and his insolent director marched back to the set arm in arm. Von clicked his heels and kissed the hand of his imperious leading lady. Jack Gilbert, who played no favorites and despised L.B., Von, and Mae with equal passion, was photographed with a malevolent smile on his face. As they approached the big "orgy" scene, an uneasy peace held the unstable *Merry Widow* set together.

Maurice and I didn't know what an orgy was, but from the way everybody in the studio was talking about it, we knew it was something we had to see. But the set was "closed"—Von's sets were always off limits to outsiders, including even Mayer and Thalberg—so we missed the big orgy scene, though we hoped to get a peek at it in one of the projection or cutting rooms to which we had access. We could lean over the shoulders of friendly cutters and see all sorts of filmic wonders on the tiny screen of the moviola. We could see them shortening a shot on that ingenious little machine and then running it through again to study the effect of the reedited rhythm. Most of the cutters were conscientious, knowledgeable, congenial technicians, and in their cluttered cutting rooms we felt an air of sanity dramatically absent from Von Stroheim's *Merry Widow* set.

Even tighter security was to be established for a scene in which Mae Murray was to dance in a tight-fitting gown with décolletage almost but not quite revealing her celebrated bosom. The set was to be cleared of all but the essential technicians. To Von Stroheim's credit, he was trying to break out of the American corset of prudery and censorship. He had studied Freud and Jung and Krafft-Ebing and was years ahead of his time in conceiving scenes that scorned our superficial approach to "sex appeal," exploring instead the raw power of sex.

When the stage was dark, we lifted the giant latch and sneaked inside.

216

Lights flooded a vast nineteenth-century Viennese ballroom set and there was the flamboyant Merry Widow herself beginning to move slowly and sensuously to the lush music of the orchestra. We didn't dare creep too close for fear of being caught by the terrible-tempered Von. If he was bold enough to tell off L.B. Mayer—to his face, while everybody else did it behind his back—what would he do to a pair of small, uninvited boyeurs, the sons of the high-and-mighty movie executives he loathed? We watched as Von Stroheim barked his command. A perfectionist who would shoot a thousand feet to get ten precious seconds of film, he ordered his star to do the dance again. As the exotic music struck up again, to the staccato command of "Action!"—which sounded in Von Stroheim's guttural accent like "*Achtung!*"—the golden-haired Ziegfeld beauty went into her act. The musky aroma of sex filled the stage; Maurice and I were ready to be seduced vicariously. Then we were rudely awakened from our dream: A second assistant director shouted, "Hey, you kids! You don't belong in here! Now get out! And stay out! It's a closed set! Mr. Von Stroheim's orders!"

We were herded out the large stage door, shutting us off from Von's passionate world. The sensuous lure of that set had a stronger effect on us than any sense of being in on film history, on a creative tug-of-war between Von Stroheim and his constant antagonist, the Front Office. When Von the Headstrong stormed off the Metro lot in a fury because they took away his cutting rights on *The Merry Widow,* L.B. retaliated by canceling Von's percentage of the profits.

So when the picture created a riot in staid Pasadena—where police stopped the screening in the middle of the seduction scene—Von wasn't there. The cops held L.B. responsible and wanted to book him at the station house. When Father heard of it, he laughed: Louie the Pious being arrested for salacious filmmaking! But L.B.'s tongue was soaked in honey. Of course he realized the scene was an insult to American morality, he assured the officers. That's why he had chosen to preview it "in God-fearing Pasadena. Von Stroheim obviously had exceeded the bounds of decency. Exposing such licentiousness to the right-thinking people of Pasadena was the best guide to editing it so as not to offend the morals of America."

Whenever a studio washed its hands of the dynamic, spendthrift, inspired but uncontrollable Von Stroheim, another studio took him on. Now it was "my" studio's turn. *The Merry Widow* made him a hot property: a calculated risk because of his cavalier disregard of costs, but still "bankable." His behavior on *The Wedding March* repeated his *Merry Widow* performance, only this time it was even more extreme. Vienna, vintage 1914, was resurrected on the back lot. A relative of Emperor Franz Josef, brought over to affirm the authenticity of the sets, swore he could not tell them from the Alt Wien he knew. Von Stroheim's creative hunger for cinematic realism, so exactingly achieved in *Greed,* drove set- and costume-designers mad. No slipshod "Hollywood license" was permitted. Von Stroheim, perfectionist, madman, or both, knew every detail of the period he was recreating. A minute error on a uniform, an anachronistic touch on a period gown would call down his wrath. And to be on the receiving end of his fury was to be stunned by thunder and struck by lightning. Extras and underlings literally trembled in his presence. I too was so afraid of the head-shaved, bullnecked Von that even though I saw him frequently during the seemingly endless shooting of *The Wedding March,* I never dared approach him for his autograph. Erich von Stroheim was the Last Tycoon of silent directors, a satanic Galahad in search of some cinematic Holy Grail, an obsessed Quixote forever tilting his lance at the hated Front Office my father represented.

In fairness to B.P., he had his own feeling for realism and he kept trying to slip honest, realistic films into the schedule. He admired Von's dedication to *Greed,* even though he joined the MGM brass in deploring his determination to release the film as a forty-reel, ten-hour monster. Veteran screenwriter June Mathis had slimmed it down to a ten-reel version we had seen in the Rapf projection room.

My father felt that *Greed* represented a highwater mark in American cinematic realism, with scenes that would never be forgotten. Relentless, brutally honest, it was unrelieved by the commercial touches usually inserted to leaven tragic material. B.P. was convinced that every talented director striving for realism owed a debt to Von Stroheim. But B.P. also believed that he was pigheaded in insisting on his ten-hour version, and that piling detail on detail, no matter how brilliant those details were, finally became self-defeating. Watching the shortened version—even though sections were necessarily jumpy and bridged with subtitles—Maurice and I were inclined to agree with our fathers: Von Stroheim was brilliant, innovative, and original but driven to excessive, needless expenditure.

Many years later, when Von became a cult figure, he was described as a martyr of cinematic purity destroyed by crass studio bosses like Mayer, Thalberg, and my father. That can be argued from either side. In the great days of the silents, there was no director who could match him in combining uncompromising realism with an erotic imagination that made his films so sensuous they became emotionally disturbing. Father realized that in Von Stroheim he was dealing with an authentic genius and not merely a temperamental egomaniac. And, to give B.P.'s side of the controversy as I remember it, he was ready to give Von as free a hand as possible, *provided*—and that was always the rub between Von and the Front Office—he could hold *The Wedding March* within the prescribed budget and shooting schedule.

Von Stroheim promised to do his best, because he already had struck out at two of the Big Three, filmmaking was his passion, and where else but here in Hollywood could he find the million or more dollars he needed for each of his extravagant dreams? I watched him work on the Paramount backlot, terrorizing thousands of extras and driving his crew as mercilessly as he drove himself. In those pre-union days, he would often shoot all day, through the night and into the dawn, driving his staggering, bleary-eyed troops onward like a film-crazed Napoleon.

Soon my father was coming home shouting a string of epithets, building to an explosive "That goddamn lunatic Von Stroheim!" At the rate he was going, that #$&&*!! s.o.b. would take five years to finish his ¢&*$#! s.o.b.'n *Wedding March*. He had warned Von that at his snail's pace of perfectionism, the two leads—Von himself, and his favorite dramatic actress Zasu Pitts—would be ready to play the parents, if not the grandparents, of the bride and groom by the time the obsessed director got them to the altar.

Von indulged in demented whims worthy of a Paul the First, the mad czar of eighteenth-century Russia. He had ordered silk underwear for a thousand extras, even though these costly underthings would never be seen by the camera, arguing that this inner sense of well-being would make his background people feel more truly aristocratic in the luxurious prewar court of Emperor Franz Josef. In silk underwear they were no longer ciphers, lowly five-dollar-a-day extras who would be back on the Hollywood streets looking for work when the sequence was (finally) concluded. Like all of Von Stroheim's theories, even the most extreme, this one was provocative. The "silk-underwear" dispute has been refuted as myth by the Von Stroheim authorities and/or apologists who insist it was one of the many alleged aberrations invented by the "money men" to cut the ground from under the feet of a genius who refused to bend to The System. I only know that at the time my father—caught between Von's cavalier approach to money and Adolph Zukor's realistic concern for that commodity—came home with the news that Von had put in an order to the costume department for those silk undergarments and B.P. had thundered back that he could not justify any expenditures that could not actually be seen on the screen. Father was already getting those panic signals from the New York office—"If you can't control him, take him off the picture!"

Von Stroheim, B.P. protested, wanted it both ways. He wanted a limitless amount of Paramount money without having to answer as to how it was spent. Indeed, as an artist he felt an inalienable right to an open-ended call on the Paramount bank, just as he had looked on Universal and MGM as boundlessly wealthy patrons who should consider themselves fortunate to be allowed to underwrite his fantasies.

"He's a genius!" Von Stroheim's Army cheered him on.

"He's a raving lunatic!" the studio managers fought back.

"He's both," Father agreed as he tried to mediate between an irresistible force and an immovable object.

At the end of two tempestuous years, B.P. finally had to call a halt to the shooting, and to add insult to injury—just as Thalberg and Mayer had cut Von down at MGM—he turned the cutting over to the other "Von," our Jewish-American Joe von Sternberg. Father had been impressed with Von Sternberg's first picture, *Salvation Hunters,* an intensely individualistic effort, sordid, uncompromising, with a masterful use of mood photography. Joe was as quirky as Erich, if slightly more tractable, and soon he would be directing for my old man some of the more memorable films of the late Twenties and early Thirties: *Underworld, The Last Command, Morocco,* and *An American Tragedy.* He would become world-famous as Marlene Dietrich's director/Svengali, and in the mid-Thirties he would collaborate with B.P. on a daring if faulted *Crime and Punishment,* a book from which Father had read aloud on our literary Sundays at home.

Once again, as with *Greed* and *The Merry Widow,* Von Stroheim felt that his *Wedding March* had been mutilated, indeed castrated by the hated Front Office. He had shot one hundred reels of film which he had planned to edit into *two* four- or five-hour pictures. His natural medium seemed to be the ten-hour film, a monstrous form that marked him as a madman in those days of the classic ninety-minute silents. Was Von a demented genius, as Father believed, or *the* master of all directors, too far ahead of his time? The day would come when Soviet Russia would release *War and Peace* in two long sittings, along the lines that Von Stroheim had projected forty years earlier. And when James Michener's *Centennial* would be shown on television for a total of twenty-four hours.

Unfortunately for Von Stroheim, neither the American public, the Paramount exchequer, nor the patience of my father were ready for him. Though New York critics singled out particular sequences in *The Wedding March* as "incomparable," and *The New York Times* described him as a cinematic Zola, the sad truth was that no major studio would take a chance with him again. A crusty independent, Joe Kennedy, the very good friend of Gloria Swanson, was willing to gamble on him for *Queen Kelly,* but the picture was abandoned halfway through. He was never to finish another Hollywood film. And even in Europe, in what should have been a more congenial atmosphere, never again was he able to mount a picture of his own. Artistically frustrated, he eked out a living as an actor. In films like *Grand Illusion* and *Sunset Boulevard,* he left indelible performances. For the rest of his life he would act, he would write novels and scenarios, and he would agonize over all the marvelous films he would never be permitted to make.

21

WATCHING A *Ben Hur* in the making, a Greta Garbo or a Lon Chaney creating film history, a bizarre figure like Von Stroheim in action was simply part of our daily life—along with rooting for the flamboyant Trojans of U.S.C. in their crimson-and-gold football uniforms as they struggled heroically against the Fighting Irish of Notre Dame or the California Golden Bears. Irreverently we sang "Fight On for Old S.C.—The Halfback Wants His Sal-a-ree . . ."

When the Golden Age of the silent screen was reaching its end, our western edge of Los Angeles was still so rural that we could safely take our bikes and pedal from Lorraine to Larchmont, bordered by great pepper trees. Every Saturday afternoon at the Larchmont Theatre we could watch our favorite star, not the ones our fathers launched, nourished, cussed, and profited from, but the intrepid western hero, Art Acord. When the silents fell with a resounding crash, Art Acord was one of the hundreds of marquee names caught in the switches. He went galloping off into the sunset of total obscurity. When I was old enough to begin to play the "Whatever-Happened-To?" game, I got a familiar answer: Having silently lassoed his last cattle rustler and having silently saved his last golden-haired damsel in distress, Art found himself overcome by a world he thought he had conquered. The offscreen fade-out was suicide.

Darkness was always lurking behind the bright, leaving a subliminal shadow on our minds. We would roughhouse with the MGM comedy team, English music-hall comedian George K. Arthur and his tall, glowering sidekick, Karl Dane, who had been discovered as a carpenter on the MGM backlot. Scoring in a serious role in King Vidor's *The Big Parade,* he had gone on to comedy roles; Arthur and Dane were Harry Rapf's and MGM's answer to Father's Beery & Hatton comedies at Paramount. But the advent of sound had sneaked up on Karl Dane. Suddenly he wasn't a five-thousand-dollar-a-week talking actor, he was an unemployed ex-carpenter with a guttural Scandinavian accent. There seemed nothing else to do except put a revolver to his head. Tom Forman, one of Father's favorite directors from those sunny days at the Selig Zoo, grabbed the same one-way ticket when he was declared "*Not Okay for Sound*" in a new age of cinematic progress that had turned its back on Tom's silent Preferred Pictures.

Although we were aware of the dramatic rising and falling of these tides of fortune, the painful exit of Charles Ray, Gilbert, Von Stroheim, Charles King, or Buster Keaton—and what a mixed bag were those vaulters and tumblers!—they were still peripheral to the center of our existence, the elaborate fun and games that gave pleasure to our growing days. We loved track-and-field meets as much as we did those emotional Saturday-afternoon football games. We held our own meets in the open lots on Lorraine, clocking ourselves with expensive stopwatches and keeping personal records. Then we doubled as reporters, hailing these activities in our own sports paper: RAPF SETS NEW HIGH JUMP RECORD AT FOUR FEET EIGHT!; SCHULBERG WINS STANDING B.J. WITH FIVE FEET TWO! New events were constantly added to our friendly but intense competition. We bought miniature turtles and staged turtle meets in our respective bathtubs—usually mine since Grandmother Rapf took as dim a view of this sport as she did of our other activities.

Radio reception was still an exciting experience. Maurice had an RCA about two feet long with a slanting face, and I had a Superheterodyne more than three feet long with so many different dials it is a wonder that I—outstandingly unmechanical—ever learned to operate it. With our earphones clamped to our heads we would bend over our sets, moving our tuning dials a fraction of a fraction of an inch until we would hear a telltale squeak that meant a distant signal trying to get through. There were no networks in those days, and not too many local stations to overpower us, and so when local stations *Star-Spangled-Banner*ed off the air at midnight, the airwaves would be free for the power station of the East, KDKA in Pittsburgh, WJZ in New York, WBZ in Boston. . . .

As we grew more accomplished at this delicate all-night job, we began to extend our reception range to England, Australia, and finally Japan.

When motion-picture songs came in with the groundbreaking *The Jazz Singer,* Maurice and I would monitor the radio to keep track of how many times our studios' songs were broadcast, how many plays for his "Pagan Love Song" or "Singin' in the Rain" compared to my "Beyond the Blue Horizon" or "My Future Just Passed."

On almost every level but one we competed with intensity. Jumping, running, criticizing current films, and writing copy, jokes, and songs for our private newspaper, our talents seemed virtually interchangeable. But in the esoteric field of music, Maurice was clearly my master. Just as, if you put a hammer in my hand, I would invariably hit not the nail but the fingers holding it, so it was for me with musical instruments. Maurice's parents insisted that he learn to play the piano, and under the determined surveillance of his grandmother, who saw to it that he practiced the prescribed hour a day, he learned to play acceptably. My mother soon discovered that the best I could do with the piano was to turn on the switch that started the rolls.

So they bought me an expensive, gleaming saxophone, with its mysterious keyboard that only inspired madmen like Lester Young and Stan Getz can solve. When the sax was turned in for a trumpet, the trumpet for a trombone, and still no music came forth, a string instrument was suggested. When I failed to conquer the mandolin, my mother took it over and I was given a banjo. A small fortune was lavished on instruments and frustrated teachers. Still no music issued from the Paramount prince. After several years, my mother on her mandolin and her music-resistant son on his banjo were able to play a duet, more or less together, of "Mighty Lak a Rose."

Fortunately for us, there were no tape recorders in those days, and so the world has been spared any relic of our musicales. But I remember the earnestness with which Mother picked at her shiny mandolin, and the boredom that engulfed me as I failed to master yet another instrument. Still Ad pressed on as she did with all things cultural. We had to be complete people in the Grecian sense, at home with intellectuals and artistes and on the playing fields. My sister Sonya was given a far more elegant instrument, a harp, which she mastered with about as much proficiency as I brought to the saxophone, the piano, and the banjo. But who could resist the image of little Sonya, ethereal and painfully shy,

225

dressed for her role in a long, flowered Victorian gown, bending toward the harp that towered above her yellow curls? Mother was so proud of her creation that she hired a successful local portraitist, Stewart Robertson—an artist of the court, so to speak—to preserve Sonya and her harp in an oil painting that oozed affluence and culture.

But commerce went hand in hand with culture in our multipurposed life. Those were the days when houses were rising from the vacant lots all over Windsor Square, and once in a while a carpenter or bricklayer sweating under the winter sun would ask us for a drink of water. With hundreds of laborers building mansions for our expanding city, it struck me that a profitable business might be set up selling orange juice fresh from our kitchen. With lumber and canvas from the studio, my Uncle Joe built us an impressive orange juice stand. The oldest of Mother's brothers, Joe was strong and useful with his hands. He liked to boast of how he had beaten off Cossack assailants in his native village. But like Grandpa Max, he was a fish out of water in this new world. He could not cope with the urgent challenge of Hollywood that his young brother Sam and my father found so exciting.

The thirsty workmen were grateful for our cold orange juice, and at the lunch hour Maurice and I did a brisk business. Since the oranges came from our own kitchen, obligingly squeezed by Anna the cook, who also supplied the punch bowl, the ice, and the small glasses, Father estimated that at five cents a glass the household was a nickel behind on every transaction. But this economic logic was lost on us, as we pocketed our nickels.

Allowed, in the permissive climate of California, to operate motor vehicles at age 14, I soon owned a Ford Model A roadster, and with this new freedom came a significant expansion in our soft-drink business. Driving all the way down Sunset Boulevard to its source at the old Mexican Plaza, we found a wholesale bottling works in East Los Angeles, not far from the now-abandoned Mayer-Schulberg Studio. We would buy cases of root beer, orange pop, and cherry soda, selling them on our quiet, tree-lined Lorraine Boulevard at twice the cost, thereby encouraging Mother to believe that I was not only an athlete and a scholar but also a respecter of the almighty dollar, in which she placed as much trust as she did in Freud and Jung and such social heroes as Upton Sinclair and Lincoln Steffens.

Branching out from our soft-drink business, Maurice and I next directed our multi-talents to the magazine field, pressing subscriptions to

226

The Saturday Evening Post, The Ladies' Home Journal, and *The Country Gentleman* on our parents' friends who were too embarrassed to refuse. When that guest list was exhausted, we took to the streets, hawking our wares on the bustling corner of Western Avenue near what was then the Fox Studio.

To commemorate a new contract bringing him more than half a million dollars a year, B.P. ordered a custom-made town car that became for many years the bane of his children's existence. The body was a model of an 18th-century coach, laced with gold bric-a-brac, incongruously placed on a Lincoln chassis with a 16-cylinder engine. On either side of the door to our royal coach were two genuine antique lanterns. The interior was a jewel box, large enough for three on the plush rear seat, with two small circular jump seats that folded into the carpeted floor. Over each of the small rear windows was a small cut-glass vase in which fresh tea roses were placed every morning. There was also a delicate telephone with which we could communicate with James, our liveried chauffeur, a lean, ruddy-faced English war veteran who carried himself with the dash of Errol Flynn and indeed bore some resemblance to that irrepressible Tasmanian.

That automotive hybrid with its powerful engine from Detroit and its Hollywood replica of an Empire coach was an unlikely vehicle from which to peddle magazines. But forbidden to drive my new Model A into the dangerous traffic of Western Avenue, and laden with my magazines, I had no choice but to be driven to my corner in that gaudy symbol of conspicuous consumption. I never sat in that car in an upright position. To avoid the humiliation of being seen by passengers in ordinary vehicles, I always traveled on the floor, folded more or less into the fetal position. "Dressed down" in old knickers and a worn shirt, I would huddle there clutching my bagful of magazines. Near Western Avenue, as James opened the door for me, I made my escape in a manner that Lon Chaney might have admired. From my prone position on the floor I would crawl out onto the curb, move away from the car as quickly as I could, and then suddenly rise from my knees and stride away rapidly as if I had nothing to do with that $18,000 monster.

Once I was out on that Western Avenue corner I became the typical small-fry solicitor. Only my vocal pitch sounded like this: "G-get your S-saturday Evening Post—C-country G-G-G [soft *g* was always one of my most difficult consonants] Gentle-man L-Ladies' Home J-J-Journal?" Passersby must have felt pity for my affliction. Perhaps they thought I was retarded or that I had a harelip and was saving my nickels for an operation, for I was able to lighten my load of magazines through the afternoon. But it was a nerve-wracking job, as I always had to keep an eye out for dirty Alex and his Wilton Place yahoos. Our little nemesis, Pancho Villa, Jr., he was my chief tormentor at the Wilton Place Grammar School. Here on the Avenue he led a small band of outlaws who frankly terrified me. Once I saw them coming, just as James was driving to get me. Tucking my bundle of unsold magazines under my arm, I ran for my life down Third Street toward Van Ness. James saw me, stopped, flung open the door of the town car, and I dove in, hugging the floor as he drove home.

I was not the only member of the family to be a floor-rider in this glorious carriage. Whenever my sister Sonya was sent off in that car she would also hide on the floor, as ashamed of its ostentation as was I.

One night, in the car with my parents, I was all dressed up and forced to sit on the jump seat. We were on our way to the opening of one of Dad's pictures, *Old Ironsides,* at Grauman's Egyptian Theater. The ornate entranceway on Hollywood Boulevard was jammed with frenzied fans pushing against the barricades for a glimpse of their idols—Ronald Colman, Vilma Banky, Billie Dove, Jackie Coogan. . . . Suddenly a young girl, breaking through the barricades, ran toward our car which was caught in the star-studded traffic. The fan jumped onto the single step beneath the carriage door. There I was, with parents in evening clothes, in a fabulous chauffeur-driven carriage of gold. That was all a star-blinded fanatic needed to see.

"Who are you? Who are you?" she shouted at me. "Are you a movie star?" I shook my head. A slight drizzle added an extra note of madness to this searchlight circus.

"Who are you!"

It was not a question but a command. For those timeless seconds I belonged to her.

"I-I'm n-nobody," I stammered.

"Nobody?" She was moving along with us, her face peering over the half-lowered window, growing suspicious of elusive movie stars who high-hatted their fans.

"Are you sure? Do I know your name?"

I shook my head. "I-I'm not in the m-movies. I'm n-nobody j-just like you."

She stared at me and then suddenly accepted me, with a kind of ecstasy, as if miraculously the nobodies were inside this golden carriage riding with the greats. Still clinging to the coach, she turned around and shouted to the crowd pressing forward behind her. "He says he's nobody!" Her voice rose triumphantly. "Just like us!"

That was as close as I ever came to egalitarianism in Father's dream machine.

22

To COUNTERBALANCE OUR princely position, Maurice and I found an outlet for our pent-up energies on Halloween. A favorite target was the large red-brick Edwardian home of the Listicos on the corner. Mr. Listico, constantly overseeing his beautifully manicured lawns and hedges, was on the lookout for us. "Hey, you kids, stay off my grass!" he was always shouting at us.

One Halloween we decided to get even. From a mansion going up on Wilshire Boulevard we carried a barrel of wet cement. Then we collected garbage from neighboring houses, dragged it up the bricked entranceway to Mr. Listico's front door, and covered it with the cement. Hearing sounds within, we turned and ran. Panting, I hurried into the house and turned on the player piano. Moments later came a knock on the door: the police, asking for my father. It was one of the nights he happened to be home. I ran up the stairs and hid under my bed. After a while, I crawled to the doorway to listen. Father was doing his best to save me from reform school. Creeping out into the hallway, I peered down the banister. Father was reaching into his pocket and handing the officers some money. Their tone softened. He offered them some of his blimp-sized Upmann cigars. I heard the mingled chuckling of grown men who understand each other. The best sound of all was the front door closing behind them. Then I heard Father's footsteps coming up the stairs. I was more anxious than frightened because he had never struck me.

Perhaps because of his own human weaknesses he could not bring himself to sit in judgment on me. His permissiveness was instinctive and emotional where Mother's was theoretical and intellectual. Father simply explained to me that although he had managed to persuade the police not to arrest us, we would have to atone by removing the hardened cement and decaying garbage within, and by forfeiting next month's allowance to pay for the damage.

I never forgot Father's understanding, nor forgave Mr. Listico for calling the cops.

Another enemy was Rabbi Magnin, who presided over the local Temple B'nai B'rith, a position of grandeur he continues to enjoy an incredible half-century later. Today the Temple is a magnificent dome on Wilshire Boulevard, a monument to the affluent religiosity of Los Angeles. But in those days it was housed in an unprepossessing block-long two-story building in downtown Los Angeles. Instead of the traditional Hebrew school for youngsters, we had Sunday School, viewed as outright heresy by our Orthodox grandfathers.

But if the Rabbi's Sunday activities scandalized the bearded fathers of the studio bosses, it had charms for the young bosses themselves. Louie Mayer, William Fox, and the other moguls were happy to contribute large sums for front-row pews, and Rabbi Magnin rewarded them with flattery that poured like honey, and with a sanctimonious air that played up to their image of a man of God. Magnin was the right rabbi in the right temple in the right city at the right moment in time. If he had not presided over our B'nai B'rith, God and Louie B. Mayer—whose overpowering presences tended to overlap—would have had to create him. Or maybe they did.

Since my father had inherited his father's lack of interest in the religion of their ancestors, and since Mother gave lip service to the High Holy Days but had her head in other clouds, the teachings of Judaism meant little or nothing to me. Still, there was an irresistible force that drew me to B'nai B'rith every Sunday. Her name was Elsie Brick. Our Sunday School teacher. The first woman I was ever in love with. I should say *we* were ever in love with. Since Maurice and I were now accustomed to doing everything together, it followed that we should become mutually devoted to Elsie Brick. Still fearful of girls our own age—we would run from our houses to hide under a spreading evergreen whenever one appeared—and wary of those predatory little animals called starlets, in Elsie Brick we discovered an altogether different and superior female specimen. She had about her a dark and intense yet ethereal Rebecca-like beauty. Looking back, I realize that she was in her early twenties. But she was old enough for us not to feel challenged in offering her our love. Thus an innocent *ménage à trois* formed in our heads. In some cloud-banked kingdom of youth the three of us would live happily ever after.

Our Sunday School lessons began with the creation of the Earth, according to the Hebrews. I don't think we yet knew the difference between fact and fancy, law and legend. There was, for instance, something about Miss Brick's account of the origin of man that struck us as a little fishy. The Lord created Adam in His image, the lonely Adam gave up one of his ribs to form Eve, and the two of them gave birth to Cain and Abel. So far so good. But after Cain killed his brother, there should have been only three people left on earth. Yet Cain goes forth to the land of Nod and finds a wife, from whom came Enoch who begat Irad who begat Mehujael who begat Methushael, who begat Lamech, who took unto himself two wives, Adah and Zillah.

Well, we asked our divine Elsie, if Adam and Eve were the first two people on earth, where could Cain's wife possibly have come from? Why weren't her parents as famous as Adam and Eve? Why did our Bible ignore them? And later, if Lamech was a descendent of the original Adam and Eve, where did he find Adah and Zillah? Who were *their* ancestors, and why weren't they mentioned in the opening chapter? Where were they during all those goings-on in the Garden of Eden?

Miss Brick did her sweet, vague best to explain away these discrepancies, but each Sunday Maurice and I pressed on with our questions. We never did understand—if Adam, Eve, and Cain were the only three people on earth—what was meant by the biblical threat to Cain: "Whoever finds him shall kill him"? Where would the avengers come from in an unpeopled world?

Sunday after Sunday we laid intellectual siege to the biblical loyalty of Elsie Brick. No fact in Deuteronomy or Joshua or Judges was accepted on face value. Why, we demanded, did the walls of Jericho come tumbling down on the seventh day of the siege by Joshua and his forty thousand nomadic troops? Was the sound of Jewish trumpets and the shouts of Joshua's legions sufficient to bring down those walls thirty feet high and six to twelve feet thick? Was God really staging these miracles so that the Jews could conquer their enemies and occupy the Promised Land as prophesied on the eve of their exodus from Egypt? Or was this simply a Jewish folktale written after the fact to justify the conquests of the children of Judah?

While we constantly challenged Elsie Brick's biblical teachings we tried to think of new ways to express our devotion. One Sunday morning we decided to pick flowers from our gardens and to present them to her before the class would assemble. We were so eager for precious minutes of privacy with Elsie that we arrived fully half an hour before class was to begin.

Depositing our bouquet on Miss Brick's desk, we waited impatiently for her arrival. With nothing to do but inspect the empty classroom, we noticed for the first time a trapdoor in the floor. Finally managing to pry it open, we discovered beneath our feet an underground world—not a basement but a crawl-space, typical of southern Californian construction, about three feet deep. In our Sunday best we lowered ourselves down and pulled the trapdoor shut behind us. Around us spread a labyrinth of pipes and cobwebs that only boys could love. It was dark and we had to crawl over and under the pipes, along the dirt on which the temple had been built years before. Preoccupied with our explorations, we lost track of time until suddenly we became aware of footsteps above our heads as our classmates took their seats. We had hoped to resurface before their arrival. Now we were trapped. As we huddled down there in indecision, Miss Brick began to call the roll. When she got to "Rapf," Maurice cupped his hands to his mouth and called up through the floor, "Here." A murmur ran through the classroom. After a pause, Miss Brick continued. At "Schulberg," I also raised my head to the dark underside of the classroom floor: "Here." Again a murmur of surprise and confusion ran through the class. "Maurice . . . ? Buddy . . . ? Where are you?"

We heard the voice of our beloved but remained silent. After a minute or two of mystified speculation, Miss Brick took up the morning lesson. As she was reminding us of the moral leadership of the Chosen People, somehow we found the courage to dramatize, under the floor of the temple, the laws that came down to us from the Lord at Mount Sinai. "This is the voice of Moses," I began, in my best ghostly tone, "bringing you the Ten Commandments. . . ." My speech teacher would have been interested to hear that; assuming a new personality, impersonating Moses himself, I found my words flowed easily, without hesitation.

Then Maurice took over and intoned through the cracks in the floor: "Thou shalt have no other gods before Me. . . ." and right on through all those fearful "Thou shalt not's . . ." It was not exactly

234

applause that we heard from the other side of the floor but a collective murmur of approval that encouraged us to go on. Unmindful of the dirt and the cobwebbed darkness, we were exhilarated with the prospects that lay before us. For our underground crawl-space extended the length and breadth of the building. Before us lay new worlds, or classrooms, to conquer. So we crawled to a new position under the adjoining classroom and again went into our brother act on Moses and the Ten Commandments.

This was so successful that we decided to expand our presentation. Under the next classroom we gave them Joshua—oh, we had done our homework despite our rebellion—and in our now-practiced biblical voices went on intoning: "I say unto you people of Jericho, surrender now or we shall march around your city for six days—and on the seventh day when we blow our trumpets and all shout together in one great voice, your walls will come tumbling down. . . !"

We were all the Jewish heroes, Moses and Joshua, Judah and Ehud, as we crawled euphorically from classroom to classroom, showing off our knowledge of the violent history that Jehovah and Rabbi Magnin called holy. Overcome with our powers we crawled back to our own classroom, crying out, "Moses has returned!" By this time our act was such a hit that we were getting requests on small pieces of paper folded and pushed through cracks in the floor. "Do Isaiah. . . ." "Do King Hezekiah. . . ." We were hidden acrobats of the Torah. But then a fat, clumsy boy—Joseph Ray, a name I would always remember—pushed his request down, and, in character, performed his furtive act so unfurtively that with a sudden movement the trapdoor was raised and we found ourselves staring up into the face of our beloved. Now livid with fury.

"All right, you two! Climb out of there! This second!"

Rising from the mud like twin Calibans we climbed up onto the classroom floor. Our Sunday suits were smeared with dirt, and the moldy underside of the building we had navigated on hands and knees had left grotesque streaks across our faces. As our pudgy Judas closed the trapdoor, our classmates were too frightened to laugh at our discomfiture.

We waited in pain while Miss Brick quickly wrote a note, slipped it into an envelope, and handed it to me. "Take this to Rabbi Magnin," she said, and abruptly turned away.

The Jews on their long march into Babylonian captivity could hardly have felt more uncertain of their fate than their Hollywood descendants, as the deflated prophets trudged the long mile to the office of Rabbi Magnin.

After what seemed an interminable limbo in his outer office we were finally summoned to our audience with the Rabbi. In his flowing black robe he loomed like Jehovah Himself calling down God's vengeance on the backsliders and the disbelievers. We had left him no choice but to call our parents and threaten them with our expulsion from Temple B'nai B'rith.

I got off with a light lecture from my parents. Maurice was beaten by his grandmother, tongue-lashed by Tina and Harry, locked in his room immediately after school, and forbidden to see me.

Life quickly lost its flavor when I was barred from contact with Maurice. It wasn't fun to bring in a new long-distance radio station if I couldn't pick up the phone immediately to boast of that latest wireless conquest. It wasn't fun to race my turtles alone, or clock myself in the 50-yard dash alone, or watch rushes of Father's then-current million-dollar gamble, *Wings,* if I couldn't use it in my open-ended debate with Maurice as to the respective merits of Paramount and MGM.

Meanwhile, suspense mounted as we approached the impending Sunday morning service at B'nai B'rith. Maurice's father had spent more time with Rabbi Magnin that week than he had with L.B. He assured him of the depth of Maurice's compunction, and of his son's sincere desire to return to the fold. And so it came to pass that Rabbi Magnin granted us permission to come unto the temple on probation. And it so happened that this observance fell on the last Sunday of the month when children and parents alike were called together in common assembly. I always felt that this was a day dedicated not only to the glory of God but to Rabbi Magnin's as well. Like a peacock he seemed to expand in his rabbinical robes, delivering his sermon with a kind of professional piety that always made me feel he was auditioning for L. B. Mayer and Harry Warner. Here we all were, the children of Israel, again divided into tribes, Mayer-Thalberg, Warners, Fox, Laemmle, Lasky-Schulberg, all enjoying His largesse in the New Jerusalem called Hollywood.

Our rabbi's message ended with a flourish. And then, as was his practice, he clutched the lapels of his robe, leaned forward on his toes in a familiar gesture of self-satisfaction and said, "Now, if any of you students, or parents, have any questions. . . ?"

236

Mine was among the first half-dozen hands to be raised, but my signal was studiously avoided. The questions were all soft ones for which Rabbi Magnin had ready eloquent answers. He was happy to expand on God's self-revelation to Moses. And on the contemporary value of the Ten Commandments. And on the true meaning of manna from Heaven. Finally, when all the raised hands had been answered, only mine was left. Over his fistfuls of robe, Rabbi Magnin glowered, pressed his lips together, and finally acknowledged me.

"Schulberg."

My legs were shaking, my hands were trembling, I could feel the cold sweat on my forehead and the words were like chicken bones in my throat. But for some reason I had to get them out.

"R-R-Rabbi, h-h-how d-did the J-Jews g-g-g-go to the t-t-t . . ." It seemed I would never get the word out; when it finally emerged it was with the force of a shotgun: "TOILET . . . in the desert?"

My question hung there in the silence as if the air was too oppressive to let it fall. In a dramatic show of loyalty—for the price he had to pay for defiance was far greater than mine—Maurice stood up with me: "Yes, Rabbi—how *did* the Jews go to the toilet in the desert?"

Again, knuckles tightened in the fists holding the folds of the temple robe. How dare these two little gadflies mock their faith and upstage their rabbi? But Magnin said merely, "If you two young men will go to my chambers and wait for me, I will see you at the conclusion of the service."

With the eyes of the entire congregation drilling holes in our backs we edged into the side aisle and retreated from the hall.

Again the long wait, then the heavy steps down the corridor informing us that doom was approaching.

"Now," Rabbi Magnin began in a tone surprisingly reasonable, "if you had asked your question out of genuine curiosity, I could have answered it in terms of rabbinical scholarship. I could have told you that we Jews were the first people in the ancient world to have any concept of sanitation and bodily cleanliness. On the flight from Egypt through the desert our ancestors were required to walk thirty paces away from the caravan to take care of their bodily functions, and to dig a hole in the sand and then cover it up. They kept themselves as clean as they possibly could under those difficult circumstances."

There was a long, dangerous pause. When he spoke again his tone had hardened. "But unfortunately I think you asked the question not from any sincere desire for knowledge, but only to mock your God and your faith. What you did was blasphemous and unforgivable. I will inform your parents that you are as of this moment expelled for all time from B'nai B'rith."

Thus we were driven from the Temple. When she heard the news, Grandmother Rapf set up such a howl that I thought Maurice might be the first Jew to be nailed to the cross since the days of the Romans. The possibility that he would be driven from the House of Magnin before Bar Mitzvah loomed as a tragedy even darker than, say, Harry Rapf's being driven from the House of Mayer. All communication between Maurice and me was severed again while his parents implored the rabbi to take Maurice back into the fold. At last Magnin relented and Maurice was allowed to return and resume the studies that would technically convert him from boyhood to manhood.

Since my parents accepted my expulsion with much more equanimity, I was left to struggle into man's estate without help from the Lord and/or Rabbi Magnin. Locked out of the temple I went through a period when I no longer considered myself Jewish because, as I would try to explain, "Rabbi Magnin kicked me out." And all through my teens I considered myself un- or non-Jewish. It would take Adolf Hitler to bring me back to a sense of identification with the culture of my forebears. When I learned that German bullyboys were beating up Jews in the streets, breaking the windows of their shops, forcing them to wear yellow stars, and finally pushing them into sealed cattle cars and gas chambers, I realized of course that I was one of them. But there were curious years of limbo when I felt that I had been excommunicated.

I did not surrender all of my Jewish ties, however. In my biweekly attendance at the prizefights with my father, I still continued to identify with and root for Jewish boxers. All the movie celebrities were ringside, for on Friday nights it was no longer the *shul* but the Hollywood Legion Stadium where you would find the studio heads and the big-name stars and directors. The night Mushy Callahan (born Morris Scheer) won a close decision over the local Irish hero, Ace Hudkins, Father managed to squeeze me into the victory celebration in the dressing room. When Mushy presented me with the gloves with which he had held off the bull-like rushes of Hudkins, I had to fight back tears of pride.

Those gloves hung on the wall above my bed until I was ready for college, the closest thing to a religious symbol I had in those days. If I have been accused of making a religion of boxing, blame it on my youth and Mushy Callahan.

When I heard that my father had invited the great lightweight champion, Tony Canzoneri, to tour Paramount Studio, I asked to be his guide. Not wanting him to know I was the boss's son, I posed as a mailroom boy assigned to take him from set to set. What a thrill to stand beside Tony Canzoneri and introduce him to movie stars as the champion of the world. His warmest reception was on the set of the Marx Brothers, especially from Chico and Zeppo the gamblers, ardent fight fans from the East. But it was there I came a cropper. When the cameras started rolling for the next take the zany Marxes made me laugh out loud, ruining the take. The assistant director wheeled with a snarl that all A.D.'s used to cultivate in those days. "For Christ's sake! I said *quiet*! Who the hell's that?" He turned around. "Oh, it's you, Buddy. You ought to know better. Do that again and you're barred from the set—even if your old man *is* the boss!"

I introduced him to Canzoneri, and the A.D. in turn introduced the smiling little champ to the entire crew. "Jeez," Canzoneri said, "I only have three guys in my corner. These guys have thirty. I had no idea it took this many to make a movie." Tony clowned with the Marx Brothers and all was forgiven. On the way to the next set, to meet Richard Arlen and Esther Ralston, the champ asked me why I hadn't told him I was the boss's son. There he was, a man who had beaten the best lightweights in the world, impressed with a kid whose old man ran a movie studio. Only the kid who took movie stars in stride had put Tony Canzoneri up there on a pedestal with Jack Dempsey and The Great Benny Leonard. Falling stars were part of his daily life. He would save his tears for a feisty little champion like Canzoneri, who years later would be found dead, alone, in a five-dollar Manhattan hotel room.

23

EVEN GRAND MASTERS of motion-picture trivia who know the names of the second unit director of *Gone With the Wind* and Humphrey Bogart's stand-in on *Casablanca* draw a blank on this question: "Who was George Bancroft?"

It happened again the other day. My niece, a bright avant-garde movie producer, wanted to know about the stars her grandfather had discovered before she was born. Clara Bow she'd heard of, vaguely. But George Bancroft? Not a clue. And yet there was a time when that name had risen like a surfer's dream-wave and then had come pounding down across America and on around the world. "You mean you *never* heard of George Bancroft?" I pressed her. "Never," this member of the Wertmüller and Scorcese generation confessed.

"He was the world's number-one box-office star, bigger than Gilbert and Colman, Beery and Barthelmess and all the rest of them!"

I had been more involved with him than with any of Father's other stars. I had been there at the birth of George Bancroft as a world figure and I had traveled with him at the height of his fame.

Underworld, which brought George Bancroft overnight acclaim, was an example of Father's filmmaking at its best. He was proud to have bought a gangster story—he claimed it to be the daddy of them all!—by Ben Hecht. *Underworld* was to be made on a low budget, starring Bancroft, then considered a mere feature player, and Evelyn Brent, a sultry, dark-haired heroine of a dozen Paramount melodramas. To direct the picture Father turned to Joe von Sternberg.

The vicious, unrelenting, but loyal lord of the underworld, treated not as the conventional heavy but as a new kind of cult hero, made *Underworld* an overnight sensation, creating national and even international life-styles. In big cities, box offices opened an hour earlier and stayed open an hour later to accommodate the unexpected demand. All but forgotten now, *Underworld* was then as much of a milestone as *The Great Train Robbery, The Birth of a Nation,* and *The Big Parade.* The moment that *Underworld* hit the screen, gangster movies were in. Big, bumbling, rugged-faced George Bancroft became the forerunner of that immortal backfield of good baddies, Jimmy Cagney, Eddie G. Robinson, John Garfield, and Bogie. George was the first of the anti-hero heroes to walk curly-lipped into machine gun fire and who died not only oozing blood from his noble mouth but with epigrammatic fade-outs like "Mother of God, is this the end of Ricco?"

Father knew he had a gold mine in Bancroft, and the imperious, inscrutable Joe von Sternberg was now established as a star director. So B.P. assigned them to further explorations and exploitations of the underworld in *The Drag Net, The Docks of New York,* and *Thunderbolt.* Father often said that Von Sternberg was as impossible with success as he had been in his years of struggle for recognition. Of George Bancroft, on the other hand, to say that fame went to his head is understatement. Like fire down a cotton suit it spread to his chest, his pelvis, and down to his toes. As *Underworld* drew rave notices and lines around the block from New York to Rome, George Bancroft began to talk differently, walk differently, eat differently, think differently. I could see it in the way he drove through the main studio gate to his redecorated dressing room. When he waved at old Mac, the gateman who had been there forever, George's little flip of the hand was not so much patronizing as what one would expect of a British monarch acknowledging the salute of a loyal subject. Fame not only turned Bancroft's head, it seeped into his acting, as I would see for myself when Von Sternberg was directing Parmount's king of the underworld in *The Drag Net.*

Von Sternberg had a way of talking to his actors as if they were slightly retarded children, and in his approach to Bancroft we should strike the adverb. "Now George, this is a very simple scene. We should be able to get it in one take. All you have to do is walk up that flight of stairs. You think you've thrown your pursuers off the track so you are relatively relaxed. But they've been tailing you. Now, the camera is going to be on your back, but when I say 'Bang!' that's when you get it. You grab the banister and twist around, until you're facing the camera. As you slip down the steps you try to reach for your gun. But I'll say 'Bang!—Bang!' again, and that's it. I don't think we even have to rehearse it. Just give it to me as real as you can. Now George, are you sure you understand what I'm saying?"

George looked at his director with his expressive St. Bernard eyes. "Yes, Joe."

So the commander-in-chief cracked the order to his aide-de-camp, the assistant director called "Quiet!", Joe told his head cameraman—Hal Rosson, one of the best—to start filming, and at the crisp command, "Action!", Father's overnight number-one box-office star started up the creaky stairs of a realistic-looking boardinghouse. It was an impressive sight, the hulking George Bancroft, all six-foot-two and two hundred pounds of him, charging up that stairway. At the third step, Von Sternberg's voice rang out. "Bang!!" But George didn't fall. In fact, he didn't even flinch. He kept right on going. "Bang!!" Joe shouted again. George Bancroft paused a moment, as if distracted by a random thought, and went on climbing the stairs.

"God damn it, George!" Von Sternberg screamed. "What's the matter with you—are you deaf?" His voice filled the cavernous set. "*Bang!—Bang!*"

Still George didn't fall. Instead he stopped and turned those expressive brown eyes on the Napoleonic Von Sternberg. Then he spoke in the quiet voice of the ultrareasonable. "Don't shout at me, Joe. Of course I heard you. But just remember this: One shot can't stop Bancroft."

It became one of our favorite Schulberg family lines. At home Sonya and I would take turns playing the domineering Von Sternberg shouting "Bang!" while the other took over the swaggering gangster idol: "One shot can't stop Bancroft."

When I went to the preview with my father, there came that desperate moment on the stairs. In the picture it turned out exactly as Von Sternberg had planned it. George could keep on walking up those stairs with all the sense of invulnerability that his gangster roles and the powers of stardom had invested in him, but Joe had the final say. All he had to do was establish George on the stairs, cut away for a moment, and then cut back to Bancroft on the decisive "*Bang!*" that made him grab the banister and twist forward. Thanks to judicious cutting, one shot did indeed bring down the mighty Bancroft. The audience would never know that their rugged hero up there on the silver screen was a muscular presence who had come to believe in his own invincibility.

When I saw it on the screen, with George reacting to the first shot, I tried but was unable to choke back my laughter. Father tried to shush me. I was destroying one of the most dramatic moments in the picture. People were looking around at me. I held my hand over my mouth until the fit passed.

As George's fame kept mounting to tidal-wave proportions, so did his pretensions. Von Sternberg's defense was simply to ignore the antics of his star. Nobody could acquire instant deafness more quickly than Joe. They made a remarkable pair, Bancroft whom fame had transformed into an impregnable fortress, and Von Sternberg whose artistic arrogance regarded all actors as empty-headed puppets to be jerked this way and that in the firm grip of the puppeteer.

Frustrated by the Von Sternberg freeze, George would invariably turn to my father as a higher court of appeal. A vital part of B.P.'s job was to cope with his box-office stars, keeping them happy or at least content enough to show up on time for their eight o'clock calls, charming them without surrendering to their often unreasonable demands or complaints. Those were still the days of block booking, and "four Bancrofts" had been sold in advance to movie houses all over the world. So B.P. had to baby George, humor him, and hear him out. Whenever George asked him to fire "that little monster Von Sternberg," Father would play for time. Why didn't they think about it and meet over the weekend to discuss it further? Then Father would turn around and say to his director, "For Christ' sake, Joe, if George wants to do one more take, once in a while give in to him. Sure, we know he's a moron, but after all his popularity is helping to pay our salaries." And if George kept coming, as he came constantly to Father's royal chambers, with ideas for future roles he wanted to play—for now he was convinced that his dramatic range was boundless, from Ahab to Zoroaster—B.P. would smile, offer George one of his Upmanns, and say, "Interesting idea, George, why don't we think about it. . . . "

A blue-eyed tower of charm and patience at the studio, Father let go at home in his ritual walk around the dinner table with scotch highball in hand. "That stupid sonofabitch George is driving me out of my goddamn mind!" he'd shout in a voice that must have been heard from one end of Windsor Square to the other. Sometimes I was afraid that our

244

genteel neighbors would think my parents were fighting when Father was only crying out at his studio tormentors. There were some who were vicious and some who were openly defiant and some who were secretly conniving and conspiratorial, but that season George was the worst of all: as ever-present and persistent and noisy as an overgrown horsefly. At school, kids who marveled at his powers in *Underworld, The Drag Net,* and *Thunderbolt* would say, "Gee, you're lucky, you actually know George Bancroft!" And while I was admitting "Y-y-yes I do," I was thinking to myself, "If you only knew!" Their idol had feet of clay that went all the way up to his head.

One evening Father came home saying, "Ad, if I don't get away from George for at least a couple of weeks, I'm going to crack. I'm not exaggerating—his stupid ideas for new bits of characterization, new scenes, new pictures to make are driving me out of my mind."

Since there was a slight lull in the frenetic fifty-picture-a-year schedule and since Father had put together what he considered a dependable team of supervisors (the fancy new name for associate producers), he thought this would be an opportune time to take a vacation. Although Ad didn't agree with Ben's estimate of his producing staff—she thought they were mostly sycophants whose greatest talent lay in their knowing how to play up to Father's weaknesses, which were wide-ranging, rather than to shore up his strengths, which were impressive—she welcomed the idea.

"Let's go to Europe," Mother suggested, "and take the children." What she had in mind was a cultural holiday, museums and art galleries, Shakespeare at Stratford, the Louvre, the sea- and history-soaked wonders of Venice, the Italian opera and the Caesarean splendors of Rome. Over dinner they talked out the elaborate itinerary, from the Tower of London to the Tower of Pisa, from the English Channel to the Adriatic, from the Savoy to the Adlon to the George V to the Excelsior—our version of that most spendthrift and splendiferous British institution, the Grand Tour.

Father liked his culture too, but for him the ideal vacation was sneaking over the Mexican border to the gambling casinos at Agua Caliente. Traveling with Ad, the children, and their nurse was not his idea of getting away from it all. But he'd go along with anything if it spelled temporary relief from the agony of daily exposure to the ever-expanding ego of George Bancroft.

Our trip was planned like an official journey of state. Steamer trunks and suitcases were packed with changes of clothing for the five of us for every possible occasion, from formal affairs to beachside picnics, and duly labeled: *The Santa Fe Chief—The Ile-de-France—The Hotel Savoy* . . . Our itinerary, the size of a movie script, arrived from the studio Transportation Department, complete with the name of the head of the Paramount office in every one of the eight foreign capitals we would be visiting. The studio even provided us with books from Research so that we could read up on the histories and cultures of the cities and countries we'd be visiting. With our minds and our steamer trunks overpacked, the Schulbergs were ready for their European invasion. Mother kept telling Sonya and me, and even little Stuart, how much we would profit culturally and intellectually from the long journey, and Father's home-from-the-studio mood lightened dramatically as we reached Departure Day minus one. Then it happened.

Fifteen hours before we were to board the luxurious *Santa Fe Chief,* George Bancroft came shambling into Father's throne room. "B.P.," he announced, "I've got great news. We're going with ya!"

Father began to stammer, as he frequently did under pressure. "G-G-George, that would be great, but I'm afraid it's a little late— w-w-we've got a complicated schedule—thirty different reservations. . . ."

"Don't worry, we're all set!" George talked through B.P.'s protestations with his wide-screen smile. "I just checked with Transportation. We're on the *Chief* with you, in the same car! And we've got a stateroom on the *Ile-de-France,* in the same corridor. We couldn't get on the same floor with you at the Savoy, but we're in the suite right above yours. All you have to do is open the window and call 'George' and I'll pop right down. Isn't that swell? We're booked with you all the way, the Blue Train, the George Sank, right down to the Excelsior in Rome and back on the *DaVinci.* That's how it's gonna be for the rest of our lives—the Bancrofts and the Schulbergs like *this!*" George held up two long thick fingers pressed together in a gesture of inseparability.

The next day as our trunks and bags were being loaded onto the *Chief,* a truck drove right across the station platform and parked alongside our Pullman car. Two men began unloading several dozen heavy wooden cases wrapped in brown paper. We watched from our three connecting drawing rooms, having already settled in for our four-day train ride to New York. The Bancrofts, we had begun to learn, were habitually late. The pride of the Santa Fe line had to delay its departure a few precious minutes while the mysterious cases were handed up to the Pullman platform.

"George, what the hell have you got in those boxes?" B.P. wanted to know.

"My scotch," George said.

"George," Father spoke to him softly as he might to a five-year-old child, a five-year-old with a bottle-a-day habit. "All you need is half a dozen bottles. In less than a week we'll be on the *Ile-de-France*. Five days later we'll be in London. The *home* of scotch whiskey, George. Not bootleg stuff. The real thing." Father looked at the half-dozen cases still waiting to be unloaded from the truck. "Tell them to take that back and keep it for you. I just can't let you bring all that bootleg booze to England."

"Now Ben," George said with those box-office brown eyes, "I don't care what you say about the scotch over there, I trust Eddie Kaye."

Eddie Kaye was our studio bootlegger. He was a marvel of offbeat casting, jockey-size at five feet two, a hundred and ten pounds, with a falsetto voice. Legend had it that Eddie had been castrated by rival gangsters who resented his muscling in on their lucrative studio bootleg preserve. He always expressed deep devotion to me, which he begged to prove by offering to "take care of" any enemies I might have. "Anybody gives you a hard time—just tell me who ya wanna hit, Buddy—I'll get 'em in a dark alley—I'll break their legs—I'll . . ." Tiny Eddie Kaye represented the real Hollywood underworld, but audiences would have rocked with laughter if they had seen him on the screen. They wanted George Bancroft who looked every inch the killer. They would never believe that under that formidable exterior beat the heart of a marshmallow, while under the child-size hairless chest of Eddie Kaye beat the heart of your friendly neighborhood sadist.

"I trust Eddie Kaye" became another Bancroftism. Big George was loyal to his trust. He not only drank Eddie Kaye's finest throughout the four-day journey to New York, but made sure that it was installed in his spacious stateroom on the *Ile*. He drank Eddie Kaye all the way across the Atlantic and right into his suite at the Savoy. I'm not sure whether or not he brought his trusted bottle of Eddie Kaye to the captain's table on the *Ile-de-France,* but I'm sure he would have if he could. George Bancroft, my father used to say, had the courage and the simple faith of profound ignorance.

On that ocean voyage George and I had many serious conversations. That was the only kind of conversation George knew. He liked to talk and he had a favorite word: *facsimile*. I don't know where he had picked it up, and clearly he had never looked it up, but there was something touching about the loving way he rolled it around on his tongue before delivering it. "You know, Buddy," he'd say, leaning on the ship's railing and squinting his eyes at the horizon, "that sunset is a facsimile . . . of the first play that Tava [his wife] and I ever did together. An absolute facsimile . . . "

I would nod. I had learned to nod and half-listen to George. "You know, Buddy," he said, always with that thoughtful squinting of the eyes, "this trip to Europe is a facsimile of the wonderful relationship I have with your father. And that I'm going to have with you as you grow older. An absolute facsimile."

Father and Mother had encouraged me from childhood to look up any word I didn't understand. I was to drag that growing list all the way to prep school with me, and beyond, until I had compiled what amounted to my own personal dictionary. So I knew what *facsimile* meant. And I knew that poor, world-famous George didn't know what the hell he was talking about. At times I had an impulse to tell him. But there were at least three reasons for resisting the temptation. I had learned enough of studio politics to know that the boss's son doesn't offend his father's bread winning stars. In the second place I knew that George Bancroft was basically harmless. And finally I was too timid to correct him even if I had wanted to. With my stammering, my natural form of expression was to write things down.

George didn't know it but I was working on my first novel on the *Ile-de-France*. I had invented a brilliant plot, about a murderer who leaves no fingerprints because he has only one hand, and his weapon is the hook fitted on to his stump. Every afternoon I would retire to the desk in my stateroom and add a few more pages. I thought "The Hook" was bound for greatness because it drew on scenes that had most impressed me in the works of Dostoevsky, Dickens, Stevenson, and some of the other masters Father had read to us in those Sunday sessions. In addition, my central character inevitably resembled George Bancroft. In my walking dreams, my novel would be published—naturally to critical acclaim—and then would be snapped up by Paramount for a film starring George Bancroft. I even considered adopting Father's *nom de plume* from his days as a fledgling short-story writer, and calling myself Oliver P. Drexel, Jr.

This dream of artistic collaboration was in Bancroft's mind too. "Buddy," he said to me on the morning of our landfall on the English coast, "this is a momentous day, the arrival of the Bancrofts and the Schulbergs in England. In fact it's a facsimile of an idea I had when I was trying to get off to sleep last night." Stardom had made George so sensitive, his wife Octavia confided to us, that she lulled him to sleep by stroking his cheek with peach fuzz. "Peach fuzz!" Father exploded. "His head is so thick I don't think Gene Tunney could put him to sleep with a straight right to the jaw!"

Despite his intellectual shortcomings, there was something consistently affecting about George Bancroft. He was so predictably and vulnerably full of himself. Even though at fifty he was more than ten years older than Father, having achieved his fame at an age when most stars had already begun to fade, our box-office hero had total faith that he would outlast B.P. as a Paramount power, unto the next generation when I would be ready to take over the studio. Oh, we were a potent team as we leaned on the railing of that luxurious ocean liner and stared out at the blue-green vastness full of whitecaps and facsimiles.

George, incidentally, was not the only celebrity to hold forth on the *Ile-de-France*. There was also Young Stribling, the heavyweight contender from Georgia, "the King of the Canebrakes," one of the fistic phenoms of the day. Only 25, he was already a nine-year veteran of well over two hundred professional fights. Now he was on his way to London to fight an Italian giant seven inches taller and a hundred pounds heavier, at that time an unknown freak discovered in a traveling circus, but soon to become world famous: Primo Carnera. After we met together at the Captain's table, Young Stribling offered to spar with me on the deck and to teach me some of the finer points of the Manly Art.

George Bancroft looked on thoughtfully, observing that Young Stribling was a facsimile of an idea he had for a motion picture in which he would play the Georgia Peach when Stribling went on to win the championship of the world. By that time, in another facsimile, I would be out of high school and ready to write and produce this epic fight film.

Young Stribling showed me how to place my left and tuck my chin in behind my cocked right hand, and promised to get us ringside seats for his battle with the Italian strongman known affectionately as The

Ambling Alp. Father's spirits rose considerably. If he had George Bancroft on his back, at least he had the celebrated Young Stribling at his side.

Disembarking at Southampton was a madhouse. The sporting fraternity was there to receive and interview Young Stribling. And all the rest of England had turned out to surround and embrace George Bancroft. He needed a police escort to clear the way for him to get off the gangplank and onto the train for London. His fame was such that custom inspection was waived, and the Bancrofts reached their drawing room in the style of royalty. Even their cases of Eddie Kaye scotch moved along with them without mishap. When we reached the London terminal, the crowd scene was repeated. English reserve was forgotten as fans closed in and tried to lay hands on him, crying "Go'ge! Go'ge, gimme a kiss!—Sign this!—Shake me hand! Go'ge. . . !" As we moved into the lobby of the Savoy, wild-eyed fans jostled with photographers and reporters. One of the latter managed to get in a question, "Mr. Bancroft, now that you're in England, what are you most looking forward to seeing?" After one of those dramatic pauses—"Bancroft pauses" we had come to call them—George said, "I have come here to see your underworld."

I exchanged looks with my family. Father was wearing his "I'm going to murder George Bancroft" look. The look on the British reporters' faces reflected studied self-control. But when George looked into the faces pressed around him, all he saw was a mirror reflecting his own.

On our first night in London, the noted actress Peggy Wood, a close friend of Ad and Ben's, was opening in Noel Coward's *Bitter Sweet*. The Schulbergs and the Bancrofts were to be her guests, both for the performance and for dinner afterward. Aware of George's chronic unpunctuality, due in large measure to that steady flow of Eddie Kaye's finest, Father had forewarned him as he would a child, in a tone that even I found myself adopting, "Now George, here's what you should do—stop drinking at five and take a nap, as I want you to look well in the pictures they'll be taking of you and Peggy. At six o'clock start dressing. Remember it's white tie. You and Tava meet us in the lobby at seven. Seven on the dot. Peggy's been nice enough to give us her house seats. Now let's be in them ten minutes before curtain. Are you listening to me, George?"

George smiled the big, open smile beloved on all five continents. "Gotcha, B.P."

At seven, Father phoned upstairs to say we were leaving our suite and heading for the elevator. Were George and Tava ready? B.P. was sure he could hear the familiar tinkle of ice in the highball glasses as George boomed, "Yup, we're just about ready. Tava's putting the finishing touches on her makeup. We'll be down in five minutes, B.P."

In the lobby, with my young, slender father elegant in white tie, Mother looking like a doe-eyed movie star in her chiffon evening gown, Bancroft's five minutes ticked on to ten and to fifteen. Father strode to the house phone.

"George, for Christ' sake!"

Gurgle, tinkle. "On our way down, B.P."

Seven-thirty brought Father's ultimatum that we were leaving without them. At seven-thirty-three, just as we were on our way to the revolving door and the waiting limousine, George and Octavia emerged serenely from the elevator.

"George, this is unforgivable. As one star to another, you owe it to Miss Wood to be punctual. It's the height of professional discourtesy. How could you do this to her?"

Again the big brown innocent eyes begged understanding while the resonant and now well-oiled voice spoke these words: "Now Ben, I've only been in this country a couple of hours. How do you expect me to know their customs?"

For Bancroftisms there were no answers. That evening Peggy Wood, always a gracious lady, held the curtain for fifteen minutes, the additional time required by George Bancroft to adjust himself to the strange customs of his English cousins.

Next day the head of Paramount's London office showed us some of the principal sights of the city. We began with a lovely view of the Paramount emblem, stars forming a graceful circle around an impressive mountain over the company's "flagship" theater and office building. Eventually we worked our way to Westminster Abbey. The Bancrofts had declined this sightseeing trip, preferring to sleep late. When Father reprimanded George gently at the end of the day, George defended himself on the grounds of privacy. It was no fun being mobbed wherever he went. The night before, he had been pushed and pulled and had bits of his expensive full-dress suit torn off for souvenirs. So Father assured him that for their visit to the Tower of London next morning he would make special arrangements through the Paramount office; a team of English bobbies trained in crowd-control would be provided, as well as a special approach to the rear of the Tower.

Father told George we were leaving the hotel next morning at nine, while advising our Paramount guides to pick us up at ten. George was instructed to lean back in the middle of the rear seat of the limousine, so as to remain as inconspicuous as possible. Thus we drove uneventfully toward the Tower without inciting any local pedestrians. So far, so good. But as the Tower came into view a few blocks ahead, George began to stir and lean forward, peering out into the street over my shoulder. At that moment, a young pedestrian, happening to glance into the car, could not believe his starstruck eyes. "Go'ge! That really you, Go'ge? Blimey. . . ! Hi, Go'ge! Go'ge!"

His cries attracted other passersby until soon there were a dozen faces at the window. George leaned forward, presenting that famous face to them. It was like honey to flies. Now there were twenty, fifty, a hundred . . . you could see them buzzing with their revelation: "It's Go'ge! Go'ge Bancroft!!" The limousine was surrounded, a spontaneous Limey version of a Hollywood opening. The narrow street was clogged and tight-lipped bobbies tried to push back the crowd to clear a way for our car. Suddenly a large hand reached down over my shoulder and found the handle of the door. The rear door of the limousine swung open, and George Bancroft flung himself out of the car and into the midst of that churning human sea.

Later we would laugh about it, the crowd-shy George Bancroft literally throwing himself to the wolves of fame. But at that moment we watched in amazement and horror as George's head bobbed along like a loosened buoy in an angry sea. It was half an hour before we found him again, in the Tower of London where the intrepid bobbies had rescued him from the crowd. He was battered and torn and flushed with victory.

"George, goddammit, you could have been killed out there," Father scolded him, promising us that this was the last time he would ever urge the Bancrofts to join us in our sightseeing.

"I'm sorry, B.P.," George was still panting, "but after all, they're my public. I owe that to 'em."

The London leg of the Grand Tour was full of turmoil. It led to the first real fight I'd ever had with my father. It had to do with another theater evening. The Stratford Theater was doing *Twelfth Night* and Father had a ticket for me. I told him I couldn't go because I had to pick the college football games coming up that Saturday for my weekly contest with Maurice. We picked the scores of a hundred college football games, all the way from the Trojans of Southern California and the Fighting Irish of Notre Dame to struggles involving Slippery Rock and Bowling Green. It was hard work at best, with all the available sports sections to provide vital intelligence. But all I could find in London was the Paris edition of the *New York Herald-Tribune,* and so I was under a great deal of pressure, especially since my predictions had to be postmarked before the day of the game.

My usually permissive father began to raise his voice. An evening like this was exactly why we had come to Europe, to see all the good things that never came to Hollywood. He had had to use his influence to get these seats. The theater had been sold out for weeks. It would be a dramatic experience I would remember all my life. I was to put away that silly list of football games, he insisted, and open my mind to Shakespeare. When I tried to explain that if I did not get my football picks in the mail that night I would break a vital link in the continuity of my gridiron competition with Maurice, he tried to lift me bodily out of my chair. I squirmed out of his grasp and suddenly he slapped me across the face. My eyes smarted with tears, falling upon the paper on which I was inscribing those thoughtful numbers: "Washington State 21—Idaho 7 . . ." I shouted at him: "Leave me alone, you sonofabitch! I never wanted to come on this crazy trip anyway!"

He tried to drag me down the hallway to the main door of the suite but I fought back. There was another terrible scene at the door. "All right, Buddy, I'm sorry I hit you. But for the last time—you're coming with us to *Twelfth Night.*"

"I'm staying here and picking football games!"

"You know what's going to happen to you?—you're going to grow up to be one of those typical, stupid Hollywood kids who collects autographs from morons like George Bancroft and sings 'Fight On for Old S.C.!' Your mother and I may have been poor, but we knew what was important in life. We would have saved up all year to see something like the production we're seeing tonight."

"Dad, you don't understand. I've *got* to pick these football games."

Father's bulging, sensitive eyes would have destroyed me if I had not been armored in self-righteousness. "All right, be an idiot," he said. "It's that goddamn California sunshine. It makes everybody football and tennis crazy." The last word I heard was "Idiot!" Then the door slammed with what seemed to me at the time a tragic finality.

But in time, family relations were repaired by the tribulations we suffered in common from the Bancrofts. Father forgave my cultural lapse sufficiently to take me to the Young Stribling-Primo Carnera bout, which attracted great attention at the time. Sandwiched among the English fancy, I saw the largest fighter I had ever seen win an awkward and unsatisfactory decision on a foul in the fourth round. Father had bet on Stribling because he had watched the Georgian train. In the gym he had looked stylish and hard to hit, and Father had made one of his casually reckless wagers—a thousand pounds, he admitted later. The ungainly stray from a small Italian circus had been awarded a most peculiar decision, claiming he had been hit low by what seemed to us at ringside to be an invisible punch. They repeated their act again a few weeks later, in Paris, this time with Stribling winning on a foul. By now I had seen enough fights to learn one of the sad realities of the sweet science: Every so often the fix was in.

In the case of hapless Primo Carnera, as we would learn in time, the fix was always in, right up to the championship of the world he would win from Jack Sharkey. But when the mob who owned him had made their point, and the handcuffs were removed from his opponents, he was defenseless, thrown to lions like Max Baer and Joe Louis.

In Paris, George repeated his London performance. When the attentive but cynical French press asked him what he most wanted to see in the City of Light, he told them he wanted to see its underworld. In overflowing press conferences in Prague and Budapest, he was a great block of consistency: Take me to see your underworld. In Budapest this particularly infuriated my father. Budapest, of course, was one of the flourishing centers of European theater. Again the Schulbergs and the Bancrofts were invited to the homes of the leading playwrights, the Vajdas, the Zilahys, the Biros, and to the openings of their plays in a theater world that rivaled London's and New York's. Again Big George was late for those openings, and failed to catch the names of Hungarian stars who considered themselves as famous in their smaller but highly artistic world as he was in his global fishbowl. George was a constant embarrassment, and we even blamed our growing family tensions on his overbearing presence. In one luxurious *wagon-lit* drawing room there was an un-Schulberglike chain reaction of face-slapping that began with Sonya's striking little Stuart, my striking Sonya, Father reacting against my reddened cheek, and Mother making some Freudian observations to Ben as to how intrafamily trauma could scar our emotional life, triggering a parental shouting match. When our nurse Ruth, who had replaced

Wilma, burst into helpless sobs, the Schulbergs focused their frustrations on her.

The prospect of seeing Europe for the first time had flushed Ruth with an enthusiasm that waned quickly once we disembarked. As insensitive to Europe as the Bancrofts, she had spent most of her time with a long face sending postcards home and wishing she hadn't come. Little Stuart was fidgety, Sonya was moody, and I was just old enough to resent having a nurse along at all—especially a clod who cared nothing about football games, or reading Robert Benchley, or meeting Young Stribling, or even listening to the records I had brought along. My favorite was an English hit that went, "I lift up my finger and I say 'Now now tweet tweet come come . . .'" By now everybody was begging me not to play it, and Ruth went so far as to threaten to break it.

Mother and Father, momentarily united, turned on Ruth with the accusation that if she had been doing her job instead of moping, if she had taken little Stuart off to play somewhere so that he and Sonya could be peacefully separated, this family explosion never would have happened. To which Ruth answered, perhaps with more reason on her part than any of us appreciated at the time, that she was up to here with little Stuart and moody Sonya and crazy Buddy, sick of all of us, fed up with Europe in general and ready to go home to some place that made sense, like Oxnard, California. She was put off at the next depot, and walked contemptuously out of our lives.

Things were a little more peaceful without Ruth. But Father's number-one star was still breathing down our necks, still dreaming of the future partnership of Bancroft & Schulberg, Jr. In Vienna the Bancroft style drove Father to the wall of ultimate exasperation. Once again George had told the press he was not interested in seeing their famous St. Stephan's Cathedral, he really had no interest in palaces and opera houses and art museums and all the other cultural wonders of which Vienna was so proud. "What I've come here for is to see your underworld."

That did it. Father decided on a desperate ploy. The next stop on our itinerary was to be Venice, but he canceled that leg of the journey and instead we took off for Biarritz without letting George and Tava in on the secret. There was jubilation in the Schulberg drawing rooms as Bancroftless we sped our way to the French coast. Father's mood soared as he pictured the Bancrofts finding themselves on the train to Venice. He and Mother even played casino without arguing over the cards. She invariably won, a canny and cautious player, and he played with his usual unmathematical abandon, a trait that had made him one of the favorite pigeons at the big games in Hollywood. (I would watch with a sense of wonder and unease as fifteen and twenty thousand of his dollars went flying off to shrewder pockets at a single sitting.) It was a hilarious trip to Biarritz as we exchanged our favorite Bancroftisms, which seemed to improve with each retelling, like listening to Father read Robert Benchley out loud.

The Bancrofts finally caught up with us again in Rome, where we made an official tour of the Paramount facilities, the Colosseum, the Spanish Steps, and some of the other interesting sites of that old, provincial city. Always a great convincer—who else could run a big movie studio?—Ben expressed indignation that their travel plans had been fouled up. When Transportation had changed the itinerary at the last moment, he had assumed that the Bancrofts had also been informed. As always, George was understanding. I have never known anyone who could look so thoughtfully understanding.

Back in Hollywood the Bancroft parade marched on. Another film— *The Docks of New York*—another success. With Humphrey Bogart still playing the clean-cut WASP juvenile complete with white flannels and tennis racket, George Bancroft was riding high as the world's favorite tough guy. At a wrap-up party on the set, I watched as George singled out a lowly bit-player hovering in lonely anonymity near the bar. "Well, are you enjoying the party, young man?" George asked with professional affability several sizes larger than life.

"Yes, Mr. Bancroft," muttered the awestruck unknown. "Been in pictures long?" George kept the conversational ball rolling. "No sir," said the neophyte. "In fact, this is my first one." "Is that so!" George seemed delighted to hear it. "Well, that's why I came over. I just wanted you to know that George Bancroft talks to everybody." And I had a new Bancroftism for our collection.

Bancroft continued to star in tough-guy movies through the early Thirties, but now the gangster film was hitting its stride and Warner's had begun to take over the field with Cagney in *Public Enemy*. After Paul Muni scored in Howard Hughes's *Scarface,* they would make super-tough guys of Bogey and John (né Jules) Garfield. Now every studio was in the *Underworld* business and George was no longer Mr. Underworld.

George had been signed to a seven-year contract that began at one thousand a week, with each year's option raising his salary an additional thousand. But his weekly salary for the seventh-and-final year under the original contract called for a raise from $6,000 to $7,500. By this time he was still a "name" but far from Number One. Responsible to Lasky and Zukor and the awesome power of New York, whence the banking capital flowed, Father felt he could not recommend picking up George's option at a cost of $380,000 a year. But George was still a valuable property, and so B.P. suggested that George be kept on at his present salary of $6,000 a week, or $312,000 for the coming year.

When George heard this from Father, he grew red in the face. He couldn't believe that Father would insult him like that. He insisted that rival studios had offered him $10,000 a week if he could get out of his contract but he had felt a loyalty to B.P. and the Company. Now, where was their loyalty to him? It wasn't a question of loyalty, Father argued, but of hard dollars and cents. In fact, he offered to show George the box-office receipts on all his pictures from the beginning. Then he could see for himself how far grosses had fallen off. But Bancroft refused to look or listen. Father begged him to take the six thousand. "George, please listen to me, you'll never make more money in your life."

George looked at him with those big, brown, hurt, and now angry eyes, "Ben, I can't believe this—I thought you were my friend."

"George, now I'm going to level with you. Lasky and Zukor don't want me to keep you on even at six thousand a week. I know it hurts but it's a fact. I've been fighting for you."

George drew himself up to his full six feet two and squared his broad shoulders. "I don't need anybody to fight my battles. I can walk over to Metro right now and double my salary! I'll be bigger over there than Wallie Beery."

"George, for your sake, I hope you're right," Father said. "But this is a nutty business. It's not a facsimile of anything, George. It's its own crazy world. You're not Number One any more. And you never will be again."

George Bancroft turned on his heel and walked out of Father's office, cleaned out his deluxe dressing room, went home to Tava's soothing ministrations, let all the other studios know he was now open to their offers, and waited for the telephone to ring. But Hollywood was a cluster of small but powerful feudal states run by half a dozen men. While constantly conspiring against each other, these feudal lords met at least once a week around an apparently congenial poker table. In a room filled with the smoke of the finest Havana cigars and the aroma of the most expensive scotch that could be smuggled in, a casually pejorative comment could make or break a star's career. So the word was out that

George Bancroft refused to budge from his self-appraised salary of $7,500 a week. Teeth clenched to the soggy end of a giant Upmann, a man who was a hundred times tougher offstage than George Bancroft could ever simulate on camera raised the ante another five hundred and said, "Fuck 'im! He's washed up! who needs 'im?" That's the way Eddie Mannix of MGM talked, and Harry Cohn of Columbia. The glamour capital of the world was as tough a company town as could be found in the coal fields of Pennsylvania or West Virginia. The men behind the movies carried brass knuckles and never hesitated to use them in the crunch.

When George Bancroft had been off the screen for six months, a studio felt they had a good all-star role for him and offered him $25,000 for a six-week guarantee. Nothing doing, said George. His price was $7,500 a week, take it or leave it. When he had been off the screen a year, he was offered $20,000 for a five-week job. No deal, said George, my price is seventy-five hundred a week. Sulking, stonewalling, peach-fuzzed, he was finally forced to accept bit parts that gnawed at his pride. When he finally came back to work for my father again, in *Wedding Present, A Doctor's Diary,* and *John Meade's Woman,* starring B.P.'s new find, Eddie Arnold, in a role that would have been considered tailor-made for Bancroft five years earlier, George accepted $250 a week. But when he finished his last scene, on a job that began on Monday and wound up on Friday, he asked if he could come to Father's office. "Ben," George said, "I think I've got an interesting idea for an entirely different kind of screen credit. Instead of putting my name in the cast list, how about putting just a big question mark and then we'll run a nationwide contest on 'Guess Who's Playing This Part?' People who may have forgotten me will scratch their heads and say, 'My God, that's our old favorite, George Bancroft! They should bring him back in a picture of his own!' And then, Ben, we'll find a great story, maybe get Ben Hecht to write it, maybe Eddie Arnold and I could co-star, we'll play two brothers who become rival gangsters in love with the same girl, one hit picture, B.P., that's all it takes, and then I'll be right back there on top again."

Father had to tell George, as gently as he could, that the "Guess Who?" contest would be laughed out of theater lobbies. It would only remind the public of how precipitately the great George Bancroft had tumbled from the top of the mountain. George *Bancroft* had become George *Who*? and all the promotional horses and all the publicity men couldn't put the *Underworld* superstar together again.

24

ONE DAY I was approaching the inter-
section of our quiet Lorraine and stately Wilshire Boulevards when the
wail of saxophones attracted my attention to *two* white Pierce-Arrows
cruising down Wilshire in tandem. In the rear seat of the chauffeur-
driven lead car was the handsome, ruddy-faced, ever-grinning Mickey
Neilan, with his arm around a dark-haired beauty, Father's obstreperous
Gloria Swanson. And in the motorized chariot behind them, another
chauffeur drove half a dozen jazzmen of the Abe Lyman Orchestra,
there to serenade the royal couple wherever they went, and believe me
they went everywhere, from the raucous all-night Plantation Club to the
decorous gingerbread castle of the Hotel Del Coronado.

I waved from my bike and Mickey, whom I had known all the way
from the early Pickford-Famous Players days to those cross-country
extravaganzas on the *Chief,* waved back with his broad, infectious Irish
grin. The entire scene was over in a few ticks of the stopwatch I carried in
my pocket, but the moment still shines like a diamond in the crown of
memory. Did I know then, as I sat on my bike absorbing the splendors
not of a mogul but of an irrepressible Irish king, that his silver train of
Pierce-Arrows was doomed to sweep down Wilshire Boulevard until it
reached the Palisades and plunged into the obscurity of the sea? There
must have been something more than a casual wave to a famous director
with whom I was only marginally acquainted to make that moment so
memorable. A little bird of reality seemed to be cawing, "Too much . . .
too soon . . . too good to last . . ."

The reality bird may have been the voice of my mother who never lost her ghetto sense of survival. Facing the gusty winds of Hollywood, she would bend but never break. She might spend sums of money on clothes and houses, American antiques, private schools, travel, and favorite forward-looking charities but she spent wisely, with care and taste, keeping a ledger of investments, determined never to return to the poverty of an impractical father and a trapped mother. While Father didn't spend money so much as he flung it away by the fistful.

I went up to do the math homework I loathed, leaving Father at the card table with Zeppo Marx. Zeppo was the rather good-looking one who played the inane romantic leads in the Marx Brothers comedies: the only Marx brother who wasn't funny. Whatever frustrations Zeppo may have suffered in front of the cameras, eclipsed as he was by Groucho, Harpo, and Chico, he more than compensated for them with an aggressive card sense that made him the terror of the moguls. He could destroy the smartest of them, with a deck of cards in lieu of a pistol.

When I came down for breakfast next morning at seven o'clock, Father and Zeppo were just winding up the game and settling accounts. I watched as Father wrote out a check for $22,000. He was potted from all-night drinking (while cool-head Zep kept mental record of every card discarded), and I remember his hearty laugh. He loved laughing as much as he did living and losing.

I went off to school with a troubled mind. I wasn't worried about our going broke. It never occurred to me that such losses could drain the plentiful Schulberg reservoir until it would be as dry as the Los Angeles River. At that time Father's hold on the studio still seemed secure. I knew Hollywood was a roller coaster, but I was too busy or complacent to worry about the Schulbergs ever hurtling off the track. But over there on Western Avenue I had seen a lot of kids who were poor. South of Wilshire Boulevard, in the streets around Pico, I had seen Mexicans and Japanese who worked as gardeners, fruit-pickers, street vendors. I lay no claim to premature social consciousness. I could see that there were people on the bottom, in the middle, and at the top but I was too young, too rich, and too obsessed with my own activities to have much time left for social analysis. So it was less a process of thinking than of feeling that there was something not quite right in Mickey Neilan's go-for-broke world of white Pierce-Arrows, and Father's embarrassing and totally unnecessary custom-made town car, or $22,000 tossed away on a friendly game of chance. Something was rotten—whispered my little reality bird—in the state of Hollywood.

260

When I came down for breakfast on another school morning I found one of Father's favorite writers, Herman Mankiewicz (a refugee from the New York *World* and the Algonquin Round Table, known later for his screenplay of *Citizen Kane*), winding up a casino duel with B.P. There was genius in Mank—"a spoiled priest," Scott Fitzgerald would call him—but at the card table he was no Zeppo Marx. This time Mank was the loser, out $15,000, and since Father was making five times the salary Mank was earning as a screenwriter, he arranged to have installments taken out of Mank's weekly paychecks for the next three months until they were even again.

Here were two of Hollywood's more sophisticated intellects playing like kids with tens of thousands of dollars that never seemed real to them. It was like funny money you could buy in the ten-cent store. But Mother knew it was real, and although I was drawn to Father's style, his unique combination of intellectual curiosity and robust joy of life, his superiority to the moguls I knew as tough, selfish, ignorant, and mean, I was shocked by the vulgarity of his mindless gambling. Not that I coveted the money myself. But the waste of it, seemingly for the sheer sake of waste, was not easy to understand. Maurice's father may not have had the searching mind, the education, and the literary leanings of mine, but at least he didn't drink as if the scotch faucet was being turned off in the morning, and he didn't squander four-figure money on the flip of a card.

One Monday morning after Father had played through a weekend poker game with a motley group of Reno professionals and Hollywood high rollers, I asked him in their presence how he could bear losing almost $10,000. Maybe I could understand it if he won, I said, but losing that kind of money—or more—week after week (when he could have bought San Fernando Valley or given it to the poor) was beyond my comprehension. "Buddy, you don't understand," Father tried to define it: "Winning and losing is the same thing. It doesn't matter. It's the excitement of playing."

I felt baffled and frustrated. But the daughter of Nick the Greek—somehow she materialized like one of those unbelievable/believable creations of Lewis Carroll—spiritedly seconded B.P. "Your father's so right!" she shouted at me. "If you're a real gambler, you never care if you win or lose. It's the excitement, the thrill, everything riding on how you play your hand—and then the turn of a card!"

I had heard a lot about Father's gambling, mostly through laments from Ad, but I had never thought about it deeply before. Ad's theory was that Father was basically a sensitive and serious man who knew in his heart that nobody was worth $11,000 a week, that he was wracked with guilt and self-doubt about earning that kind of money when his father had been lucky to make five or six dollars a week and when his own brothers Louie and Arthur were struggling to keep a small toy business alive in The Bronx. Father's sisters were also married to men whose lives ran on the rim of failure. Only Ben had broken through the money barrier into a stratosphere shining with dollar signs instead of stars.

Whatever the explanation. Father was from his premature grey hair to his pedicured pink toenails a gambling man. One Sunday evening after a disastrous Saturday night at the Clover Club, the fever was still in him. Sometimes, in need of action, he would play (and lose) to Mother. But this time in desperation he offered to flip me for half a dollar. I lost. Double or nothing? I lost again. To make the confrontation more bizarre, it all took place—for some reason I can no longer remember—in the bathroom. What I do remember is that I kept losing. I might win an occasional flip, but it seemed as if three out of four times I was on the wrong side of the coin. Suddenly B.P. was doing to me what Zeppo Marx and the pros from Reno to Caliente had been doing to him for years.

When I got too far behind he gave me a chance to get even by raising the bets to a dollar. And when I still came up a loser, he offered to double the ante again. After all, I reassured myself, sooner or later the law of averages would have to assert itself. So I accepted. But nervously. I was betting to win. The Jaffe side of me was worried about losing so much money. I didn't think in terms of Father's eleven-thousand-dollars-a-week, although I would have to think about it later as I tried to find my own place in society. All the fathers of the boys I played with in Windsor Square were making thousands of dollars a week. When I heard my father mention someone as "only making" a thousand a week, I associated the figure with actors, directors, or writers in the lower brackets.

Still, my sense of values was attuned to my own five-dollar-a-week allowance, and what I could earn from my soft-drink business with Maurice, and the extra payments (or cultural bribes) I'd get from Mother for reading the classics. So as this bathroom gambling session with Father escalated from the innocent flip of the coin with which it had begun, I suddenly heard Father telling me I was out two hundred dollars. "How about it, Buddy. Double or nothing?"

"N-n-n-n . . ." I shook my head NO. I was still thinking like a non-gambler. In terms of real money. How could I pay back $400? It would take me six months of self-deprivation. I went on losing until my debt reached $250. Father was flushed with victory. Like a losing fighter who finally finds himself in the ring with someone he can lick. I was flushed, too, but with fear of losing. It never occurred to me that Father would say, "That's all right, Buddy, forget it, we were only playing." That was the human side of him, and when he was human he was extremely human. But when he was gambling he was as crazed as Dostoevsky at the roulette tables in Wiesbaden.

Dostoevsky was in that bathroom with us. Father had read aloud to me and urged me to start reading myself the short novels of the Russian master. All his life he dreamt of doing *The Eternal Husband* as a film, and while I was still in high school we made some stabs at breaking it down together into screenplay form. So I felt a kinship to Dostoevsky, not only through his work (though the major novels were still in store for me)but through his life as Father revealed it to me in bits and pieces. That's how I knew that our Feodor had gone to Wiesbaden to make a fortune on the turn of the wheel, had lost stake after stake until he was virtually pauperized again, and had gone away not defeated and suicidal but strangely exhilarated. No wonder Father and Feodor, in my young mind, became a single image of paternity. "Five hundred rubles," Dostoevsky was saying with that mad glint in the eye. "Double or nothing!"

I managed to mumble "Double" and won. On the next toss of the coin I would either owe or win a thousand dollars, a modest weekly paycheck at the studio but a towering fortune to the young man Ad had taught the difference between Hollywood money and the real thing. When I looked up at Father-Feodor, and felt him almost trembling with anticipation of the next toss, something within me cracked, and I cried out, "I don't want to! I don't want to play anymore. Let's stop! Can't we stop?!"

The outburst had an immediate effect. It was able to reach Father and bring him back to sanity. "I'm sorry, Buddy," he said quietly, "I shouldn't be teaching you to gamble. Ad would kill me."

25

EACH ME TO *gamble*! Father was so intelligent in some ways, the equal, perhaps the superior, of Irving Thalberg as Hollywood's resident intellectual. But so crazy-dumb in other ways. Didn't he know that he was teaching me *not* to gamble, at least for the obscene stakes he had a passion for losing? Didn't he know that I would become as obsessed with the size of his losses as he was—for totally opposite reasons, his emotional compass pointing 180 degrees away from mine?

The point-counterpoint of gambling is that while it may be wildly self-destructive, it can also inspire the taking of creative chances. And while Father's (and Von Sternberg's) *Crime and Punishment* was hardly in a class with Dostoevsky's original, it suggested the same drive that had propelled the Russian novelist to psychological depths as yet un-fathomed, and that prodded my father to bet on hands still unproven. I am thinking not only of *Underworld,* where he gambled and won, but of *Wings.* In Jesse Lasky, Jr.'s account of his own and his father's Holly-wood careers, there is a curious omission: my father. Young Jesse has been one of my good friends; I know him as a charming and talented man. But he manages to describe the ordeal of producing *Wings* as if it were entirely the product of his father's courage and creativity. From the starting gate to the backstretch and down to the wire, B.P. doesn't get a single call. In an odd postscript to the saga, young Jesse has my father asking the director Bill Wellman after *Wings* is finished who the tall, handsome, shyly appealing guy is who makes a memorable little gesture before flying off into the wild blue yonder for his final dogfight. And in Jesse's myopic version, Bill Wellman's answer is, "Hell, if you don't know—I don't, either!"

Sons are understandably vulnerable to fabulous fathers and so that's how it must have been told in the Lasky domain. But the story doesn't wash. B.P. had already cast Gary Cooper opposite his prize discovery of the Twenties, Clara Bow, both in *It* and in *Children of Divorce,* and had fought for Coop against the directors who insisted he was "wooden" and "couldn't act." In those days, thank God, producers didn't protect themselves by having test audiences twist dials to indicate their reactions—*cool—warmer—getting hot*—as the film played on. Father used a more direct approach. In *Wings,* Gary Cooper was still a featured player, with a role subordinate to Richard Arlen's and Buddy Rogers's. But Father was quick to notice that none of the Paramount stars stirred the hearts of the front-office secretaries—and other parts of their anatomy—like Gary Cooper.

Long before the stardom that came to him in the Thirties, and the superstardom that swept him on from the Forties to the Sixties, Coop was the secret dream and in many cases the literal love of the entire studio secretarial pool. All typing stopped, all eyes turned to devour what Father's main secretary described as "the most beautiful hunk of man who ever walked down this hall!" My father's second secretary, the pleasingly plump, happy-dispositioned Jean Baer, carried on a semi-secret (or as secret as those things could be in the studio fishbowl) affair with Gary for years. He was never a flamboyant swordsman like Errol Flynn or (though this may come as a surprise to outsiders) Freddie March. But, for all his quiet speech and diffident ways, Coop might have been the Babe Ruth of the Hollywood boudoir league. It was whispered down the studio corridors that he had the endowments of Hercules and the staying powers of Job. It was local gossip that during his romance (as we used to call it) with Lupe Velez, the Mexican pepper pot was so jealous of her prized possession that she would meet him at the door when he came home from the studio, unbutton his fly, and, spirited primitive that she was, sniff suspiciously for the scent of rival perfumes.

Anyway, in every meaning of Miss Glyn's provocative two-letter word, Cooper had It, and Father was one of the first to recognize it and to guide him from supporting to starring roles. At least that's the way the Cooper legend spun its golden threads through the Schulberg household. And in his memoirs in *Life,* Coop—like Gary Grant and the rare few among a legion of ingrates—acknowledged his debt to B.P. as the first producer to recognize his potential and give him his break.

Wings was an embattled picture, both on the screen where the vicious dogfights between the American and German fighter planes of World War I were reenacted for the first time, and behind the scenes where a running battle was fought between the West Coast studio (where Jesse Lasky loyally supported B.P.) and the ever-threatening New York office of Adolph Zukor. Father had wanted to do an air picture for a long time. The seed may have been planted when we were coming home from New York through the Panama Canal and the news was radioed to our ship, the *President Van Buren,* that Lindbergh had landed safely in Paris. The *Van Buren* went berserk. Passengers who had never spoken to each other kissed and hugged, and nearly everyone on board got gloriously drunk. Father had been so carried away with the historic 33-hour flight of our Lone Eagle that he had wound up in the wrong stateroom with a young homeymooner who had lost track of her bridegroom in the shipboard excitement.

From the moment that the single-prop one-seater *Spirit of St. Louis* touched down at Le Bourget, America became instantly air-minded. People treasured envelopes that arrived by airmail, and sporting types offered great sums to aviators who would fly them from Salt Lake City to Los Angeles in an open cockpit. After Harding, Teapot Dome, splitting headaches from bathtub gin, the cynicism of the American press, and the nihilism embraced by the so-called "lost generation," America seemed to be born again in the individual triumph of the modest, diffident (Cooperlike) hero of the skies. When Lindbergh came to Hollywood that year, world-famous movie stars crowded around him like kids, begging for his autograph. My parents took me to the reception for him at the Ambassador Hotel and his autograph in my precious red-leather book gave me vicarious celebrity when I showed it off at school. Of course Father wanted to make a picture of what everybody was hailing as "the greatest single exploit in the history of the world."

But Lindy, our blue-eyed young god, was positively un-American in his determination not to cash in on his overnight fame. Willing to be feted by Doug Fairbanks, Mary Pickford, Marion Davies, and the rest of our local peerage, he was unapproachable on the subject of turning over his life story to the whims of the movie moguls.

One of Father's writer friends was John Monk Saunders, who had lost a leg after being shot down by a Von Richtofen fighter-pilot in an air-duel over St.-Mihiel. Saunders, married to the beauteous Fay Wray (later of *King Kong* fame), was one of those literate, colorful romantics spawned by the Great War. With gusto he told us about his adventures in the days when fliers jousted with each other through the clouds with all the dash and aplomb of knights of old. Father, who loved to play his hunches, told Saunders that if he wrote the story, Paramount would buy it. Thus the first motion picture of the world's first battles in the air was launched. The story—two fellows in love with the same girl—was the plot Hollywood war-films seemed unable to avoid. But B.P. felt a simple story line would allow for more footage of the dogfights that had never been seen before.

Jesse Lasky backed B.P. on the crucial decision to add *Wings* to the Paramount production schedule for the coming year. "We will make the first epic of the air, the *Big Parade* of the Lafayette Escadrille," Lasky announced with the same ebullience with which he had backed C. B. De Mille when they had rented that old barn in the wilds of uninhabited Hollywood to make *The Squaw Man* almost fifteen years earlier.

With that kind of encouragement, Father assigned his favorite writing team to the project, Buddy Leighton and his talented wife Hope Loring. As the only producer at that time who had served his apprenticeship as a screenwriter, B.P. had a built-in appreciation of the writer's contribution to the finished film. He drummed into me that unless the writer's structure is sound, the plot has its own logic and power, and its characters are believable, intriguing, and *vital,* the combined cinematic genius of John Ford, King Vidor, and Lewis Milestone couldn't bring the script to life. In time Buddy Leighton would become a producer, as most good writers became producers or directors in self-defense, in protest against their well-paid serfdom. But just as I learned, at 525 Lorraine and at the Studio, the answer to that frequent question, "What do producers do?", I also saw with my own eyes and heard with my own ears how much more the writers were doing than the public would ever know.

I had already learned that not all actors and actresses were the bastards and bitches Father liked to call them. Gary Cooper was always nice to me on the set (nice to everybody, it seemed to me), and Cary Grant parked his Model A roadster in our driveway to deliver one of my favorite dogs, a young Airedale called "Gent." Richard Arlen, who would play one of the leading roles in *Wings,* took me boating with his bride-to-be, Jobyna Ralston, who had a supporting role in that picture but was never to achieve the stardom of her sister Esther.

But my admiration was reserved for the Buddy Leightons and the Hope Lorings. Sometimes, fighting panic, I would show them and other writers who came to the house some of my groping efforts at short stories and poems. It was their praise and Father's I hoped to earn. In turn I'd be allowed to read their scripts and sometimes even be asked for comments. I never spoke up at the story conferences. But sometimes Father would ask me what I thought of their scripts, or of a particular scene or character. I was learning to read with a pencil in my hand—to make notes in the margin. To this day I am unable to read a novel without a pencil in hand for marginal comments. I can still see Father reading a script in the library with a pencil in one hand and a highball within reach of the other. That is how I thought reading was done.

While *Wings* was in the works, a brash young second-unit and special-effects director intercepted Father in the long corridor between the reception desk and his office. That's where underlings he couldn't crowd into his daily schedule would be able to steal a minute moving along at his shoulder as he hurried on to the protective presence of his secretaries. (When the Hungarian playwright Ernst Vajda—pronounced *Voida*— was imported to Paramount, and in turn brought his brother Victor, they would lurk in this corridor and pounce on Father for impromptu story conferences whenever he appeared. Father's only defense was to add to his bathroom repertoire a little number entitled "Oh, you can't avoid a Voida in the hall. . . !")

An active member of this corridor army was the impetuous and then-unknown William Wellman, called "Wild Bill" because he was thought to be slightly crazed as a result of a steel plate in his head.

"B.P.," Wild Bill ran up to him one day, "you've got to let me direct *Wings*."

"That's asking the impossible," Father told him. "In the first place we haven't got a green light from New York to make the picture yet. And if we do sell them on it, it will be our first picture costing over a million. Can you imagine the look on Zukor's face if we tell him we're putting all that money in the hands of an unknown director?"

"Fuck 'im!" said Wild Bill, who had brought back from France not only a wild temperament but a World War vocabulary. I was in the Lafayette Escadrille. I know what it is to be in one of those fuckin' dogfights! In fact, I've got a fuckin' plate in my head to prove it!"

"And when I tell Mr. Zukor I've chosen you to direct *Wings* he'll say we both have plates in our heads," Father told him.

"Fuck 'im! I thought *you* were the boss of the studio!"

"I am," Father said, "but it's like the Army, Bill. Jesse Lasky is the Chief of Staff, and Mr. Zukor is the President, the Commander-in-Chief. What I *can* do—if we get the go-ahead we're working on—is to put you in charge of all the aerial photography. Even if it's called second unit it will be a good credit. After all, two-thirds of this picture will be in the air. In fact, right now the whole thing's in the air."

"Fuck second unit," Wellman said. "If anybody directs *Wings,* it's Wellman. That picture is *mine.* My own life story. I'll tear this joint apart if I don't get the chance."

Day after day Bill Wellman would be waiting in that front-office corridor to pounce on Father and pump the same message into him until "Wellman—*Wings,* Wellman—*Wings* . . ." began to throb in B.P.'s brain like an overplayed radio commercial. Finally the green light flashed from the New York office! Lasky had convinced Zukor, who in turn had convinced his Board of Directors to let B.P. put *Wings* into production. Now came the vital question. Whom would you assign to direct it? Vic Fleming was a big name on the lot. And James Cruze. Or should they try to borrow King Vidor from MGM?

B.P. heard himself saying, "I think we should use Bill Wellman."

"Bill *who?*"

And then Father, whose own resistance finally had given way to his gambling instinct, his flair for the dramatic, and his feeling for the underdog, ran through the now-familiar lexicon of Wellman's virtues. "I've got to play my hunch. Every once in a while a director comes along who's born to make a certain picture. Bill fought in those air-battles we'll be staging in *Wings.* He'll be able to show Buddy [Rogers] and Dick [Arlen] and Coop how it felt to climb into those fighter planes and how they acted between missions when they were afraid that every night they had on the ground might be their last. Bill knows what it's like to be shot down by a Von Richtofen ace—he has a steel plate in his head!"

If the Schulberg household had had its own Hollywood Smithsonian, that celebrated steel plate would have been one of our principal exhibits. For Father loved to tell that story. A slender cigar-wielding St. George fighting the dragons of New York, he could tell it four or five times in succession, usually to guests at his bar, but sometimes only to Sonya and me for want of a fresher audience. Although his obsessive repetition may sound boring, it was like a passionate pilgrim's sharing a stirring episode from the Crusades with his family.

And so it came to pass that Adolph Zukor, the little man with the overall power, called my father and said in his quiet voice, "Ben, so you still want to use Wellman? If it's all right with Jesse, I don't care—I think everybody who stays out there in Hollywood too long gets a little *meshugah*. New York never heard of Wellman. New York feels you're taking a terrible gamble. You're putting a million dollars of our money in the hands of a boy who's never handled an epic before, who's only made two C pictures in his whole life."

"Mr. Zukor," Father said, "if Wellman doesn't do a great job with this picture—if he doesn't make it the picture of the year—you can have my resignation. So help me God, if Wellman's a flop with *Wings,* I'll quit."

"You won't have to quit," Zukor warned, "you'll be fired first."

"It's a deal, Mr. Zukor," Father said, always excited by high stakes. "And this is one bet both sides can win."

Wild Bill Wellman threw himself into *Wings* with all the zeal he had promised. The picture was dedicated "to those young warriors of the sky whose wings are folded about them forever," and the realism of the air-battles impressed the critics and amazed the public. In a creative transition between silence and sound, subtitles were still used in place of audible dialogue, but when the fighter planes took off the audience could hear the roar of the engines, and when one of the aviators was shot down they could hear the haunting whine of his fatal descent. Because these sounds came from a screen that had been silent for thirty years, they had more effect than they would ever have again.

All over the world *Wings* was hailed as a cinematic milestone, and with that one big chance Wild Bill Wellman was up there with the big boys like Ford and Cruze, Fleming and Vidor. He would go on to *Nothing Sacred, The Ox-Bow Incident,* an impressive list of well-directed hits. *Wings* won the first Academy Award for best picture of the year, and that spring at the white-tie dinner at the Hollywood Roosevelt Hotel the bibulous Wild Bill threw his arms around my father. "B.P., I just want you to know, I'll never forget what you did for me. I owe everything to you. If you ever want me for anything, just holler. I'll work for you for nothing!"

There would be other nights of triumph for Father before the fire burned to ash, but never again would he sit down to a table and draw a royal flush. For in addition to *Wings,* the first Best Actor award went to his foreign import, the rotund and unforgettable Emil Jannings, for *The Way of All Flesh.* One night in the studio projection room a year or so before, we had seen a brilliant German film called *The Last Laugh,* starring Jannings as the self-important, elegantly uniformed doorman of the Hotel Adlon in Berlin. What was unique about the film was that it was not interrupted by a single subtitle. Yet without a word to prompt or distract us, we knew at every moment what Jannings's imperious door-man was thinking and feeling. He ruled over his domain between the curb and the revolving door as if he were the commander-in-chief of the entire world. When he opened the door of a limousine and bowed to arriving guests, it was a gesture not of servility but of the gracious hospitality of an overlord. When he escorted people to his grand revolv-ing door, he was inviting them into his palace. And when he went home to his dingy room in a tenement, he enjoyed another kind of adulation. To the tenement dwellers his arrival was the highlight of their day. They adored the magnificence of his uniform and the overbearing benevolence with which he wore it. Here was a symbol of the power they would never have and could only taste vicariously through their proximity to this great man.

Then, one day, the hotel manager sees Jannings stumble under a heavy trunk he is carrying into the lobby. Deciding that the world's greatest doorman is too old for the job, he assigns him an easier job as an attendant in the lavatory. But Jannings has to exchange his field-marshal's uniform for a shapeless white smock. We see the pride of the man seeping out of him like air from a huge balloon. Before our eyes Jannings becomes just another fat, stooped, defeated old man. We suffer with him as he goes back to face his former subjects in the tenement. Seeing him without his uniform, they feel deprived of the grandeur that has given meaning to their meaningless lives. So they turn on him, taunt him—a deposed king dragged to the guillotine. He goes back to the hotel to die in the lavatory; no longer is there any reason to go on living.

And that—an unexpected subtitle informed us—is how the story really ended. But since Hollywood loves its happy endings, this picture would give us one: A millionaire who dies in the hotel wills his fortune to the doorman. And so we have Jannings at the second fade-out, once more a swaggering, self-important figure, with a lovely lady on his arm, obsequiously helped into his limousine in front of the Adlon Hotel by a new uniformed doorman who will never be quite so grand as the original.

When the lights came on, instead of the usual postscreening chatter, there was a long, thoughtful silence. Here was genius at work. With subtle shadings of self-deprecating humor (poignantly directed by F. W. Murnau), Jannings had done for drama what Chaplin had done for comedy.

The film had a profound impact on the Schulbergs. I saw in it the kind of mood I had been working for in my short story, "Ugly." I related to it much more than to the romantic, surefire happy endings Hollywood was grinding out. I was proud of Father for saying that evening that he would like to sign Jannings and bring him over for a series of pictures in the European mode. Despite the support of Lasky, who reigned from his palatial beach house at Santa Monica, again there was opposition from New York. *The Last Laugh* might be a work of art, Zukor and his principal Wall Street backer Otto Kahn acknowledged, but this was the picture *business* and who the hell ever heard of Emil Jannings in Oshkosh?

This was the kind of argument B.P. warmed to. Even if a Jannings picture only broke even in the States, he assured Mr. Zukor, it would more than get its money back in Europe where Jannings was a box-office name and where audiences would be curious to see how Hollywood treated him. Ordered to hold the picture to a modest budget, Father was allowed to proceed. The result was *The Way of All Flesh,* for which the Paramount writers Jules Furthman and Lajos Biro were advised to study the dramatic elements of *The Last Laugh* (and of another Jannings tragedy, *Variety*) and adapt them to an American setting.

Father asked me, half-teasingly, half-seriously, if I approved of the scenario. I told him the part was perfect for Jannings: a smalltown bank teller, a model family man slavishly loyal to the bank he has served for twenty years. Everything about him speaks of punctuality and responsibility—up on the ring of seven, breakfast and paternal encouragement to the children at seven-thirty, at his post in the bank precisely at the same time every morning—the personification of bourgeois dependability and pride. He loves his boss, he loves his bank, he loves his job, he loves his wife and kids, he loves his life. In the overall scheme his job may be a minor one but he is bloated with self-importance.

One day his manager calls him in to say the bank must deliver a packet of thousand-dollar security notes to the main branch in Chicago, a job that calls for the utmost in reliability. That's why Jannings has been chosen for the assignment. He is reluctant to interrupt the daily routine to which he is addicted. But as a good soldier he conscientiously takes his seat on the train to Chicago.

Joining him in the compartment is Phyllis Haver, as provocative a little blonde as ever strutted down the aisle of a Pullman car. (Father had recruited her from the ranks of Mack Sennett's Bathing Beauties.) Jannings cannot resist posing as a bank manager rather than a lowly teller. Champagne flows. His first taste of the high life. When he wakes up in the bedroom of a roadhouse and searches frantically for his precious bank notes, they are gone.

Jannings can never return to face the music. He becomes a derelict, stripped of all pride, a trembling hulk so different from the self-righteous Mr. Perfect at the beginning as to be almost unrecognizable. On Christmas Eve—in these pessimistic "European" pictures it is always Christmas Eve—Jannings can't resist coming home to see his family. He stares in the window and watches his wife and children trimming the Christmas tree. There is a picture of him lovingly framed on the mantle. (Oh, yes, a man was found on the railroad tracks with Jannings's identification papers, and Jannings is believed to be dead.)

We see the broad, stooped back of Jannings, suffering. In a reverse angle, we see a close-up of his crushed, unshaven face at the window, suffering. There have been some pretty good sufferers in the movies down the years but I can't think of a single star who could suffer in the same league with Emil Jannings. We previewed the picture in San Francisco, where B.P. was testing it before a more sophisticated audience than the same old small-towners on whom still-unreleased pictures were usually sneaked in Glendale, Long Beach, and San Bernardino.

The San Francisco audience had anticipated the Hollywood happy ending that *The Last Laugh* had both ridiculed and exploited. But when Emil Jannings turned away from that fatherless Christmas scene, and went on drifting down the road like a porpoise-bodied, uncomedic Chaplin, there was a standing ovation.

When it opened in New York, the *Times* review could not have been more glowing if Father had written it himself: "A great artistic triumph . . . rivals both *The Last Laugh* and *Variety* . . . a marvel of simplicity . . . a poignant character study that bristles with carefully thought-out details . . . Jannings excels his previous screen contributions . . . never falters in his delineation . . ."

So it had come as no surprise to us that Jannings won the first Best Actor award that championship season. Ben and Ad came home late from that celebration at the Hollywood Roosevelt. After the presentations there had been dancing and drinking. I could hear Father's infectious laughter as he poured himself a nightcap that Mother was urging him not to take. In the morning, like the first chirps of the songbirds heralding the dawn, we would hear the familiar sound of Father's throwing up in the bathroom. There was always something reassuring about that sound. It meant that Father was safely home, sobering up, and getting ready to go back to work. The ritual of regurgitation would be followed by song. From my yellow bed with its ornately carved headboard I could sing along with his hangover anthem:

"Haitch—Hay—Dubble—Rrr—I . . . G-A-N spells Harrigan . . ."

Father had a lot to sing about that morning, because not only had *Wings, Underworld,* and *The Way of All Flesh* strengthened his (and Lasky's) hand, but Jannings was now an American marquee name.

The next two pictures he made with Jannings would always remain with me. In *The Last Command,* Jannings played a White Russian refugee general who has drifted to Hollywood where he is surviving as an extra. Typecast as a Czarist commander in a movie about the Soviet Revolution, his mind flashes back to his actual participation in the fighting that destroyed his life. On the Hollywood set, a replica of the battlefield from which he once had fled for his life, reality collides with make-believe until the general cracks under the pressure, forgets he is only acting out a minor role in a movie, and, once again the powerful White Russian commander of the past, runs amuck trying to rally his forces. Through the swirling snow (salt spread by the prop men and whirled about by a wind machine), he hurls himself against the barbed wire and collapses in the artificial snow where he dies of a heart attack.

I was on the set that day and the effect was unforgettable, a dream performance of a dream situation in a dream setting that was strangely believable, fusing fact with fiction in the style of Pirandello. There was not only a play within a play, but an outer play as well, as Emil Jannings and the director Von Sternberg could not bear each other, each one too egocentric and overbearing for the other. If Von Sternberg treated his actors like puppets, Jannings treated his directors like pawns. Jannings would throw tantrums equal to anything he created before the cameras, and Von Sternberg would pointedly ignore him: Von had perfected a cold disdain for actors who displeased him. Unable to get his way, or even a reaction from his haughty director, Jannings would stalk off to his dressing room to sulk. Sometimes he would storm into Father's office to protest Von Sternberg's maddening indifference. "Now we've got a *German* George Bancroft," Father would say, "another big baby whose wife pampers him and who doesn't know how lucky he is that we pick the right stories for him, the best writers, the best supporting cast, and put him in the hands of a Joe von Sternberg."

Von Sternberg told us he would never work with Jannings again, but when the advent of sound drove Jannings with his thick Teutonic accent back to his homeland, whom did he send for to direct him in *The Blue Angel?* Von Sternberg. And of course Joe accepted the job, making film history with the German bit-player he chose for the role of the leggy music-hall performer who leads Jannings, a dignified professor, down the road to self-abasement. On the wings of *The Blue Angel* Von Sternberg would return to Paramount with the protégée he seemed to have created out of common middle-class German clay—Marlene Dietrich. In *Morocco, Shanghai Express, The Scarlet Empress, The Devil Is a Woman,* the pudgy Fräulein was transformed into the tantalizing European sex symbol who was to become an ageless superstar.

Marlene literally used to sit at the feet of Von Sternberg in those days when directors behaved and dressed like field marshals. When they would come to the house Joe would do all the talking—a verbose intellectual with a genuine feeling for art and a habit of talking in philosophical abstractions that challenged you to follow them. Indeed, like a fox of the mind he seemed to delight in disappearing through the intellectual underbrush, throwing his yapping pursuers off the scent.

Not as flamboyant as Von Stroheim, in his own self-contained way he was just as outrageous, pulling his superiority around him like the heavy long overcoat he affected even in sunny California. He was an intellectual bully to whom all actors were fools and all producers idiots.

Most of the famous employees who came to 525 Lorraine played up to me, a few out of genuine fondness for children, others to make an impression on Father. But Von Sternberg made no concession to me whatsoever. He never bothered to ask me how I was doing in school, what I was writing, or who I thought would win the big game on Saturday.

At his best, he was one of the few motion-picture directors able to bridge the gap between Hollywood practicality and the art form as it had been developing in Europe. At his worst, he was arrogant and self-indulgent. This may be the voice of a father's son, but I always felt that after he left Paramount and parted company with B.P. in the mid-Thirties, the great promise of his career began to deteriorate. Of course he would have denied this with all his vehemence and sarcasm, insisting that front-office guidance—or interference—was destructive to his art.

In truth, it would be difficult to know how to assign the blame for the version of *Crime and Punishment* Joe directed for B.P., with Peter Lorre as Raskolnikov, Marian Marsh as Sonya. For it was not only miscast, but misdirected as well. Von Sternberg was a connoisseur of modern painting and sculpture and although he had made marvelous films with Bancroft, Jannings, and Dietrich, he was increasingly interested in the camera as a medium of abstract art. He had come to films as an experimenter and he was always more interested in his photographic effects than in the story he had to tell, or the characters his films could explore. Snobbish, impatient, unreasonable—dedicated artist inextricably intertwined with the poseur—his contempt for his inferiors (which seemed to include everyone in the world with the possible exception of Picasso, Matisse, Kandinsky, and Klee) left an indelible impression on me. He wore his long woolen overcoat like a suit of armor and what had once been a sensitive Jewish face was fixed in an imperious sneer. He was the giant-artist Gulliver pinned to earth by a throng of money-minded Lilliputians, and the disdainful look in the eye, the set of the mouth, the very droop of the mustache contrived to put us all in our places, from marquee name to studio chieftain to stammering teenager.

What he could not succeed in doing in his films (after *The Blue Angel*), he tried to project in the architecture of his own home. Built of concrete and great walls of glass, it was shaped in the form of an enormous *S* encircled by a moat. This Von Sternberg creation seemed the ideal monument to himself. "Don't talk to me, don't touch me, stay out," it warned Hollywood. Unless you were Charlie Chaplin, or Arnold Schoenberg or Thomas Mann, the drawbridge was raised against you at the Sternberg *schloss*.

What stands out in my mind about Marlene when she came to our house with Joe was her manner of dressing. She was the first woman I ever saw who wore pants—later when they became fashionable we called them slacks. In fact, she was wearing an entire suit and tie. It may have been that the silent Marlene we knew in our house was content to let her bizarre wardrobe speak for her because she was new to America and had still to perfect her English, although even the most articulate would have an uphill battle when Josef von Sternberg was holding the floor.

By coincidence Marlene came to America on the *Bremen,* where she became friends with my late wife Geraldine Brooks's parents, Jimmy and Bianca. Their memories of her in those early years are quite different from mine. Although Jimmy was head of the Brooks Costume Company and lived his life among Broadway stars, he was charmingly stagestruck. With his snapping blue eyes, his flirtatious and irresistible smile, this incorrigibly happy-go-lucky extrovert immediately ingratiated himself with Marlene. Not yet the self-assured superstar she was to become by the end of the decade, she welcomed the attention of the gregarious Jimmy and his stylish little wife, Bianca. They dined together, took their constitutional walks around the decks together, played the ship's games together. Jimmy nicknamed her Dutchy, which she enjoyed—it sounded breezy and American. Even when she had achieved her new status as the world's sexiest grandmother, Marlene continued to send letters to them signed "Dutchy."

On that *Bremen* crossing, Dutchy presented Bianca with a bunch of violets every day. Bianca was touched by their new friend's thoughtfulness, although she wondered if Dutchy wasn't revealing a touch of guilt because her behavior with Jimmy had been provoking shipboard gossip. One afternoon Dutchy invited Bianca to her cabin, offered her a glass of champagne, and showed her a book—on lesbian lovemaking. Bianca liked to think of herself as an F. Scott Fitzgerald jazz baby but the flapper exterior concealed the morality of a West End Avenue matron. With this, her first real pass from a member of her own sex, she reverted to her upper-class German-Jewish background. Her shock only amused the sexually ecumenical Marlene. "In Europe it doesn't matter if you're a man or a woman," Marlene explained. "We make love with anyone we find attractive."

Jimmy was so amused to learn that it was Bianca that Marlene was trying to lure to her cabin, and not him, that they remained lifelong friends. The first time they all went to a Broadway opening together, Marlene appeared in white tie and tails, complete with silk opera hat—courtesy of the Brooks Costume Company—a costume that became an overnight sensation and was to become her theatrical trademark. Actually she favored men's clothes because they were cheaper to rent than elegant gowns. Later, Brooks did make many of the slinky, see-through, spangled costumes she introduced as her Vegas "uniform."

Today most movie stars choose to dress down in jeans and T-shirts, but in those days, top names like Crawford, Swanson, and Dietrich were conscious of giving performances every time they appeared in public and they dressed the part. The masculine but sexy look was Marlene's contribution to our folk-film culture. Once she emerged from behind the father figure of Von Sternberg, she blossomed into a new kind of femme fatale able to parody her own sexuality without losing its powers. Giftedly, wickedly on the make, Marlene was able to recreate herself as an American fantasy of how a sexy European woman looks, sounds, and acts. A strange continuity moves through my life, for when I first met Geraldine Brooks, as her baby-sitter, she was a stagestruck six-year-old who would manage to extend her bedtime by perching on a bar stool, tilting her father's top hat on her head, crossing her little knees, and singing a song her "Aunt Dutchy" had taught her: "Fah-ling een luff a-gane—never vant-ed to—vot am I to do?—caan't help eet. . . . "

While Marlene rode her rising wave of sensual self-mockery and Joe von Sternberg retreated to London and then Japan in search of his elusive cinematic muse, Father's other German star, Emil Jannings, decided that having to speak English in the new talkies was too much of a challenge. So he came to say goodbye with fervent avowal of love for all the Schulbergs and an open invitation for us to be his houseguests whenever we came to Germany. After all, Emil insisted, he was a *landsman,* or at least half-*landsman,* having been born in Brooklyn of a Jewish mother who took him to Europe when he was still a child.

Yet, when Hitler and his Brown Shirts came to power and Jannings's professional status if not his life was endangered, he went to court and became a certified member of the Master Race by declaring that he had been born out of wedlock to an Aryan maid in the Jannings household. Which prompted Father to say, "I've known a lot of bastards in this business, but this is the first time I ever heard of anyone going to court to make it official."

26

AS MUCH DRAMA as Sternberg, Dietrich, and Jannings generated on the screen, in the studio, and in their private lives, it often seemed as if the world-famous lived less dramatic lives than the servants with whom Sonya and I spent so much of our time.

Our nurse Wilma had been our substitute mother while Ad occupied herself with her Godmothers' League, her birth-control clinic, her Friday Morning Club, and Hollywood's first progressive school.

While Mother was busy with her life, Father with his, and I lived my intense existence with Maurice at school and on the tennis courts, there were two lonely souls in our household: Sonya, of whose presence Father seemed almost totally unaware, and Wilma, who was never able to make the adjustment from New York to Hollywood. Back east she had had family and friends, but here among the palm trees, the orange blossoms, and the wide-open spaces of early Hollywood she felt painfully uprooted and homesick. I had outgrown Wilma. And Windsor Square was so quiet that little Sonya could play safely with Marjorie Lesser and the daughters of other movie producers without Wilma's having to take her to a park. Besides, with separate rooms for the three children, and Ad's youngest brother Sam now in residence, there was no longer room for Wilma in the main house, so an apartment had been set up for her over the garage. The work on it was done by the studio carpenters and electricians, and probably charged to studio overhead, a form of corruption that Hollywood had winked at from the beginning.

I don't know exactly how it began—I was too much concerned with my own problems of growing up at the time—but somehow Wilma became involved with one of the studio electricians, a big, ruddy-faced, healthy-looking fellow whose name was George. Wilma had always been a stay-at-home: Even on her days off she hadn't seemed to know what to do with herself in Los Angeles. Her problem (I would learn later) was her color, that lovely light coffee-color that I had always found so appealing. Too light to feel comfortable among black people, she was still too dark for the whites.

When she developed a relationship with the big electrician, I felt a twinge of ambiguous jealousy I wasn't able to put into words. I long ago had outgrown Wilma and hardly had time to talk to her with all our activities. But children, like cats, seem to be born conservatives. They want to keep their world exactly as they discovered it. I wanted Wilma to go on living in her apartment over the garage. I didn't want her going off with any man.

One day when I came home from school I heard Mother talking to her in the library. I lingered in the hallway, at first not meaning to eavesdrop but then held by their conversation. They were talking about George, or rather, Mother was talking and Wilma was listening.

"Wilma, I know he says he loves you, and he wants to marry you," Mother was saying, "but your parents are giving you the right advice. Even if you tell him you're—" there was a discreet pause—"what your background is, and he says it doesn't matter, believe me in time it will. Especially if you have children. And they turn out to be—well, the color of your sister. Or your father. It might not matter to people of intelligence and education. But is it fair to the children themselves? They could go through hell, raised out here in a white neighborhood. And sooner or later, it's bound to affect your relationship with George."

There was a soft protest from Wilma—always so gentle and passive—and then I heard quiet crying. I peered in. Wilma had her head on Mother's shoulder. It looked like one of those four-handkerchief scenes from an Eddie Goulding movie. Except that there weren't any colored people in the movies unless they were dancing and singing as in King Vidor's *Hallelujah!,* or in there for watermelon jokes like Stepin Fetchit (born Lincoln Peary).

Wilma must have accepted Mother's well-meaning if negative advice. For I became aware of the fact that George wasn't calling on her anymore. She was totally "ours" again. When I came home from school I would often see her on the little balcony over the garage, slowly rocking back and forth, nodding at me with a smile of gentle resignation. She would sometimes call down to me and I would go up and tell her how school was going, or about some new movie I had seen. She seemed quieter than ever, and then she slipped into some mysterious sort of illness. She was steadily losing weight. It was as if the light was slowly flickering out of her. And then one day I heard that Wilma was very ill and that she was leaving us, going back to New York where her family could take care of her.

Thirty years later, Wilma might have been able to settle down with George and make a life of her own in southern California. But in the late Twenties (and after), Hollywood was as lily-white as Mississippi. There was no place in the life pattern for a serious light-colored girl like Wilma. How many other Wilmas must there have been, lost between an alien white culture that would not accept them and an underground black culture yet to be discovered.

27

F WILMA WAS my second mother, my paternal surrogate was James, the English butler-chauffeur who was with us for several years and who drove that hated gold bric-a-brac royal coach in which Sonya and I tried to melt into the floor.

When Wilma went east, James took over the apartment over the garage and I spent as much time up there with him as I could. He was tall, athletically built, and with a great deal of physical confidence, something I was anxious to develop. It seemed to me that there was nothing in the world—at least nothing important—that James hadn't done. He had been a machine gunner in the British Army and had killed his share of Krauts. As a merchant seaman he had sailed the seven seas. The first time I saw him undressed, getting out of his tight-necked grey uniform, I noticed colored pictures on his muscular arms—the first tattooing I had ever seen. The one beneath his right shoulder was an elaborate heart on which was inscribed the word MOTHER. The other arm was decorated with the figure of a naked woman with blue script winding artistically around it to spell MARGIE. He explained to me that it was the work of little needles depositing different colored inks under the skin. Didn't that hurt? He gave a manly shrug. What's a little pain? After what he had seen in the trenches? Doughboys running back toward their own lines with their guts spilling out like spaghetti? Knife fights in the alleys of Hong Kong in which Limey sailors and thieving Chinks cut each other up until they were slipping and falling in each other's blood?

As our robust chauffeur with the look and accent of Errol Flynn talked on about blood and guts, I began to see little white pinwheels inside my eyes. Throughout my adolescence I had an embarrassing tendency to faint. Once I was downtown near the old Main Street Gym, after watching the workouts of some of my favorite local boxers. Suddenly those little pinwheels began to spin until they were wider and wider, spinning around me like a hundred metaphysical hula hoops. I leaned against the wall of a building and slowly slipped to the pavement. A half-seen stranger helped me to my feet, and in a few moments my mind was clear again, like a fighter recovering from a ten-second concussion. When I went home that day I was too ashamed to confess my momentary lapse, although I knew that Father had also suffered from these spells in his youth. Had I inherited this weakness along with my stammering?

Another time I was at the Friday-night Hollywood Legion fights with my father in one of his prized regular seats in the first press row, when a tall, skinny-legged Mexican fighter, whose name I remember only as Tony, started to bleed from the corner of his left eye. Blood kept running down from his eye, blinding his vision and smearing his face. At the end of each round the referee would go over to examine the injury. Tony's handlers would protest that the wound was not serious, and the fight was allowed to continue. Now the eye was a bloody mess, an angry pool of blood that no longer resembled an eye. Father and other first-row fans held their programs up against their faces to protect them from the spray of blood. I heard the screaming, I saw our Mexican sexpot, hysteric Lupe Velez, pounding the apron of the ring to urge on her blinded compatriot, watched the terrible wound in his face grow larger and larger, and suddenly I felt as if I was inside that eye and this time I saw red circles spinning, spinning, spinning. . . . When I came to I was in the fighters' dressing room, stretched out on a rubbing table and the old gargoyle of a trainer I had known for years was bringing me to with smelling salts. "Okay, kid? Don't feel too bad. Everybody gets knocked out sooner or later." Everybody in the dressing room, even the Mexican kid with a red hole for an eye, cracked up. I wanted to crawl into one of the lockers and hide. But I went back to my ringside seat.

So now I gritted my teeth and weathered James's goriest tales because I believed that he had been the boxing champion of his regiment, and later of the entire British merchant marine. When Georges Carpentier, the light-heavyweight champion who had figured in the first million-dollar gate with Jack Dempsey, came to London to meet the English champion, James had sparred with the French hero and (according to James) had done so well that he had been urged to turn pro.

James still had his old pair of heavy sparring gloves and one day he made me a present of them, beautifully aged red-leather boxing gloves. On the back lawn James showed me the stance, how to hold my hands so I was ready to jab with my left and protect my chin with my right, how to balance on my toes so I could move back and forth like a dancer, how to punch harder by pivoting on my left foot and corkscrewing my left wrist as my hook landed. James would use his own body as a heavy bag, urging me to punch him in the belly as hard as I could. I would punch him so hard that it would sting my hands right through the gloves, and James would say, "Now again, only harder, keep your hands close to your sides and throw your whole body into it. Like this!" And my marvelous James would whistle punches into the air that would have KO'd Gorgeous Georges Carpentier himself. When I hit James again, and he said, "Hey, that's better, I could really feel that one!" I felt the way Dad must have felt when *Wings* won the Academy Award.

James seemed to grow more and more fond of me as he became practically a member of the family. He even offered to take me camping, but my parents didn't feel they could spare him from his chauffeur-and-butler duties. Someday, he promised, when he had a vacation, he would take me up into the Sierras and teach me how to hunt and fish and live off the land. It seemed as if there was nothing of a practical nature that James didn't know how to do. When he drove us up to Lake Arrowhead, he made his own trout rod from a sapling, and with a red fish egg on the point of a bent pin he caught several small trout in a deep pool under a five-foot waterfall. Father, of course, spent the entire weekend in the playroom of the Lodge losing at poker with Joe Schenck and other members of the rich inner circle. James was the ideal outdoor counterpart, healthy, ruddy, energetic, resourceful. He attracted so many interested looks from our actress friends and producers' wives that B.P.— who loved to discover "unknowns"—half-seriously suggested that he take a screen test. But James said a refreshing No. He had no desire to go into the movies, he was quite content with the job he had. The spaces in my family life were more than filled by Maurice as a surrogate brother and James as a surrogate father.

One afternoon, I was downtown with my mother taking a music lesson, she on her mandolin, me on my banjo—still struggling with "Mighty Lak a Rose." We had taken Mother's Marmon rather than the hated town car and James, ever helpful, had volunteered to put the extra time to practical advantage by washing all the windows. Usually we had a special window-washer in to do this job, but James suggested that it was a waste of money, and besides he had been a professional window-washer. The panes of 525 Lorraine would be pristine by the time we returned.

After a desultory hour with our music teacher, whose winces were barely suppressed as we misfingered our chords, we drove home to find our usually quiet Lorraine Boulevard lined with police cars. Policemen were on our lawn pacing the driveway, and stationed at our front door.

"Mrs. Schulberg, I'm sorry to have to tell you this, but your house has been burglarized. Detective McMahon would like you to walk through it room by room and point out what is missing."

The first thing that was missing was James. With our gold petit-point Lincoln coach. From the maid's quarters we heard a terrible wailing and we hurried to Paula's room to find our stocky German maid thrashing on the floor, kicking and screaming. She began to sob out her story. James had not only cleaned out the entire house, he had even taken her piggy bank into which she had stuffed her life's savings.

We hurried up to the master bedroom and found that James had taken all the household cash: several thousand dollars, all of Mother's jewels, diamond brooches, pearl necklaces, sapphire rings, Father's wardrobe of expensive Eddie Schmidt suits and monogrammed silk shirts, a gold watch inset with tiny diamonds, even his most recent box of dollar-a-smoke H. Upmann Corona Coronas from Havana.

I ran to my room, found a few things missing, my radio, antique revolver, and a Civil War sword. Under my bed, mysteriously, were a blackjack and an auto wrench. Downstairs the cook, Lucille, was shouting that all the silver was gone, utensils, platters, serving dishes, goblets. . . . It didn't seem possible that one man could have accomplished all this in a few hours.

While Mother tried to soothe Paula and the other servants, I sat on my bed and stared at the floor. Tears were stinging the corners of my eyes, but not for the cash and the jewels and the silver. James had stolen something much more precious. God, but I had thought he liked me! In fact I had taken it for granted he was crazy about me. Now who was going to box with me and tell me man-to-man stories of high adventure? His apartment above the garage had been an exciting world in which I felt a bond I had never known with my busy father. Father would show me off at the fights and story conferences, projection-room rushes and previews. But that was different. It was as if B.P. was my studio father and James was my real father. And now James had driven off into the outside world without even a last goodbye.

It was a lonely feeling having the police ask me questions about him. Suddenly he wasn't James any more. They were asking questions about a stranger, the suspect, the burglar, the perpetrator. "This is no amateur job," the police were agreeing, almost in admiration. "We're dealing with a cool customer who knew every corner of this house and exactly what he was doing every minute."

From the accounts we pieced together from Paula and Lucille, James had used the window-washing as a cover-up for his systematic looting of the household. To empty the dirty water he had made countless trips to the garage. A pail of dirty water was an ingenious place to hide the valuables he was removing from all the rooms. On each trip to the garage, ostensibly to pour the soapy water down the drain, he would hide the loot in the town car. The afternoon had been an exercise in ingenuity. He must have passed the servants a hundred times as he went back and forth with his water pails. How cool he had been, how sure of himself as he paused to make little jokes with them in his charming English way.

"Don't worry, how far can he go in that town car?" Detective Mc-Mahon reassured us. "We've sent out a description of the vehicle and the driver. He'll never get over the city line."

Of course the city lines of Los Angeles are no ordinary municipal borders. In those days it was not yet the nation's third largest city in terms of population, but it was surely the largest in terms of square miles, running forty miles from north to south and an even greater distance from grubby East Los Angeles to the mansions rising precariously on the palisades above the Pacific. Even before they had attracted the bodies to populate the rolling open country, the city fathers had grandiose ideas for establishing a city-state. So we didn't think it would be that easy to check our elusive James at the city line.

But while we all huddled together in the looted house (even the silver and marble ashtrays had been removed from the sunken living room and the tiled library), a detective arrived with the news that our gold bric-a-brac coach had been found, abandoned in a lonely sidestreet in the southeast section of the city. All of the stolen goods had been removed. It was strongly suspected that James was headed for the long and under-protected Mexican border between Tijuana and Mexicali, a favorite no-man's-land for smugglers, escaped convicts, and outlaws. Without a trace, James managed to disappear with virtually all the Schulbergs' worldly goods.

A year later, we heard he had been apprehended at last, on a great estate on Long Island where he had pulled a similar caper. Either the New York police were more efficient or there were fewer avenues of escape from Long Island. At any rate he was caught red-handed, or blue-shirted, for he was actually wearing one of Father's powder-blue monogrammed silk shirts.

Sometime later there appeared in *The American Weekly,* the sensational Sunday magazine section of the Hearst newspaper chain, a most illuminating how-to article by my erstwhile mentor. James, we were fascinated to learn, was a second-story man of international celebrity. His game was to gain access to a prosperous household as a charming and efficient butler-chauffeur, ingratiate himself with the family, stay long enough to win their confidence completely, and then at the appointed moment, clean them out. He would then sail off and live the good life on some tropical island for the next six months to a year, masquerading as a British blue blood of independent means. As I read it I could see him bamboozling his new island friends as easily as he had bamboozled us. When he began to run out of fluid wealth, he would go to an area he had never worked before and begin the charming-servant routine all over again.

It was a tantalizing piece. He had the same felicity for writing he had for everything else. He was one of those irresistible scoundrels who could have been a success at anything he put his mind to, but, James admitted, he found life more interesting as a second-story man.

In every household—his tone was more boastful than confessional— he would look for the weakest link in the family chain. It might be a wife or servant who found him sexually attractive. It could be a wandering husband with whom James would buddy up, smoothly covering for him as he went about his chauffeur duties. In our household, he pointed out, while he had flirted experimentally with Paula, he decided early on to involve me in his caper. In search of a father-surrogate, I was a pushover for his blandishments. Quickly scouting me as gullible and naive, and noting both the favoritism that Mother bestowed on me and the pride-*cum*-guilt that Father felt toward his much-admired but rather neglected firstborn, he had decided that I was the key to the Schulberg vault. He had done his job so well that in a matter of months I was as emotionally dependent on him as I had been on Wilma during my childhood. And he was able to have the run of the house because Mother and Dad felt grateful to him for filling the emotional vacuum their busy schedules created.

Once he had won my devotion and their gratitude, it was, as he put it, "easy fruit." He had only to bide his time until the golden apple fell into his hands.

He had almost struck several months earlier—and here his confession cleared up a family mystery. One night Mother was giving one of her grand dinner parties. The all-powerful Louella O. Parsons, self-styled "Gay Illiterate," had dubbed Ad "one of Hollywood's most gracious hostesses," and Mother vied with Bessie Lasky and Norma Shearer Thalberg as a leader of local society. Present at this elegant sit-down dinner were Charlie Chaplin and Paulette Goddard, the Ernst Lubitsches, Dietrich and Von Sternberg, the recently arrived Broadway star Ruth Chatterton, and the latest English import, Ralph Forbes— lovely targets all.

Impeccably, James served the rare roast beef from a large silver platter, poured the Lafitte Rothschild into delicate glasses we had bought in Venice on our Grand Tour—and then, after the glittering company had raised their glasses in a witty toast, the lights went out. After a few anxious minutes the lights came on again and James reappeared to explain that a fuse had blown and he had gone down to the cellar to replace it.

In his *American Weekly* article, James confessed what had really happened. Hearing from my mother of the distinguished company who would be present that night, he had decided to throw the light switch and then at gunpoint remove from our guests their cash and valuables. Windsor Square had its own private security patrol, with a signal alert to its neighborhood headquarters. James had taken the precaution of disconnecting it. But just before he was ready to set up these movie stars in a true-life drama, a late guest, Hector Turnbull, arrived. Turnbull was a writer-producer at the studio and one of Father's favorites. He was also well-built and rugged and there was something about his late arrival that threw off James's timing and confidence. Once the lights were out, he confessed, he lost his nerve and decided to turn them back on, invent the story of the blown fuse, and wait for a safer opportunity.

The next morning, Mother had lectured James for some slight derelictions the night before. After the brief blackout he had spilled a bit of wine when filling the glass for Mr. Turnbull, and he had not seemed as attentive to his butlering duties as he had been at many other formal dinners. James had apologized profusely, protesting that he loved the job, loved me and the younger children, and that his one ambition was to make this his permanent home.

Through the following month he was the model chauffeur-butler-second father. In his room over the garage, what wonderful tales he would spin. While I was sitting there at his feet in adolescent rapture, he was weighing the possibilities of taking me to the mountains and holding me for ransom. But deciding that was also too risky, he finally settled on his ingenious window-washing scheme.

His published confession was an even greater blow to us than the actual burglary because the act exposed our nouveau-riche grandiosity, pomposity, and vulnerability. From the inside out we seemed to ourselves a serious, intelligent, creative family, superior to the clichéd foibles of such Hollywood boss-families as the Mayers, the Warners, and the Laemmles. L.B. was a tyrant, Jack Warner was a loudmouthed vaudevillian, and Uncle Carl Laemmle—although one of Hollywood's original "mound builders"—pretty much a joke for the way he surrounded himself with boatloads of relatives from Laupheim, his birthplace in Bavaria.

But here were the literate if profligate B.P., the cultured and resourceful Adeline, and their trusting little genius of a son being ripped off and publicly exposed to millions of Hearst readers as "easy fruit."

IV

KINGS

28

ВUT IF JAMES thought he had the last
laugh, leave it to Mother for the last word. With a thorough inventory
plus total recall, she presented Father's pal and insurance agent Artie
Stebbins with a claim that brought in a generous bounty she closed her
pretty pink-nailed claws around before Father could dump it on the
gaming tables at the Clover Club.

Although—or perhaps because—Artie was a crony of Ben's from the
New York-Benny Leonard days, he handed over the insurance check
directly to Ad, who as usual had decided how she was going to invest the
windfall.

Over the years the filmmakers had been moving west, from downtown
Los Angeles to Hollywood, from Hollywood to Beverly Hills, then all
the way out Wilshire and Sunset Boulevards to Santa Monica. Hearst
had built a winter palace there for Marion Davies, and soon other
mansions rose alongside it on the beach looking out on the green and
often seaweed-clogged Pacific. The MGM triumvirate, Mayer, Thalberg, and Rapf, soon followed Hearst's example, and so did Jesse Lasky,
Jack Warner, and most of our other feudal lords.

Although relations between B.P. and L.B. grew increasingly strained
as their studios fought each other for Hollywood supremacy, Ad managed to maintain our friendship with the Mayer family. Louie's wife
Margaret was sweet but somehow lost as the simple days of Mission
Road and the Mayer-Schulberg Studio were left behind, and the once
rough-talking Louie took elocution lessons and cultivated his friend-

ships with Hearst, President Hoover, and Republican leaders. Ad enjoyed her role as intellectual mentor and social guide to the Mayer daughters, Edith and Irene, and the four of us, with introspective little Sonya tagging along, enjoyed elaborate picnics at Catalina Island. Even then the Mayer girls seemed to have little respect for poor Margaret. ("Poor," incidentally, was a Hollywood adjective frequently applied to studio widows who rarely saw their husbands, who were either busy working into the night or playing into the day. The word became so attached to the first name of the wife of the brilliant and erratic Herman Mankiewicz that no one ever referred to her as Sarah. It was always "Poorsarah." To this day I am unable to think of that quiet, intelligent, long-suffering sister-in-law of director-writer Joe Mankiewicz, and mother of talented sons Don and Frank, without "*Poorsarah*" flashing in my mind.)

At one of the brunches at the Mayers', with Father discreetly absent and presumably working at the studio, Mrs. Bowes (wife of the amateur-hour radio impresario Major Bowes) mentioned a new beach area that was opening up twenty miles north of Santa Monica. It was called Malibu, and belonged to the Rindge Estate, which had inherited one of the sprawling land grants into which Spanish California had been divided. The Rindge Estate had been a self-contained enclave with its own castle on a promontory overlooking the bay, and sullen armed guards to keep the curious away. Now a choice private beach was being opened to the public at last.

In character, Mother suggested that we look at this *terra incognita* that very afternoon. We motored up the narrow, winding road under the trecherous clay palisades until we reached the pastoral waterfront of Malibu. From the foothills ran a freshwater stream that spilled into a crescent-shaped lagoon between the imposing Rindge mansion and the isolated beach. On the other side of the coast road, several thousand acres of rich land were under cultivation by Japanese farmers. On a knoll rising above the foothills was a monastery. Below it, near the deserted beach, was a jerry-built office where an energetic salesman with the country smarts, Art Smith, was waiting for his first customers.

The price seemed high: $10,000 for a 90-foot oceanfront lot that could only be rented for 99 years but not bought outright. The Rindge executors, said to be anti-Semitic and not eager to sell their precious sand to low-life movie people, knew a good thing when they had it. Unspoiled southern California ocean country less than an hour away from thc Hollywood cluster. Usually Ad was a cautious buyer, feeling she had to compensate for B.P.'s impetuosity. But she too knew a good thing when she saw it. While Mrs. Bowes thought this undeveloped beach too remote, Ad decided to sign up for three lots in what is now the heart of The Colony of aging movie stars and unshaven rock stars.

Still drawing on the insurance check that James's creative burglary had bestowed on us, Ad built a tasteful Cape Cod house across the three lots, called Green Gate Cottage. She filled it with her precious Early American furniture and some innovative interior decorating, such as canopied single beds set in an alcove back to back. My room on the second floor offered a marvelous view of the Japanese farms stretching to the foot of the mountains. From my window I would watch those diminutive farmers tirelessly working their quarter-mile rows of vegetables. Sometimes I would walk along the edge of their farms but they never seemed to notice me. How calm and patient was their labor, how different from the panics and manics of the Hollywood world on which our welfare depended.

I don't think I was yet aware of the deep split in my attitude toward Hollywood. I seemed a typical scion of Hollywood success, film- and sports-addicted, proud of Mother's foresight in building the first house at Malibu, and, across the dirt road running the length of the beach, the first tennis court. There I practiced my serve, sharpened my backhand, scrupulously listed my victories, and agonized over my defeats from sunup until the after-dinner matches which we played under arc lights.

But with all the dreams of silver trophies that danced in my head, there was another dream, represented by a Currier and Ives print on my bedroom wall. It showed an early 19th-century manor house shaded by great trees and looking out on a rolling lawn that ran down to the banks of a great river called the Hudson. An old man in a frock coat was sitting on a wrought-iron bench in thoughtful contemplation of this pastoral scene. In old-fashioned type the caption read: "Sunnyside, Home of Washington Irving at Tarrytown." The picture had a hypnotic effect. Having read *The Legend of Sleepy Hollow*, I could picture old Mr. Irving in white wig and black frock coat putting to paper with his quill pen his marvelous story of Ichabod Crane and the Headless Horseman. I would stare at the picture when I woke up in the morning, and whenever I felt upset because my first serve wasn't going in or I feared having to read aloud in class the following day, or I wondered why I was still so afraid of girls that I wouldn't allow one inside the sacred confines of my Model A, or I worried about Father's latest gambling escapade, or the fact that he seemed to be having new difficulties with that constant ogre, New York—whenever any of these fears penetrated what seemed to be my paradisaical existence at Green Gate Cottage on Malibu Beach, I would lose myself in that print of Sunnyside and join the scholarly Washington Irving in his stately retreat on the beautiful river.

All we had in my hometown was a dried-up joke of a waterway, the Los Angeles River. And although Father's writers lived in nice houses, in the Hollywood hills or on the flats of Beverly, they did not seem to enjoy the kind of peaceful, creative life I pictured as Washington Irving's. Instead of the luxury of writing exactly what they pleased in the comfort of a book-lined study, with a fire crackling in the fireplace, Father's writers (and he often boasted he had the best) had to do their work according to order and have it ready on demand.

Now that we had the Malibu house as well as the house on Lorraine, there would sometimes be story conferences in the big high-ceilinged living room overlooking the sea. There were writers who were gifted talkers, basically performers, who would leap to their feet and bring a seemingly empty situation or set of characters to life. But the life would turn stillborn the moment the story-conference whip tried to put his histrionics on paper. The writing ranks were full of phonies who had mastered the art of the story conference but who struck out at the typewriter. Father liked to think he could separate the real ones from the fakers, but he was often fooled.

Sitting there silently, taking it all in, I would watch in fascination as a self-propelled writer-performer rose dramatically from his chair to act out his brainstorm. It was a ritual going back to the earliest days of storytelling around the campfire. The little audience falls into rapt silence as the volunteer problem-solver takes over. Half-a-dozen inspired ad-libbers come to mind, foremost among them Eddie Goulding, the veteran English writer-director whose scenario credits went all the way back to *Tol'able David* in the early Twenties, and who had established himself as one of the major studio dependables from whom stories poured like Niagara over the Falls.

"The night is cold and wet," Eddie would intone, his theater-trained British accent giving dramatic emphasis to the scene. He would cross to the door to make a theatrical entrance, the collar of his expensive navy-blue blazer turned up around his neck, his shoulders hunched against the imaginary night air. This was long before the days of the

298

Actors Studio, but here was a brilliant *impro,* with Eddie assuming the posture and inner feeling of a prodigal husband who has gone off on a fling because he suspected his wife of infidelity, only to learn too late that his decision had been based on circumstantial evidence planted by the heavy. Everyone watched in awe as Eddie Goulding staggered back into our living room and begged for forgiveness. "That's it, you've got it, Christ, Eddie, you've licked it!" Father would cry out in relief.

Sometimes the scene would go into the ailing picture just as Maestro Goulding or one of his eloquent colleagues would imagine it. More often, it would set up a chain reaction of "improvements" which would twist the story in the opposite direction from its original concept—if indeed the original charade could be so dignified. Sometimes, following the departure of weary supervisors, battered writers, and harried story editors, Father would reconstruct an Eddie Goulding brainstorm to a jury that sometimes consisted of Sonya, little Stuart, and me, and realize in the telling that the silver-tongued Goulding had sold him a bag of three-dollar bills. Sometimes Father's own storytelling abilities would embellish the "idea" with sufficient stock graces to save it.

There was the time when Father was desperate for a story for Jeanette MacDonald. It was the old problem of the starting date, the picture presold to theaters before it was even a gleam in a writer's fevered eye. Eddie Goulding to the rescue. Eddie paced up and down, reeling off his story, playing all the parts, each one a potential Oscar-winner. "Eddie, you've saved us," Father told him. "If you can put it down in five pages and bring it to me tomorrow morning, you'll have a check for twenty-five thousand dollars."

The flamboyant Eddie Goulding jumped into his Packard roadster, called his favorite leading lady of the moment, and headed for the Trocadero and a night on the town. It was champagne for all his friends to celebrate the $25,000 he was to pick up in my father's office as a result of his ad-lib presentation. By the time he got back to his stucco castle in Beverly Hills, the morning sun was rediscovering the palm trees. In the arms of his blonde companion he fell into a deep and luxurious sleep where champagne bubbles waltzed with thousand-dollar bills. A few hours later, B.P.'s secretary, Henrietta Cohn, knowing Goulding's habits, phoned him to be sure he was on his way to his vital appointment. With his five pages. Five pages! Eddie didn't even have five lines. In fact, he realized as the cold spray of the glassed-in shower brought him back to the real world, he didn't have the faintest notion of what his story was all about. All he could remember of that faraway Malibu conference was that he had leapt to his feet with a cry of "Eureka!" and my father had promised to reward him with $25,000. Everything in between had vanished like the golden bubbles in his champagne.

Half artist, half charlatan (the ideal Hollywood mix), Eddie tried to make it on bluff as he had so often. So he told B.P. that he had not brought in the five-page outline as promised because overnight he had thought up something that he liked even better. He began to improvise a completely new story, but a few minutes into it, Father stopped him. "Eddie, we've made that story three times. But what you told me at Malibu had freshness, a new twist. I'll call in Henrietta—you can dictate it to her. And still get your twenty-five grand."

Cornered, and practically speechless for the first time in his spectacular career (he was to direct *Grand Hotel, Dark Victory,* and the remake of *Of Human Bondage*), Eddie finally confessed that he hadn't the faintest notion of the story-conference inspiration.

"Eddie, next time you get a brainstorm, promise me you'll write it down before you go out to celebrate," Father lectured him. Then he suggested a solution: that Eddie come to the Lorraine house that night (now we were back in Hollywood after our weekend at the beach), that they gather the story conferees together and, with each member contributing what he or she remembered, reconstruct the continuity that led up to Eddie Goulding's providential creation. It was like one of those S. S. Van Dine mysteries where all of the suspects are gathered in the drawing room to recite the details leading up to the crime, whereupon the master sleuth, Philo Vance, gets the flash that puts it all together.

Once again Eddie leapt to his feet with his "Wait a minute! I've got it! It's come back to me—" and proceeded to tell his story of the day before, only this time Father didn't take a chance on Eddie's quixotic ways. He had his assistant Geoffrey Shurlock (later the congenial chief censor for the Breen Office) take it all down as Eddie reenacted it. But when the Goulding brainstorm was finally committed to paper, it seemed to have lost something in translation. In fact, when Father read the handful of pages, he gave it that one-word verdict I was to hear so often, whether the work was mine or the thousand-dollar-a-day Ben Hecht's: "Lousy!"

That was one of the familiar discoveries of the story conference. The talented actor who could galvanize his small audience could get away with murder, and just as often the gifted writer who had a genuine but inaudible contribution was drowned out. Of course it's tempting to satirize the story conference as Moss Hart and George Kaufman did in their irreverent *Once in a Lifetime* and as the mysterious Graham brothers did in their scandalous roman à clef, *Queer People*. But along with the honey-throated medicine men like Eddie Goulding, there were a lot of good story minds like Buddy Leighton and Hope Loring, Jules Furthman, young David Selznick, and Ben Hecht who helped hammer out with Father what they called "a straight dramatic line."

Of course the phonies were the ones we laughed and talked about. At MGM there was a story genius, Bob Hopkins, who had truly mastered the shorthand of the surefire movie. Maurice and I would watch him in awe. He probably had an office somewhere, a cubbyhole in the Writers' Building. But his arena was the studio commissary, the barbershop. the vital avenues from the executive offices to the parking areas where chauffeured limousines waited for the sultans and sub-sultans who ruled the lot. In his writer's uniform of checkerboard sports jacket and baggy grey slacks he would wait in ambush for a Louie Mayer, an Irving Thalberg, a Harry Rapf, a Hunt Stromberg, and grabbing him by the arm, confront him with his double whammy. One of his most famous was "Earthquake—San Francisco—Gable and MacDonald—can't you see it, L.B. [or Harry or Irving]?—Clark's on one side of the street, Jeanette's on the other—goddamn street splits right between them—it's gotta be but terrific!"

That's how one of Metro's blockbusters was born, for that time the studio brass recognized a hot idea when they heard it. When one of Hoppy's telegraphic brainstorms was given official recognition, he had a way of waving his hand in an imperious gesture, "Okay—now put a word man on it." The poor wretch—the one who had to take those bare bones, not even a recognizable skeleton, and somehow build and flesh out a 90-minute feature. Meanwhile the irrepressible Hoppy, as much a part of the studio scene as the front gate and the backlot, would be back at his old stand, the barbershop and the commissary, peddling his wares.

Every major studio had a Hoppy. Warners had two of them, Darryl Zanuck and Jerry Wald. They weren't writers but their busy minds bubbled with story ideas—ideas torn from the front pages or borrowed from cocktail-party shoptalk or twisteroos of ideas already sold. Hungry and without shame, they were eager studio beavers like Hoppy. Except that Hoppy was content with his life as a sidewalk catalyst and Darryl and Jerry were men with bigger dreams—glib *toreros* who discovered in the big studio compound the perfect arena for their hyperthyroid energies. Given the Hollywood in which I was raised, it was inevitable that young doers like Darryl and Jerry would soon graduate from *novilleros* to full matadors who cut screen credits instead of ears and tail and then took over the arena itself as front-office impresarios. They were all around us, the Hoppies in the barbershop and the Darryls and the Jerrys racing up the golden stairs.

29

JUST AS HOLLYWOOD had been growing up around me, or I within it, so it was with Malibu. First our sprawling "Early American" cottage was the only house on the half-moon beach. But an odd mix of Hollywood celebrities began to build comfortable two-story houses all along the beach on either side of us. As for the Capras next door, if I hadn't know that Frank was one of Hollywood's leading directors I never would have guessed it. He had none of the hauteur of a Griffith, a Von Sternberg, a DeMille. He wasn't a madcap like Wellman or a character like Jack Ford or Alfred Hitchcock. He lacked the flamboyance of Leo McCarey and the European cynicism of Ernst Lubitsch. He was down-to-earth, hardworking, seemingly always smiling. Born a Catholic, now converted to Christian Science with his endearing wife Lucille, he liked to spend his evenings quietly reading or studying his scripts. Just as we idealize the Girl (or Boy) Next Door, the Capras were the perfect Couple Next Door. Sometimes if the waves were rolling in, I would body-surf them to the beach for an hour, then run up and down the beach, feeling the salt and the sun soaking into my skin. If I saw Frank and Lucille at their picture window, I would wave, and sometimes drop in. They made me feel welcome, they liked me for myself, and not for what my father could do for them.

Frank didn't need B.P., although he was always neighborly with him. Frank made movies that were great box-office successes and won Academy Awards, and he was probably earning as many thousands of dollars a week as Father. His father had been as poor and illiterate a

Sicilian immigrant as my grandfather Max had been a poor and unworldly ghetto Jew. The difference was that Frank seemed to know instinctively that the gods or his God were smiling on him. Now that he had fought his way up from the poverty of his childhood, selling news-papers to see him through a downtown Los Angeles high school, he knew the value of a dollar and he and Lucille lived comfortably but without ostentation. To me, the Capras were symbols of sobriety and sanity for whom all-night drinking or gambling and losing ten thou-sand dollars a session were inconceivable. It was a comforting thought that right next door lived a man who could be famous, creative, and rich without going crazy. He and Lucille gave me a sense of values (one of Mother's favorite words) impossible to get from my rich and famous but erratic father.

The same could hardly be said of the other neighbors. When Clara Bow built a bungalow on the south end of the beach and moved in with her current lover, her roommate-secretary, and her all-night party pals, late at night I could hear the beat and saxophone wailing of jazz and the laughter from many mouths even though her place was half a dozen houses away.

To the other side of Green Gate Cottage the ageless Gloria Swanson lived with the Marquis de la Falaise, who seemed to be in the business of bartering his title for a life of luxury with glamorous movie stars who thought they had everything in life except that title. Either there were a lot of Marquises de la Falaise or he played marital musical chairs with—was it Mae Murray, Constance Bennett?...It wasn't easy to keep up with them. There were all-night parties at the Marquis's, but they were drinking champagne instead of Clara's scotch and beer. Whatever they were drinking, Maurice and I disapproved. In the Hollywood of wild parties and three-day binges, the more they partied and binged the more prudish we became. Self-appointed judges of misbehavior, we could not have been more square if we had been card-carrying members of the Emporia, Kansas, 4-H Club. Women, it seemed to us, were sinful little schemers who would do anything to get within the studio gates, and on to the couch and the seven-year contract. The studio heads were ogres who clawed their way to the top over the backs of competitor-victims. They used their total power to womanize and manipulate, although Jack Warner did it with a laugh and Louie Mayer with a tear.

The two top intellectuals in town were Irving Thalberg, the sickly saint who never drank, who worked twenty hours a day, and was faithful to his beautiful bride Norma Shearer and to his mother who continued to live with them—frail, self-contained Irving who burned with a Jesuitical faith in the world religion of motion pictures; and B.P., a more profound reader and a more original mind but with all the traits that Irving piously disavowed: drinking, gambling, and wenching. In his good years, those Lorraine-Malibu years, Father worked almost as hard as Irving. But he also loved to laugh. Stand-up comics used to be delighted when he took a ringside table. We didn't get the best of the New York comics, because oddly enough Hollywood was a gambling and a party town but not much of a nightclub town. But when Joe E. Lewis brought his unique, half-stewed mumbling style to the Sunset Strip, B.P. would be there leading the laughter. One evening I was driving down Sunset Boulevard, past the Trocadero, when I actually heard laughter so loud that I was sure it was my father's. I parked my roadster and there he was, at a big ringside table with half a dozen of his studio cronies. One of these was Felix Young, who had owned restaurants and nightclubs in New York, a dandy with a breezy but polished style who endeared himself to B.P. by borrowing large sums of money from him with which to open newer and splashier cafés. Father finally thought it would be more economical to put him on the payroll as an associate producer. Like so many Hollywooders I knew, Felix could live in high style, with the choicest of wines, Eddie Schmidt suits like Father's, and opulent motorcars when he didn't have a dollar in the bank.

Once Felix had called from the Lincoln Street jail, where he had been booked for fraud—Felix could sweet-talk a cardinal out of his red hat. Father had rushed down with the bail money. That must have been about the time Father decided to make Felix (Feel, we called him) a Paramount producer. B.P.'s pals (like Felix) talked about his great personal loyalties and his boundless generosity. To which Mother countered: "Why is it that Ben is so brilliant—one of the three highest-paid people in Hollywood—and still so full of insecurity? He seems to need people around him who tell him what he wants to hear—instead of first-rate minds like Paul Bern and the other bright people Irving has around him."

Father would fight back eloquently, without the trace of a stammer. "Stop picking on Felix. As a matter of fact, he's a smart showman. But why don't you mention young David [Selznick], Buddy Leighton, Lloyd Sheldon, who was a damn good newspaperman? I have a better staff than Irving's—and if you want to know something, I'm making better pictures than Irving. He's not responsible for the entire program the way I am—he's smart enough to pick off the plums. It's Harry Rapf who makes the bread-and-butter pictures—the Wallie Beery-Marie Dresslers and the Joan Crawfords. . . ."

"Harry Rapf is a lucky ignoramus," Mother would say. "And that's what you mostly have around you, too—lucky ignoramuses who never tell you you're wrong."

It was one of those endless family arguments neither could win because both were right. I took it all in, at first without any sense of pain or foreboding because it was all part of the Paramount-MGM air I breathed, not unlike the "My father's studio makes better pictures than your father's" game I used to play with Maurice. And the edges of the argument were softened by the fact that the cast of advisors they were arguing about had become either Malibu neighbors or constant weekend visitors. Felix Young rented a house as close to ours as possible and was constantly on our tennis court. Young David Selznick, who struck me then as an eager, alert St. Bernard, often dropped in with a young actress who was very pretty and very shy—I would be surprised later to see how bright and perky and outspoken Jean Arthur would seem in the knowing hands of Frank Capra when they did *Mr. Deeds.* I remember a Sunday afternoon when she sat on the floor and listened with a lovely and I thought loyal intensity while David was busy talking enthusiastically, as was his style, about some new picture-idea. Studio and home were virtually interchangeable. The people Mother attacked as hangers-on and Father defended as indispensable (or vice versa) were around us all the time. I couldn't help noticing that some of the people whom Mother accused of being the most flagrant hangers-on were the same ones who went out of their way to be my friends, too. So she was undoubtedly right a lot of the time. She might have been able to help Father separate the creative wheat from the fawning chaff. Even I, an emotionally retarded Buddy-in-Wonderland, was beginning to spot the difference. The trouble with Ad was the trouble with most people who are much more often right than wrong—that human and almost irresistible need to trumpet one's hits over one's misses.

And of course when Ad would confront Father with a Felix Young (or directors like Louis Gasnier or Marion Gering who she thought would bring him down), he would counter with low blows: "How about your goddamn brother, Sam? I've made him studio manager. Do you think he's any smarter than all these *schmucks,* as you call them? I catch hell because of Sam. I attack Louie's nepotism—well, he does have his whole goddam family on his payroll, even Jerry, the one he hates—and I have to stand up to Lasky and Zukor about making your brother studio manager!"

"Now, Ben, that's not fair. Sam may not be intelligent but he's very smart. He's worked hard to learn the business. He's learned a lot from both of us since we brought him out from New York. Everybody says he's one of the best studio managers in the business."

Those were the sunshine days before my mother and her brother, my very savvy Uncle Sam Jaffe, had developed a blood-knot hatred for each other.

"Who's everybody?" Ben would storm back, "You and Milly?" (Milly, Sam's very pretty, dark- and frizzy-haired wife from the Bronx, was studying Culture I and II with Ad the great mother hen. She had been added to the brood of Freudian- and art-oriented protégées—Rosabelle Laemmle, Sylvia Thalberg, and the Mayer girls—Ad liked to think she was hatching and rearing.)

Sam and Milly were now regulars at our Sunday brunches, our tennis tournaments, our perpetual rattle of Ping-Pong matches, our family feasts, celebrations of hit pictures, and smoldering quarrels. It was fascinating to see how quickly immigrants—not from the Old Country now but from the Bronx—could acquire the look and the speech of what passed in those days for Hollywood quality, as determined by the Ad Schulbergs and the Bessie Laskys. When Milly, our new aunt, had stepped down from the *Santa Fe Chief* and into our lives for the first time, she looked the typical gum-chewing, coarse-haired, cheaply dressed New York highschool girl. But now her hair was sleek, pulled back into a chignon, her deep tan gave her an unexpected Egyptian beauty, and she quickly learned the language of this self-contained little kingdom. For some reason the conjunction *but* was in favor, and soon Milly was using it just as effectively as the rest of us. Asked, "How do you like this new dress?" the answer would be, "I think it's *but* adorable!" References to death took over the conversation, in a most casual way. "Want to hear this," Milly (and the others) would say, "this is going to but kill you." Whereupon a choice piece of gossip—what Sara had heard from Martha about whom Jean Harlow was doing it with behind Paul Bern's back (or Norma Shearer behind Irving's)—to which the answer would be, "It's but unbelievable! I can't *stand* it!" Sometimes it seemed as if everything that we couldn't *stand* we stood every day.

Aunt Milly had joined our circle as a result of Uncle Sam's liaison with the ubiquitous Clara Bow. When his family began to fear that he was seriously considering marriage with this *meshuganah shiksa,* the word went out that young Sam must be saved by finding him a Nice Jewish Girl. A certified NJG was my new Aunt Milly from New York. Milly would flower in Hollywood, growing more chic, outdoing Mother at U.C.L.A., and eventually outdistancing her in such fields as modern art and classical music. The day would come—after Sam had made his fortune taking over and expanding Mother's agency business—when he and Milly would move to London's exclusive Eaton Square because they found Hollywood stultifying. But in those early years of their marriage, Aunt Milly was still fascinated with our Babylon-by-the-sea.

Along the beach, as the Colony continued to sprout houses in both directions, were people who might be described today as Far-out, Kooks, or Swingers. But in those days they just seemed our normal everyday Hollywood screwballs. Edmund Lowe, who came to stardom as Captain Flagg in *What Price Glory?*—famous for his "Sez you-Sez me" confrontation with Victor McLaglen's Sergeant Quirk—lived with his wife Lilyan Tashman (when he was not on our tennis court) in a candy-cane house on the north side of the beach, where the Rapfs had also moved from Santa Monica. Eddie Lowe was tall, dark, and handsome, the leading-man ideal of the period, and Lil was a stylish, sexy, slender blonde who had a passion for red and white. The Tashman-Lowe house was Christmas eternal, red-and-white striped furniture, red-and-white striped walls: From the kitchen to the master bedroom no other color interrupted its candy-box perfection. The cotton-white, apple-red beach house seemed to say, Let us be gay, let us be bright, live for today and the party tonight.

Nights at the Tashman-Lowe candy box were given over to parties—drinking and singing around the white baby grand. To keep her sinuous and famous figure, Lilyan was known for her habit of going to the powder room during the revels and putting her slender fingers down her lovely throat to induce vomiting—or *upchucking* as it was more decorously described. Lilyan was no rowdy Clara or golden chorine like Marion Davies. She was always chic, smartly turned out, a modish girl at play rather than a playgirl. Even that self-appointed social arbiter, Ad Schulberg, approved of Lil Tashman. She was always bright and friendly with me, would call me in for a soft drink if she saw me riding the waves or jogging along the beach. But whenever I looked at this sinuous Jewish princess of the sun, I thought of the self-induced retching in the candy-striped bathroom.

When she died, still looking as high-style as ever, her friends explained that she had only planted the story of the forced upchucking to conceal the true cause—cancer of the stomach.

30

ANOTHER MEMORABLE NEIGHBOR in
the early Malibu colony was Adela Rogers St. John, once married to
screen comic Al St. John. Adela was the female counterpart of the two-
fisted drinker/hard-nosed newspaperman, a sob sister who could give
lessons to Ben Hecht, Charlie MacArthur, and the free-spirited news-
hawks they created in *The Front Page*. Adela's old man, Earl Rogers,
was the original Great Mouthpiece from Denver: She had been raised in
knowledge of what the real world of homicide and grand larceny was all
about. Accordingly, when she wrapped her stories in tinsel and fan-
magazine gush, she knew what she was prettying. Give her a typewriter
and twenty minutes and she could write you a thousand words that
would tickle or touch your heart. She was a formidable word-machine
who could more than hold her own in the male-dominated world of the
early Thirties. And just as successful producers and directors had
shapely mistresses, Adela had a gorgeous piece of beefcake by the name
of Enzio Fiermonte.

Fiermonte was an Italian pugilist, reputed (by Adela) to be the heavyweight champion of Italy. According to the Malibu legend, Primo
Carnera had been afraid to fight him. And that was understandable, for
although he was not built to the proportions of the peasant Goliath,
Adela's tiger displayed chest, arms, and legs that might have been
sculpted by Michelangelo. He would hurl that great physique into the
waves and then come leaping out with all those marvelous muscles
glistening with the spray of the sea and the bronze of the sun. Sometimes

I would trot behind him on the beach, as the incoming breakers licked at his golden feet. My own arms grew thinner, my legs spindlier, my chest seemed to shrink as I tried to keep up with this heroic specimen. Please God, I'd pray as he ran on until I would have to stop and gasp for breath, when I grow up if only I could look just a little like the champion of Malibu—Enzio Fiermonte. . . .

There was another handsome heavyweight in town, another pugilistic sun-god named Pat Doyle, who was said to be one of the brace of lovers fancied by Mae West. His muscles were also celebrated as those of a coming champion of the world. And so Doyle-Fiermonte seemed a natural match for the local Legion Stadium. For the heavyweight championship of Hollywood.

Hollywood turned out in style for the big event between these two invincibles. The Mexican bombshell, Lupe Velez, flashed her diamonds. Mae West wore white sable under the hot lights. The biggest stars in town gave the apprehensive Adela the good luck sign.

Doyle—introduced as the Irish Thrush—wore a green satin robe with a golden harp embroidered on his back. Fiermonte matched him in sartorial splendor with a rainbow robe of the Italian national colors.

The Hollywood Legion band played the Irish and Italian anthems while both gladiators stood patriotically at attention. From Father's precious seats in the front row of the working press, I watched Enzio cross himself in his corner, throw several ominous punches into the air, turn to blow a gallant little kiss to Adela, and stride forward to meet his Irish rival. That was to be the most aggressive gesture the Italian Adonis made that night. In the center of the ring his magnificent jaw made contact with the Irish hero's overhand right, and before some of the distinguished audience had settled back into their seats, Fiermonte was writhing on the canvas. Some final flick of machismo brought him to his feet at the count of nine but moments later he was back on the canvas again, sleeping soundly like a Malibu sun-worshipper improving his tan.

Although the magnificent Fiermonte had come to the end of his pugilistic career, his Hollywood adventures were not quite at an end. Soon after his abbreviated battle with Mr. Doyle, we discovered that he had been playing hooky from his marriage with one of the princesses of the Astor fortune. That aggrieved lady was charging desertion and suing Adela for alienation of affections. There was a brief period when the fallen gladiator took refuge in our Malibu house while the process servers laid siege to Adela's. In time Sr. Fiermonte removed his bronze muscles from the

Hollywood scene. But along with the kept women in a town awash in money searching for new ways to be spent faster, there were almost as many kept men, splendid-looking fellows who played excellent tennis, filled their bathing trunks and their double-breasted blazers to perfection, and who could play all the roles from gigolo to business manager to itinerant husband.

There were many dens of iniquity in early Malibu Beach. In the bathroom of Adela Rogers's house an unexpected scandal was revealed. Cigarette smoke seeped from under the locked bathroom door. Pounding on it, the two irate mothers and inveterate smokers, Ad and Adela, demanded that the culprits come out. After a long silence, the 11-year-old girl perpetrators—our Sonya and Adela's Elaine—emerged, their hands figuratively raised above their heads, the half-smoked evidence of their guilt already swirling to the bottom of the toilet bowl.

A few years later, Elaine escaped her driving superachiever of a mother by becoming the child-bride of author Paul Gallico. Sonya escaped into the tower room of our beach house where she wrote poetry and stared pensively at the sea and the Japanese farmland. Smack in the middle of the movie colony, she was a wistful, bony-kneed, fatherless Emily Dickinson, pursuing some inner or secret life. I was both athlete and scholar—at least so my parents boasted—and Stuart was small, round, and cute, already a remarkable raconteur. Between these two rather formidable slices of sibling sandwich, Sonya was an almost invisible ingredient. I was writing, I was perfecting my backhand, I was even asked my opinion of new movie ideas. Baby Stuart could hold master-storytellers in thrall—a Mark Twain in short pants—with his long-winded but never boring anecdotes. When Father was home he smiled proudly on Stuart. I don't remember his smiling on Sonya. Uncle Sam Jaffe enjoyed Stuart and played tennis with me, but teased Sonya as an amateur matador teases a half-terrified, half-furious fighting calf. "Sam, stop," she would warn, raising a small hand to slap him, using an accent that was neither English nor American but distinctly her own, just as she then called B.P. not "Dad" or "Daddy" or "Father" but "Faith," a term that always sounded more accusing than endearing, and from which he always recoiled.

So Sonya's secret retreat was the tower room, where she developed a sensibility and a literary sophistication that was more finely developed and more fragile than either Stuart's or mine.

Another den belonged to a mysterious fellow down the road, Tod

Browning, who had come to Hollywood as had we, in its ranch-house and orchard days, an old circus hand who got into the movie game as an actor and go-fer for D. W. Griffith, and who had an affinity for darkness, evil, and malignant creatures. *London After Midnight* was his forte, and *Dracula,* and at Maurice's studio we watched him make *Freaks,* a bleak circus movie in which the heroes were not the clowns and the high-wire artistes but the midgets, the hermaphrodites, and an armless and legless thing that drew pictures with a pencil in its teeth. There was a certain glee in the way Tod Browning went about making this picture that made us think of him as Count Dracula on Stage Ten. Those freaks were all over the set and it sent shivers through us to look at them. But he enjoyed it too much. The marathon dance was in vogue then and we went a few times to the Santa Monica Pier to watch the young unemployed zombies drag themselves around the floor in a slow-motion *danse macabre* that earned them a handful of desperate dollars. (One of our local novelists, Horace McCoy, was to describe this minuet of misery in *They Shoot Horses, Don't They?*) If a couple succumbed to motionlessness, they were instantly disqualified, but it was permissible for one contestant to drag his unconscious partner along the floor. Compared to this humiliation of the human spirit, a prizefight seemed as ennobling as the tragedies of Shakespeare.

Even more appalling than the victims on the dance floor were the regulars, affluent resident sadists in the same front-row seats every night, cheering on their favorites who kept fainting and occasionally throwing up from exhaustion. One of the most dedicated of the regulars was Tod Browning, who never missed a night and who got that same manic gleam in his eyes as when he was directing *Freaks*. It was whispered around Green Gate Cottage that Tod Browning was a bona fide sadist and that we should not allow him to entice us into the dark interior of his brooding beach house. In later years he put up a sign, "Tod's Little Acre," and seemed quite harmless as he literally cultivated his garden on the east bank of the old dirt road.

The Malibu Colony was both wild and naive, and what passed for sophistication was a kind of gold-rush free-spirited individuality. Along that historic dirt road was another Malibu pioneer, Fred Beetson, second-in-command of the Hays (later Breen) Office, official overseer of film morality and unofficial guardian of the moviemakers' personal morality. Fred was another of the early colonists who seemed to loathe the surf and sand. On the narrow road behind the row of beach houses he would take his stand in the morning, with a scotch highball somehow permanently attached to his right hand. He would chat and gossip with passersby and invite them in to join him in a glass. He never seemed to be altogether drunk or altogether sober. He was what he was, Fred Beetson of the Hays Office, forever stationed there with a highball in his hand.

Many years after leaving Malibu, I decided to drive out there on a sentimental journey to old Green Gate Cottage. It was a weekday in the off-season, and the beach was deserted. I stopped at the familiar fence, opened the gate, and from the front deck stooped down and peered under the drawn window shade into the living room. The furniture was different, changed for the worse I thought, "modern," no longer Early American. As I stared in at that room full of familiar ghosts, an accusing voice interrupted my reverie. "What are you up to?"

I found myself facing a uniformed beach patrolman.

"I just stopped by to look at my house," I said.

"This house belongs to Mr. Breen."

"No, it really belongs to me," I said. "It will always belong to me."

"You're coming with me," said the beach patrol.

Passively, or perversely, I followed as he led me to his car. "Get in," he ordered. "I'm taking you to the Highway Patrol."

We drove in silence for a long thirty seconds. Atavistic pride urged me to insist on my sentimental rights. Damn it, it *was* my house. Mr. Joe Holier-Than-Thou Breen of the Production Code might hold the deed to the house and now be residing there, but I had seen it rise from the empty sand. Ad had given it the warm Early American look that had come to be a more natural expression for her than the musty, crowded, hand-me-down furnishings of the Lower East Side from which she had escaped. It was my house, scene of elaborate Sunday brunches, furious tennis matches, exhilarating body-surfing, of adolescent apprehension at the sound of expensive chips clacking and adult voices rising in alcoholic bickering that would swell and break into anger as surely as the waves of Malibu mounted and tumbled over into white foam rushing up to our homey picket fence.

It was the house where the radio in my room initiated me into the mysteries of political conventions and election nights, where I heard in sadness the returns that gave the election to Herbert Hoover over Al Smith, a friend of Zukor's and a political hero of my father's. It was in that beach-house bedroom that I first read Molnar's novel, *The Paul Street Boys,* and wept so hard at the end that I had to lock the door so no one would see my weakness. If a house is paid for not in dollars but in

315

memories, then ineluctably the house that I had been caught staring into was forever mine.

But as we drove on, subjective courage capitulated to realistic cowardice.

"When I say it is my house, I mean, my family built it, I grew up here, the Colony grew around me."

There was a constabulary silence, then: "Is there anybody here who can identify you?"

Who was left? The shade of Clara Bow? Lawrence Tibbett, who used to take me sailing? The glamorous ghost of Lilyan Tashman? Suddenly it came to me: "Fred Beetson. I used to know Mr. Beetson. Is he still here?"

A dozen yards ahead of us the question answered itself. There he was, old Fred himself, still planted where I had left him, holding his highball glass like a liberty torch.

"Fred!" I shouted and started to escape from my captor.

"Buddy, where you been? C'mon, I'll buy you a drink!"

Reluctantly, with the possessive spirit of the good cop, the Colony patrolman released me to the custody of the drink-and-let-drink custodian of motion-picture morality.

31

WHEN ALL OF Mother's psychia-
trists and all of Father's Hollywood vocal therapists couldn't mend my
broken speech, I was allowed to drop out of public school, where my
peers never seemed to tire of the humor inherent in imitating a chronic
stammer. At the Los Angeles Coaching School, run by a venerable
monster by the name of Macurda, there were only five or six students to
a teacher, and the faculty was better able to cope with problems like
mine. The other students were either misfits of one sort or another, or
professional working children who could benefit from the concentrated
and abbreviated schedule. Instead of languishing in a thirty-student
classroom until three P.M., we were out at noon. Inevitably, Maurice
became restive at the most conventional public school. Meanwhile I
found it difficult to fill in the three hours until our daily partnership was
reunited. Over the usual objections of Grandma Rapf, Maurice's parents
surprisingly gave him permission to join me at the Coaching School.

After we dutifully put in our three hours, Maurice and I would grab a
bite at a lunch counter and rush downtown to the theater district to see
the current movies. Armed with our gold passes we would race from
feature to feature, and since movies averaged ninety minutes in those
days, we often managed to take in four in the course of a single afternoon. No daily film critic could have worked harder. Miles of celluloid
streamed through our minds. We saw the godawful (30 percent), the
passable (45 percent), the good (15 percent), and the better-than-good to
excellent (that happy 10 percent), and we argued their merits with the

knowledge if not the style of a Robert E. Sherwood, a pioneer of serious film criticism. Our heads were stockpiled with ammunition in the war between our fathers' studios. I would argue that my father was smarter than Thalberg because Irving had given up on Von Sternberg while B.P. had made him one of our top directors. Maurice would counter by reminding me that my father had used Wallace Beery in routine comedies teamed with Raymond Hatton while *his* father had realized the dramatic potential of that grizzled alumnus of Mack Sennett slapstick. And indeed his old man's *Min and Bill* comedies with Beery and Marie Dressler put the burly comic on the road to dramatic success in *The Champ, The Big House,* and *Grand Hotel.*

Seeing movies all afternoon, watching rushes and rough cuts in our fathers' projection rooms, taking the Red Car (halfway between a streetcar and a short-line *Super Chief*) to the previews at Glendale, Burbank, and Pasadena, we couldn't help becoming premature or self-appointed experts on the art of the cinema. We knew why Charlie Chaplin was almost as funny but somehow not as moving in *The Circus* as he had been in *The Gold Rush.* We traded names like picture cards of major-league baseball players. My father thought he might have "a blonde Clara Bow" in gum-chewing, wisecracking Alice White, who stole *Gentlemen Prefer Blondes* from Ruth Taylor. Maurice thought Alice White was a flash-in-the-pan compared to Sally O'Neill and that "my" Esther Ralston would never have the star power of "his" Norma Shearer. We argued the relative merits of two Jewish charmers, *my* Evelyn Brent and *his* Carmel Myers, and of two suave leading men, *my* Adolphe Menjou and *his* Ronald Colman. Seeing almost all of the four to five hundred pictures Hollywood was grinding out every year, we could name not only the top ten but the top one hundred actors and actresses, including names still far down the list like Janet Gaynor, Mary Astor, Lionel Barrymore, and William Powell.

Both studios managed each year to make a handful of classics and a truckful of turkeys. Often it seemed a dead heat as to which studio could make the worst pictures. I cringed for *Hula,* a carbon copy of a carbon-copy Clara Bow story, where everybody gets drunk and Clara inevitably takes off her clothes and dances on a table. Maurice was unable to come to the defense of a weirdo Tod Browning picture, *The Unknown,* in which Lon Chaney cuts off his arms to prove his love for Joan Crawford and thinks this sacrifice will induce her to marry him. On the other hand there were honorable failures like Father's *Old Ironsides,* in which Jim Cruze and the screenwriters effectively recreated the atmosphere of the three-masted U.S.S. *Constitution,* sailing into battle against the Tripoli pirates. I had crossed from the mainland to Catalina Island on a replica of Old Ironsides, and had spent an idyllic summer on location there. I watched the veteran Cruze maneuver those unwieldy sailing ships, took swimming lessons from the Olympic champion Duke Kahanamoku, and received the obligatory attention of the cast: Wallace Beery as the burly bos'n, George Bancroft (hot from *Underworld*) as an embattled gunner, with Charley Farrell and Esther Ralston supplying the somewhat implausible "love interest." The formidable black heavyweight George Godfrey, also aboard, talked fights and sparred with me. I was in a Paramount paradise.

Also with us on location was Dorothy Arzner, one of Paramount's best film editors, whom Ad was urging Ben to promote to the ranks of directors. Soon she would get that chance—follow the path of the original, Lois Weber—and become one of the top directors of the Thirties and Forties.

It had been Father's expectation that *Old Ironsides* would do for the canvas Navy what MGM's *The Big Parade* had done for the doughboys of the Great War. He thought it had everything, the romantic involvement of our fledgling Navy in a war against pirates, a score so stirring that I could hum it all my life, and a dramatic technical innovation: the curtains on stage rolling back to reveal a superscreen more than twice as large as the standard 12 x 18.

Expecting the bows he had taken for *Beau Geste* and *Underworld,* Father was bewildered and angry when the picture was praised by the critics but ignored by the public. As self-appointed experts, Maurice and I knew what was wrong with *Old Ironsides.* It was too long. It was strong on history and production values but short on story and character development; it insisted on being an epic. Judicious editing by the incisive Dorothy Arzner would have helped, but Father had fallen into one of those prevalent Hollywood traps Mother kept warning him against: self-deception. Seduced by his own press-agentry, he persisted in overpraising *Old Ironsides* and was gallantly prepared to go down with the ship.

32

ALTHOUGH WE WERE already on a feverish schedule that left us only á few hours a night for sleep, Maurice and I discovered still another hobby that soon became a passion: racing pigeons.

Mr. Nettles, the pigeon man, sold us our first pair of Belgian thoroughbreds, the original king and queen of our racing stable. Eddie and Peggy came from a noble line. Mr. Nettles had shown us how to differentiate them from their plebeian cousins, the culls in city parks. Our pair had broader chests and stronger wings, stood more erect, had a thick wattle (or white fleshy tissue) circling the eyes and over the beak. Once you had a close look at a thoroughbred racing pigeon, you could no more mistake it for a park pigeon than you would a racehorse for the lead pony that accompanies it to the starting gate. With Eddie and Peggy, Maurice and I were launching on a great adventure into the world of "serious birds."

To build a pigeon house at the far end of our backyard, although we could have "borrowed" the materials from the studio, we preferred the bolder crime of filching the tar paper, wire screening, and wood; with so many houses still being built around us, it was irresistible to creep at night into construction sites. Our rationale was primitive socialism. The mansions going up on or near Wilshire Boulevard were larger than ours. A banker was building one with twenty rooms in an architectural style best described as Southern California Moorish. These new arrivals at Windsor Square could obviously afford whatever we needed for Eddie and Peggy's dream house.

321

Following the instructions in our "pigeon bible" (by Elmer C. Rice), my dependable Uncle Joe built us a model loft that would last for years. Near the roof was an entranceway, with bars that moved in but not out so our birds could "home" into the loft but would not be able to fly out again until we released them.

Maurice and I were proud voyeurs as Eddie and Peggy began their elaborate mating ceremony, he puffing out his chest, spreading his tail and strutting while she coquettishly turned her head away. We could almost see her flouncing her crinoline petticoats. Finally, they held each others' beaks, their necks throbbing in a pigeon soul kiss. Then she hunched down on the floor of the loft; he mounted her with a flashing of wings. In a few seconds it was over. He strutted off like a matador accepting the *olé's!* of the crowd while she sauntered away with a practical "Well, at least *that's* taken care of."

In due course, two small white eggs arrived. For weeks we waited while Eddie and Peggy sat their eight-hour shifts. There was no protest from this husband that a woman's place is in the home. We learned that the male accepts an equal share of the domestic responsibilities and that thoroughbred pigeons are mated for life. The philandering that flourished among *homo sapiens Hollywoodiensis* was practically unknown to homing pigeons.

On schedule our first two squabs were born. We noticed the activity in the nest and hurried into the loft to welcome the first entries in our racing stable. (Since Eddie and Peggy were from Mr. Nettles's loft, they would always "home" there and so had to remain caged. But now we would have our own sleek thoroughbreds homing to 525 Lorraine.) Not that those featherless little bodies with oversized heads and feet bore anything but the most ludicrous resemblance to mature homing pigeons. Their heads wobbled like mechanical toys as we inspected them like proud parents. We slipped metal bands identifying our loft over their rubbery toes and onto their tiny legs, where they would remain until death.

We watched the first of our Lorraine homers enjoying their frequent daily meals as the parents flew from the feeder to the nest to regurgitate the "milk" of cracked corn and other grain into the eager, celluloid-like beaks of their young. In a week the squabs had doubled their size; in two weeks the nest was too small for them and their parents. Eddie and Peggy used the adjoining nest box. Every mated pair needed two nest boxes, since they often laid a second pair of eggs while the first set of squabs was still fattening in the other nest.

One morning we noticed an unusual commotion in the nest. Our squabs were screeching as if they were being killed. Eddie and Peggy were also in the nest and seemed to be attacking them. What they were actually doing was driving them out. The parents had a new nest to attend to now. The moment had come for the month-old children to go out on their own. But the children had other ideas. In terror and confusion, they protested through wide-open beaks, and flopped their unused wings so as not to lose their balance on the ledge of the nesting box. But they were no match for their parents. With a sickening thud (for they had yet to learn they could fly), they tumbled out onto the floor of the coop.

Hungry, frantic, abandoned, they ignored the feeder and fluttered their immature wings to beg their parents' attention. Whenever Eddie and Peggy flew down to the feeder, the squabs hurried over to them with beaks wide open. But Eddie and Peggy pecked at them and drove them away. Their cries were piteous; at night they would huddle together in a corner of the coop. On the third day, prolonged hunger drew them to the feeder.

We were learning along with them. We bought another pair so as not to inbreed. We (or rather Uncle Joe) built a second coop so we could separate the homebred birds from their parents. We set up books to trace the bloodlines and to record their individual homing and racing performances. For homing pigeons must be bred, trained, and raced as carefully as four-footed sons of Man o' War and Seabiscuit.

Soon pigeon racing began to crowd out our other intense hobbies. Still tuning into the early-morning radio stations in Australia or Japan, we managed to meet at our loft at dawn to release our fledglings first one block away, then four blocks, then up to Melrose near the studio, a mile away. We watched as our young birds circled over our heads, round and round until the little compass in their heads clicked *there*; then they winged straight home, pushing the movable bars and flying into their loft. Occasionally a backslider would land in a tree or on a rooftop. If he or she persisted in this dereliction, we would try to trade or sell the sluggard. Other birds would "home" but, instead of flying right in and going to the feeder, would dawdle on the convenient roof of our tea-house. As we lengthened the training flights to five miles, ten—rising ever earlier to drive that distance—some birds would never make it back at all. Although homing was an instinct, it had to be developed with care.

Soon we were driving 25 miles out of provincial Los Angeles, fragrant with orange groves. We watched our birds circle under an impeccable blue sky and then aim themselves like arrows flying at sixty miles an hour. Then we raced them home. Joy it was to see them swoop down through the movable entranceway for a well-earned breakfast: cracked corn and fresh water. A homing pigeon will starve to death before giving up the homeward flight, even five hundred miles. Legendary homer heroes used for messenger service in the Great War managed to complete their missions even when fatally wounded.

As our young racers matured, their range outdistanced our ability to drive them 50 to 75 miles and still get back in time for school. We began to impose on friends motoring up to Santa Barbara, or down to Tijuana on weekend forays. Would they mind pulling off the road a moment to release our birds? We'd pick up the empty cages at their homes when they returned. As we grew more professional, entering our best in the formal races of the Sierra Racing Pigeon Club, we'd entrust our sleek champions to a railroad conductor on the old *Santa Fe,* who—for a modest fee—would release them from the baggage car when the train stopped at Victorville a hundred miles away.

When our homers streaked in from their first long flight, we were as proud as the owners of a winning three-year-old Kentucky colt headed for Churchill Downs. We learned how to breed our own thoroughbreds, selecting the superior young males and females and confining them in a mating box. There they would stare at each other through a partition. When they were ready for the next act of Boy Meets Girl, we removed the partition. Nature prevailed.

One day a strange white pigeon followed our birds into their coop. It was almost a third larger than any of our thoroughbreds and looked more like a sea gull than a homing pigeon. We released him with a new class of young birds we were training. To our surprise Whitey returned, first from a mile, then five. Had we discovered a new species of homing pigeon, even bigger and stronger than our Belgian blue bloods? As we increased the distance to 25 and 50 miles, he continued to lead the new trainees back. He had only one bad habit. Instead of flying directly into the coop through the movable bars, he would land on the slanting roof of the nearby teahouse and preen himself. In pigeon races each entry has a rubber racing band on his leg which must be inserted into the official racing-pigeon clock as soon as he returns to his coop. Like horse and foot races, it is a sport of precious seconds; and we had learned to work with quick-fingered efficiency to grab our birds and stop the clock. So we tried to train the powerful but erratic Whitey by not feeding him the night before a long flight and by scattering cracked corn on the landing platform leading to the loft entrance.

When we thought Whitey was ready, we entered him in one of the major races in southern California. Two hundred miles over the rugged San Bernardino mountains. Depending on weather conditions, a fast bird would make it home in about four hours.

Half an hour before E.T.A., Maurice and I set up our vigil, our eyes trained on a sea-blue sky. In those smogless years, we could see the rim of the yellow-brown mountain range rising behind Hollywood, dividing us from the rolling country of Ventura Valley.

Flying over those hills and down into Windsor Square a fluttering speck appeared—Whitey! Home in less than four hours—record time over those mountains. We crouched near the door to the coop, ready to punch the racing band into our racing clock the moment we could slip it off his leg. But there we waited, and waited, while a self-satisfied Whitey preened himself on the teahouse roof. While the winning seconds ticked away on our racing clock, he refused all our blandishments. Fifteen minutes later, when our first group of entries appeared, Whitey condescended to follow them into the coop.

When we rushed our clock to the club headquarters, our fears were confirmed. If Whitey could have been timed from the second he landed on the teahouse roof, we would have won! Less tenderhearted or more professional pigeon-trainers would have consigned Whitey to the nearest butcher shop. Hard-nosed breeders, like Mr. Nettles, told us it was a waste of valuable grain to maintain a homer who wasn't literally up to scratch. A quick twist of the neck and a one-way trip to the stew pot was the common fate of the reluctant racer. But our birds were pets with names and personalities. Losing them in races and long training flights was painful enough. How could we sentence them to cold-blooded execution? Handy Uncle Joe built us more coops as our flock expanded.

There was a reassuring sense of order to our racing-pigeon world, so different from the movie world that was our larger nest. There we knew of the fractured if not broken marriages, and the flashy studio pimps— the casting directors and the favored agents who served up pretty hopefuls to the studio bosses like squabs on toast. Again and again we saw last year's stars transformed into this year's flops; careers hung by a golden but flimsy thread. While everybody wanted to get close to L. B. Mayer and Irving Thalberg, Jesse Lasky, and B. P. Schulberg, those moguls lived in daily anxiety. L.B. was wary of Irving, and Father woke up each morning with new fears about the machinations of "New York." Clara Bow was worried about gaining weight and Gloria Swanson was worried about losing box-office appeal. Margaret Mayer was worried about losing her self-righteous L.B. to studio starlets. Harry Rapf was worried that his position as the Number Three man in the MGM hierarchy was being undermined by the Thalberg henchmen. Like rival principalities, each major studio intrigued against all the others, and at the same time was a house divided, a hive of enemy camps.

It seemed no accident that the studios were built along a major geological fault and that from time to time actual tremors cracked our windows and made the hanging lamps swing like pendulums. Had we built our magnificent castles of stucco on shifting sands? With our 16-cylinder cars, our liveried chauffeurs, and movie stars for dinner companions and tennis partners, we would seem to have nothing to worry about. Yet the smell of fear mingled with the scent of orange blossoms. Apart from the innate fascination of homing pigeons, our dedication to our loft stemmed from the stability we found in our thoroughbred family. Here we could play God to our growing flock, sending our prize birds off to fly great distances, and choosing the pairs to be mated for life.

But even in this well-ordered world there were aberrations. One of our hens, whom we called Mary, turned out to be a natural-born slut who refused to accept the prevailing marital arrangement and instead set up a little back-street nest in a rear corner of the pigeon house. There she would occasionally distract a roving male from his domestic duties. Mary came from a good family and we tried our best to imbue her with the morality of our feathered bourgeoisie. But she was a dedicated jezebel. We kept her as a curiosity and grew fond of her, though her behavior was more like Clara Bow's than Bessie Lasky's.

All through high school we would maintain our meticulously structured pigeon organization. Different bloodlines were separated as carefully as they are in Navajo clans. Each homer in our racing stable had its own page in our book of records. Our vigilance and enthusiasm never slacked until we moved on to college, when we had no choice but to turn the project over to little Stu and Maurice's kid brother, Matty.

When we returned, order had turned to chaos. The partitions between the cages had been removed, and the separate groups were irrevocably mingled. Squabs had been born and raised without records of their bloodlines and flight performances. It was like the Fall of the Roman Empire: our carefully constructed civilization of homing pigeons in ruins. And finally, in our absence, the final blow: Unable to care for the growing and now chaotic flock, our younger brothers submitted to the advice of our parents that the pigeon population be liquidated; and, instead of a dignified sale to pigeon fanciers, they were sent off in a tumbril to the neighborhood butcher at fifty cents a head.

But in my mind those noble descendants of Eddie and Peggy are forever airborne, flying their great circles and homing hundreds of miles, unique among the creatures whose wings inspired the myth of angels.

33

OING FROM THE small, exclusive Coaching School to teeming Los Angeles High was like being wrenched out of the nursery and thrown into the real world. L.A. High was the largest public school in the city, with 3,500 students, including almost 800 freshmen, or "scrubs" as we were called. Halfway between Wilshire Boulevard where the rich people lived, and Pico, where the Mexican, Japanese, some Negroes, and poor whites clustered in modest stucco bungalows and small frame houses, "L.A." was the classic Southern California melting pot.

At recess there was a riot around the flagpole in front of the three-story neo-Gothic building on Olympic. I watched a lynch mob of older boys in howling pursuit of a hapless "scrub." It seemed he had made the mistake of wearing corduroys to school: Cords, the dirtier the better, were the special uniforms of the privileged seniors. The offending scrub had his cords ripped from his body and run to the top of the flagpole where they waved along with Old Glory. Then a disciplined group of seniors in respectably worn and soiled cords descended on the mob, and restored order. These authority figures, I learned, were members of the Senior Board. Their word, Maurice explained to me, was law. If you got out of hand, if you tried to cut in on the cafeteria lunch line, if you were wandering around one of the corridors after the classroom bell, the Senior Boardman could either give you a stern warning or send you to Mr. Ault.

Mr. Ault was a Dickensian disciplinarian, a one-man judge, prosecutor, and jury dedicated to the Napoleonic Code—guilty until proven innocent. But in Mr. Ault's court, proof was inadmissible. A few days after matriculating, I was late for my nine A.M. homeroom. Of course it had not been my fault: My Model A wouldn't start. By the time I got the chauffeur to drive me in the hated town car I was five minutes late. The bespectacled, narrow-faced Mr. Ault handed out demerit slips with the finality of a Rabbi Magnin. At the end of the first month I was doing what they called "detention study-hall duty." At Urban Military, I had had to do makeup drills on Saturdays. At B'nai B'rith, the righteous rabbi literally had driven me from the Temple. Now Mr. Ault. "Oh, so you're back again," he would greet me when I came to report my latest delinquency. I simply added Mr. Ault to my hate list and tried to stay out of trouble.

That wasn't easy; from Mother's Lower East Side "socialism" and my childhood rooting for underdogs, I had developed a resistance to self-important despots. I had no politics except the rub-off from the avant-garde interests of my mother and the Al Smith-sidewalks-of-New York democracy of my father. But I knew that I didn't like President Hoover or our Republican Governor Merriam or William Randolph Hearst. I didn't like people who used power for self-aggrandizement. I didn't like the way Oscar the Bootblack was always being goosed. I didn't like the way little people were pushed around in the studio, or the way crimes by Hollywood "names" could be covered up because Eddie Mannix, the MGM hatchet man, and the inner circle of studio bosses had the district attorney in their pocket.

Men in frayed white collars were half-heartedly selling apples on street corners. We read about breadlines and farm foreclosures. But the Depression hadn't really touched us yet. Father had lost a million dollars in Paramount stock, but he went blithely on drawing that monster weekly salary and blowing most and sometimes all of it at the Clover Club. I was more concerned with improving my backhand at tennis and with cheering the L.A. Romans on the gridiron than with the mounting pressure of social injustice.

A few weeks into my life at L.A. High, a specter began to haunt me again: having to read aloud. In the English class, our teacher, Mrs. Loomis, would start with the A's—we were seated in alphabetical order—with each student having to read a paragraph or a stanza of a boring classic like *Idylls of the King*. I would watch the big round clock over the door and pray that time would run out before my ordeal began. Cold sweat would form on my forehead, little white spots would spin in back of my eyes until I was sure I was going to faint. Once, when the public reading was only two seats ahead of me, I went to Mrs. Loomis, told her I felt ill, and asked for permission to go home. She said I could if I brought a written excuse from my family doctor to Mr. Ault. I got an excuse from the studio doctor, Dr. Strathern, who would sign anything, and back at school next day I begged Mrs. Loomis not to make me read out loud.

She thought I would get over my nervousness if I gave myself a chance and practiced at home. She didn't seem to understand that it was no problem for me to read out loud to myself at home. It was the pressure of reading or talking to other people that undid me. Mrs. Loomis agreed to skip over me in the reading assignment, but in return for this privilege I had to attend a special class for—she didn't call us misfits, but that's what we were. It was a primitive catchall for anybody with any sort of handicap. There was one boy with a harelip, another with a head too large for his body, and a third, a gentle, husky kid called Tom, who was slightly retarded and whom I often took to movies in the afternoon when Maurice was busy. Strangely, I don't remember any girls in that little gathering of freaks. Maybe we segregated ones were further segregated as to sex. Or maybe my fear of girls blocked them out of my memory.

The kindly but primitive lady therapist couldn't help me stop stammering, any more than she could give the poor hydrocephalic kid across the table a normal head. I see a dozen of us gathered there around that long conference table, as if caught in a frieze by an artist of the grotesque like Goya or Daumier. In one way, though, the freak class was helpful. In my English class, as I prayed that the sweep-second hand would save me from having to read out loud to my snickering peers, I could feel terribly sorry for myself. What had I done to suffer this terrible affliction? Why could Maurice talk, and all my other friends, Buddy Lesser, big Fred Funk, Bud Blumberg? And why was little Stuart so fluent that he was on his way to being a polished monologist? "I had them in the palm of my hand," this fat little seven-year-old confided in me after holding a group of sophisticated adults spellbound with an anecdote he had spun into a thirty-minute cliff-hanger. But surrounded by the harelipped, the deformed, and one poor boy who stammered so desperately that efforts to talk made him spit and slobber, I felt that my speech defect was something I could learn to live with. The freak class was a lesson in humility. No matter how much pain I thought I was suffering, others in the room had deeper wounds.

But my powers of perspective failed me utterly when I had to face another senseless highschool requirement: To pass eleventh-grade English, we all had to participate in a debate. Sides were chosen and debate issues assigned. My subject—Resolved, that commercial advertising is deleterious to radio broadcasting—stirred the social reformer drowsing within me in the California sun. I buried my terror of public speaking in a mountain of research. I sacrificed my afternoon tennis lessons and hours of practice to read every book on radio I could find at our big downtown public library. I became a hive of indignation at the evils of commercial radio. Carried away by my mission, I wondered if a combination of encyclopedic knowledge and strong feeling might provide the magic formula to break through the speech-defect barrier.

The night before the debate I was unable to sleep. At four A.M. I was practicing my delivery. I thought of all my lessons from various therapists over the years: Take a deep breath like a singer before you begin. Use a singsong cadence that relaxes the vocal chords. Remember Mother's Coué-like optimism: "I—can—do—enn-ee-thing—I really —want to do. . . ." I reread my voluminous notes. Demosthenes, Daniel Webster, and William Jennings Bryan rolled into a single oratorical genius could not have been better prepared.

In English class that morning, I leaned forward in my seat like a boxer waiting for the opening bell of a championship fight. Numb with anticipation. *Clang.* I heard my name and went to the center of the ring, or rather to the front of the class. Sixty curious eyes were staring at me, sixty skeptical ears waiting for me to begin. A terrible hush fell over the crowded room. I opened my mouth for the first broadside in the denunciation that would demolish the excesses of commercial broadcasting for all time. From my mouth came . . . silence. A silence so prolonged that it seemed to take on some agonized life of its own. Five seconds? Five minutes? Five years? I could feel the muscles inside my neck braided together like the thick strands of a rope. I felt myself strangling in silence. They had kicked the stool out from under me and I was hanging by the cords in my neck. White circles spun like dizzying pinwheels behind my eyes and I was both resigned to and hoping for a fainting spell. There was laughter, nervous and malicious, and I wished I were back in the freak class among my own kind. At least we didn't laugh at each other up there.

I must have blacked out without fainting because the next thing I knew I was walking home. Crossing broad Wilshire Boulevard into the peace and safety of palm-treed Lorraine, I was suddenly aware of a cold wet feeling in my pants and realized what had happened. My God, had it happened while I was standing there in front of the class with silence stuck crossways in my throat like a fishbone? Is that when the class started laughing at me? Not that they needed scatological encouragement. Watching me squirm there with my mouth open and no words coming out was funny enough.

After I got home and hit the punching bag for a few minutes I felt a little better. Then I released our racing pigeons and watched them fly in great circles. When Maurice got back from school, we practiced the standing broad jump, worked on our prediction of the score of the U.S.C.-Stanford track meet that coming Saturday, timed ourselves running around the block, and wrote a song: "Things that go up—are sure to come down—my love reached the blue skies—then fell to the ground. . . ."

That night I did my homework with the earphones on, listening to the blow-by-blow of the Speedy Dado-Pete Sarmiento fight, and hating arithmetic which never would have any meaning for me, and that English class because English was my best subject. After all, it had helped Father become a writer, and although everybody at the studio seemed to expect me to take over Paramount as soon as I got through college, like Junior Laemmle at Universal, my parents expected me to become a writer. Writers don't have to know algebra unless they want to know how *n* for novel equals *x* in royalties, and even then it won't do them any good. And writers didn't have to debate. Even if Mother pointed out that Father had stammered on to victory. Writers write—or at least they did in the golden days before they were expected to go out on the media circuit and shill for their own books—because that is their way of not having to talk.

In the morning, up at dawn to exercise our flock, I wished I could stay there in safety for the rest of the day. When I went in for breakfast I told our cook I wasn't hungry. I went back to my room and decided to be sick. When Mother came in to remind me that it was time to leave for school, I told her I was sick to my stomach. And I was—with a severe case of not wanting to return to the scene of my shame where I would have to face my peers. Rhymes with jeers and fears. I was allowed to take the day off and crawl back into bed. Shutting my door against the world of talk transformed the room into an island of peace and security.

I was reading *The Old Curiosity Shop* and thinking that the most subtle and satisfying of all human pleasures is to be able to lose yourself in a good big book you hope will never end. How deeply my own humiliation was sublimated in the suffering of Little Nell and her poor old helpless grandfather. I cried through whole chapters as the sad tale carried me along until Little Nell breathed her last. Evil had triumphed as it always seemed to in the good books and the rare good movie. The good die young, Dickens seemed to be telling us: Oppressors prosper.

I had such a fine cry in bed all day with *The Old Curiosity Shop* that next day I decided to hang onto my bellyache and read *David Copperfield.* If I had been able to have my way, I think I would have stayed in that cozy bed forever reading big rich novels one after another. I didn't have to write a little essay to explain to my teacher how much I enjoyed them. Or define the theme. Or describe the characters. Just the reading of them was justification and pleasure enough. That's why I resented the very English classes in which I was expected to excel. Devouring Dickens in bed or just reading a good short story by De Maupassant or Chekhov was all the "English" I needed. The rest was rote, and cant, and stale obligation.

34

WHEN IT SEEMED as if I might stay sick indefinitely, Mother decided I was having a benign nervous breakdown. A family trip was prescribed, this time to Mexico. Once again we piled into connecting drawing rooms and went clicking along day after day through the sun-tortured Southwest and the state of Texas that threatened to stretch on to the equator. Again my parents played an incessant game of casino, which sometimes seemed to be their favorite medium of communication, while I raced back and forth through the train with Sonya and enjoyed the observation car.

At the disappointing, muddy-brown Rio Grande, in an elaborate hour-long maneuver, our Pullman car was attached to the Mexican version of the *Super Chief—el Maximo Jefe,* you might say. The first entry in my diary as we crossed the Mexican border was "I hate Mexico," a lesson in humility since the day would come when Mexico would be my second home. The Revolution that had begun with the furious peasant armies of Villa and Zapata had fought itself out. The great haciendas had been broken up and the tyranny of Diaz had been overthrown. But although the songs of the Revolution and the heroes it inspired were the stuff of legend, all I could see through my young Hollywood eyes was a hunger that made the poverty of South Los Angeles look like Hearstian grandeur.

Rolling through the wilds of northern Mexico in the privacy of our drawing rooms, the family was drawn together in a ceremony of laughter as Father would interrupt the casino game (in which Mother seemed to lick him three hands out of four) to read us our Benchleys. Robert Benchley, the *Life* and *New Yorker* humorist, could make us scream and gasp and grab ourselves in laughter. Even when we knew the words of the sketches by heart, we wanted to hear them again. We wanted to, we needed to, laugh out loud.

When our train slowed to a stop at a village, its station platform seemed a fetid open-air version of my freak class at L.A. High, multiplied by hundreds. Mothers in black *rebozos* held up babies with swollen bellies and flies on their festered eyes, and extended gnarled hands palms upward in the attitude of the supplicant. Some of the children were mutilated and an American businessman in our parlor car asserted that mothers cut the fingers or toes off babies at birth to make them more appealing to affluent passengers. Was this true, or just another *gringo* canard? Certainly there were ragtag armies of the mutilated on those rural station platforms: pockmarked heads without ears, women without arms, men and women who stared blindly through eyes glazed with glaucoma.

Some were not beggers but merchants selling tomatoes and avocados, spiny green fruit and tortillas in a cloud of flies. The poor Mexican passengers who of course could not afford to eat in the dining car would buy this fly-encrusted mess and hurry back with it to their hard wooden seats. And I had been uneasy about Oscar the Bootblack! Compared to this company of the crippled and the blind, he was a king.

At one station, outside Guadalajara, I saw from my comfortable drawing-room window a creature more hideous than anything I had ever seen in a Tod Browning movie. At first it looked like some sort of awkward ball rolling over and over across the station platform toward our Pullman. But as I stared at it through the windows, I realized it was not a ball but a man, or what was left of one. The arms and the legs were gone but there were shoulders and knees, and on these it, or rather he, propelled himself forward in a series of somersaults. No one on the platform paid the slightest attention. He must have been a familiar sight, plying his trade like all of the other lost Mexicans drawn here to the station in the backwash of the Revolution.

When he reached the edge of the platform he stopped rolling and looked up at us. A little boy with enormous black eyes took off a tattered straw hat and held it out to us. I asked my father if I could go out and put some money in his hat. "I don't think it's safe to go out there," Mother said. "And anyway, we'll be pulling out any minute." And as

336

happened so often, in practical terms she was right. As I went to the end of our parlor car, feeling in my pocket for a twenty-five-cent piece to put in the straw hat of the little boy with the big eyes, the train suddenly lurched forward and began rolling south again. I didn't think of it then as a single moment in a life of well-intentioned but futile gestures. I only remember the rolling stub of a man and the child with the big straw hat forever held out in front of him, watching without expression—or rather with a look of such historic resignation that it would haunt me all my life.

The nightmare train rolled on into the Mexican darkness. There was a man aboard with the hard fat muscle of a plainclothesman. He wore a brown double-breasted suit with a flowered tie, high black shoes, and a tan stiff-brimmed hat to prove he was middle-class. He had an important black mustache and a way of walking and sitting that was intimidating. He was, we learned, the man who had killed Pancho Villa. I regarded him with awe. I had known actors like George Bancroft, who played killers on the screen but were marshmallow-soft under their makeup and their costumes. And I had met Jack Dempsey when he came calling on Estelle Taylor, the sultry brunette actress who was Mother's friend. The champion who had been so fierce, even vicious, in the ring turned out to be a friendly and easygoing guy who spoke in an unexpected falsetto, and who didn't seem to be mad at anybody except his ex-manager Jack Kearns. Movie heavies and famous pugs had nothing in common with the man who had murdered Pancho Villa. When he looked at you he was not interested in you. He wanted nothing from you except your life if he was paid to take it. He didn't act menacing, or try to be menacing. He just sat there. Intact. He *was*.

There were two Mexican ladies on our train who were dressed in black. Not because they were in mourning as I first thought, but because they were highborn and rich. Two elderly sisters. Their only ornaments were black ebony crucifixes trimmed in silver and hanging from silver chains. We knew they were *upper*-upper-class because they were so snooty you could almost hear them sniff as Mexicans with brown skins (*mestizos* with Indian blood) passed them in the corridors. For the first day they sniffed at us just as they did at all the others. But when they heard that Father was the grand *jefe* of a Hollywood movie studio, they decided to strike up a conversation. It began in the dining car when we happened to sit at tables across the aisle from each other.

"Dolores del Rio?" asked the elder of the two sisters. She spoke the name in Spanish with an air of infinite refinement. We all looked at each other in astonishment. Father responded with the social charm that was one of his trademarks. "Yes, Señora, we know Dolores del Rio."

The ladies nodded to each other and the conversation continued.

"Lupe Velez?"

How many times had we seen the tempestuous Lupe in the front row at the Hollywood Legion Stadium, pounding on the blood-stained canvas of the ring and screaming profane Mexican incantations at brown-skinned countrymen who were failing to live up to her high standards of combat? One night we had seen her stand up and cup her hands to shout some words of pugilistic wisdom to a light, handsome, Mexican-Indian lightweight named Rojas. Rojas turned to look at Lupe. Lupe was easy to look at. In fact he had been openly flirting with her between rounds. Even I, who professed to hate girls, and who was surrounded by young women whose profession it was to be pretty, often found myself staring at Lupe. So Rojas turned his head and looked down the better to hear Lupe's advice. It was the last thing he heard for several minutes as he lay unconscious on the canvas, his head so close to Lupe's that she could have reached out and cradled her fallen gladiator in her arms. Instead she was screaming "*Hijo*! Get up, you son-of-a-beech. . . !"

"Yes, Señoras," my father smiled his most ingratiating smile, "we also know Lupe Velez."

The aged sisters shook their heads and made polite clucking noises of disapproval.

"Dolores del Rio, *si,*" said the elder. "Lupe Velez, *no!*"

"Del Rio, *si,* Velez, *no!*" her sister seconded the verdict.

There was no more to be said on that subject, or indeed any other, for those were the only words we had in common. Later that afternoon when we passed each other in the Pullman corridor, our new Mexican friends rewarded us with the slightest of bows, the faintest of smiles, and their considered opinion of life in Hollywood: "Dolores del Rio, *si*! Lupe Velez, *no!*"

We felt we were selling poor Lupe short but, after all, this was a long journey down through the cactus country and the parched plains of Sonora and one had to be sociable. So we nodded in agreement. Next morning at breakfast we greeted each other like old friends.

"Dolores del Rio, *si*!" said the elder sister. "Lupe Velez, *no!*" said the younger. Poor, hot-tempered, lovable Lupe didn't get a single vote all the way to Mexico City.

338

I wanted to know why the ladies felt so strongly about the respective qualities of our two leading Mexican actresses. Dolores, my father explained, was a daughter of the Mexican aristocracy. Her father was a wealthy banker. Her mother was one of the Asunsolos, distinguished in the arts. But Lupe's mother had been a walker of the streets. (With all his vices, Father refrained from the vulgarisms commonly associated with Hollywood speech.) Lupe herself had made her theatrical debut in the raunchy burlesque houses of the city. Stagedoor Juanitos panted for her favors and Mama Velez would sell her for the evening to the highest bidder. Her price soared to thousands of pesos. Hence, Dolores, *si,* Lupe, *no*!

Another flash of memory of that primordial journey to Mexico: In Durango, when we stopped at nightfall, our American businessman know-it-all tour guide explained that an armored car was being added to the train, with a detachment of soldiers, because the Yaqui Indians were on the warpath (just like a John Ford movie!) and had been swooping down on horseback, stopping trains, making the passengers line up outside their cars, then taking all their possessions and sometimes even their clothes. Everybody in the first-class cars became very friendly, drawn together in a communion of fear. Passengers sat up through the night, waiting for the Yaqui attack. But the Indians never obliged. They were up there in their mountains, waiting, perhaps for another Revolution. We could see the glow of tiny fires or perhaps candlelight from the paneless windows of the distant one-room adobe huts in the foothills.

In the armored car, soldiers in sloppy uniforms dozed over their rifles inherited from the Great War. I watched the killer of Pancho Villa snoring in his parlor chair and as his broad chest hunched up his coat jacket I could see the silver holster of the .45 he carried on his hip.

As we pulled into the big station in Mexico City, we saw two men of swarthy complexion, wearing serapes over their business suits, hug each other tightly while pounding each other's backs. That, Mother explained, is how Mexican men greet one another. When we stepped off the train, one of the backpounders turned to greet us. He was the Paramount representative in Mexico, he said with a bow as he presented his card, "*Bienvenido a Mehico!*"

In the limousine on our way to the hotel, our host pointed out various sights of the strange and, to me, filthy-looking city.

"Were you born here?" Mother asked.

"Born here? Whaddya think I am?" Our host lapsed into perfect New Yorkese: "I'm a *landsman*. My name is Kaplan. I came down seven years ago and married a Mexican girl—from an old Jewish family. Did you know the oldest *shul* in North America is right here in Mexico City? Before you leave I'll bring you home for a nice kosher meal. Even the chili peppers are kosher!"

That night after dinner we took a walk with Sr. Kaplan. Turning off the main street, the Paseo de la Reforma, which Maximilian and Carlotta had built to resemble the Champs Elysées, we looked into the open doorways of ancient houses where candles were burning before small altars. We saw women on their knees praying to the figure of a dark Madonna. We had arrived, our Jewish-Mexican guide explained, at a tense and historic moment. The assassin of President-elect General Obregón—a young Catholic fanatic named José de León Toral—was to be executed at sunrise. Although the Catholic Church had been banned by the Revolutionary Party now ruling Mexico, and priests were not allowed to wear their cassocks in public, the Church still had millions of adherents, especially women, who considered Toral a martyr to the cause of the *Cristeros*. Sr. Kaplan did not think the Toral affair would touch off a new insurrection. The provisional President, Portes Gil, had the Army behind him and even though there were organized bands of *Cristeros,* especially in the back country, Sr. Kaplan was not too worried.

"Every couple of months we have a little revolution, but I think we've seen the last of the big ones," he assured us. "The generals who led the old Revolution are mostly interested in getting rich now. There may be some shoot-'em-ups on election day, but no Pancho Villas: Too many people died. They say the Mexicans are in love with death but even they get sick of dying. No, this Toral thing will blow over. But the trouble is, a situation like this knocks the hell out of our business. The Mexicans are great movie fans. They love our Westerns and the costume pictures and you should hear 'em laugh at the slapstick comedies. But when they set up army patrols like tonight, it's murder at the box office."

Sr. Kaplan spoke politely in his perfect Mexican Spanish to sinister groups of soldiers at various intersections of the broad and silent boulevard. I pictured the young assassin—a cartoonist for a Catholic paper, Kaplan had told us—praying on his knees in his dark prison cell as he waited for dawn and the firing squad. I had seen things like this in the movies, but somehow the movies made it seem glossier and more melodramatic than it really was. There was something casual, almost matter-of-fact in the way the brown-skinned *soldados* fingered their old old-fashioned rifles or leaned against a lamp post to smoke a cigarette. What history would record as a critical counter-revolution put down by an aggressive government dictatorship was for us a quiet stroll through the dark streets of an ancient city a million miles from the laundered estates of Windsor Square.

After the execution, when the authorities were satisfied that the *Cristeros* were not taking to the streets, the people poured out into the parks and onto the sidewalks filled with vendors selling newspapers, cheap candies, lottery tickets. . . . With his happy blend of Bronx and Latin enthusiasm, Sr. Kaplan took us on the round of tourist attractions. We drove out to Teotihuacan to marvel at those architectural improbabilities, the Pyramids of the Sun and the Moon. I was not yet a quasi- or would-be archeologist, but the seeds were planted as I sweated my way up the largest pyramid this side of Cheops'.

Dutifully we boated through the floating gardens of Xochimilco, another marvel of pre-Columbian ingenuity. At Sr. Kaplan's urging, we even submitted ourselves to our first bullfight. But even our many nights at prizefights had not prepared us for this bloody spectacle. As the first scrawny horse was toppled over and the cruel spear of the picador brought forth a gushing well of blood from the shoulder muscles of the bull stubbornly pushing against the pain, Mother looked away, I stared at my clenched fingers trying not to faint, and Father chewed on his big cigar and grew very pale. With an unannounced but unanimous vote, we all rose and started up the wide aisle toward the exit. *Aficionados* voiced their resentment of *gringo* queasiness as we hurried toward the safety of the tunnel. Years later, when I came to embrace rather than reject Mexico, I would learn to accept the *corrida* as the ultimate expression of her orgiastic culture. But on that initial escape from what seemed to me the butchery in the arena, I was simply reinforced in my dread of Mexico as a country of vicious extremes where the people were dedicated to blood-lust and death was a way of life.

When Sr. Kaplan took us to the famous House of Tiles, the palatial sixteenth-century home of the Marquis del Valle—now transformed by American ingenuity into Sanborn's, a flourishing restaurant, gift shop, and drugstore—I was distracted by the human carpet of beggars sleeping on newspapers in the entranceway. Our indefatigable Sr. Kaplan nimbly stepped through them, waving us to follow. It was unnerving to try to find room to set down first one foot and then another among the faces, arms, legs, and ragged bodies of old men, women, and children. By the time we had managed to gain entrance to the brilliant, high-ceilinged interior, entirely decorated in colonial tile, Sr. Kaplan's description of its history and architectural elegance was tainted by the reality of the homeless lying outside. As we looked at the expensive menu, I could not get them out of my mind. But Sr. Kaplan chatted on about theater grosses and the rosy prospects for Paramount distribution if only the *Mehicanos* would put their *pistolas* away and settle down to business.

As our Mexican holiday drew to a close, it was still beggars rather than box office that said *Mexico* to me. It was still sad-eyed mothers in dusty *rebozos,* with one baby at the breast and another swelling in the belly, squatting outside the massive cathedral, palms reaching toward us for a pinch of the gold they pictured in our pockets.

I hated the relationship: Walk rich among the poor! I blamed the Church for flaunting all that gold and leaving its children to starve in its very courtyard. In Hollywood I had seen many who were hungry for fame and the main chance, and at L.A. High there were Negroes, Mexicans, and a few Japanese dressed shabbily in what were probably hand-me-downs. But raised in my celluloid cocoon, I had never looked into the eyes of the truly hungry.

35

OME ON LORRAINE, between the challenges of L.A. High and the battles of "The Stude," as we called the studio, I was beset by demons of insecurity and haunted by goals I could only strain for but never reach. As the new editor-in-chief of *The Blue-and-White,* one of the few highschool dailies in the country, I was dedicated to perfect typographical makeup of the front page, which meant writing heads, subheads, and the accompanying copy to exact count, so the right-hand column would precisely match the left. Maurice and I had developed this journalistic perfectionism but he was gone now: A semester ahead of me, he was off on an aircraft carrier, doing go-fer duty on a service movie his father was making for MGM. I alone was left to battle the porpoise-bodied, sarcastic print-shop teacher, Mr. Vaughan. Since I refused to lock up the paper until even the most minute imbalance had been corrected, Mr. Vaughan would bellow and rage against being kept in the print shop beyond the day's closing bell. "Fifty years from now do you think anyone's gonna give a damn if the lower heads on the left are one em lower than the right?" the black-aproned printer would bluster. Although intimidated by his size and sound, I never bent to his wrath. I had two potent allies, the spirit of my absent "brother," Maurice, and the presence of Miss Katherine Carr, our homely little dynamo of a journalism teacher who relentlessly drilled into us the "who-what-when-where-how's" of reportorial clarity. Her brother was Harry Carr, the illustrious columnist for the *Los Angeles Times,* and so, as I dummied, supervised, rewrote, and squeezed into shape our daily bugle, I felt a titillating sense of connection with the exciting world of professional journalism. In fact, I lost my amateur standing when Miss Carr arranged for me to be a sports stringer for the *Times*. I gloried in such dispatches as:

"Trailing by 13-7 at the half, the fighting Romans of L.A. High came roaring back in the final minutes to score a dramatic 14-13 victory over the Hollywood Sheiks at Housh Field Friday afternoon."

Each gridiron struggle was a personal victory for this 17-year-old veteran, summing up 60 minutes of football in five bristling lines that bore the imitable stamp of Grantland Rice. At the rate of five cents a word I was earning three or four dollars a week, and with my scrapbook of reportorial accomplishment I was able to line up similar assignments with the weekly neighborhood papers, *The Los Angeles Tribune, The Hollywood News,* and *The Beverly Hills Citizen.* The little checks I collected every week gave me a heady sense of following in Father's footsteps.

But editing my little daily or describing the heroic feats of valor of my peers still left me panting for glory in the field. I would happily have traded all the bylines and editorial honors for a varsity letter in football, tennis, or track. I was a willing but marginal athlete. I scrimmaged with the "B" football team but was never in the lineup. I ran an indifferent 660 on the Class B track team. My one hope for glory was in tennis; on weekends I logged twenty sets in a day, turning on our court lights to play on into the night. On our highschool tennis team, I was ranked eighth or tenth, and since the top four played the singles matches and usually two of the four doubles as well, my main chance to get into the lineup was on the third or fourth doubles team. My aspirations rode on the slender shoulders of our Number Three, a graceful player with the improbable name of Yale Katz.

As soon as the paper was put to bed and the disgruntled Mr. Vaughan liberated from his print-shop prison, I would rush to the school tennis courts to practice with Yale or to play in one of the seemingly endless rounds of elimination matches that would decide my fate.

If I had a silver spoon in my mouth, I was gagging on it. Nothing came easy to me. My peers at L.A. High were almost all accomplished sheiks into whose arms pretty little girls fell like ripe oranges. But Maurice and I had developed a pathological fear of breaking through the sex barrier. We had to force ourselves even to talk to the girls on our newspaper staff.

At least there we had a chain of command and a daily professional imperative to force us out of our tight little corner.

As we approached my seventeenth birthday, our friends mutinied against our traditional mode of celebration: a free-for-all fight in the dark in the Rapf projection room. They insisted on bringing their dates to a less pugnacious party. Literally going down fighting, I was forced to give in . . . and faced the agony of deciding what girl to ask. She would be my first date. The second girl I asked—and I only knew two—accepted.

As I recorded in my diary: "Jeez! I tremble every time I think of that party tomorrow night. But as Maurice preached but didn't practice: Why cut out half of the world's population, because of a silly prejudice?"

And so I faced my first G-day: "After the Hollywood-L.A. meet we won, I dressed hurriedly and called for Bella Codon. I was rather burned up but rather liked the idea. It was all so new to me. We had supper at my house and then went to see *Seventeen* at school. The play was well done. In the car I was rather shy and did little talking. However I could hardly be blamed—this being my first time. After the show we came home and everyone danced—but me. That is what hurt the most. I felt like a wallflower. The party broke up at 12:00. I took Bella home. She seemed pretty nice though was not very talkative. They say: 'Every time there is a lull in the conversation a Jewish child is born.' In that case we raised up a great race of Jews this evening. That's how much we talked. However it was a new feeling and one, I must confess, that I rather enjoyed, despite my embarrassment and uncomfort. Got to bed around 1:00."

Jack of all sports, master of none, I was unexpectedly summoned back to the track team by Coach Philo Chambers, who had given up on me. It seemed our best half-miler, Beverly Keim, who could just shade two minutes flat, was overmatched against McCarthy of Fairfax High, a champion middle-distance runner. Chamber's strategy was to put me in as a "rabbit," instructed to run the first quarter-mile as fast as I could in hope of fooling McCarthy into thinking I was some sort of phenomenal unknown who might steal the race from him. Then as I fell back, Beverly Keim could come on and pass him in the stretch.

That week I was back on the track training hard for this desperate assignment. Suddenly finding myself "in" with Keim and the senior stars gave me the confidence to do something I had never done before. There was a small dark-haired girl in my homeroom class, Penny, who looked awfully cute. Once in a while she would glance at me and I would look away. Now I stopped her in the hall, managed to mention that I would be running in the Fairfax meet Friday. I wondered if she would like to see it and then meet me for a malt after the race.

My first "pass" at a strange girl, but isn't that what all varsity trackmen did? When she promised to be there, I intensified my training to the point of frenzy.

The night before the meet, my family took me to Victor Hugo's, the fanciest restaurant in town, where I could not resist the *fettucine verde*. Back in bed I ran my race against McCarthy again and again, coming in a courageous third as our strategy swept Keim to victory.

Toward morning I slept a few hours and woke like a lathered race-horse. I sleepwalked from class to class. Then I was on the track, proud and trembling in my powder-blue-and-white L.A. High track shirt, sandwiched between Keim and McCarthy. At the gun I sprang forward like all my heroes. My legs were spinning like wheels—I knew I had never run so fast before. But no matter how fast I ran, McCarthy was at my heels. After 300 yards, I knew I was in a nightmare. In fact, I was almost hoping it *was* a nightmare from which I would awaken. For no matter how hard I tried to step up the pace, to run even faster, there was no way I could run away from McCarthy. While my legs were churning—the muscles beginning to tighten—I could feel him loping along easily behind me. He was playing with me, he was toying with me. I was no rabbit outrunning a greyhound, I was a mouse and he was a lithe, graceful predator cat.

At the end of the first quarter-mile we were in front of the grandstand again, and there was Schulberg of L.A. leading McCarthy of Fairfax by an air-sucking yard.

There was a smattering of applause and scattered cheers. But I was unable to romanticize about Penny up there rooting me on. I had too strong a case of McCarthyitis. After 600 yards I literally didn't know whether I was still running or not. I thought McCarthy was passing me and loping on but I wasn't sure. I had a strong sensation that my brain was frying like hamburger, and also that my head had no connection with the rest of my body. At the 660 mark was a small section of bleacher seats that blocked a view of the track from the main stands. My sub-conscious must have welcomed it as an oasis, for the moment I came to it I blacked out, rolled off the track, and threw up Victor Hugo's *fettucine*. I didn't realize I was on a stretcher until I was carried into the dressing room. There I heard that McCarthy had won easily, in record time, with Keim a respectable second.

Next time I passed Penny in the corridor, she was walking with a letterman. I was relieved that she didn't seem to notice me. We never spoke to each other again.

Sports and movies were my daily addiction. But it was the availability of movies at "Father's stude" or the Rapfs' that sharpened our critical senses: "*Once in a Lifetime,* a burlesque on the movies which contained millions of laughs and not a little truth." . . . "*Min and Bill:* Harry Rapf's picture deftly combines comedy and tragedy. Dressler, Beery, and Rambeau excellent." . . . "In Dad's projection room tonight I saw one of the finest moving pictures I have ever seen: SKIPPY. Jackie Cooper and little Bobby Coogan are both marvelous in it. The story was human and even when it was over I couldn't stop crying."

Skippy had been one of Father's favorite projects, the Percy Crosby comic strip brought to life, the kind of small-budget film done with loving care that B.P. believed in and that could be slipped almost secretly into a fifty-picture schedule featuring million-dollar epics and extravaganzas. To write *Skippy,* Father had taken the advice of his gifted drinking-and-gambling crony, Herman Mankiewicz, and assigned Mank's younger brother, Joe, to do an original screenplay. Still in his early twenties, only a few years out of Columbia (the college, not Harry Cohn's castle), Joe had already written a couple of successful scripts for Paramount. In *Skippy,* he came up with what Father considered a little masterpiece. In addition to Jackie Cooper and the five-year-old Bobby Coogan, there was the film-wise Mitzi Green and the specialist in snotnose child heavies, Jackie Searl. Skippy is a doctor's son; his little pal Sooky lives in shantytown on the wrong side of the tracks. When the mean dogcatcher's son grabs Sooky's little dog, an endearing but unlicensed mongrel, they first go searching for him, with Sooky describing him as "always lickin' ya!" Their struggles to raise the three dollars to save the life of Sooky's dog had the projection room in tears. And when the boys finally manage to amass that much money, only to learn that this urchin dog of the urchin kid has already been destroyed, I thought of our own beloved dogs, Bozo and Gent, and could bear no more.

From Maine to Manchuria, ferment was in the air. The usually tractable and patriotic veterans of the A.E.F. were marching on Washington to demand their bonus; General MacArthur was ordering his troops to open fire on them. Mussolini was rattling his sword at the world, ranting that Fascism was the answer for the twentieth century. The Klan was marching openly through the South, Ford was having his workers beaten up for trying to organize his flivver plants, a fascist Black Legion was forming in Detroit, and a former screenwriter of my father's, William Dudley Pelley, was organizing his anti-Semitic Silver Shirts right on our doorstep.

While the world was going smash on a dozen fronts, I was obsessed with my tennis match against Manual Arts. My diary gives Yale Katz and his shaky partner twenty lines to record another disaster: Needing our match to win the overall victory, we are even in sets and four-all in the third. Our Roman teammates are on the sidelines trying to root us home. Joe Davis, our Number One, a ranked junior player, is shouting encouragement. And once more I choke in the clutch and double-fault the match away. The stars of the team turn away. My partner and pal, Yale Katz, can't look at me. Coach Crumley—my lifeline to athletic respectability—walks off without a backward glance.

With the terrible stink of defeat clinging to me like the persistent odor of skunk, I slunk home to my haven on Lorraine.

348

36

HE STORY OF what I omitted from my simpleton diary that crucial spring of '31 is more telling than what I included. Missing were not only the millions of unemployed, the dispossessed farmers, the armies of fascist bullyboys; something personal and central to my life was also missing: Father—almost a non-person.

An entry devoted to Maurice, Miss Carr, Coach Crumley, and Yale Katz ends with three mysterious words: "Saw Dad tonight." Where had Father been and what kind of talk did we have together when he surfaced at last? Troubled by his absence, I concocted a cover-up. I agonize over my San Pedro match and again call on God to help me win it. "My last real chance! I must make good on it!" And then: "Mr. [Louis] Weitzenkorn [author of *Five Star Final*] and [Uncle] Sam [Jaffe] were over for supper. Dad was not here. I believe he is sleeping at the Ambassador for a while to concentrate on his work since he maintained that he was disturbed too much here." If I was aware of the backstage drama at our cozy little mansion, I imposed on myself a censorship as tight as the Hays Office's.

On a sunny Sunday in June, with our Negro cook, Lucille, serving up sumptuous late breakfasts of creamy waffles and Canadian bacon, life at Green Gate Cottage to an outsider must have seemed like Hollywood heaven. I could trade forehands with Freddie March and Edmund Lowe, trounce Jeanette MacDonald at Ping-Pong, ride the breakers with Frank Capra, have Lawrence Tibbett sing booming arias at me as we fished in his sleek motorboat off the Malibu pier. I could go sailing with the elegant leading man, Neil Hamilton, and drop in for a Coke at any movie star's beach house, from gum-chewing Clara Bow's on the south to high-style Lilyan Tashman's on the northern boundary of our principality. Could a 17-year-old possibly ask for more?

The answer is as simple as the plot of a four-hanky Andy Hardy movie: *Yes*—for Dad and Mom to act like parents in an L. B. Mayer family picture and live together. One Sunday early in June comes a tight-lipped but ominous entry: "Mom and Dad quarreled tonight before supper. I am worried about them." And on the following day: "Tonight Mother and Dad had an awful quarrel before they went to the preview. I happened to hear them and never before did I realize how serious the matter was. I hate to go into detail here; the facts hurt me that much! They left a few minutes ago with Sam and Milly. Incidentally their fight gave me a great idea for a short story."

There beats the double heart of the child writer, gloating over the literary possibilities of the very event that is eating him alive. Next day I recorded: "Dad and Mother are okey again but Mother seems sad."

"Okey" meant that Mother and Father were back under the same roof for the sake of appearances. An uneasy truce had been declared.

Father was having trouble at the studio—the perennial power struggle with New York, intensified because Walter Wanger was running a rival studio of the Company's back east in Astoria. Mr. Zukor himself was involved in a far-off Wall Street power fight brought on in some mysterious way by the Depression. In bed with my radio earphones on so Mother would think I was asleep, I lay there worrying. I had tuned in old Aimee Semple MacPherson. Even though I knew little or nothing of the outside world, I knew that Sister Aimee was another of our gaggle of spiritual frauds, a female Elmer Gantry decked out in Hollywood tinsel. . . .

Then I was hearing other voices, closer to home: from my parents' bedroom directly across the hall. I had heard Mother and Father argue before, had heard Ad nag him about his gambling or his tendency to surround himself with sycophants. But this time, even before I grasped what they were shouting about, I knew this was deeper and more dangerous.

"Now Ad, now Ad, be fair—God damn it, Ad!" Usually loud only when laughing or singing or retelling a favorite story, Father's voice was trying to smother Mother's attack. But she would not let go of her prey. She had it in her teeth now and she was going for the jugular like all mothers protecting the lair. I put my earphones aside, sneaked out of bed, and crept to the door.

"*Hoor!*" The word spat into the night with a venom I had never heard from Mother before. "She's nothing but a little *hoor.* Cheap little *kike!*" Father's "Now goddamnit, Ad!"'s were ineffective punctuations. Gone now was all the understanding from Mother's five-foot shelf of psycho-analysis. It made me tremble. Who was this *hoor?* Who was this *little kike,* who was the mysterious third point to the triangle? When the name *Sylvia* flashed through the angry words, I became more fright-ened of what I was beginning to understand. It was Sylvia Sidney— Father's luscious little plum-blossom, recently plucked from the New York stage.

Puritanical Hansels steeped in middle-class morality, Maurice and I saw Hollywood both as Baghdad and Our Town where, at the end of the working day, Dads come home to Moms—or should. If most males look back on their first sexual experience as a milestone on their road to manhood, for me from that moment at the door it was the shock of *Sylvia Sidney.* As I listened in the dark I felt no Oedipal leap of joy—at last my chance to move in on old Dad and take his wife! I felt: Oh my God! He's going to leave home and live with *Sylvia Sidney*—how can I get Mom and Dad to stay together?

The verbal battle built to its inevitable crescendo of screams, shrieks, accusations—the fearful orchestration of domesticity undone. Then the slamming of the door. An ominous silence. I wondered if Father had gone to the bar or back to the Ambassador Hotel and the sultry young *hoor* whom movie fans were just beginning to take to their hearts. I crawled back into bed and began to cry.

37

IN THE COURSE of righteous curiosity, I was to learn more about Sylvia Sidney. Her Hollywood debut, ironically, owed more to Mother's talent-scouting abilities than to Father's. On a trip to New York, taking in all the plays, Ben and Ad had seen the 20-year-old Sylvia in the risqué hit, *Strictly Dishonorable.* Mother prided herself on her ability to spot upcoming actors, directors, and writers who were still "unknowns." And so that evening, it was Ad who raved about young Sidney's promise and urged that they go back to her dressing room to introduce themselves. It could have been a scene from one of Father's movies: the stylish matron in her middle thirties and the elegant, prematurely grey, articulate tycoon at the height of his power and confidence, going backstage to introduce themselves to the fetching ingenue.

Now that the Pola Negris and the Clara Bows were giving way to a new breed who could both dazzle and speak, B.P. was anxious to keep his studio abreast of L.B.'s, and so it was logical that he would back Mother's judgment and sign young Sylvia before Mayer and Thalberg or the Warner Brothers snapped her up.

I watched Mother's new rival on the set of *City Streets,* sitting close to my father while one of his new favorite directors, the brooding Rouben Mamoulian, put her through her paces. I sat with Father, Sylvia, and Mamoulian in the intimacy of the projection room, never sensing that the drama going on around me was more intense than the acting on the screen.

I must say, for both Father and Mother, that until the night their shouting brought me to my bedroom door, their public behavior had been so "correct" that even a greater sophisticate than their firstborn would have been deceived. Whenever I saw Father with Sylvia Sidney, or with any of his other glamorous leading ladies for that matter, he was always a model of decorum. And Mother, no matter what the provocation and humiliation, never took her children into her confidence, or tried to enlist our sympathies against our wandering "Pate," as my sister now insisted on calling him. With a courage bordering on hypocrisy, Mother went sweetly on, pretending that Father's habitual and now extended absences from home were due simply to the intense pressure of work at the studio.

My diary continued to be as evasive and self-protective as Mother's daily cheerfulness. An occasional "worried about Mom and Dad" is as much as I would permit it to reveal of what was happening to our life.

But it was festering inside, so deeply that I could not share the pain of it even with Maurice, although we had shared every other experience from the age of ten. This time, when Father left home, I knew the reason and, as the dutiful elder son—and dedicated prude—I was determined to do something about it. It never occurred to me, of course, that my father and his young protégée might be in love. I loved our dog Gent and I loved to watch our homing pigeons circling high above their loft. I loved to watch the graceful half-miler, Eastman of Stanford, breeze toward the finish line, and I loved to watch a director who knew what he was doing—like King Vidor or Ernst Lubitsch—take control of his set. I loved to reel in a ten-pound bass from the Malibu kelp and I loved to "sleep over" at Maurice's and talk about everything we liked or hated and feared until the tropical morning light began to creep under the window shades. Of loves we had many but of love we knew nothing. "Love" was what an actor professed to an actress on the movie screen. Clara Bow with Buddy Rogers in the big fade-out smooch. But that my 40-year-old father and the 20-year-old *gamine* could be physically, romantically, passionately, and even tragically in love was something my mind was as closed to as the big studio gate was to outsiders peering in.

I would give Miss Sidney no quarter. In my eyes there was nothing she could do to redeem herself, nothing to modify my preconception that Sylvia Sidney was simply the latest (and in Father's case the most destructive) of the pretty little vampires who sucked his blood to fatten their studio careers. I had no idea how long Father's liaison with Sidney

354

had been going on, but I knew that discretion on Mother's part would not protect us from the country-club gossip and the wits who held forth in the studio commissary. If I had been living in a small midwestern town—well, maybe that's what our Hollywood was—I could not have been more "mortified" by the public scandal that I knew was spreading from one end of the principality to the other, from Malibu to Culver City. I was a palm-tree Puritan.

From the sound of the midnight battle in the bedroom, I knew that Father's studio cronies were in on It, and that of course Ad's brother, Uncle Sam the studio manager, knew about It, as did his wife Milly, who loved to check in every morning for a detailed exchange of the news of the day with Poorsarah Mankiewicz, Herman's wife. For Poorsarah and the ubiquitous Mank, no matter how much they owed to my father, also had a responsibility to their reputation as gossipmongers of a high order. So I could imagine those daily Aunt Milly-Poorsarah shovel-sessions. I could hear Milly's stylized outcry, "I don't be-leeve it!" Mildred Jaffe, Mother's little protégée, who matriculated at Ad Schulberg University and eventually (inevitably) challenged her as our local Queen of Arts. We lived among orange groves that were really poison trees. I would even hear forked-tongue gossip that Aunt Milly had succumbed to the undeniable charms of my father.

Open *Modern Screen,* say, for the period when I was feeling the first shock waves of Father's intrigue with Sylvia Sidney, and all on one page we read: "Garbo has a new girl friend—an exotic, amazing person" (Mercedes Acosta); "Latest inside facts about the suit the ex-Mrs. Sternberg is bringing against Marlene"; "Fast and furious rumors about Joan and Doug (Jr.)"; "Betty Compson and Hugh Trevor tell the world they'll never marry"; "Wedding of Paul Whiteman and Margaret Livingston took place last month but as we go to press rumor has it that there is a rift between them." I dreaded the issue that would blazon the Schulberg rift.

I went to my punching bag and hit it hard, seeing the provocative little face of Sylvia Sidney bobbing in front of me. Or I would belt her Mamma for good luck. For I had heard—rightly or wrongly didn't matter to me then—that her mother Sophie was with them, encouraging the affair. It was all part of the obscenity, it seemed to me: Mrs. Kosow serving as madam for her dewy-eyed siren, both on the make for big studio success.

From my mother I had learned to take everything hard, the working and the playing. Pleasure was to be earned and life pursued with Mosaic zeal. Working for A's in Taking It Hard, I took the stone of Sylvia Sydney to bed with me, swallowed it for breakfast with my cornflakes, felt it stick in my throat as I went through the big studio gate. It didn't help at all that I found Sylvia painfully appealing, with a New York waif-like quality that was coming into style with the Depression—a kind of female John Garfield. Or that she could play a working-class role like Roberta in *An American Tragedy* with exciting sexuality. I watched the scene in which her socially ambitious lover, Clyde (Phillips Holmes), takes her for a boat ride on the lake (our studio tank), and decides to drown her so he can marry the debutante (Frances Dee) who represents high society and, for him, upward social mobility. In the famous Dreiser scene, premeditated murder is ironically avoided when the boat tips over accidentally and Roberta drowns.

How good it felt to watch that drowning scene and to see Sylvia pitched into the "lake," floundering and going under. What an ideal solution! If only I could take Sylvia rowing in Westlake Park, tip the boat over, watch the little homewrecker go down for the third time, and swim to shore insisting it was an accident. The perfect crime. The family saved. I not only watched that scene being filmed, but studied it again on the screen when Father ran the rushes a few doors down from his big office. I listened to Father and Von Sternberg dissect the scene, which take was best, and how to intensify suspense through intercutting— Sylvia nagging about her "condition" and Phillips nervously trying to work himself up to the act of desperation. Father was blowing smoke from his big cigar and insisting that while Sylvia should of course look pregnant and haggard, she must still look sexy and beautiful; after all it was she—and not lovely but somehow "too nice" Frances Dee—who was on her way to stardom.

I listened, sucking it deep into myself, living Phillips Holmes's role vicariously. But the would-be murderer was careful to keep these feelings to himself.

38

WHEN I WENT back to Father's office with him, we talked for a few minutes about my summer job—instead of my working as a sports stringer for the *Los Angeles Times,* he thought it was time for me to take my first "regular" job. Maurice was going to work at MGM, so it seemed fitting that I should enroll at Paramount. B.P. suggested I break in with the publicity department, as he had with Adolph Zukor in the old Famous Players days. He had done the same thing for Zukor's son, Eugene. "The old man," as Zukor *père* was called, sent his son to B.P. for assignment in the minuscule publicity department of the New York office. "Do you know how to write a publicity release?" Father asked him. Young Gene wasn't sure. "Well, here's some paper," B.P. said, "and there's a typewriter. Sit down and write one." Gene sat down in panic, not even sure he could type his own name. Then B.P. gave him some facts—the new Mary Pickford picture, the title, the featured players, the theater in which it would open. Years later Gene would say that he never forgot that experience, akin to Sam Goldwyn's challenge to an aspiring scenarist, "So you're a writer? Here's a pencil. Write."

As soon as I got my highschool diploma, I was given a week off to recover from graduation before reporting to Tect Carle, an experienced publicity man in the flourishing department headed by veteran newsman Arch Reeves. "It won't be a snap job," Father promised. "I've told Arch to work the hell out of you. And to fire you if you don't pull your weight. Just the way I told Mr. Zukor I would fire Gene. It's what I call 'enlightened nepotism.'"

My literate old man, never at a loss for words or clever phrases, kept at me to enlarge my vocabulary, to read (*all* of Dickens, *all* of Melville and Twain . . .), and to "Here's a pencil—there's a typewriter—*write!*"

This was what I loved about my old man. You couldn't dismiss him as a boozer, a gambler, a wencher. He had intellect, and at his best, in the good years, he used it well. I sat in that big office and one part of my mind despised him for what he was doing to my mother, and to my sister and little brother, with this Sidney thing. If only I could kill that part of him and keep intact the intellect, the literary bent, the filmmaking skill, the creative drive. . . .

Burlesques and satires of Hollywood like *Once in a Lifetime* had reinforced the stereotype of the movie producer as an illiterate cloak-and-suiter who could say with the profane Harry Cohn of Columbia, "When my ass begins to itch, that's what tells me there's something wrong with the story." As Mank liked to point out, "The trouble with this business is that people like Harry Cohn think the taste of the American public is wired to their ass." But what the satanic Mankiewicz said about Father was quite the opposite. "The trouble with your old man," he confided to me in his book-cluttered office at the studio, "is that he's read too goddamn many books. That can get you in a lot of trouble out here. B.P. should have stayed in New York [where Mank had served as drama critic of *The World*], and if only he hadn't sent for me out here, I might have been writing *Once in a Lifetime* with George [Kaufman]."

Poor Mank, Hollywood's Ambrose Bierce, was a spendthrift in every way, including brilliant lines which he wasted on studio commissary quips, cocktail chatter, and story-conference ripostes. It was typical of a play Mank had written and submitted to my father, who passed it on to me, that the stage directions sparkled with witticisms that outdazzled the dialogue.

Sitting in on a story conference with my father and Mank was enlightening entertainment. I listened to Father and his other top writers analyzing *The Strange Case of Dr. Jekyll and Mr. Hyde* in the language of cinema. These weren't ignoramuses butchering the classics; they were men and women who knew their Stevenson and were serious about bringing his work to the screen as authentically as possible. "Don't change Stevenson just for the fun of rewriting him," Father was urging. "You can kill a classic with 'improvements.' A big, sprawling novel, say *Bleak House,* you have to pare down to a continuity that will hold an audience for ninety or a hundred minutes. But remember, *Jekyll and Hyde* already has a continuity. We don't have to waste time hammering out a story line. What you have to do is visualize it, think of every scene as the camera will see it and not as you—or Stevenson—would describe it in prose.

"We've got the makings of a great picture. A great story, a great director [Rouben Mamoulian], a great cast [Fredric March and Miriam Hopkins], and a great cameraman in Karl [Struss]. But take it from an old scriptwriter, every one of us is only as good as our script. You can build the most beautiful building in the world, I don't care if it's Monticello or the Taj Mahal—but if it doesn't have a solid foundation, down it falls."

Father didn't deliver this from behind the big mahogany desk, but on his feet pacing as was his habit, twirling the gold chain of his diamond-studded watch clockwise around his index finger, then counterclockwise in what seemed a hypnotic perpetual motion.

He wasn't stammering now. He was eloquent. His face was slightly flushed. His eyes, always bulging a little, gleamed with excitement. A lot of boiler-plate comedies and "mellers" had to be ground out by the majors to fill the public hunger for at least one new movie a day. Television was still almost twenty years away and America went to the movies virtually en masse. But *Jekyll and Hyde* was different. Here was a chance to please Bob Sherwood, make the coveted Ten Best list, and still bring Paramount the profit it needed to keep its head above water in these tricky Depression days.

Watching B.P. send his scenarists back to the Writers' Building all fired up to do or die for Paramount, I was reminded of Pat O'Brien playing Knute Rockne in that jockstrap classic, *The Spirit of Notre Dame*: "Men, you're going out there in the second half and win it for the Gipper!"

Sometimes when one story conference was over, I had a few moments alone with my father before the next began. He did work deep into the night. It wasn't all booze-time and poker and play with Sylvia. A studio head functioned in a pressure cooker of unrealistic starting dates, impossible demands from New York, and the vicious competition of the rival "majors." In the early Thirties, Hollywood was still working a six-day week—the long weekend had not yet become a way of life. But even before the unions won the five-day-forty, the mogul reminded me of a hamster in his cage running in place to keep up with himself. There was no way that a man in charge of a schedule geared to producing movies on the average of one a week, year in, year out, could have time for family or friends who were not also his working associates, or for creative diversion away from the movie machine. With rare exceptions like Irving Thalberg, who was a mama's boy with a weak heart, the demands of the dream factory drove the studio heads to manic behavior. In the wenching or gambling or drinking of Jack Warner, Dave Selznick (only a junior mogul then), Harry Cohn, and B.P., there was a fevered quality, an unquiet desperation. The casino tables, the casting couch, the studio bootleggers, and the private bars more lavish than the best of the speakeasies offered swift surcease to these pressure people. The gaming rooms of the Clover Club were a study in ten-thousand-a-week anxieties.

Graduating from L.A. High was like adolescent menopause. Somehow I had survived my tennis disasters, my traumatic exposure to the half-mile on the track team, my stammering breakdown in English debate, my dread of having to take girls to school dances or squire them to parties. I had learned to write declarative sentences for the daily, and to run it efficiently. I had quietly fought my way up through a teeming interracial high school to become a member of the various status groups that ran it. As a first-rate editor and a third-rate athlete, I had become a campus figure. If my poetry was at a standstill, my short stories seemed to be improving. Even my hard taskmaster of a father, when I could catch him between rushes or conferences or drinks, would mutter an occasional, "Not bad. Better than the last one. But still not quite De Maupassant." At least he wasn't slamming it down on the dining-room table and pronouncing it "Lousy!" Mother, on the other hand, was her consistent Coué self. I had started on a level somewhere between De Maupassant and Tolstoy, and "Day by day in every way you're getting better and better!"

Somehow I had managed to get through high school without a single serious date, coping with the graduation dance by being the first to volunteer to rush down to the basement for extra floor wax, and to provide whatever auxiliary services a veteran wallflower could invent. In that last week before we headed off to our respective studios for our summer jobs, Maurice and I were still talking late into the night, determined to solve our "girl" problem. In a later day we undoubtedly would have been marked as queers. But we knew that we felt no sexual attraction to each other or to other boys. We had simply—well, not so simply—built a fear of the opposite sex into a cult. Just as we had once run from the house and camped out under a tree on our pastoral Hollywood block if a girl our age arrived with our parents' friends, so now we clung to our companionship and all the games of our youth. But the growing pains were setting in.

39

THAT SUMMER IN the Paramount publicity department, my beat was to collect items and boiler-plate news stories on up-and-coming stars like Buddy Rogers, Richard Arlen, Gary Cooper, Kay Francis, Nancy Carroll. . . . It should have been an easy job. After all, the names I was to write squibs about were the same ones who were in and out of our Malibu house every weekend. I didn't have to introduce myself.

My first interview was with Gary Cooper, who had just finished playing opposite Father's aging It Girl, Clara Bow. Of all the hot young stars Paramount was building, Coop was the hottest. His small but poignant part in *Wings* had been one of those instant star-makers. Under the shambling, "shucks-Ma" shyness was a smoldering sexuality. Clara Bow had had *it* from the moment the imperious Elinor Glyn dubbed her our Jazz Baby Queen. Gary of course was born with *it*; Father's service to the Cooper cult was simply to observe how women swarmed around him at the previews, and how movie stars and secretaries alike knelt at his big, slow, western-walking feet.

Like the lame leading the blind, the stammerer developed a lengthy interview from this young yup-'n'-mebbe man. Coop was ill at ease talking about movies and acting, but truly at home on the range, for he had been raised on a ranch in Montana owned by his father, a county judge, and so was more secure with ranch hands and cattle, bear-tracking, and mountain climbing than he was with scenarios, fancy studio front-offices, and movie sets. As an actor he seemed naturally embarrassed: His instinct was to act as if he were trying to escape from the camera. Therein lay his inimitable quality. The talented Cary Grant, the gifted Freddie March, the inspired Jack Barrymore could all talk circles around him but inside those circles there was the laconic, nonverbal, seemingly inadvertently sexual movie star who knew the ways of the camera by always seeming to wish it wasn't there.

In my Model A roadster, I raced back from Coop's stucco "Spanish" bungalow in Beverly Hills (the Hollywood architecture *à la mode* of the early Thirties), eager to roll paper into my typewriter and pound out my first big interview. A few hours later I had produced eight pages of what seemed to me brilliant reportage-biography. Everything I had learned from my father, from Miss Carr, and from Father's writers, genius-type newspapermen like Mank and Ben Hecht, flowed into it. With a heady sense of having completed a masterpiece, I gave it to Teet Carle. He leafed through it with what struck me as obscene haste, rolled a piece of yellow paper into the Underwood, pounded on it for about thirty seconds, ripped it from the roller, and handed it to me. My two thousand words now read:

> Gary Cooper, Paramount's rising young star now playing the "love interest" to Claudette Colbert in the forthcoming *His Woman,* is one of Hollywood's few real-life cowboys, having been raised on his father Judge Cooper's ranch in Montana.

When I glanced at it, I felt stammery inside. "That's all you wanted?" "Papers use little fillers like that all over the country," my mentor mentored.

"I could have done that without leaving the office."

"That's all right. It's not bad. Just too long. Too many words from a man who's not supposed to talk. We'll file it and use it for background."

Teet turned back to his own typewriter and started punching out more copy. I sat and stared at my typewriter. Had Teet given me the Cooper assignment just to get rid of me for a few hours? For so many years the "Stude" had been my playground. Now that it had become my first workground, I was acutely sensitive to my reason for being there. The sweet-and-sour smell of nepotism. The Depression was finally reaching its bony fingers into Lotusland. Even veteran reporters with families were out of work. But the "Stude" had to give me a job. I was the boss's son.

Maybe it would have been easier to run copy and write my little sports squibs for the L.A. *Times*. Here I had to prove that I could be as good at this job as my father had been at his when Edwin S. Porter brought him to Famous Players. In twenty years my father had gone from teenage copyboy and cub reporter to two-reel screenplays and flashy publicity capers, to become the boss of bosses (under founders Zukor and Lasky) of one of the two biggest film factories in the world. How was the 17-year-old son going to live up to those sycophantic inscriptions in his autograph book, "Hoping you'll grow up to be as great a man as your father"? Father was making eleven thousand a week, not counting stock options and Christmas bonuses, and his son seemed to have only two choices, either to try to live up to and maybe surpass the achievements of his old man—or give up and become a bum like his Grandfather Simon.

Having been surrounded by so many lushes and idlers from childhood days, I didn't want to be a bum. I had to show Teet Carle and my father that—nepotism be damned—they had a bargain.

After a few weeks of writing better and better copy, some of it passing through Teet's hands with a minimum of red-penciling, a few planted virtually unscathed in papers around the country, I had passed my first test and was ready for bigger things.

Teet's idea was to plant in one of the popular fan magazines— *Modern Screen* or *Photoplay*—a feature article on what some fifty of Paramount's most famous stars and directors had wanted to do before they stumbled into moviemaking. I warmed to the subject. Here was something a little less cut-and-dried than the stock releases I had learned to knock out. Since there was still no way of preparing for a movie career, most film stars and directors had simply stumbled, backed, or lucked into Hollywood fame.

John Ford (honest handle, Sean Aloysius O'Fearna) was the son of a saloonkeeper in a small town in Maine. After his elder brother Francis had worked his way to the wide-open Hollywood of 1913 as an itinerant actor, he was able to get young Sean a job right out of high school as a day laborer at Universal. Jack (Sean) was tough and wanted to go to sea. He had nothing but disdain for the Griffiths of his day (although he had had a bit as one of the Klansmen in *The Birth of a Nation*). But he found himself assisting his brother in directing two-reelers, and moving on to direct low-budget Westerns (Harry Carey, Buck Jones, etc.) through the silent days.

And Marion Marshall Morrison, otherwise known as John Wayne, was a football star at U.S.C. whose bruising tackles won him a job after graduation as a studio "grip" for John Ford. "Duke" Morrison had about as much interest in becoming a movie star as he had in dancing with the Russian Ballet. He was just a big, strong, raw-faced handyman until the canny O'Fearna decided to stick that ruddy bourbon-and-branch-water face in *front* of the camera—and another cult figure was on his way.

The crap-game aspect of film fame appealed to me. Undaunted by Teet's diminution of my Gary Cooper feature, I was after another summer masterpiece. Notebook in hand, I prowled the studio lot to corner my victims. I knew all the gathering spots: the barbershop, the gym, Oscar's bootblack stand; the open square bordered by star dressing rooms on the left and the Writers' Building on the right; the enormous gossipy commissary. . . .

Trying to grab interviews on the various sets was more difficult, for actors were often edgy, directors demanding, and their officious assistants would snap "Quiet!" even at the boss's son. Sometimes I would try to follow them into their dressing rooms. I tagged along with Freddie March, figuring he'd be easy since I played so much tennis with him at Malibu. But right at the door he reached out and grabbed a blonde bit-player and pulled her past me. "I wanted to be a banker, Buddy, but this is more fun!" The door slammed them in and me out. Of all the stars I saw running in the sex derby—not excluding Errol Flynn and the improbable Peter Lorre—Freddie was the most outrageous. He would simply reach out his dressing-room door and pull them in. In public he would grab them in private places. Absolutely out of control. Laughing, screaming, outrageous. But the moment he took his place in front of the camera he was all business, one of the great pros who could play everything from light comedy to heavy tragedy, from *Nothing Sacred* to *Jekyll and Hyde, A Star Is Born,* and *Best Years.* . . .

I stepped back from the impromptu frolic going on inside and conscientiously made my notes: Freddie McIntyre Bickel from Racine and the University of Wisconsin might have been a banker if his good looks hadn't drifted him into modeling, from there to midwestern stock companies, and on to the New York stage. I could fill in the rest of the story while we rested from hard-fought competition on our Malibu court.

Jack Oakie (Lewis D. Offield), the country-boy comic who had become one of the Paramount dependables in racy hits like *Sweetie* and *The Wild Party,* was easier. He liked to hang around Oscar's and clown for passersby. "What did I want to be before I got to be a ham movie actor? Well, first I tried selling Eskimo pies to Eskimos, but—"

"Please, Jack," I told him. "This is a serious piece. I really want to do it well."

"Oh, you d-d-do?" he mimicked me good-naturedly, even though that little joke always rankled. "Well, believe it or not, Mrs. Offield's little boy was a whiz at math and put in a couple of years on the New York Stock Exchange. Remember the New York Stock Exchange? It was fun while it lasted. Then somebody saw me getting laughs at a party and I drifted into stock—" *Drifted* was becoming the key word of movie-star careers. "Next thing I knew I was making funny faces for B. P. Schulberg. Hey, how about telling your old man I want to play romantic leads, I'm getting sick of clowning around as the pal of the guy who always gets the girl." Then he gave Oscar an exuberant goose, Oscar accommodated with a squeak and a ludicrous leap, and my quarry went swaggering back to the set.

I caught the ladylike Lily Cauchoin (Claudette Colbert) in the wardrobe department, where she was trying on costumes for the next Chevalier musical. "What did I want to be when I was growing up? An actress!" she said, and swept by me. Tallulah Bankhead I cornered at Lucey's, the speakeasy-restaurant across the street. "Darling, what did I want to be before I became an actress?" A dirty laugh erupted from that still-lovely throat. "I couldn't decide between a Mother Superior, a whore, and President of the United States. I hope you'll put down in your notes that I'd be damned good at all three!"

I spotted Peggy Shannon getting out of a red roadster near the entrance to the Studio. Since she was being groomed to replace B.P.'s self-destructive Clara Bow, naturally she had to drive a red roadster. She was a marvelous-looking Irish girl, with red hair and unsubtle sex appeal. "What did I want to be. . . ?" Like a breezy Hecht-MacArthur reporter, I waited, notebook in hand, with one foot on the running board. If Father should happen to look out, he could see me from the open stained-glass windows of his big office. ". . . I wanted to be a great swimmer like Gertrude Ederle. I was in junior high when she swam the English Channel. Overnight she was famous. But then I realized . . . I hated to get my hair wet!" She laughed, a lovely, no underpants laugh, and gunned her jazzy little car down Marathon Street to the studio gate.

Day after day I persevered, cornering stars whose fame would last down the years, others doomed to careers of fluttering brevity. I was into my third notebook when I started knocking on doors in the Writers' Building. A gravel-voiced "Come in!" brought me into the presence of Grover Jones and William Slavens McNutt, a pair of barrel-bellied ex-newspapermen who had risen to the top of the Paramount writers' roster—earning four thousand a week as a team, writing original stories and preparing screenplays for the stars under contract.

It was one of those steamy Hollywood summer days, and when I barged in, there were Father's $400-a-day writers sitting on the floor in their BVD's, a bottle of scotch balanced on a pile of scripts, playing cards. The office reeked of sweat, booze, and studio stucco.

When they recognized me they threw down their cards in disgust. "What the fuck are you doing in here, spying for your old man? Tell 'im he'll have his fuckin' script by Friday. Now amscray!"

Bill McNutt was shuffling the cards, dangerously. When I told the two besotted geniuses the reason for my mission, a series of ribald invocations poured from their lips. "My big ambition was to marry the madam of the local whorehouse!" "And mine was to bugger the piano player of the Bijou Theater!" I decided if I didn't beat it out of there, they might hurl me through the window into the wilting flower beds below. I shut the door behind me and retreated into the hallway. As I worked my way down the corridors of the buildings, I met with similar if less explosive rejections. Writers were either writing or reading or playing, and whatever they were doing they tended to greet my interruption with sarcastic wit. Some invented ribald answers, others simply said they didn't have time for such nonsense. I felt discouraged. An assignment I thought I could finish in a week was turning into a project that could devour the rest of the summer.

One person who did have time for me—nothing but time, it seemed—was a man whom many consider the authentic genius of silent motion pictures. Sergei Eisenstein. I found him wandering the second-floor corridor of the Paramount front-office building. Eisenstein had come to Hollywood from an avant-garde film conference in Switzerland—after a stop in New York, where he presented Adolph Zukor with letters from people like H. G. Wells and George Bernard Shaw. Zukor had politely passed Eisenstein on to Jesse Lasky, who passed him over to my father.

Father, a political liberal in the reactionary world of Mayer and Hearst, welcomed the idea of adding the great Eisenstein to the Paramount roster. Mother, with her Rivington Street-cum-Fabian socialism, was also impressed by Eisenstein's intellectual credentials. In fact, she had played hostess to the Russian master, considering him a cultural catch on a level with Count Keyserling and the other international philosophers who frequently held forth at her Friday Morning Club.

On a stone bench in the studio garden, Eisenstein told me that his father had been a well-known architect, a profession he had planned to follow. Then he had become a painter and stage designer, in time a stage director, then an assistant to the Russian film directors who were creating their own form of social cinema in the revolutionary Twenties. I listened carefully, for in Father's projection room I had seen not only *Potemkin* but *Ten Days That Shook the World,* great silent films that put *montage* into the language, with the intercutting of vivid images creating a new cinematic experience.

I had heard Father's version of Eisenstein's "failures" at Paramount. Now I took notes from the source himself. His first idea had been to make a film about a city made entirely of glass—in which everyone could look into everyone else's private life. But this had been abandoned as impractical—"My God, B.P." Father had been warned by studio manager Uncle Sam, a pragmatist, "it would cost us a million dollars to build that city, and we couldn't use it as a standing set and write off the cost against other pictures, like our ocean liner, our castle, or our New York street."

Next, Eisenstein and his team had worked enthusiastically on *Sutter's Gold,* which Father hoped would become a social classic like *Greed* or *Modern Times.* But Eisenstein and his collaborators were convinced Marxists, and their story of how the gold discovered at Sutter's ranch destroyed a legitimate pioneer was too radical for the money men in New York who had the final say on studio decisions.

Each script Eisenstein had worked out with his meticulous eye for visual detail. Turning to *An American Tragedy,* he had discussed the novel with Dreiser. He had been impressed with my father's knowledge of the book. (Despite two strikeouts he spoke warmly of my father, with a kind of good-natured condescension, surprised by his literacy, but not surprised that he would have to defer to the financial bosses who pulled the strings.) In the end, *Tragedy* also would be snapped from Eisenstein and he would leave our studio—to its shame—without ever having made a picture.

In retrospect, Eisenstein was one of those whose genius cannot accommodate *any* social system—as ill-fated for Zukor-Lasky capitalism as for Stalin's communism. And in between, soon after my interview with him, came his painfully expensive fiasco for socialist-independent Upton Sinclair, no less: the aborted *Thunder Over Mexico*. Eisenstein may have been to the movies what Michelangelo was to painting. But for all his great knowledge and insight, he lacked patrons.

That afternoon on the Paramount lot I found an Eisenstein who had wanted to be a painter with oils and now had moved on to a dedication to painting with moving-picture frames—becoming a mosaicist of moving pictures, as much an innovator in the late Twenties and early Thirties as was D. W. Griffith ten years earlier. Eisenstein had no illusions about what Paramount could do—and *not* do—for him and his revolutionary theories of filmmaking. He realized he was a misfit on a lot where box-office talents like Lubitsch's and Von Sternberg's could be so much more easily exploited. There was something about him that was not so much defeated as bemusedly resigned, like a chess master who had somehow wandered by mistake into the old Ebbets Field of the rowdy Brooklyn Dodgers and decided to sit through the game.

At the typewriter in my corner of Teet Carle's office, I began transcribing my notes on Eisenstein. Of Soviet Russia I knew only the vague bits I had picked up from my mother's socialist sympathies for Upton Sinclair and Lincoln Steffens. I wondered why Eisenstein was wandering the corridors of Father's studio when he could have been making another *Ten Days That Shook the World* in his own country. When I asked him about Father's idea of making *War and Peace* with the cooperation of the Soviet Film Trust, Eisenstein said, "An interesting idea. But I don't want to be limited to Russian subjects." He found Hollywood itself a fascinating place. He wanted to explore California and the West, and even if *Sutter's Gold* had been ingloriously shelved, he had not given up the idea of doing his own kind of socially oriented Western.

I was on my way to a full-scale appraisal of Paramount's most unusual (if unused) acquisition when I was interrupted by a question from Teet Carle. "Buddy, how are you coming on your piece—what the stars wanted to do before they got into pictures?"

I had a fistful of notes, I told Teet, but there were at least two dozen I still hadn't interviewed.

"I need that piece by the end of the day," Teet said as sternly as a nice man can. And then he did what studio people called a double take—

"Buddy, you don't mean you're actually going around asking all the stars personally what their first ambition was?"

"Well, isn't that what you asked me to do? I've cornered as many as I could, but—"

He stared at me dumbfounded. "Buddy, that would take all summer! What I meant for you to do was sit down and make it up. Like—Marlene Dietrich wanted to be a kindergarten teacher. Maurice Chevalier wanted to be a pastry cook. . . . Just think of the opposite of what they seem now. . . . Just make it colorful and catchy. You're not writing this for *Vanity Fair*. It's for a lousy fan magazine. Mitzi Green wanted to be the first girl jockey. That kind of thing. You think the stars mind? It's all part of the game. Now get going."

A few hours of furious invention and I had it in hand. It turned out to be fun! In my studio cubbyhole I could play God: "Gloria Swanson wanted to be a Red Cross nurse and go overseas with the Rainbow Division in the Great War. . . ." The fact that she had been a 15-year-old starlet for the pioneer Essanay Studio in Chicago three years before we got into that war no longer got in my way. Never again in that first summer of studio work would I let an obtrusive fact clog the spinning wheels of the publicity machine. If I wanted to study the tormented career of a Sergei Eisenstein, I would have to do it on my own time.

When Budd was at Deerfield Academy he decided to write a book about lynching.
He turned for advice to Clarence Darrow, who answered him promptly with a letter
suggesting that he get his information from Walter White at the NAACP.

▲ The L.A. High School Tennis Team spring, 1931. Budd Schulberg is kneeling extreme right. Kneeling second from left is Budd's doubles partner, Yale Katz, who later became a prominent physician and subsequently a suicide.

◄ Budd after he won the Malibu Beach Tennis Tournament from Irwin Gelsey (on the right). The cup was donated by Frank Capra. Gelsey, assistant to Walter Wanger, was Paramount's Tennis Champion.

Sylvia Sidney with another of B.P.'s discoveries, Cary Grant, in *Thirty-Day-Princess*

B.P. and Sylvia Sidney, *circa 1932*

Mrs. Eddie Goulding; her husband, the celebrated British writer-director; and his agent and friend Ad in St. Moritz, when Budd's parents were separating (1932) and Ad was travelling on her own. ▼

▲ The 1930 wedding of two of Hollywood's "noble" families: the Mayers and the Selznicks. Mayer's biographer, Bosley Crowther, described this as a "quiet" wedding—but although L.B. was less than delighted with his newest son-in-law, pride compelled him to make it the nuptial event of the year. The bride is Irene Mayer; the groom is David O. Selznick. To the groom's right is his brother, Myron, the first important film agent. To the left of the bride is her father, L.B. Behind the bride and groom is Rabbi Edgar F. Magnin, who three years before had expelled Budd from his Temple.

To L.B.'s left is Irene's sister, Edith, and the man with the glasses in the same row is her husband, William Goetz. In the cluster of people to the right of Myron Selznick, the farthest right is B.P. Schulberg; the second woman to the right is Janet Gaynor, first Academy Award-winning actress. Immediately below this group is another royal couple, Norma Shearer and Irving Thalberg. Above and to the right of the Thalbergs is screenwriter Herman Mankiewicz (*Citizen Kane)*, a B.P. Schulberg import from New York. At the extreme left, the third up from the bottom, is MGM's hatchet man, Eddie Mannix.

Budd Schulberg at about the time he left for Dartmouth (1932)

40

OF COURSE, THE one star on the lot I would not have interviewed if I had tripped over her was Sylvia Sidney. If I knew she was working on a set, even one I was eager to see, I would avoid it like the pox. A plague that would carry her off to the Hollywood Cemetery around the corner is what I wished for that little predator. While I didn't exonerate my father, it was easier to focus my callow but bone-deep hatred on a stranger, an outsider, an intruder.

I took my problem to Felix Young, despite the fact that Mother always looked down on him as a poseur and a hanger-on with his fancy cologne, his raffish clothes, and his *eppis*-elegant speech. "Superficial" was Mother's word for our friend Feel, and she may have been right that there was more style than substance in Father's handpicked supervisor. And she may also have been right to assume that as a sycophant, without any noticeable qualifications except charm and panache, he would have to take Father's side in the liaison. Mother even accused him of going further, of actually encouraging the affair and serving as a "beard" when Father and "the Sidney woman" appeared in public.

Nevertheless, Felix would listen, and so in his spacious office overlooking the studio quadrangle I poured out my feelings. In a few months I would be leaving Hollywood on my own for the first time since our arrival. (I had been accepted provisionally, at a far-off place called Dartmouth, but the consensus was that I was too young, emotionally unprepared for the great leap from Hollywood to Hanover; so, to ease the culture shock, I was to put in a transitional year at Deerfield

Academy in Massachusetts.) But, I told Felix, the tension between Father and Mother was now so intense—with constant bickering, open fighting, and Dad's frequent disappearances—that I felt the family structure would tear apart if I weren't there to hold it together. I simply had to make Father see the light. Otherwise, I pleaded with my Victorian morality, what would happen to Sonya, a gentle, introspective, and already somehow *lost* 11-year-old, and little Stuart, who was only seven, and needed his family to develop normally? Because B.P., married to his work, had never been a real *father*-father, I felt responsible for my only sister and only brother. Not that I ever spent much time with them. Hardly a better "father" to them than their actual father, I moralized about them far more than I actually helped them. But, in my mind at least, I had become the family linchpin. How could I go east, with our home life in such disarray? I'm afraid I had read too much Dickens. Without me, I could see Father disintegrating into a hopeless drunk, Mother thrown on the mercies of a heartless society, and poor Sonya and Stuart winding up in the county orphanage.

Suave and soothing, Felix did his best to reassure me. I was too young to understand these things. No one was as perfect as I thought they should be. Maybe the best thing for me to do was not to interfere, try not to take it so hard, concentrate on my own job of doing well at Deerfield and developing my writing. Did I know Father thought I showed signs of becoming a better writer than he had been at my age—when he was on the threshold of his own career?

Although Felix spoke with genuine concern, it wasn't good enough. I begged him to talk to Father about giving up Sidney. Make him realize how he was destroying our family and my peace of mind. Otherwise, I warned Feel, I was determined to take things into my own hands. I would call Mother and Father together before I left, and if I did not succeed in getting them to promise to bury their differences and resume life together, I would cancel my trip east and stay home to keep them together. And also, I told Feel, I was considering going to Sylvia Sidney myself, telling her off, and—I added almost casually—threatening to kill her unless she left Father alone.

By this time my moral guide had switched from Dickens to Dostoevsky. Felix urged me not to do anything foolish and promised to help put our house back together.

Working hard at the studio, playing furious tennis on Malibu weekends, I was unable to take Felix Young's advice not to worry so much about Sidney. Dad still took me to the Friday-night fights, but tension between us spoiled the old excitement when we rooted together for our Jewish champions. He was still living with us, technically, but Sylvia and her mother had rented a large house just outside the Malibu Colony, only a few miles south, and it was now an open secret as to where he spent his time away from the studio. It was a knife twist in the wound to have to pass her place on the Pacific Highway on the way to our once-peaceful Green Gate Cottage.

By this time, in place of my jazzy Model-A roadster, I had inherited Father's Dusenberg phaeton. A notoriously poor driver, he found it easier to operate his Lincoln roadster. For some reason, maybe becuase of his erratic habits, he did not like to use the chauffeur. It made him self-conscious, he said, to have someone sitting in a car waiting for hours while he watched rushes, went off the lot for occasional luncheon meetings at Perino's or Victor Hugo's, stopped at the Clover Club, or (though he didn't admit this) went on his nocturnal prowls.

Driving back from the studio in midtown Hollywood, once I reached the two-lane Coast Road I would gun that fifteen-thousand-dollar toy until the murky ocean on my left and the sunbaked palisades on my right were falling away behind me at a speed of almost one hundred miles an hour. That was a *real* Duzie. Sold later to a professional antique-car collector, it turns up occasionally in movies trying to recapture the look of luxury in the early Thirties.

I felt I was paying for that car pretty dearly by having to drive it past Miss Sidney's beach house in order to reach our two-story "cottage." Sometimes I would slow down, stare at the forbidding fence of the Sidney house and think dark thoughts about what was happening within. There must be some way I could put death into that house! Like using the tomcod I caught off the pier, lacing them with strychnine and leaving them at the gate with a clever note: "Dear Dad, I was thinking of you when I caught these fish, and . . ." Or I would wonder if I could sneak something lethal into the groceries being delivered from the Malibu store. Or should I simply barge in and drag my father out? If Father thought he could buy me off with a Dusenberg . . . I gunned it to the floor and raced on into the Colony. Mother was there, taking a tennis lesson. I felt sorry for her. I told her how well things were going at the "Stude"—at least my little corner of it.

She said she was anxious about Father. Careful not to mention Sidney, she went on: "I'm worried about his concentration." Not since he entered The Industry was he in greater need of it. No longer was moviemaking the carefree carnival it had seemed in the Twenties. The invisible intrigue of finance capital was setting in. Until now, Famous Players-Lasky, despite its Wall Street backing, had been a personal company, with Zukor in New York and Lasky in Hollywood maintaining almost as much control as when they had founded the company some twenty years earlier. But the innovation of *sound,* plus the delayed pinch of the Depression, was throwing The Industry into its first convulsion. Soundproofing the giant stages, investing in new equipment both for production and exhibition sent costs soaring, while profits were pinwheeling down like a fighter plane crashing in *Wings.* The hundred shares of stock that Father had given me for my fifteenth birthday when it was selling at 75, and that he had been sure would be worth more than twice as much by the time I finished high school, had plunged to 1. Insiders who were backing it on margin—like the free-spirited Lasky, one of the more lovable of the moguls—were losing much more than their shirts; they were losing their oceanfront mansions.

Overexpansion and the pressure of the times had led to a vicious power fight for control of the Company. In the early days, when Hodkinson and his Paramount chain had tried to absorb Famous Players-Lasky, Zukor and his henchmen had turned the tables and swallowed Paramount instead. This time the opposition was tougher—Sam Katz, of Balaban and Katz, the Chicago theater chain, was moving in on the Company, through his (and Paramount's) subsidiary, Publix; so was Sidney Kent, the self-made ex-boiler stoker from Lincoln, Nebraska, whom Zukor had put in charge of distribution in the early twenties. The battle for control of the stock between Katz and Kent made pawns of the patriarchal Zukor and the flamboyant Lasky, while Father was at the mercy of them all. In this internecine struggle, the cautious Zukor would survive, if never again the power he had been, and poor Jesse, overextended and outmaneuvered, would come crashing down, forced out of the Company that had mushroomed from the amalgamation of his Jesse Lasky Feature Play Company with Zukor's Famous Players. When Sam Katz had outfoxed (or, as B.P. said, outkatzed) rival Sidney Kent, Lasky lost his champion. But tough little Zukor hadn't been a banty East Side fighter for nothing. Exiled to South America for a while, he was kicked upstairs as chairman of the board.

As a studio politician, Father was more like Lasky than like Zukor, more impetuous and partisan, less cautious and shrewd. He had a disturbing habit of saying what he thought and, on his third or fourth highball, of saying it a little too loudly. Mother, on the other hand, was battle-tough like Zukor. She was a lady now, but she knew the "gracious living" to which she had become accustomed demanded *gelt,* as her poor relations would have put it. And to make, keep, and expand *gelt* demanded self-discipline and forethought—hers.

With the collapse of the old Paramount, with heads as high as Lasky's rolling into the basket, she was convinced that only her own highly developed art of survival could keep Ben's head from tumbling after Jesse's. Concerned for him because she loved him with the fierce devotion of Ruth for Boaz, she was also dedicated to the preservation of that half-a-million-dollar annual income on which she was determined to build a family dynasty.

"Schulberg has the best mind in the whole industry," Mother would say to me, using the surname as a First Lady might in lieu of saying "The President." "He's much better-read than Irving [Thalberg, our patron saint]. But Irving knows how to protect himself, even against Louie [Mayer]. Schulberg is reckless. He loves to take chances. He goes out of his way to make enemies of powerful people who might be helpful to him later. I know he doesn't like to hear it, but right now Schulberg needs me more than ever."

From the beach house a few miles south of us, the one I had marked in my mind with a scarlet *A,* I could almost hear "Schulberg" saying, "Buddy, your mother is right. But she'll say the same thing nine straight times, until comes the tenth, you're so sick of hearing yourself say, 'You're right, Ad, you're right!' that you want to do just the opposite!"

Once they had been two prongs of a tuning fork producing a single sound. Now the prongs had been pried apart.

At this critical moment in his personal and professional life, Father had to make a key address at the Company's convention in Denver. Over at MGM, Louie Mayer—with the chestbeating and crocodile tears for which he deserved an Oscar—had begged his employees to accept a 50 percent cut to keep the studio solvent. Secretaries and office boys complained in private (to avoid the wrath of hatchet man Eddie Mannix) that L.B.'s cutting his salary from a million to half a million a year was not the same as cutting theirs from forty dollars a week to twenty. At Paramount, *New York* (now becoming *Chicago*) was in favor of a similar cut. Father resisted the cut not only for himself, but for the army of employees at the bottom of the ladder. Instead he advocated shutting down the Astoria studio where Walter Wanger reigned as his opposite number. There was wasteful duplication, Father charged, and the eastern studio had not justified its existence.

"Dad will be back tomorrow," read my Malibu diary. "Everything turned out fine. He won't have to take the cut (or all the others either) and Walter Wanger is out. I believe the Eastern Studio is to be closed, so Dad must have enjoyed great success at his Denver confabs."

Despite Mother's fears, he had held on to his room at the top. While admitting that the recent product had not lived up to expectations, he had held out rosy prospects for 1932, with Chevalier and Jeanette MacDonald, the Marx Brothers, Dietrich, Lubitsch, Powell and Lombard, Cary Grant, and another important discovery, Sylvia Sidney. . . . From the divided convention, he had received a standing ovation and a nearly unanimous vote of confidence. His studio court circle had met his train at Pasadena and in the traditional sleek black limousine had driven him back to Paramount in triumph. So, according to Father, Mother's alarums had been only another example of her overprotectiveness. She had to feel that she was in command, the power behind the throne, "what every woman knows," and that without her he would fall from his high wire.

Too busy cranking out publicity releases to cope with my diary, I returned to it on my last payday at the "Stude": "Quit work today. Hated to leave the old place. Mr. Reeve said I had made good. Played tennis all day in preparation for the tournament . . . the best Saturday tennis of my life. . . ."

Next day's entry: "WON THE CUP! An all-star audience of actors, actresses, producers, and directors filled the pavilion. Father arrived alone, looking both dapper and slightly hung over in his Sunday whites, waving his impressive Upmann like a royal wand as he greeted famous employees and guests from rival studios. Mother was coolly correct. I felt ashamed at this public acknowledgment of their separation, at the first gathering both had attended since the rupture. Still I was grateful to them for being there rooting for me."

Winning the silver Capra Cup in doubles was a major challenge to this marginal athlete who would have traded three Freddie Marches for one Ellsworth Vines. With the seriousness of a Wimbledon finalist, I had turned in early, jogged and wind-sprinted the length of the beach before breakfast, cooled off in the ocean rolling up toward our fence, run through calisthenics, and knelt in the quiet of my bedroom in desperate prayer.

The shy exterior of the child stammerer hid a fierce if largely frustrated competitiveness. Now that I had proved in the Paramount publicity department that I was no mere "producer's son," I wanted—oh, how I wanted!—that cup: my Holy Grail. Proof that I was not a flawed but a true knight of Malibu.

At the end of a triumphant day the would-be jock (rather than the would-be Melville) recorded: "First set, marched through them 6-0. Then tired and lost 6-2. In the last set they led 3-1 and 40-0 and things looked black. I played my best here, driving every serve. Even at 4-all, we went on to win. What a match. Three times today we won games after trailing 0-40. That's what I call fight!"

Back in the Schulberg beach house, a victory party was in progress. There was a supper buffet with the gleaming silver trophy, surrounded by flowers cut from our garden, as the centerpiece. The finest whiskey our studio bootlegger could supply inspired alcoholic laughter. Couples were dancing to the current hits as played by our local favorite, Abe Lyman and his Orchestra.

The redheaded Irwin Gelsey, our studio tennis-champ, "drank a lot and was a riot." Gelsey entertained with imitations of the eccentricities of "our crowd," drawing screams with his impersonation of our Hungarian star Paul Lukas, who invariably cried "Out!" the moment his opponent's racket met the ball. Looking around at our Beautiful People, vintage '31, laughing it up, drinking it up, there to make merry in the house of the influential forty-year-old hostess, a familiar sound was missing: the hearty laughter of my father. He could outlaugh all the professional laughers at the party, Jack Oakie, Frank Fay, and Eddie Lowe (from whom he won $800 that day, betting me to win at 5 to 8). Exulting in athletic victory while feeling trapped in our domestic triangle, in adolescent dismay I watched Mother dancing with Gelsey and her other admirers.

Next day, my sober diary reports: "Drove into town to the Studio. Said goodbye to the publicity department again." Since I had said my goodbyes to everyone I knew, from publicity chief Arch Reeve to the lowest mail clerks, what more was there to say two days later? But the "Stude" had been my nest ever since I could remember. Now I was going off alone into the Eastern Unknown. At lunch I said goodbye to the commissary—to the stars and the Writers' Table, to the cutters and the cameramen, to the grips and the secretaries, to eager mailroom boys, some of whom I would know later as producers and hot-shot agents. From the world-famous to the lowly, my extended family. Was I over-dramatizing these goodbyes, like Sarah Bernhardt's ceremonies of fare-well? Or was it the realization that I was finally taking leave of my Hollywood childhood, still innocent but no longer an Innocent?

Back in the office of our unofficial family counselor, "I talked to Felix Young again. More trouble brewing—I'm not even putting it in here—that's how important it is. Felix has been nice about it and is trying to help—but it is almost too late—Jesus Christ! Got all choked up when I spoke to him. Oh my God. Why is there so much dissension in this God-damned world?"

That evening Mother, Sonya, and I picked up the Viertels, Mother's kind of people: Berthold, a poet-dreamer who had been a distinguished German stage director before he became an unlikely Hollywood movie director when B.P. signed him for a series of pictures; Salka, a former actress for Max Reinhardt, a strong, assertive personality, definitely the wearer of the pants in that family, soon to become Garbo's confidante, favorite film writer, and—some whispered—lover.

Next day I went to MGM with Maurice—now set for Stanford—for another round of farewells. Metro had been our other playground from grammar-school days; we had roughhoused with George K. Arthur, joked with Slickum, Metro's answer to Paramount's Oscar the Boot-black, gaped at Greta Garbo. I had exchanged stutters with Marion Davies and had been privileged to sit at the long executive dining table where the eloquent, illiterate L. B. Mayer presided with an unctuous authority I despised. Around him were his court, tough men like ex-bouncer Eddie Mannix and agent-pimp (with a touch of *Little Caesar*) Frank Orsatti.

In contrast to "my" studio, the atmosphere of the ruling circle at Metro was oppressively totalitarian. The most heinous crimes could be committed and covered up. Mannix was the studio's hit man; Irving Thalberg, vice-president in charge of quality at MGM, was as much of a tyrant as L.B., though he ruled his half of the studio with a softer touch. Maurice's father Harry, the program-picture *maven,* lacked the drive for power that kept Mayer and Thalberg at the top—and also at each other's throats. A favorite victim of the cruel wit of the Writers' Table, because of his enormous nose and his Goldwynlike malapropisms, Harry was a crude but gentle man who knew his show business, from Joan Crawford musicals to Wallie Beery-Marie Dressler-Polly Moran comedies. My parents, and the Hollywood literati in general, looked down on him as an ignoramus, but I thought of him as a warmhearted father-figure who may have lacked my father's erudition but was more dependable domestically. I didn't know at the time that Joan Crawford had been Harry Rapf's "Sylvia Sidney" and that a second domestic crisis was brewing on Lorraine Boulevard. The Crawford affair was a fairly well-kept secret while Father and Sidney, with their provocative Malibu arrangement, invited the attention of the gossipmongers.

At Metro, L.B., with the elocution he had developed so doggedly, told me to give his good wishes "to Ad, a wonderful woman and a fine mother." Although it was an open secret that Orsatti and the casting directors fed him a regular supply of starlets, Mayer seemed to be running on a platform of Motherhood and Family Togetherness. As if my father did not exist, L.B. suggested that if there was no place for me at Paramount when I came back from prep school, I could always join Maurice at MGM.

In his paternalistic tyranny, there seemed to be not the slightest doubt in Mayer's mind that we would return for grooming as eventual producers. It even struck me as a form of bribery, to lure me away from his enemies, B.P. and Paramount. I doubt that L.B. had ever read a book, but he knew his Machiavelli: master of on-cue emotionalism, of threats sweetened with flattery, of divide and rule. Sharing Father's contempt for him, I treated him like a dangerous enemy, promising to drop in on him and his wife Margaret (of whom I was fond and for whom I felt sorry) when I returned.

Then I recrossed undeveloped West Los Angeles to have my first shave at—where else?—the Paramount studio barbershop. I had done my first boxing in the studio gym, and when I broke my arm at L.A. High in a frenzied effort to clear five feet in the high jump, it had been to the studio clinic that I rushed, to Dr. Strathern, who obligingly set my left arm without lining up the palm of my hand with the inside of my elbow. I would carry the twisted arm with me all my life, but as with so many Hollywood flaws, no one ever seemed to notice. In the barbershop, head barber Bill Ring boasted that he would remind me of my first shave when I returned from college to take over the studio. Even in those troubled Paramount days, no one on the lot entertained any doubts about the rights of divine succession. I was the Prince of Marathon Street, shyness, stutter, and all.

I called my parents together for a farewell showdown. It took place, with great solemnity, in the library of the Lorraine house. How could I go east with any peace of mind, I challenged them, if Father was still living away from home? Unless they gave me their promise to reconcile, I would cancel my trip.

Mother cried a little and Father stammered that they both were proud of me, hoped I would concentrate on my studies and writing at Deerfield, and try to worry less about their personal differences.

After an hour, I went up to my room with a sinking feeling that I had failed. The best I was able to get from Father was that he loved all of us and would do his best to work things out. In my bedroom I punched my bag lackadaisically, looked out at my flock of pigeons, fingered my old long-distance Superheterodyne, and cryptically confided to my diary, "Spoke to Dad and Mom but somehow couldn't tell them in just the words I had chosen previously."

That night, after packing the four books I had chosen for the long drive east—*Famous Russian Short Stories,* Emil Ludwig's *Genius and Character,* Herbert Asbury's *Gangs of New York,* and Francis Wallace's football novel, *Huddle*—overexcited and deeply upset I indulged in dreams of glory as to how I would settle the Sidney affair. If I could not bring myself to poison or drown her, there must be some other way.

The next day was ritual: The Last Swim. The Last Talk with Maurice. The Last Talk with Mom. The last of the last farewells. One would have thought I was leaving for Darkest Africa with slim hope of survival. I took my Dusenberg out for a Last Spin because I would be driving a democratic Chevy across the country to New England. I did some farewelling along the beach mansions of Santa Monica, including Margaret Mayer, whom I found alone in their big house, painting a crude still life.

On my way back the Duzie was racing along when suddenly, as if with an impulse of its own, it braked to a halt at the Sidney house. In a kind of trance, the young driver got out of his chariot and strode toward the gate. To his surprise it was open. As if sleepwalking, he followed the wooden walk until it brought him to a side porch. Slowly he walked up the steps and through a screen door. There on an oversized couch facing the ocean sat Sylvia Sidney, with her mother. And pacing, scotch highball in one hand, a big cigar in the other, was Father, apparently just returned from the studio.

He was in mid-sentence when he saw me. Undoubtedly reciting the tribulations of the day, which had been mounting as company enemies kept sniping, and other stars complained that B.P. was picking the choice roles for Sylvia at their expense. Now, as I materialized in this alien place, the eyes of my father bulged in disbelief. Sylvia and her mother stared, waiting to see what I would do.

I was waiting, too. I have never known a sensation like this, before or since. I must have been, quite simply, possessed. I could feel a trembling all through my body. When I finally spoke, it was with a new voice—and words I had never used before, certainly not to my father:

"You son of a bitch! You're coming home with me. Right now, you son of a bitch!"

I was grabbing Father by the arm and pulling him toward the door. My body and my spirit were stronger than his. I pulled him out through the screen door, down the wooden walkway, and out to the Dusenberg. At the running board he resisted, but I had the door open and pushed him in. The Duzie sprang forward like a trusty steed and I, in my own mind, must have been Malibu's Galahad, strengthened by ten because my heart was pure. I dragged Father out of the car and up the walk to Green Gate Cottage. At the entrance to the house he tried to pull away. "Buddy, I can't! I can't!"

I was merciless: "Go on, get in there, you yellow son of a bitch!"

As possessed in his way as I was in mine, Father walked through the doorway and into the house.

I ran ahead of him to alert Mother.

"Mom, he's home! I brought Dad home!"

If Dad had wanted to walk out now, I would not have had the strength to stop him. But he stayed. He asked where Sonya and Stuart were. Sonc was down the beach with Adela Rogers's precocious daughter, Elaine, and Stu was up the beach with Maurice's little brother, Matty. Mother and Father sat facing each other, making polite conversation about my imminent drive east. Mother urged me to write down the numbers of all my traveler's checks, and Father warned me not to pick up strangers. There were so many people out of work now, on the bum, and possibly dangerous. "What I'm worried about," I said, "is what'll happen to you."

There was an awkward silence and I decided to leave them alone. Upstairs, I stared out at the ocean that had been our front yard since Ad first discovered Malibu. To the south I could see the rickety pier where Maurice and I had caught hundreds of tomcod. Then I looked out at the manicured Japanese farms that stretched behind us all the way to the green foothills. I wondered if I should pack my tennis cup, decided that would be ostentatious, reread the latest version of "Ugly" that my U.S.C. mentor Mrs. Stanton thought "almost ready for a 'little magazine,'" and gazed at my favorite print of Washington Irving's ivy-covered castle on the Hudson. I would rather have his life, I thought to myself, than that of a Hollywood mogul. I couldn't help wondering what would have happened if my father had persevered as a writer and never moved up through the ranks of Famous Players to his glamorous but precarious sunken office. Would his drinking and gambling and Sidneying have been this excessive? Knowing nothing but Hollywood, having been exposed all my life to its opportunists, sycophants, pimps, and "hoors," and wanting to absolve my father as much as possible, I was inclined to shift the blame to the impersonal amalgam we called "Hollywood."

At dinner that evening there was forced gaiety as Lucille showed off with her rare roast beef, popovers, glazed sweet potatoes, and chocolate soufflé. Father was sober, very sober. I was too self- or family-absorbed to wonder how he had explained to Sylvia his continued absence from her hearth.

Already caught up in his story conferences and rushes, he didn't accompany me to the railroad station—but I went in style in the chauffeur-driven Lincoln gold bric-a-brac town car, with Mother, Sonya, Uncle Sam, and of course Maurice to see me off on the crack overnight *Lark* to San Francisco. There I would hitch up with Rudy Pacht, the husky, easygoing all-city fullback from Hollywood High who was driving east with me, he to Dartmouth, where I would follow if I made good at Deerfield. Heading north through miles of orange groves that were still the landmark of outer Los Angeles, I wrote in my diary with solemnity: "I am going through a great deal before I see them again. After the train pulled out I cried—just a bit. Then I read quite late."

41

ROSS-COUNTRY DRIVING IN the early Thirties, only a little less adventurous than in covered-wagon days, offered scenery instead of speed. As we bounced along the narrow road that twisted up the Pacific Coast into Oregon, there was time for the awesome redwoods and the great pines holding the coastline against a white-water ocean. Sometimes the engine boiled over and the tires went flat. Daily crises brought us close to the people and the land. There were sleepy towns with names that ran round and round in the mind like half-remembered poetry: Ukiah . . . Fortuna . . . Eureka . . . Our ratty car was like a pinto pony, driven all day to the point of exhaustion. A list of expenses for an average day on the road is a faded snapshot of the times:

Aug. 22 [1931]

Hotel	$1.00
Gas	3.00
Breakfast	.50
Lunch	.45
Candy	.10
Soda	.15
Supper	.75
Stamps	.05
Post cards	.05
Tip	.10
Total	$6.15

We toured the campuses of Oregon and Oregon State Universities, swam in the Columbus River (lunch 20¢, supper 45¢), and when, out of gas, we coasted into Pendleton, it was almost as if I had reversed course onto the studio back lot. "Pendleton," wrote the road-battered Hollywood prince, "is a typical little western town, with everyone wearing half-gallon hats and blank expressions—as if they've been around their cows so long they've begun to look like them."

Across the Montana border, "the road gave up any ambition of being a road . . . result was a rocky lane which vibrated every bone in my body. Troy, where we had a tough roast beef (65¢), is undoubtedly the World's Worst Place. Lacking one paved street, the burg is a typical old-western town with a pack of booted hicks lounging on the corner. The houses are most dilapidated and even the women look run-down."

We were averaging 15 miles an hour now, hugging a narrow dirt road winding around a mountain. A lumber truck approaching from the opposite direction provoked a life-and-death crisis. Shouted at to move over, I complied until my left wheels were hanging over the edge, in the air, Harold Lloyd-style. Later, in a Montana ranch town, "The movie house is a rattrap of 100 seats. The picture, *Ship of Hate*, typifies both the town and the theater." Since American ingenuity was yet to present us with one of our great cultural forward thrusts, the motel, we stayed in dusty two-story hotels where the going rate was one dollar a night. "There is a rope tied to my bed which is to be thrown out the window and slid down in case of fire. I don't know which I'd rather do—slide down the rope or fry." And before sinking down into his lumpy bed, the western-weary traveler makes a final observation: "Montana is beautiful virgin country—but the roads are more virgin than beautiful."

To a Los Angeleno raised on Westerns of Art Acord, Tom Mix, Tim McCoy, and Hoot Gibson, the real West, or at least the one-tacky-hotel western town, was an eyesore. Missing our Hollywood bungalow courts, I complained that we were motoring back into the 1880s. In a sleepy stopover named Challott, where the only restaurant bore the faded legend EATS, the most prominent sign in town read "Funeral Parlor. Nice Assortment of Caskets." On the way to Yellowstone National Park we not only ran out of gas but had a flat; when the car fell off its flimsy jack into a road of tar softened by summer heat, we waited for hours until a good samaritan arrived in a wood truck and not only jacked us up but siphoned a gallon of gas from his own tank.

At Old Faithful, the mysterious geyser that goes off every sixty minutes according to its own primordial clock, more serious disaster brushed our shoulder, although we would not feel its grip until the following day. It seemed a happy coincidence that we met Ralph Cohn, son of Jack Cohn, the nicer of the two brothers who ran Columbia. Ralph was on his way to Cornell with his roommate Bernie and, considering the hazards of western auto travel, it seemed logical that we drive on in tandem.

The wisdom of this decision proved out almost immediately. While we were giving high marks to the beauty of Teton National Park, our car ran out of gas again. When two gallons had been siphoned from Ralph's and it still refused to start, we had to be towed ignominiously into Jackson, the first truly wild-west town I had ever seen. Horsepower came mostly from horses there, tied to hitching posts while their riders shouldered through the swinging doors of the side-by-side saloons that opened on the raised wooden walkway. I was used to seeing people getting drunk in their homes, and Father staggering in from casinos and "speaks," but in those days of national Prohibition, these were the first wide-open bars I had ever seen. The town, we were told, had a population of 333, of which the entire male population seemed to be in a state of extreme inebriation. The lone gas-station attendant was drunk, and stared at our dead engine and admitted he "don't know how to fix the damn thing." When I asked if the Sheriff might be able to help us out, he pointed with an oily finger: "Most of the time he's drunk. You'll find 'im in one o' them saloons across the street."

Somewhere along the way Ralph and Bernie had picked up a pair of girl hitchhikers. Fairly attractive, tough country girls. We all had supper together in a greasy spoon while a would-be mechanic tinkered with our stubborn Chevy. The girls were on their way to Cheyenne, and urged Ralph and Bernie to take them along. Since the two couples were already holding hands, and since Cheyenne was directly on our route, why should there be any objection? Girl-shy and puritanical, I said I didn't like the idea. In this unreconstructed Old West, I could feel the hostility against outsiders, intensified by unspoken but unmistakable anti-Semitism, and I thought the presence of two Wyoming girls would not improve our welcome at gas stations and lunch counters. But I was outvoted by the two swains and the amiable Rudy.

Next day on the winding road from Jackson to Rock Spring, we were following Ralph's car, Rudy laughing at the ostentatious necking between both couples that had been going on for miles. Suddenly, on a sharp turn, Ralph turned his head to the girl, lost his grip on the wheel, and as we watched it like a horror show, the car went catapulting off the road and into an open field where it cartwheeled over and over, finally crashing to a halt upside down. We heard the screams and the splattering of glass, jumped out of the car, and ran toward them.

I wish I could tell a tale of schoolboy heroics, dragging bleeding victims from a burning wreck. In truth, the next thing I knew strange men were bending over me, strange hands were lifting me onto a stretcher, and it was only then that I came to, and sheepishly confessed, "No, I'm okay . . . I was in the car behind." They had found me lying near the other bodies in a dead faint. In disgust they dropped me back on the ground and turned their attention to the real victims. Silently, Rudy and I followed the ambulance into Rock Spring.

My diary picks up the thread: "Tragedy hit us hard today. A girl who we never knew existed yesterday is fighting for her life at the hospital. (Fractured skull, face lacerated by glass, arm and leg broken.) Bernie has a bad head wound and Ralph is also injured, though less seriously. The other girl, miraculously if you saw the total wreckage of the car, is only superficially bruised and cut."

So there were Rudy and I holed up in a dingy hotel in a tough little Wyoming town with the other girl, a strange and frightened trio locked together while we kept the hospital vigil. Diary scolds my lack of decision the night before: "I wanted to say *no*—but I settled for 'I'm not wild about the idea.' I didn't argue enough. I've learned a great lesson today—to follow my own inclinations from now on. Please God! Let her live! Back and forth to the hospital many times. One time almost fainted again. Everything went white. The other girl is scared to death. Why in hell didn't I say *no*? It looks lousy with these girls here and we didn't have a goddamn thing to do with it."

Maybe we didn't, but it seemed as if the whole town had put us on trial and already found us guilty. The waspish hotel clerk glared at us as we left our key at the desk next morning. Unfriendly eyes followed us through the airless lobby. The waitress shoved our eggs at us and hurried away as if we were lepers. As we walked the now-familiar route to the local hospital, the citizens of Rock Spring stared at us as if we were horned creatures sprung from the Moon. Ralph and Bernie, the architects of our fate, were isolated in their hospital beds and we, with the stranger-girl ever-present at our side, the Unholy Three, were exposed to the cold hatred of a myopic western town. (Almost fifty years later, Rock

Spring would be described as one of the most wide-open as well as paranoid towns left in the West.) Nervously, Rudy and I considered the possibility that if the girl should die, a spontaneous posse might close in on us and string us up to the nearest tree. It didn't take Houdini to read their narrow minds: *Them dirty Hollywood Jews can't keep their lecherous hands off'n our young girls.* Even the hospital staff were barely civil as they gave us the latest bulletins: Ralph would be out in a few days and Bernie would recover, but the girl's life was still in the balance.

At the drugstore the bald-headed proprietor pulled my milk-shake glass away.

"Wait a minute, I haven't f-f-finished," I protested.

"I'm closin' up," he said through tight lips, and poured the rest of my milk shake down the drain. I was convinced that he was the Head Dragon of the local Klan fixin' to do us in.

Back at the hotel, I phoned Ralph's father at his studio. Long-distance calls were still such a luxury that we hadn't thought to call home simply to report our progress along the way. Mr. Cohn was relieved about Ralph and told us how to report the accident to the insurance company. But he did not see how it would help matters for him to come to Rock Spring himself. I had been hoping he would relieve us of our embarrassing hospital watch. Instead, he advised us to get in touch with the manager of the local Rialto Theater, which played Paramount pictures, and let him guide us through our dilemma.

A few days later, when the girl was finally declared out of danger and Ralph was able to leave the hospital and keep the vigil, Rudy and I checked out of that hostile hotel, to the undisguised relief of the theater manager, torn between his obligation to come to the aid of these errant scions of Hollywood and his concern that this association would be bad for business.

We sped away from Rock Spring like prisoners going over the wall. Driving all day and all night, the nightmare West was finally behind us. The roads of Iowa were "smooth as glass—and no speed limits! No flats or lack of gas today!"

Chicago: "Same old noisy, windy place. Hitting Michigan Boulevard is like finding a pearl in a garbage can." Notre Dame: "Disappointing, with dirty-looking buildings and ragged grounds." Niagara: "Same old Falls, a beautiful sight marred by the commercialism and the crowd you have to fight through to see it. A headwaiter in full-dress refused to seat us because my cords were so dirty and badly ripped." New York, on Labor Day: "Two million people leaving the mountains and beach resorts—the last day of vacation—torturous driving, three miles an hour—a line of cars ahead of me as far as I can see. What a day I picked to drive to a city of seven million!"

42

AFTER ELEVEN HOURS' sleep and a hearty Jewish breakfast at Uncle Dave's modest flat in the Bronx—he was another of Ad's brothers—I was ready with my appraisal of New York: "As bad as ever. People busy dodging cars and outsmarting each other. A city of wise guys. I never saw a town like this, where everyone is trying to put something over on you. Felt like a real hick. A shampoo, shave, and facial made me feel like a new man." That evening I took my cousin Rosalind—"prettier than ever"—out for supper and a movie, and as we walked up Fifth Avenue "I felt a little *hamed* [our private word for *ashamed*] because I had to take her arm in mine—first time I've ever done that. But I'm still here so guess it didn't kill me." On pretty cousin Roz I was able to practice my callow social graces, learning how to hold a girl's arm and how to help her into a taxi, modest beginnings to sexual contact I somehow had managed to avoid all my years of growing up in Hollywood.

Late that night I had an important long-distance call from Mom and Dad. They were relieved that I had made it safely and that I (having inherited Father's myopic sense of direction) had been able to locate New York City all by myself. Even in my naiveté, I knew that their calling together was merely a show of matrimonial convention, to shore up their anxious son on the eve of his Eastern Adventure.

There was a long weekend at the Zukors' Mountain View Farm (three large houses, a huge swimming pool, private golf course, tennis and handball courts, a great projection room, and their own river to fish in). I swam with Maurice Chevalier, played tackle football with the caddies, and walked the golf course with Primo Carnera, in training for his big fight with Jack Sharkey.

The Zukor family and their friends seemed to have a sublime faith that with a little encouragement from the Hoover Administration, the economy would eventually pull out of its doldrums. But a long talk with Mr. Zukor himself was not about the current state of the world but about the current state of the picture business, and of Paramount in particular. He admitted that these were troubled times for Paramount, and that The Industry was going through growing pains. But he recalled the early-morning fire that had almost destroyed his Famous Players in its downtown New York infancy. Apparently if deceptively still ruler of all he surveyed, he was able to maintain a stoic confidence: "This too shall pass."

I was relieved to hear him speak so well of Father. If he had any criticism of B.P.'s indiscretions with Sylvia Sidney, or of Father's box-office record for the past year, he was too polite to voice them. Having discovered young Ben before I was born, when Father was a teenage prodigy, a natural writer and idea man, he seemed proud of Father's progress, and pleased to hear that I also had begun to write.

Monday morning, I was awakened at dawn because Mr. Zukor, still the little furrier working a 12-hour day, liked to be at his downtown New York office by nine A.M. I returned to my busy waiting-for-school-to-open life, seeing two movies a day, visiting what seemed an endless round of Schulbergs from downtown Manhattan to the Upper Bronx ("I suppose it sounds cynical but a guy gets kinda hardened, kissing 2 or 3 Schulbergs 4 or 5 times a week"), and discovering a world I had only heard about at a distance—the Broadway theater:

"*Grand Hotel* a great show, a new idea. Sam Jaffe—not *our* Sam Jaffe—steals the show. . . . *Barretts of Wimpole Street,* starring Katharine Cornell as Elizabeth Barrett Browning; the tragic family life of the dreamy Wimpole Street poetess. *Payment Deferred,* a great show. Charles Laughton gives a powerful portrayal. To watch him sit at the window and gaze at the spot where he buried the lady in the garden was enough to give anyone the willies." Not exactly Burns Mantle, but for all my Hollywood provincialism ("finally tracked down an L.A. *Times* and devoured it"), my eastern education was beginning.

As if drawn back to the scene of the crime, I couldn't resist using my gold pass at the Paramount Theater to see *An American Tragedy* again. I had seen the picture half a dozen times from the studio projection room to the sneak previews to Grauman's Chinese and on to Broadway. Dreiser's story had held a fascination for me ever since I had read it two years earlier, when Father first began thinking of doing it as a picture. Dreiser himself had come out to discuss the project and had turned out to be a terrible disappointment, not at all the literary god I had imagined but instead a difficult drunk who literally chased Mother around the dining-room table. How could the book be so real when its author was a pompous, alcoholic ass? Dreiser had turned on the picture and had even brought suit against Father and Paramount for distorting his work. But the film, for its day, was an honest effort to bring the raw, tough, searching novel to the screen. I was so proud of what I thought of as "Father's picture" that I tipped the cabdriver a quarter instead of my usual dime when he told me it was the best picture he had ever seen and that he was going back to see it a second time. To me, *An American Tragedy* reflected Father's interest in American literature, an attempt to bring to the screen the feeling for good writing he had brought to our Sunday morning reading sessions. Tackling a radical Dreiser theme was his way of reminding himself of the writer he might have been.

Of course the film had an ambivalent fascination for me: How many sons have an opportunity to stare at their father's mistress on the screen of a darkened movie palace? Watching Sylvia Sidney crinkle her face in a provocative smile, first sexually aroused, then socially rejected, watching her pout, suffer, plead, "You've got to help me, Clyde/Ben," I could understand her attraction for Father. Clara Bow had been cute and saucy, but Sylvia had a sensuous Jewish quality that reached out to me and troubled me. In that vast audience held under her spell, I knew that I was the only one involved in personal drama with her, the only one who actually wanted to kill her as Phillips Holmes was mustering his courage to do in the movie. Nor was there any release or therapy in watching her drown again.

For by this time I had heard from Father's studio friends that the enforced reconciliation had broken down. He had gone back to the other Malibu house and my mother with her sad eyes had decided to come east with the Viertels, ostensibly to see me off to Deerfield, but also to put space between herself and Father.

Homesickness induced a recurring dream of entering Grauman's Chinese to attend an opening of one of Father's pictures, or of being ushered to the studio-reserved section of an out-of-town movie house for a sneak preview, only to wake up just as the movie was beginning. I felt let down to find myself back in Uncle Dave Jaffe's apartment in the Bronx, even though they treated me like a visiting prince, lavishing lox and cream cheese, fresh bagels, and all manner of Jewish goodies on me. Warm and supportive, they were proud to show me off at the social club where they went almost every evening to play cards and *schmoos* with their neighbors. The son of the wealthiest and most glamorous of all the relatives, I was asked questions tinged with envy—what was Hollywood really like? What was it like to know Marlene Dietrich, Gary Cooper, Cary Grant? How could I explain to them that what I really missed were track meets, tennis games, homing pigeons, and parents as devoted to each other as our feathered thoroughbreds?

43

THE ARRIVAL OF my mother on the *20th Century Limited* from Chicago brought light to the tunnel between Hollywood and Deerfield. I had never felt close to her before. She had never been the kind of mother who touches and hugs and loves. She had always been too busy improving me, and then boasting about me. I felt she was claiming my accomplishments as an extension of her own ego. But now she represented home and Hollywood, and I couldn't wait to see her.

From the old Pennsylvania Station we taxied to the St. Moritz, "a fairly good hotel with a radio." Suddenly life had become richer and more glamorous. An inadvertent snob, I had found life with the New York Schulbergs and Jaffeys dingy and cramped. It had been an uncomfortable relationship because while they fawned over me, I felt their envy and their need. Father's sister Val had a husband, Charley Beckman, who had the smell of failure on his clothes and on his breath, and who was always looking to Father for another loan. Mother's brother, Dave, was a sweet, sentimental man with none of her drive and intelligence; he and Aunt Ray were counting on Ad to bring them to Hollywood and set him up in business. We were the glamorous relatives from sunny California who could open the golden door. Grateful to them for taking me in when I arrived alone and intimidated by New York, I pretended a humility I did not feel.

That day at the plush rooftop restaurant of the St. Moritz overlooking

Central Park, dining with the intellectual Viertels, listening to talk of the latest books, plays, and films in work, I felt more at home. Hollywood was sunshine, open fields along Sunset Boulevard, blue-green waves delivering our bodies to the Malibu beach; the unforgettable smell and mysterious darkness of a studio stage and the staccato "Cut! How was that for you? Print that!"; the heady fraternity of famous and busy people gathered to toast and roast each other at favorite haunts like Henry's, Montmartre, and Victor Hugo's; the manic weekend drinking of the Mickey Neilans and the Billy Wellmans; the Ad Schulberg and Salka Viertel gatherings of literati with whom Charlie Chaplin and Greta Garbo liked to mingle. It was all the things I missed.

That afternoon my education progressed when the young couple considered Hollywood's brightest, David Selznick and his bride Irene (Mayer), learned I had never been inside a speakeasy and offered to guide me on an illicit tour. Still in his late twenties, David had a fleshy, sensuous face, an exuberant intelligence, and a feisty independence. Until his recent resignation over creative differences, he had been Father's most promising assistant. It was his contention that the major-studio "factory" system was wrong and that no man, not even a brainy young veteran like B.P., could personally oversee fifty pictures a year. Instead of the system Paramount and the others employed, with "supervisors" standing in for the studio chief but never completely responsible for the finished product, David advocated a more personal approach, with supervisors becoming full-fledged producers heading their own independent units—a system of creative decontrol.

Raised in the business as a boy-producer under the maverick, often outrageous L. J. Selznick, David was a roaring river of self-confidence. Like his scrappy brother Myron, Hollywood's first big-time agent, David was ready and eager to take on the world. He liked and admired Father but would let nothing get in the way of making his own pictures. He was bursting with ideas, books he had read, plays he had seen, his own originals. From his father he had inherited a curmudgeon resistance to authority. His memo-mania is now Hollywood legend. But those 5,000-word dictations were a natural extension of the verbal Niagara that poured from him day and night, for he was also a nocturnal force who seemed unable to stop the flow until he fell asleep from exhaustion in the early hours. Later, when I heard about Thomas Wolfe—who, like Dreiser, also chased my mother around the dining-room table—the prodigious novelist reminded me of a literary version of David Selznick, larger than life and pouring words from a bottomless well, good words, great words, needless words all gushing forth together, flooding one's mind.

David talked at you rather than with you, but you didn't mind because it was informed and entertaining talk, charged with intensity. Hailing him as the Boy Wonder, Hollywood insiders told each other that Louie Mayer had his eye on David as a counterbalance to Thalberg, who had begun his MGM career as L.B.'s protégé but who was Frankensteining into a rival. MGM had its share of son-in-law/brother-in-law supervisors. There were sinecures in the wardrobe, makeup, and sound department for relatives of Mayer, Thalberg, and Rapf. But David had no desire to go into the son-in-law business. Though he would succumb, a year or so later, for $4,000 a week and a relatively—or, B.P. would say, *un*relatively—free hand in his choice and control of productions, he was temperamentally incapable of bending the knee, even to a superpower father-in-law like L.B.

David and Irene: what an unbeatable combination they seemed as we sat around the traditional red-and-white-checkered table of a midtown "speak" that day. More sparing of speech than David, and tougher-minded, like her old man, Irene was the ideal running mate for a movie mogul on the rise. If there had been woman producers in those days, Irene would have been right up there with David. (Indeed, twenty years later, after their divorce, Irene would produce *A Streetcar Named Desire* and other hits on Broadway.)

David at 29, Irene at 24, I at 17, each of us the offspring of a Hollywood tycoon, were drawn together—despite our fathers' feuds—by our sense of belonging to a private club, the real Hollywood aristocracy. No matter that the bloodlines went back only a single generation. No matter that David was now on the outs with Father who in turn was locked in bitter warfare with L.B. We were still a family. David and Irene were like my big brother and sister who would help me grow up. They seemed so wise and strong for their age, so sure of where they were going, accepting without question their divine right to rule. And in truth, they had come here equipped to exercise their power.

In flight from Paramount and B.P., young Selznick was in New York to work out a deal with RCA's David Sarnoff to take over production at RKO, the old Joe Kennedy studio. When I returned from Deerfield next summer, he wanted me to see him about a job in the story department where I would be a step closer to screenwriting. Nepotism? Were we not chosen from birth to lead The Industry—an inevitable succession to the throne?

I drew strength from David's and Irene's support, just as they had from Mother's. Ad seemed more maternal toward Irene and her sister Edith than she was to Sonya. While Mother always thought Edith adorable, she admired Irene, whose sharp and what we then called masculine mind set her apart from the other Hollywood princesses. In the face of L.B.'s scorn of his future son-in-law, Ad had encouraged David's courtship of Irene. It suited her sense of the fitness of things. But her propensity for running other people's lives had backfired when Edith confided to Ad her feelings for Billy Goetz. Youngest brother in another Industry family also close to us, Billy was a gag man, always good for a laugh, a sidekick of Darryl Zanuck. This time Ad sided with L.B.: "I like Billy, but he's a lightweight. He's not good enough for you." Of course Edith brought this assessment back to Billy—and young Goetz, soon to be a power at 20th Century-Fox thanks to L.B.'s benevolence, had cut Ad dead ever since.

Billy would go on to become one of the entrenched Hollywood millionaires, a collector of Van Goghs, one of the shining examples of the Peter Principle. But my fierce-minded mother was relentless. Instead of ever asking herself if she could have been wrong, she would insist to the end that Billy Goetz was not good enough for adorable Edith Mayer.

But even these bitter differences were family affairs. We feuded among ourselves, helped each other, hurt each other, loved each other as do members of a large, close family. David Selznick felt about The Industry's mistreatment of his pioneer father Lewis J. as I was to feel about its treatment of my pioneer father a few years later. We were tied together. Irene and David united two of the founding families. Edith's Billy added another link. Feudal families related through marriage. Hollywood was still small enough to be held together by a single blood-knot. (When Rosabelle Laemmle, daughter of the founder of Universal, took a fancy to Irving Thalberg, Mother considered it her social duty not merely to encourage but to arrange the match. When Irving turned away from Rosabelle in favor of his MGM star Norma Shearer, Mother felt personally jilted, accused Ms. Shearer of being a "hoor"—a category to which she assigned nearly all gentile actresses but which also included Ms. Sidney—and assured Rosabelle and all of our circle that "Irving was making a terrible mistake.")

In my first speakeasy, David attacked the Hollywood assembly line and B.P.'s place in it, pointed to Father as a creative man with an artistic temperament trapped within the system. He saw the impossibility of exercising good judgment while subject to the higher authority of the New York office. "The money has to trust the talent," David insisted. "One mind has to run the show. That's what I'm asking for at RKO. Trust me or fire me. No outside interference. If I show them I can make good pictures at a profit, they should give me a free hand. Your old man has never had that at Paramount. 'Vice-President-in-Charge-of-Production' is a nice title, but what does it mean? On top of B.P. is Lasky, or was. Jesse's a sweet guy but not really tough enough for this business. On top of them is Zukor and on top of him is Kuhn-Loeb, and so it goes. Getting control of your own filmmaking—that's what we have to fight for."

David was forecasting a new creative structure in which a producer took full responsibility for only a handful of pictures a year. He sounded so right that I was worried about Father's clinging to what David insisted was an outmoded, man-killing system. Was that what drove him to his manic gambling and drinking? At heart he was a writer and a filmmaker with an independent spirit. But he had to ride the *Super Chief* to those big conventions, make speeches about "our great new program" like a politician, charm the exhibitors, play the game. He'd do it, brilliantly, eloquently, win the praise of his New York superiors, then go out and, in a drunken haze, drop fifteen thousand dollars in a crap game.

Of course David could hardly point a finger. On less than half of Father's surrealistic wages, he was another notorious loser at the Clover Club.

Midtown Manhattan was chockablock with speakeasies, but we wound up at Jack and Charlie's "21," a favorite of the literati, the theater people, and the pols. Clara Bow wasn't dancing on the table in her undies. No one was ostentatiously drunk. Indeed, it looked like a friendly restaurant-retreat for newspapermen. At a nearby table were two of the most celebrated front-pagers, Charlie MacArthur and Ben Hecht. Hecht had a couple of drinks at our table, reminisced about Father and *Underworld,* and talked to David about coming out to do a picture for him. In his late thirties, he was at the height of his ebullience and self-confidence, the archetypal breezy newspaperman turned novelist and playwright. Mank had urged me to read Hecht's racy novels for contemporary style. His and MacArthur's *The Front Page* had been the rage of Broadway. If anyone had a chance of outtalking David it was Hecht: He talked the way he wrote, rapid-fire, highly colored, highly charged. Of the scores of writers I had come to know in Hollywood—introverts, extroverts, drunks, teetotalers, the scholarly, the vulgar—Ben Hecht seemed the personification of the writer at the top of his game, the top of his world, not gnawing at and doubting himself as great writers were said to do, but with every word and every gesture indicating the animal pleasure he took in writing well.

I envied him. Dave Selznick may have been on his way to the magic circle of tycoons, but what I fantasized about was walking into Jack and Charlie's someday with a successful book behind me. I forgave Hecht his cheek and brassiness. Possibly because I had been exposed to so many Hollywood blowhards, I preferred people who talked and walked quietly and let their words speak for them. But damn it, Ben Hecht had done it, he had taken that giant step upward that almost every newspaperman dreams of and only one in a thousand manages to accomplish.

Remembering my highschool efforts, Hecht asked me how my writing was coming along, and recommended that I get a summer job on a newspaper rather than take David up on the story-department offer. "On a newspaper you get kicked around. You learn the hard way. You gotta sit down and write it, ready or not. That's how I learned to write so fast. I c'n write a novel in four weeks. A screenplay in two. Just pound it out and let the poetry take care of itself."

With Salka Viertel (Mother's constant companion) and Irving Pichel, the U.C.L.A. professor turned actor-director, I dined at The Casino in Central Park and complained, "With Paramount at 14, it's a crime to pay $25 for a dinner for four."

That night, wearing a soft evening gown, with more makeup on her eyes than I approved of, Mother had gone out to a nightclub with Pichel and the Viertels. I considered her behavior "wild," drinking martinis, smoking Camels, and flirting with men who seemed to drop in at the end of the day.

At four o'clock in the morning, Mother was still out. With Irving Pichel! I read a Fu Manchu novel in which a victim is attracted to a hotel window where a noose is dropped around his neck from a floor above. A masochistic urge drew me to the window; I thought I saw the shadow of a noose and felt a chill of fear and loneliness. Where the hell was Mom? What was wrong with people? Why in hell couldn't they stay together the way they were supposed to? I had been raised on flapper wives and philandering husbands as characters in Father's movies. But now that he was off with Sidney and Mother was out with Irving Pichel, those movies had come home.

I had browsed through Mother's extensive library on Freud, Adler, and the psychiatric pioneers. Although she had never exposed her children to sex education, she had delivered her little lectures on the interpretation of dreams and the Oedipus complex. As I paced my hotel room I realized that I was jealous of my mother's all-night escort. Through Father's delinquency, I now felt I had to fill his role. The little boy lost in the maze of Manhattan was the outraged husband waiting up for his faithless wife.

I was at the window watching the first light rediscover the trees of Central Park when I heard her come in. Back in bed, I fell into exhausted sleep dreaming I was home on our Malibu tennis court overpowering Irwin Gelsey—another of the men I suspected in Mother's new life.

That afternoon my cheerful cousin Roz took me on still another round of relatives, from my Grandmother clinging to her musty little apartment on the Lower East Side to my father's sister Val's in the Bronx. There Uncle Charley was in bed, recovering from serious burns in an automobile accident. He described the accident with such relish for detail that I suddenly pitched forward in a dead faint. It was a physical or neurological problem that would haunt me all my life. As the violent details piled on, with the morbid intensity so many victims seem to enjoy, I could feel the nausea pressing down on my face like an ether cone and then the inevitable spiral of white lines into which I was falling, falling. . .

That evening I had recovered sufficiently to go to the theater with Mother, the Viertels, and Norman Burnstine, a young relative of Father's who aspired to a studio writing job. I had also begun to suspect that he aspired to Mother. The play was *The Left Bank* by Elmer Rice. Like Father, Rice was a product of the New York intellectual ferment before the first World War. Mother had known him as Reizenstein; she had been an enthusiastic supporter of his experimental work with the Morningside Players. Sometimes I wondered if there was anyone in the artistic world whom Mother had not discovered. From that moment, she took a possessive interest in his success. With *The Adding Machine* and *Street Scene,* Rice had established himself as our foremost social dramatist.

Mother had a better eye for innovation than she had for quality. Even then when I knew very little about anything, I sensed her tendency to go off half-cocked. She did have the intuition to get there first, which was admirable. But, once there, she would rush on to the next discovery without really absorbing what she had discovered. To fill an entire wall of our library with books on psychoanalysis was an act of pioneering in the early Twenties. But I always felt her reach exceeded her grasp. It would exasperate her that Father, who had never studied psychoanalysis but had picked it up from Mother, could present Freud's ideas far more coherently. "All he knows about the subject he learned from me," she complained. "But he's so damned glib he's able to fool people."

While B.P. had the creative intellect she lacked, Ad could outdistance him in artistic ambition. He called his approach honest and hers pretentious.

At Lindy's after the play, she talked in that vague way she favored when the subject was slightly beyond her: Elmer Rice was a great playwright. She had been one of the first to realize that, when they were barely twenty years old. Here was a play, about a radical idealist, that made you think—the ideal play for me to see before leaving for Deerfield.

Over my favorite *nosh,* smoked sturgeon on toasted bagel, I shocked Mother by telling her the play was boring. What promised to be an interesting character study suffered from an obvious plot and an absence of dramatic development. It wasn't enough for a play to deal with lofty ideas. There was an obligation to be entertaining. I had learned this from a hundred story conferences, listening to good story minds like Mank and Hecht. I had been going to a writing school no college could offer and no money could buy. Having been encouraged by Father to help doctor flawed movie scripts, I had not only seen the holes but had begun my apprenticeship by trying to fill them.

Mother was impressed. At that moment, with my mouth full of sturgeon, I seemed to be more of a sage than Elmer Reizenstein. She could tell from the way I talked and the things I had written that I was destined to be a great American writer like Branch Cabell, Louis Bromfield, Sinclair Lewis, and young Thomas Wolfe. She had felt this, she said, even before I was born. Now there wasn't the slightest doubt in her mind that prep school and college would prepare me for literary glory.

From one point of view it might be considered admirable that Mother (with Father's more realistic and critical support) could take so sanguine a view of her son's future. Many of my Hollywood peers—sons and daughters of the powerful studio chieftains of the Twenties and Thirties—have complained of being made to feel unequal to their parents, their egos not strong enough to withstand the pressure of growing up with famous fathers. But with Mother working overtime on my ego, I faced another kind of danger, that of being overpraised and overstimulated to achieve. Some of the fun of growing up was stolen from me by the realization that before I had published anything except in highschool journals and local sports pages, my career already had been chosen for me. It was no longer pure joy to read Conrad and Dickens and Melville. I had to worry about following in their footsteps. And if I should fail, what would there be for me to do? It was as if Mother already had made me a success and there was no margin for failure. That was no carefree youth going off to prep school. How to put my parents together again, how to live up to Mother's extravagant confidence, and how to make my way alone in the alien world of New England made me feel like a very old man of seventeen.

44

GROWING UP WITH a sense of dramatic form, exposed to Father's daily struggles with his writers to achieve sound continuity and structure, I thought of my departure from Grand Central Station for Deerfield as a significant fade-out, and new fade-in. At the platform, instead of embracing and kissing me, Mother became my intellectual cheerleader, sending me into the literary game to run up the score for Schulberg and Jaffe U. She was remorseless in her love. She did not bestow it on the unfit. Compassion for weakness was not her way. If Sonya was shy, frightened, and unable to show off her poems to illustrious guests, poor Sonya could stay upstairs in her room. For Mother, love was confused with enabling her to shine in reflected glory.

And yet a telegram sent to Father at this moment tells of "broken heartstrings" at this first extended separation from her children. She was like a fiercely loving bitch determined that every one of her litter win a blue ribbon at the show. Of course I was expected to win Best of Show.

From the window of the train I watched New York fall away behind me. Harlem, where I was born, was becoming Negro now as Jews moved south of 110th Street or north to the greener city limits. I stared down into long, narrow, forbidding streets, watched kids playing stickball or leaning over precarious fire escapes, and wondered how different I might have been if my parents hadn't taken me west on the old *Santa Fe Chief* and planted me among the palm and citrus trees of rural Holywood.

As the train rolled into Connecticut, I began to enjoy the scarlet and golden leaves of October, unlike any I had ever seen before. Our hills at home were sunbaked brown. Although this new world appealed to me, the strangeness of it intensified my sense of transition from Hollywood insider to eastern outsider.

On the train were two Deerfield boys I had met in New York. Snooty and formal, they addressed me as "Schulberg." In the Far West we were used to instant informality. These eastern boarding-school types acted like little old men. I wondered if everybody at Deerfield would be like that. What if I found it unbearable? I wouldn't have Mother and her luxurious St. Moritz suite to return to. Even the innovator, Mother was off to Soviet Russia with Irma Weitzenkorn, pausing first to visit Latvian relatives in Dvinsk where it all began. This was in the days when Red Russia was not considered worthy of diplomatic recognition—that would come a year or two later with the new spirit of F.D.R. How did Mother arrange to travel through the Soviet Union before American passports were accepted? I could picture her marching past border patrols and insisting that the secret police guide her to her hotel in Leningrad. Maybe she used her gold Paramount pass or explained that her mission was to show my short stories to Maxim Gorky. If she had brought Gorky home to Hollywood to write screenplays for Father, it would not have surprised me.

Passport or no passport, Mother was ready for Russia. She had read Steffens on the Revolution—"I have seen the future and it works"—and the pioneer books of Maurice Hindus (*Red Bread, Humanity Uprooted*) and she didn't have any qualms about coping with Stalin. In her mind, he couldn't be any more difficult than Louie B. Mayer, whom she had eating out of her hand.

From the moment I arrived I loved the look of Deerfield, the aged-wood no-nonsense architecture of the 17th-century houses, the green meadows stretching to the great New England river, the Connecticut. Because my hometown Hollywood was so new—a beanstalk sprung up in the Twenties—I felt a reverence for the past, the old farmhouses, the village cemetery where old-fashioned homilies engraved in weathered stone stood over venerable Ebenezers and Abigails, and for the river that ran all the way from northern New Hampshire to Long Island Sound, making New England history while our California was still an Eden for aborigines.

But of course I hadn't come to Deerfield merely for scenery and tradition. There was a formidable headmaster and a demanding curriculum. I had never been exposed to that kind of tight-minded discipline; my natural response was to resist it and hate it. A loud morning bell brought rude awakening; we were herded (or so it felt to me) to group meals of what seemed prison fare, like porridge for breakfast and creamed beef on toast for lunch. I loathed having to make my bed and keep my room neat, and worst of all having to submit to the routine inspection of the house proctor. I had read enough Dickens to feel like an overgrown David Copperfield. Or Tom Brown at Rugby. No, I wasn't caned, or hazed. But in those early weeks, feeling so far from home and out of place, I took a psychological beating that made me check off the ten weeks until Christmas vacation like a prisoner counting down to the end of his sentence.

My classmates, nearly all from eastern private schools, treated me with patronizing curiosity, making me feel like a pointy-eared Martian who had mysteriously materialized in their midst. They had never encountered anyone from Hollywood before; their questions were tinged with sexual curiosity mingled with haughty disdain: They assumed that I had been raised on orgies with uninhibited starlets. Walking blindfold on a high wire, I tried to conceal the ridiculous fact that I never so much as held hands with a wicked young would-be. I had to pretend to be an accomplished Lothario or they would have thought me even stranger than I appeared. As it was, being Jewish, a stammerer, from exotic Hollywood, a newcomer to a senior class that had been together for three years, I was an obvious target for schoolboy wit. If I were not actually persona non grata, I felt myself to be persona barely grata.

At night in my monastic cell I would confess in letters to Maurice my subterfuge and my panic when hallmates asked me why I didn't have a picture of my girl, or of some of those movie kittens with whom I let them believe I frolicked. "When I come home for Christmas, I have to get a picture of a girl," I wrote Maurice, who was caught in a similar dilemma among five hundred Stanford coeds.

The heart and soul and spine and sinew of Deerfield was Mr. Frank Boyden, always referred to, English-school fashion, as "The Quid," a strong-willed, puritanical headmaster fanatical in his devotion to his school, having built it from a modest country school to a New England "prep" rivaling such long-established institutions as Hotchkiss, Choate, and Loomis. Revered as an outstanding example of New England scholarship, he considered himself a molder of young men. But in me he found unruly clay. The general attitude of the student body toward him was an amalgam of admiration, awe, and fear. Again I was made to feel strangely alone because, while others might grumble about the strictness of The Quid, I was the only one who really detested him.

Our first meeting was not exactly propitious. Father had suggested that if Deerfield lacked motion-picture equipment, he would provide projectors and a supply of Paramount films for weekend entertainment. Mr. Boyden was not overwhelmed by this offer. He would have to think about it, he said, because his time was too valuable to spend at the movies, and he did not regard them as healthy influence on the student body. I may have been hypersensitive, but in his contempt for *movies* I sensed a veiled, genteel anti-Semitism. But there was one thing movies *could* do, he acknowledged. If I could get my hands on a movie camera, I could photograph our football team in action. It might be helpful to the coaches and players to study their mistakes. And scenes of our games could be shown at the Sunday evening "sings."

The Quid was an avid booster of Deerfield athletics. It was an open secret that along with our gentleman athletes he recruited players from the working-class neighborhoods of mill towns like Holyoke and Haverhill. Most of these "ringers" lived with me in the Old Dorm to which the sloppier members of the student body were consigned. The "good boys," housed in the New Dorm, kept their rooms immaculate and were proud of the sharp creases along the edge of their beds. Visitors were invariably given a tour of the New Dorm.

Although The Quid was a stern disciplinarian, he clearly pampered the star football, baseball, and basketball players. That was fine with me, as I got along with them better than I did with the snooty aristocrats. It had been the caddies with whom I had gotten along best at Adolph Zukor's luxurious estate. And back in Hollywood I had always felt most at home with the prizefighters, the mailroom boys, and the grips. I don't know where I got my egalitarianism but it seemed deeply rooted, in ghettos where I had never lived, in pogroms I had suffered only vicariously through Mother's vague accounts and her brother Joe's painful memories.

My first Sunday at Deerfield triggered my first confrontation with The Quid. When I heard that religious services were mandatory, I went to Mr. Boyden and asked if I could be excused on the basis of my religious differences. He fixed me with a dour look, and then in a tight voice informed me that Sunday morning services were an obligation of every Deerfield boy, without exception. Deerfield, I was discovering—not unlike Hollywood at the opposite end of the spectrum—was its own world with its own law. Separation of Church and State, or Church and School, stopped at its campus boundaries.

So Sunday mornings I would sit in the rear row, huddled down in hope of escaping The Quid's inquisitorial eye. Concealed behind my prayer book were the Saturday football results; I needed all the time I could get to study comparative scores and mail my predictions to Maurice so he would have them in time for our weekly competition.

When the congregation rose for the traditional hymns, the rebel in me refused to invoke the name of Jesus. Brazenly I would substitute the word "Amos." And instead of mouthing "Amos" discreetly under my breath, the devil within me would increase the volume to make sure the worshippers around me knew I was not conforming. An obedient lad sitting next to me made a face at me and, by way of rebuttal, I pulled out his tie.

On the podium I saw The Quid staring at me in puritanical hatred. After the service he beckoned me to his side. "I know you don't believe in our faith," he intoned, "but at least you can try to be quiet so we can enjoy a solemn ceremony." He had had his eye on me, he warned. If I could not measure up to the high standards of Deerfield, I would force him to write my parents; perhaps I would do better in a western school where students were allowed to wear sloppy clothes, with behavior to match. Like my classmates, he was too genteel to mention Jews as such. But when he referred to me as "you people in Hollywood," the inflection was unmistakable. My resistance was guarded. His was the hated voice of authority, reminding me of my little war with Rabbi Magnin five years earlier. But this was different. With Mother in Russia and Father hardly even a part-time parent, I felt a need to put down new roots in this older, greener part of the world.

Three factors saved me from quitting or cracking those first ten weeks. Even though I couldn't measure up to the football varsity, I played substitute guard on the second team. I made flying tackles with gusto if not precision. I boasted to my diary that I was so covered with bumps and bruises that it was painful to crawl into bed. At a magic show one evening I fell so soundly asleep that my classmates thought I was hypnotized and did not appreciate my condition until the mystified magician failed to bring me to.

In one game, against the bulky but slow Massachusetts Aggie freshmen, I had an uncanny experience that calls to mind an Irwin Shaw football story. A willing but uninspired lineman until that particular day, I got into the game earlier than usual when a first-stringer was injured. Suddenly I felt that I could read the mind of the opposing quarterback and anticipate every play. I would charge forward, lay back and wait, or move horizontally to the other side of the line, making tackle after tackle. As my confidence grew, I felt invincible, a one-man line, able to stop their lumbering fullback and their speedier halfbacks. When I trotted to the sidelines in happy exhaustion, the embraces and loving slaps on the rump from my teammates brought tears of joy. Here at last was the athletic acclaim for which I had hungered all through high school. I didn't even mind waiting on table that evening because I was serving my peers in a new atmosphere of social acceptance.

On the following Friday afternoon our coach, convinced that he had discovered a new defensive star, put me into the starting lineup. The first play came right at me. I set myself, and let the ball-carrier slip away. The opposing quarterback decided he had found a patsy, and how right he was. Intuitive as I had been in the previous game, I was now a victim of every trap and feint. The superman of the week before was exposed as a one-day wonder. Halfway through the quarter I was benched. No more embraces, no more ego-stroking, shouts of "Attaway t' go, Schulie!" I was back where I belonged, a marginal athlete, reduced to writing anguishedly, "Why do we always come so close and always fail?"

The second factor that kept me at Deerfield was Mutt Ray. Mutt came from what was called "a good family," which is how they described the inheritors of "old money," but what was important to me was his all-around ability on the playing field. As our fullback he hit the opposing line with a ferocity that belied his size, dragging tacklers along with him yard after yard. In those hardier days when a single team played both offense and defense, he was a furious linebacker. In game after game the Deerfield line would bend or break, only to have our valiant captain plug the holes. Bulling his way to precious touchdowns, then saving the game with crushing open-field tackles, Mutt Ray was the consummate sixty-minute hero. At final gun he would often sink into unconsciousness, having survived the last quarter on guts and instinct. How I envied him as he was carried from the sidelines to the infirmary, to be treated for his weekly concussion.

Armed with the movie camera Father had provided, I was allowed to record the game from the sidelines, my third bridge to Deerfield acceptance. There was one glorious moment in the Loomis game when Ray went hurtling out of bounds, slamming my camera against my forehead and knocking me over. My head was pounding but I jumped quickly to my feet, proud to have a hand in pulling him back to his, unforgettably involved in this moment of violence. Ray winked at me and I said, "'Way to go, Mutt!"

Ray's heroics weren't limited to the football field. While the housemaster—pink-faced, bespectacled, Harvardian Mr. Allen—scrupulously saw to it that lights were out and the Old Dorm locked for the night at ten, presumably safe against the shades of Mohawk Indians left over from 17th-century raids, Mutt would be out on the prowl in search of warmhearted farm girls. Early in the morning he would creep back through a main-floor window left open for him. A genuine folk hero, he could float through space when he wanted to, and see in the dark. Of course part of his bravado was the confidence that even if he were detected, he would not suffer the punishment awaiting the ordinary Deerfield boy. The Quid loved his Deerfield eleven, and without Mutt Ray we would have been the doormat of the Mohawk Valley.

Maybe because I was such a sorry workhorse of a football player, maybe because there was something titillating about my unlikely Hollywood background, maybe because I worshipped him even more fervently than did my eastern classmates, Mutt would do me the honor of dropping in to bull in my room. Inevitably, other hallmates would appear. I began to feel a grudging acceptance. I was still teased about my stammering, my name, my life in Hollywood, and—without their ever daring to give it a name—my Jewishness. But after a month or so I did not seem quite as ludicrous or as untouchable and they in turn did not seem quite as reserved and unreachable.

There had been one early breakthrough. On the first day of school we had been encouraged to introduce ourselves to our dormitory-mates. Passing a tall, earnest-faced young man in the hall, I did my best. "Sch...Sch...Sch...oolberg, La...La...La...Hollywood" (like all stammerers, when I couldn't make it with one consonant I tried another), I offered; to which my classmate responded, "Eee...Eee...E ...ton T-t-t-Tarbell, B...buh...buh...BANGor!" I had been teased that way all my life, and was ready to strike Master T-t-Tarbell. Until I realized that here was a schoolmate who stammered even more convulsively than I did.

Since misery welcomes company, we would spend hours in our rooms at night speculating on why we couldn't talk like normal people. Why did we never stammer when we sang? Or when we were alone together? Years later Eaton Tarbell was to become one of New England's more distinguished architects. But I still see him with his earnest face twisted into verbal spasm. Strangely, it was the same look he would have at the end of the mile run when he performed on the same track team where I ran my dogged 880s. At the end, grasping for breath, we also discovered that exhaustion was a cure for our affliction. We never doubted that our disability was psychological. But there did seem to be physical solutions. Why, when we were unable to sound the opening word of a sentence, did it help to pound our feet on the floor like a jazz musician working himself up to the beat? Or similarly, to slap our hands against our thighs until the desired word broke through the barrier? And why, when no other words came out at all, were four-letter cries of frustration so easy to release?

Eaton Tarbell and Mutt Ray and my mouth-drying confrontations with Mr. Boyden gave form and substance to those first ten weeks. I would confide to my diary exactly how I felt about the self-righteous Quid. "All the athletes around here pull some awfully raw stuff, but I, for only trivial wrongs, have to be called down every day or so. Boyden wants boys to be subdued—the only-answer-when-spoken-to types of the old Mayflower days. Go to hell, Frank!"

The first semester at Deerfield was a useful lesson in hypocrisy. For while I was giving Mr. Boyden the humble *Yes sir* and *No sir* treatment, going through the motions of the apologetic penitent, I was seething inside, wishing I could use his smug ministerial face as my punching bag. It is what we call manners. We had manners in Hollywood, too, but these were more genteel (and gentile) and more sophisticated—in other words, more full of sophistry and hypocrisy. It was one of the things I had been sent to Deerfield to learn: how not to walk hard or talk loud, how to drop a scrim over my feelings.

My most serious confrontation with The Quid had come just before the Christmas vacation, when I was feeling a little giddy at the thought of being released from Deerfield discipline and joining Mother, who was returning from Russia, on the four-day journey home. Mutt Ray had suggested that after lights-out we sneak over to the mess hall and raid the huge icebox in the pantry. I was already in Mr. Boyden's black book, but how could I resist this clandestine invitation from the great Mutt Ray? Making our way into the pantry in the dark, we gorged ourselves on

412

illicit muffins and jams, ice cream and cake. But climbing back into the Old Dorm, disaster struck. Mutt made it through without difficulty, but just below the window I dropped a jar of orange marmalade and a box of saltines I had hoped to squirrel away for after-lights-out feasts. The delay and my scurrying in the bushes brought to the window a most unhappy Mr. Allen. As much as he tried to meet us halfway, this time he would have to send me to Mr. Boyden.

The Quid was terrible in his wrath. "He was so sore he was black in the face," I reported to the diary. His voice wore a long dark robe as he sat in judgment. "After the first few months I had hoped you might become more accustomed to our ways. If there is no improvement in your deportment after you return from vacation, I will not be able to recommend you for Dartmouth." I had retreated to my monastic room and added a cryptic note to my diary: "The Quid—GDHBH," which stood for God Damn His Bastard Hide, the ultimate epithet in Maurice's and my lexicon.

It was maddening to think that my fate, or at least my chances of moving on to Dartmouth, depended entirely on his judgment. Because no matter how well I did scholastically—and I was beginning to hold my own—The Quid had the power to bury my application. And now, despite Mr. Boyden, I felt a strong attraction to New England as a place and as a culture. Indeed, even Mrs. Boyden herself was a refreshing counterbalance to her Calvinistic mate. Attractively homely, in the style of Eleanor Roosevelt, she was an outgoing spirit, with a tolerance for others that made me wonder how she and The Quid ever got together. Because my mind was stubbornly resistant to algebra, or any other form of mathematics, a subject she taught, she offered to tutor me in her spare time. When I told her how useless I knew algebra would be to my life, she didn't lecture me about my Hollywood sloppiness of mind. Instead she took an eminently practical approach. Even if it made no sense for Dartmouth to demand that I get high marks in mathematics in order to be accepted, that was their rule and if Dartmouth was my choice I would have to make it my rule as well. "It's a little like taking castor oil," she insisted. "You open your mouth, Mother spoons it in, you make a face, and in a minute or two it's all forgotten." Mrs. Boyden was determined to spoon in enough algebra, geometry, and trig to get me by the College Boards: "Even if you forget it the next day as you probably will. For years I've been coaching students who hate math. I happen to love math, but it's like cauliflower or turnips—lots of people hate them, too."

"I can't swallow turnips," I said.

"I'll teach you to swallow math." Her smile came through to me encouragingly. In helping me feel I could cope with math, she also encouraged me to think I could cope with Deerfield. I was on the school paper, and while I looked down on the weekly *Scroll* as an overly sedate weekly compared to my jazzier *Blue-and-White* daily, I was proud to have made the staff. But the contrast between West Coast and East Coast journalism threatened to end my New England career almost as soon as it began. A football game between Fordham and Bucknell had resulted in two fatalities—Murphy, a former Deerfield star, dying of internal injuries a few days after the game, and his substitute Zymanski succumbing from a brain injury two days later. Two other Fordham players had been seriously injured. The Bucknell line had been recruited from the hard-muscled mining towns of western Pennsylvania, and the contest had been what present-day commentators like to refer to as "physical," for which read downright vicious. The two deaths had brought the fatalities for the season to 29! Although I still loved the feeling of trying to drive my body between opposing linemen to get at the ball-carrier, the neophyte writer in me, as well as the moralist, came up with a fiery editorial in which I compared the football stadium crowd to the bloodthirsty hordes in the Roman Colosseum rooting for the lions against the Christians.

That evening I was honored with a visit from the editor of the *Scroll,* the 250-pound "Mac" MacConaughy. Although his father was president of Wesleyan University in nearby Middletown, Mac did not at all resemble the snooty, upper-class easterners who looked down their Aryan noses at me. He enjoyed ribald jokes and Latin double entendres. The strict discipline of the school, a constant irritant to me, was to Mac merely a source of cynical amusement.

Mac flopped down on my bed, threatening to collapse it, and tossed back to me my white-heat editorial, blithely titled "Roman Holiday." "Afraid we can't use it, Schulie. Nice piece of writing. But God almighty, if I ran this in the *Scroll,* The Quid would pee in his pants. We have to write it like this: All Deerfield mourns the untimely passing of one of her outstanding sons, Robert Murphy, etcetera etcetera. All quiet and digni-fied. Make it sound like an unfortunate accident that could happen in any activity. Not like a lynching—the way you wrote it—or as if the entire Bucknell team should be indicted for premeditated murder. I wish I could run it. It would be a hell of a lot of fun. But The Quid would get my old man on the phone, and the next thing I know I can't even make it to Wesleyan."

I was discouraged. "Roman Holiday" was the strongest piece of writing I had ever done. It combined my fascination with American football with my growing awareness of American violence. If I couldn't score with a piece on a Deerfield boy dying for Fordham . . . "Look, Schulie, stop worrying about staying on the staff. Hell, you *are* the staff. You see the drool we get from all the others—" It was true that I had begun to rewrite all the limp leads and stodgy pieces in which whatever feeble news there was lay buried three or four paragraphs into the story. Mac turned to me more and more until he and I basically edited the paper together. But I had to be careful to keep a tight rein on my style, or Mac would be on my back for writing "Hollywood."

Words and writing had begun to share equal time with football and track and the compulsion to make a team. Mac delighted in using words he thought others would not comprehend. "Schulie, I think your piece would be more efficacious if it were a little less polemical, as well as less quixotic," he would say. I would nod wisely, and then secretly hurry to my dictionary to see what in hell he was talking about. Any word heard or read that I did not instantly recognize would be entered in my handwritten dictionary. In my first ten weeks at Deerfield it had grown to a thousand words I had not known on arrival. Instead of counting sheep to invite sleep I would mumble, "*Salacious . . . euphemistic . . . diaphanous . . .*" I began to realize that I had been talking and writing with a kindergarten vocabulary. Even with all the reading my parents had exposed me to, somehow I must have skipped over the words I did not know. Now they jumped up from the page and challenged me to understand them, and make them my own.

Later I would begin to understand the difference between English and American writing, learning how Mark Twain and Frank Norris and Sherwood Anderson had prepared the ground for Ernest the Strong. But in those early months at Deerfield I was happy with my *elegiacs* and *anomalies.* Already I had begun publishing short stories in the Deerfield monthly *Stockade.* A story about an old prizefighter and one about the ghosts of the victims of the Deerfield Massacre interviewed in the local cemetery established me as the school's most distinguished author, an honor not unlike that of Robinson Crusoe's winning the mayoralty of his island.

Heady with success, I decided to plunge on in the literary world.

Before I left home, Mrs. Stanton, who taught English at U.S.C., had been sufficiently impressed with my story "Ugly" to suggest I try to write a book. And my parents, with their quite different styles of enthusiasm, had agreed. The pressure was on me. And time was running. I was closing in on eighteen. If I was to be a book writer, I had better get going.

45

BUT WHAT DID I have to write about? All I knew about was growing up in Hollywood. And even though I had made some notes on Von Stroheim and Von Sternberg, on Eisenstein and Clara Bow, I knew I wasn't ready. What made me choose the subject I did remains one of those social mysteries. All I remember is that it was triggered by a book I happened to read, recommended by one of the writers who came to our house, the hard-drinking rebel Jim Tully, who liked to grouse to Mother about the honest books Hollywood was afraid to make into films. One of these was *The Autobiography of an Ex-Colored Man* by James Weldon Johnson.

It did what good books are supposed to do. I could not put it out of my mind. It made me want to write a book of my own. It is about a light-skinned "colored man," a classical musician, a cultural aristocrat traveling in the South who follows a crowd to a lynching he is only able to watch because the redneck posse takes him for white. Johnson describes the victim dragged in between two horsemen, his eyes glazed with fear and pain, already more dead than alive. No mention is made of his crime; in this atmosphere of mindless violence, it doesn't really matter. A primitive gallows is set up, but before the poor wretch can be dragged to it, an even more vicious idea takes possession of the mob: "Burn the nigger! Burn the nigger!"

While the author looks on in numb horror, the limp black body is chained to the post, drenched with gasoline, and set on fire. Cheers and sadistic laughter mingle with the screams and groans of the dying man.

417

Johnson looks around at the fiends who accept his terrified passivity for compliance, and there and then decides on a coward's escape. He will cease to be a black man. It is too dangerous and too degrading. He will go north and pass as a member of the ruling majority. This he does successfully until he falls in love with a beautiful white girl attracted to him by his sensitivity and his classical musicianship. He feels he cannot marry her without revealing his racial secret. When he does, she leaves him, bereft. Eventually they are reunited, and he lives a life of white respectability. But in the end, seeing "a small but gallant band of colored men publicly fighting for their race," he is made to feel small, weak, selfish, and empty. He has, in the final line of the book, which went into my diary and indelibly into my impressionable young mind, "sold his birthright for a mess of pottage."

The closest I had ever been to a lynching was the playful if sometimes spiteful goosing of Oscar the Bootblack at Paramount Studio. And Oscar would not scream in pain but in feigned, obsequious delight. But as I read the nightmare episode in the Johnson autobiography, I pictured Oscar chained to a stake and writhing in agony as the fire devoured his flesh. And I decided to try writing a story about it. Aware that I lacked the details of a firsthand observer, I chose to tell it through the eyes of a child carried on the shoulders of his father and not really comprehending what he is seeing. When the *Stockade* rejected it as unfit material for our precious magazine, I sent it to Mrs. Stanton, who thought it quite well done but of course in need of rewriting. With this meager encouragement, I decided on a bolder course. I would write a book about lynching, and about the persecution of the Negroes in the South. With the courage of my ignorance and the benign arrogance of youth, I wrote to Clarence Darrow. I had not yet read any of his books, but I had heard of him through my parents as a fighter for the right and a defender of underdogs.

Whatever private doubts Clarence Darrow may have had about the abilities of a prep-school teenager to write a book on lynching and the virulence of white supremacy, he answered promptly in his own handwriting:

> You can get all the information there is by writing Mr. Walter White, 69 Fifth Avenue, New York City. Sec., National Association for the Advancement of Colored People. (The N.A.A.C.P.) I am glad you are doing this work. More power to you.

A letter to Walter White also brought a quick response. One pamphlet enlightened me as to the makeup of the N.A.A.C.P. My James Weldon Johnson was a vice-president, W. E. B. DuBois edited the *Crisis,* its principal publication, and Roy Wilkins assisted Mr. White. Another pamphlet listed the *recorded* lynchings over the past forty years. Averaging as many as one a week, in the first six months of 1931 there had been *twenty-nine.* Although rape of white women was the accepted justification, fewer than 25 percent had interracial sexual implications. "Rape," according to eyewitness reports, could be anything from a familiar greeting to a questionable glance. Negroes had been lynched for arguing with white landowners over their share of the crops, for daring to strike back at their tormentors, or simply for being "uppity."

The statistics shook the mind, but the case histories told in down-home language by the families of victims stabbed the heart. Klansmen and night raiders had gone out on "nigger hunts," torturing their victims before burning them or tying ropes to their necks and throwing them over the sides of bridges. A 12-year-old had been hacked to death because a white woman had complained that he had talked to her "disrespectfully." The few whites who dared stand up to the fury of the mob were treated with equal brutality. The N.A.A.C.P. believed in fighting for justice in the courts, inside the system. But the lawyers they sent down to defend the victims of legal lynching—the thousands of blacks railroaded to Death Row and to chain gangs for life without even the trappings of a fair trial—were themselves threatened by lynch mobs not in the hate-ridden hamlets of Alabama, Georgia, and Mississippi, but even in the courtrooms themselves. Redneck judges openly sympathized with the white prosecutors, while the white audience booed and hissed the northern lawyers as if they were attending a 50-cent melodrama.

Most of these lawyers, it seemed to me, were from New York and had Jewish names. As I read the press accounts of their attempts to speak out for their illiterate and terrified clients, I tried to put myself in their place. After all, if I were going to write my book on lynching, the first of its kind—for amazingly I could find no single volume devoted entirely to this grisly subject—I really should attend one of those trials, and get the smell and feel of the subhuman mobs who terrorized the rural South and made a mockery of the Emancipation Proclamation and the 14th, 15th, and 16th Amendments.

In Father's projection room we had run Griffith's *The Birth of a*

Nation, that twisted epic glorifying the Klan in the days of Reconstruction. But I had thought of burning crosses and charred black bodies as part of the dark history of the post-Civil War period. Until I happened upon that lynch scene in the Johnson book and then reinforced it by reams of material on *this* year's atrocities, I had not imagined that the practice was just as prevalent in the early 1930s as it had been in the late 1860s. Lynch "law," I discovered, was simply a way of circumventing the abolitionist victory in the Civil War. And if the Negro dared complain about his condition, he was marked as a "bad nigger," inviting the treatment that had terrified James Weldon Johnson into going north and passing for white.

The N.A.A.C.P. reports made it clear that the fifty-odd lynchings every year were only the bloody tip of a gruesome iceberg, for local sheriffs in league with the night riders were not disposed to cite the lynchings to higher authorities. And the families of the black victims were almost always terrified into silence for fear of receiving the same treatment.

But, I learned from this extracurricular reading, a new case was scandalizing the Negro, liberal/radical, and literary communities, and the European intelligentsia, even though it had been largely ignored in our regular press. The latest victims were called the Scottsboro Boys, and although I had never heard of them until that fall, they were to become a cause célèbre of the Thirties as polarizing as Sacco-Vanzetti in the Twenties. Indeed, many of the writers speaking out in support of the nine teenage Scottsboro prisoners had also protested the execution of the two Italian immigrants. I recognized Heywood Broun, Edna St. Vincent Millay, Theodore Dreiser, Lincoln Steffens, Dorothy Parker, Sherwood Anderson, Sinclair Lewis.... To Mother's and Father's credit I was already aware of all these writers, and had met at least half of them.

I sent for everything available on the Scottsboro Boys. They were nine black back-country youths aged thirteen to nineteen, jobless and destitute, who rode a freight car in search of work in a larger town. A fistfight between them and young white hoboes who objected to sharing the boxcar had resulted in one of the white boys either jumping off or being thrown off the train and phoning the local police. When the nine "Scottsboro Boys" were taken off the train and arrested at the next stop, it was revealed that two of the "white boys" were girls dressed in baggy overalls like their fellow rod-riders.

Apparently this was all the evidence necessary to build a case that the nine black boys had raped the two white girls. The black youths had tried to explain that they did not even know the girls had been masquerading as boys. Accused of rape, the nine boys were rushed to trial in the usually sleepy Alabama hamlet of Scottsboro, while a mob of ten thousand outraged rednecks shouted for their blood. In three days they were convicted by an all-white jury and sentenced to death. Even when one of the girls—both of them had police records for prostitution—wrote a letter to a boyfriend: "Those policemen made me tell a lie . . . those Negroes did not touch me . . . I wish those Negroes are not burnt on account of me . . . ," the death sentence stood.

Mother was confident that I was working my way toward a social classic like *Uncle Tom's Cabin* or *The Jungle*, Sinclair's seminal exposé of the Chicago stockyards. But she thought I should confine my research to the pamphlets and clippings from the N.A.A.C.P. Jews were only one step up from "niggers" in the lizard eyes of the K.K.K., and she hoped I wasn't serious about attending the next Scottsboro trial, for an appeal was already underway. I may have sounded like a teenage John Brown, but except for confiding my interest in the lynching book to the maverick Mac MacConaughy, I had been careful to keep my project to myself. I was already considered peculiar enough by the "good" boys of the school. In fact, one of them had set off a stink-bomb in my room just before Christmas vacation, and the odor it gave off smacked as much of anti-Semitism as it did of rotten eggs.

My cause had not been helped greatly by Mother's visit to Deerfield on her return from Russia, and her willingness to address the student body on the subject of "The Russian Experiment." There was something delicious about a Dvinsk-to-Rivington-Street-to-Hollywood socialite leading that precious New England student body and its rather stuffy faculty through the minefields of Soviet reality. But I'm not sure I appreciated the humor of the situation. I was apprehensive that her favorable reaction to Comrade Stalin's Great Experiment would further alienate the Coolidge-minded Mr. Boyden.

But I must say this for Mom, she began with a charming anecdote. Sentimental about her first visit to her Latvian relatives since her forced departure as an infant, she pictured herself as a Lady Bountiful bestowing riches among the impoverished. Leaving behind her expensive gowns, furs, and jewels, and "dressing down" appropriately for her reunion with these backwater relations, she brought boxes of discarded coats and clothes, and bags of canned goods, cheeses, and salamis to help her poor relatives through the winter.

Arriving at the railroad station in Riga, she was approached by a uniformed chauffeur who led her to a Rolls-Royce limousine. She was driven to a 19th-century mansion far more imposing than the one she had left at 525 Lorraine. A uniformed footman greeted her at the door and helped her in with her baggage, including the hand-me-down clothes and the food packages. To her amazement, her relatives, the Schiffs, turned out to be one of the wealthiest families in the Latvian capital. The finest caviar was served before dinner, the finest wines poured by a brace of butlers for each course, and five-star cognac in the spacious paneled den. By this time it was Mother who was feeling like the poor relation as she lamely tried to explain that the secondhand clothes and tins of food were brought along as gifts for the indigent on the other side of the Russian border.

Indeed, in this Adeline-in-Wonderland turnabout, Mrs. Schiff offered Mother one of her own fur coats because she was afraid her American cousin would not be warm enough!

Mother was an exotic figure as she stood there in front of the Deerfield assembly talking of her self-propelled tour of unknown Russia, where no American civilians traveled in 1931. "I have always been something of a socialist," she began, and I could feel Mr. Boyden wince a little. That was one of the few winces I ever shared with him. And then she adopted that vague, slightly superior tone she always employed when she ventured into subjects she had not really mastered. She mentioned her socialist friends like George Sokolsky on the Lower East Side, seemingly unaware that George had swung so far to the right that he was even in favor of Japanese aggression in China. And somehow she had convinced herself that she had met Leon Trotsky when he was a New York refugee from the 1905 Revolution. That Stalin had cast out Trotsky in a bitter power struggle did not seem to deter Mother from her feeling of identification with what might be called the Sokolsky-Trotsky-Lenin-Stalin Revolution.

And yet, she did bring us a firsthand impression of the new Russia that none of us had had before. In the Old Russia of her infancy, she explained, in the days of the Czar and the Russian nobility, there were mainly two classes, the Haves and the Have-nots—on one side the city rich and the great landowners, on the other the proletarians and the serfs. Now the upper class had been swept away. The cities of Moscow

422

and Leningrad looked rather drab, but no one seemed to be starving. And in this year when so many of our own people were out of work, everybody there did seem to have a job. She had visited some of their homes, and while people lived in one room or two at the most, almost everyone she talked to seemed to think life was much better than in the days of the Czar. One of the things that impressed her was the condition of women, who had been treated like chattel before the Revolution and now were able to work in factories or get office jobs on the basis of their ability. Here Mother's old suffragist blood beat a little faster, as she spoke of having tea with a woman doctor, and also with a film technician who assured her that women were now being encouraged to follow their own careers in a way that was still denied them in capitalist countries.

Of course (Mother warmed to her subject), if you go to Russia expecting luxuries or even the middle-class comforts we take for granted, you would think life is still very hard and harsh. People have to queue up even to buy necessities, and if you travel to Russia you should bring your own cigarettes because they are impossible to buy, and also matches, soap, and even (she put it gently) sanitary tissue. But the main quality she found in Russia was hope. They had embarked on a great Five Year Plan to industrialize and modernize the country, and the people seemed to understand and accept that they would all have to sacrifice now in order to have a better life later.

Portrait of Mother as Joe Stalin's advance-woman to New England: This may have been the most favorable talk about the Soviet Union ever made in those parts. She extolled the prison system where capital punishment had been abolished and prisoners were taught useful trades, and spoke sympathetically of the liberal divorce system, whereby a partner to a marriage could end the contract simply by sending a letter to the proper authorities. This time I could almost feel Mr. Boyden's wince quivering through the hall.

Since Mother was identified as the wife of the American film producer who had offered to employ the great Eisenstein (his Hollywood frustrations were discreetly passed over), she had been invited to the Moscow film studio, and had met the famous Pudovkin and other talented directors. Even though their work was devoted to themes of social progress in step with the Five Year Plan, she assured her audience that these subjects did not appear to be forced on them, since they felt it their social responsibility to contribute their art to the success of the Plan. "Almost everyone I talked to," Mother assured her politely startled but attentive audience, "told me that no one was forcing them to do what they were doing. They were making the pictures they wanted to make and that they felt the public wanted to see." Mother had even talked to the head of the studio about Father's dream of making *War and Peace* as an American-Russian co-production.

As for the theater arts, Mother was happy to report, the classical traditions had not been swept away as most of us would think. She had watched *Swan Lake* from a red velvet box at the Bolshoi Theater, and traditional Russian operas like *Eugene Onegin* were intact, as well as the great plays of Chekhov and Gogol, Shakespeare, and even Eugene O'Neill. She had seen some excellent contemporary Russian theater as well, and although young playwrights she had met admitted that there was a certain amount of censorship, they had asked her if capitalist censorship would not prevent any Hollywood artists from presenting a positive picture of the communist system, or even a true picture of how the jobless and hungry were struggling to survive our capitalist Depression.

Of course she had found little holes in the garment of Stalinist perfection. The Russian ruble was not stable, and people would sidle up to her to trade their money for dollars on the black market. Even though she was wearing only a modest wool coat, Russian women would pause on the street to finger it admiringly, and one was so bold as to beg for it. On her last day in Moscow, a Jewish poet she had met at the film studio came nervously to her room and begged her to smuggle out a letter to distant relatives in Brooklyn—to evade the GPU. He also asked if she could help him get out of Russia by arranging a job for him in Father's Hollywood studio. She had agreed to take the letter and "loaned" him some precious American cash.

A year before the election of F.D.R. and the subsequent recognition of the Soviet Union, Mother had chalked up another "first." Having discovered Freud, John Dewey, Queen Anne furniture, and—God help us!—Sylvia Sidney, now she had discovered Soviet Russia. I confess I squirmed a little as she reminded her staid New England audience of our background in a ragged Jewish *shtetl* on the banks of the Dvina. Selfishly, I knew it would not make my acceptance at Deerfield any easier. And yet, as I watched her from the back of the hall, I had to admit that there was something gallant about her sense of adventure. When there was no way to get from here to there, no embassies or consulates to help her on her way, she was the one who made it to a land where Mr.

424

Hearst assured us they ate capitalists for breakfast. And she had come back with the courage to get up before an audience of WASPs and tell it as she thought she had seen it.

As our train rushed us westward for Christmas vacation at what seemed a breakneck speed of 75 miles an hour, I spent hours with a new book Mother had brought me from Moscow, *Short Stories out of Soviet Russia*. There were the good old standbys, Gorky and Boris Pilnyak, but also sharp new writers I had never heard of—Isaac Babel, identified as a "protégé of Gorky's"; and a satirist who dared to pull the whiskers of the Soviet bureaucracy, Zoshchenko. Far into the night I kept the light on in my Pullman berth, reading and dreaming of the day when I could be included in such an anthology. Ever since I had left Hollywood in August I had kept Ludwig's *Genius and Character* close at hand, reading, underlining, and daydreaming of literary glory. Finally I had come to the impassioned chapter on Balzac. I saw him in a loose, monklike dressing gown and nightcap, writing in frenzy through the night, trying to capture on paper the entire society of mid-19th-century France, a social realist in a day of romanticism. I copied into my notebook: "Today the writer has replaced the priest . . . he consoles, condemns, prophesies. His voice does not resound in the nave of a cathedral, it spreads thunderously from one end of the world to the other. . . . Many a word weighs more than many a victory. . . ."

When we pulled in to Albuquerque for the half-hour layover, I no longer hurried into the station as in times past. "Stayed near the train because I couldn't bear to look at those poor Indians sitting along the entrance to the Harvey House selling their ten-cent-store drums and bows," I confided to my diary. What we had done to those Indians I did not yet understand. I only knew that they had been reduced to something uncomfortably close to begging, that their trinkets were a mockery of what had been a strong culture, and that somehow *we*—white American civilization—had approached them in a spirit of lynch-and-destroy not so different from our treatment of the Negroes I had been reading about in the booklets of the N.A.A.C.P.

46

BUT IF THIS sounds as though Mother and I now spent our time worrying about the oppressed, or the future of the Five Year Plan, it is misleading. As the *Super Chief* rolled across the home-state border, the diary cheerfully shifts gears from Balzac and Babel to: "California looked marv. The sun was out and the orange trees waiting." As was the custom in those days, family and friends did not wait for the train to pull into the old Santa Fe station in downtown Los Angeles, but instead made the hour-long drive to San Bernardino to welcome us home. There were all the familiar faces: Maurice, my tennis partner cousin Phil, gawky Sonya, and plump little Stuart, along with the Jaffes and Dad. Yes, even Father had taken time off from the increasing pressures of the studio to make this sentimental journey. I carefully measured his greeting to Mother.

Home on Lorraine, surrounded by the familiar servants, pets, and pigeons, I was assured by Aunt Milly that Father would be living with us again. Since both parents seemed so anxious to please me, I wondered if I should stay home to hold our fractured family together. Father rushed back to his office, and I gathered from Uncle Sam, our studio manager, that the situation there was deteriorating. Father was still in charge of all production, but under mounting pressure now that Lasky was out and Zukor no longer in complete command. The Chicago crowd was moving in, and there were rumors that Manny Cohen—assistant to Lasky before deserting Jesse's sinking ship—was being favored to replace Father as production chief.

427

While Mother held her group spellbound with her Russian adventures, I wandered onto sets to greet actor- and director-friends, the camera crews, the grips. They all seemed happy to see me. A good sign, I thought: Father will still in power. We dropped into his projection room to see *Sooky,* a sequel to *Skippy* that seemed almost if not quite as good as the original. After a festive lunch in the commissary where I made my way from table to table, chatting with the stars, kidding with the backlot workmen, we saw another strong Paramount picture, the *Dr. Jekyll and Mr. Hyde* I knew so well from the story conferences.

Maybe, I hoped, if Father could keep on turning out pictures like these, the studio crisis would blow over. Freddie March was so convincing in the film that I decided to interview him for our Deerfield paper. He was shooting another picture now and, always amiable, never the kind of star who gave Father bad dreams, he invited me to drop by his dressing room. I waited on the set for him to finish his scene. When he strode to his dressing room, a pretty extra hurried in ahead of me. I stood there staring at the door: Nothing had changed in my absence.

When I did get into the dressing room, I found the true Jekyll behind Mr. Hyde. March was a thinking actor and a considerate man, and instead of brushing me off as a kid reporter or the boss's son who had to be tolerated, he spoke seriously and at length about his profession, and about the difference in demand and discipline between stage acting and working before a camera. In the first place, he explained, you have to think as if every member of the audience is sitting in the front row. Sometimes in the theater you have to do things which are a little too broad for first row center but perfect for the balcony; in other words, you have to play a little larger than life. On film, as Gary Cooper had sensed, you had to play smaller. But what really made screen acting more complex than stage acting, he went on, is that the continuity of a play carries you along with it; you draw strength from it and from the players around you. In film, since scenes are not shot in continuity but according to all sorts of practical demands (like getting rid of a set even if it includes the opening scene and the climax, or moving back to a studio set when an exterior scene is weathered out), you have to keep the entire script in your head. You have to play a particular scene *as if* you have already played the scenes that precede it in the script, even though they still lie ahead of you in actual production. Of course a good director, a Mamoulian, helps. But if you can't develop the continuity within you, and hold to your own inner line, you are merely doing *Smile—frown—now look slowly back over your shoulder* the way oldtime directors nursed their actors through megaphones in the silent days.

Freddie talked easily and knowledgeably, and as I scribbled it into my notebook I found myself hoping that even an old prude like The Quid wouldn't object to so serious an interview on film acting when I wrote it for the *Scroll.*

It pleased me to hear Freddie describe Father as a pleasure to work with because B.P. was literate and open-minded and, if things went wrong, the kind of studio head an actor could appeal to for intelligent advice. "The only thing he has in common with the other studio moguls is that big cigar," Freddie laughed.

When I went back to my father's office to report my success, his longtime secretary Henrietta Cohn told me not to go in: B.P. was in serious conference. I found that strange, since all my young life I had walked in on Father's conferences.

Back at the Lorraine house a little while later came a frantic phone call from Henrietta. We were not to panic but B.P. had been in a serious auto accident. Although he had been urged not to drive his Lincoln roadster home in what was described as his "condition," he had stubbornly insisted, taking his pal and crony, Zukor's son-in-law Al Kaufman, along with him. It was a drinking bout in his private office that Henrietta had not wanted me to see. Now, in a freak accident, B.P. and Al had fallen out of the car, leaving it to career crazily around and around, bumping into parked cars and knocking down lamp posts. Somehow it had finally come to rest against an obliging tree without doing any further damage. Father and Al had been rushed to the hospital. But by the time we rushed after them, Father was sitting up in his hospital bed puffing on one of his big Upmanns and laughing as he embellished the story of how his huge roadster kept going around and around while he and Al sat in the middle of Third Street, wondering if it was going to run over them, and laughing together like the Katzenjammer Kids.

Every time Father climbed into that giant Lincoln roadster, he was playing Russian roulette. He had an odd habit of stopping on the green light and starting on the red, which often brought him into interesting disputes with rival vehicles. Sometimes he turned on the headlights instead of the ignition and decided that the battery was dead. And though he lived less than ten blocks from the studio, and had driven there and back literally thousands of times, he still had trouble finding his way. his way.

Bruised and sobered, if not subdued, Father was convalescing at home next day, dropping his cigar ashes on Mother's expensive comforter, and staying in touch with his office by phone. Mother had a long face, convinced that with his position already in question at the studio, this latest escapade, gossiped from one end of Hollywood to the other, would put him in greater jeopardy. It triggered one of their familiar arguments. Ad, Ben insisted, was a born worrier. With a facility for self-justification he had developed over the years into a personal art form, he ran down the list of successful Hollywood friends, guilty of far more serious offenses, whose careers had rolled merrily along. The police who had come to the scene had laughed along with Ben and Al at the absurd turn of events. So Louella might run a bitchy item in her column because she wanted to ingratiate herself with L.B., but everybody in town would know she was only doing it to please her boss W.R. (Hearst) whose Marion Davies was an MGM star. And look at Louella's own husband, "Doccy" Martin, who not only was dead drunk every night but staggered to the hospital in that condition to perform operations without knowing whether he was supposed to remove an appendix or a kidney!

The more Mother tried to point out his shortcomings and remind him of the enemies who could undermine his hold on the studio, the more Father boasted that his production record had never been better, the studio and the exhibitors never more solidly behind him, and that he was looking forward to a banner year. Mother flew into a rage, Father raged back, and it was Punch and Judy in Hollywood; only these weren't puppets, these were my parents, this was the home I had been counting off the days at Deerfield to return to again.

Refusing a second day of recuperation, Father insisted on going back to work, bruises and all. Christmas Day found him presiding at the big party in the sunken office. It was a cast of hundreds, if not thousands, with all the glamour and power of Paramount on display, champagne popping for the Lubitsches, Mamoulian, Miriam Hopkins, Claudette Colbert. . . . Young Gary and Cary were there, Marlene dropped in, Adolphe Menjou. . . . Clara Bow, looking a little puffy, made a surprise call. The dapper, gin-complexioned Eddie Sutherland, the young up-and-coming Dave Selznicks, Norman Taurog (the pudgy, sweet-natured director of *Skippy*), the Mankiewicz brothers, even Mother's pals, Peg LeVino and Dorothy Arzner, stopped in. There was the endless popping of corks and the fine wine flowing, the flirtatious laughter and the cutting inside jokes of any high-level Christmas office party.

But there was something special about a Hollywood Christmas party, with so many world-famous people gathered together in one room, some with so much to celebrate and others with so much to fear. America was a grab bag, but everything America did seemed to be magnified in Hollywood. Even as an unformed prep-school boy, I was learning to watch it with questions in my eyes. Father may have had some good friends among all these marquee names lighting up the room. But how many would be here toasting him in bootlegger Eddie Kaye's finest imported champagne if Mother's worst fears were realized and the Chicago group, moving in, decided to push him off the throne?

Meanwhile, as it did every Christmas, a truck had dropped off at our house those outrageously expensive gifts from "Uncle Adolphe" Menjou, "Aunt Nancy" Carroll, and all the other grateful employees on the studio payroll. There had been a time when I still believed in Santa Claus and had been told by Mother that all these celebrated aunts and uncles were Santa's helpers. But now I had learned that Daddy was Santa Claus and would remain so as long as he could hold on to that grand office with the stained-glass windows.

Similar parties were going on in every executive office. I was still the prude who abstained from alcohol and extra girls, and since these were the staples of the festivities, and since I worried about Father's returning home in one piece from this marathon celebration, I couldn't throw myself into it as a homecoming teenager might have been expected to. I dropped in on Felix Young's party, over which he was presiding with the elegance and grace he would soon lend to Hollywood's favorite new restaurant, the Vendôme. Feel always made a great fuss over me, and I was enjoying the attention until I spied Sylvia Sidney among the revelers. Flushed with champagne and studio success, young Sylvia was looking particularly piquant and sexy that day. Again, a primitive desire for revenge and murder crept into my mind. I left the party.

Meanwhile, the holiday charade of parental respectability continued. My parents took me to one of those awesome openings at Grauman's Chinese, *Hell Divers* this time, and then on to the Ambassador's Coconut Grove, where stuffed monkeys swinging from fake palm trees made us all feel like extras on a studio set. Gus Arnheim played hit numbers from Father's movies, "Sweeter Than Sweet," "My Future Just Passed," the Maurice Chevalier-Jeanette MacDonald love songs. Father took a little bow and people crowded around the table to ask him favors.

The year ended not with the sound of the Arnheim trumpets but with the heavy breathing and vehement prayers of Grandfather Max. With his children—my mother and her brothers, Joe, Dave, and Sam—I watched him slowly sink away, and confided to the diary: "It was horrible waiting around for him to die. It came at 1:30, a peaceful end which anyone who must die would envy. Just falling asleep, no struggle, no pain, no sorrow. Tonight this funny old world goes on as usual, listening for Paramount songs on the radio, reading of the death of Balzac, 'his body corroded by suffering, exhausted by living, a victim to his passion for work.' There was none of that in Grandpa's life. A typical Old World Jew, he lived mainly for the synagogue. His death has double significance, for it marks the end of orthodoxy in our family. His life was the link between his age and ours. And while ours may seem more rational and based on logic, his was by far the more content. That's what I was thinking about when he was praying at the top of his voice, unafraid, trusting in his God. We scoffers will be more afraid to die, for we know not what lies beyond. Religion may not be scientific, but it is a powerful thing, the lantern that saves us from the blackness of dismay and protects us from the inky unknown of death."

By New Year's Day I had recovered sufficiently from thoughts on mortality and religious philosophy to give a detailed description of the Rose Bowl game between U.S.C. and Tulane. But the thrill of home-team victory was dampened by the post-game family conference with Mother and her brothers about Father's decision to move out again, this time not just a few miles down Malibu Beach but to the Colleen Moore mansion he had rented in Bel Air. Colleen had been one of the top stars of the Twenties, the "naughty but nice" little flapper as compared to Clara Bow's sexier version, but her career in talkies had begun to skid, her marriage was on the rocks, and she decided to go east.

B.P. never did things by halves. It was a mansion in splendid Hollywood-Iberian style with sixteen high-ceilinged rooms, several acres of rolling lawns and flower beds, a guest house that would have been ample for Father without the palatial main house, and a swimming pool as large as the one they were building near the downtown Coliseum for the 1932 Olympic Games. Mother was not only outraged at the family rupture, but at the cost of this fourth establishment, for in addition to

Lorraine and Malibu, Father had also indulged a whim to acquire an estate in Santa Barbara. He was buying real estate in all directions in those days, from Santa Barbara to Hollywood apartment houses to Palm Springs. He had dropped a million in the Crash, and Ad accused him of throwing away another million on the wheels and the cards; but, even while under fire from rivals and overseers, the money was still pouring in faster than even he could spend it.

Back on the *Santa Fe Chief* after winter vacation, I realized how much easier it was to leave home this time than the previous fall. I was growing up to the truth. Father's moving to the Colleen Moore estate probably meant the end of the "happy home life" I wanted to believe in, no matter what the hard realities should have taught me. And his difficulties with the new masters of Paramount made me worry how long he would hang on to that enormous sunken office. We had even talked about it, and Father's pink-faced optimism and infectious laughter had almost dispelled my fears. The trouble with me, he said, is that I had inherited his talent for writing and Mother's gift for worrying. The Jaffes, he charged, were great worriers. Always thinking of the worst that could happen, instead of the best. When I scolded him, with the sense of self-righteousness that seems to come to full flower in adolescence, he turned it neatly to his advantage.

"All right, Father," he'd say, managing to make of this turnabout something gay and amusing, "I'll try to do a little better, Father." Then, if there was an audience, he'd elaborate on the family joke: "Hear the way he talks to me? Buddy thinks I'm seventeen and he's thirty-nine! He came into this world frowning at me. When he was one day old I knew I was in trouble! Isn't that right, *Father?*" His laughter filled the room, turning the sense of what I was saying into entertaining nonsense.

Yes, it was almost a relief to be away from the pressures of being a self-appointed linchpin of the family and the guardian of Father's morals. Rolling eastward again on our reliable *Chief* through the sunbaked landscape of the Southwest, I actually found myself looking forward to Deerfield, to the hallmates who were not nearly so forbidding as they had seemed when I first arrived, to the winterscape that seemed a welcome contrast to the constant sunshine in which I had been raised.

47

ACK AT DEERFIELD, I acted out my Walter Mitty life on the fringe of the sports world, proved myself the school's best journalist, got by with a minimum of study, and enjoyed the camaraderie of corridor roughhousing and nocturnal raids on the commissary. I marveled at the snow, found I was able to give history reports almost without a stammer, familiarized myself with Deerfield history, and published a report on the Massacre of 1704 that won praise from Mrs. Sheldon, the local historian whose ancestors were buried in the mass grave in the local cemetery.

With the help of our Latin trot, Mac and I laughed our way through our translation of Vergil. Our real work was driving with our housemaster, Mr. Allen, to the print shop in Greenfield to put the paper to bed on Friday nights. Printer's ink was on my fingers again and neat headlines jumped into my head. We'd go to a spaghetti joint, use my gold pass to see half an hour of a current movie, and then go back to correct the galleys.

Even though I squirmed through math and the boring Sunday sermons, envied the boys allowed to visit their New England homes for weekends, and fought a running battle against Deerfield discipline, I had found my place in the school. I felt I had only one enemy now, but he was a formidable one, the Headmaster himself.

Now that Father had given the school a movie projector, Mr. Boyden had asked me if I could get a film from the studio that would be appropriate for a weekend general assembly. I thought I had pulled off a coup by obtaining a print of the latest Marx Brothers picture, *Monkey Business,* still hot from the cutting room. Here was a milestone in the history of New England film exhibition But The Quid did not see it that way. With each zany reel he became more disturbed, until finally his rigid schoolmaster's soul could take it no longer.

I took it out on my diary: "I would like to enter here that Mr. Boyden is a god damn sonofabitch. After announcing that he would show *Monkey Business,* we saw 4 reels of it. At that point he said he had enough, that he found it in vulgar bad-taste and that it should be cut off right there, before the climax! Instead, he showed some pictures of frogs and *Mickey Mouse.* What a bastard of an old Puritan he is! Am so sore tonight I don't feel like working for a week."

My alienation was compounded by my having started a composite interview with the madcap Marxes for our school magazine. I had been in on the making of the Marx Brothers' movies. I had watched them cavort on the set under the knowing eye of director Norman McLeod and had laughed at antics almost as funny off the set as on. I had watched the straight "love-interest" Marx Brother, Zeppo, relieve B.P. of countless thousands every week, for what he lacked in acting talent he more than compensated for at the card table. I had wondered at how different they were, Groucho wickedly witty and mean; Harpo the intellectual sharing his leisure time with the Gershwins, Moss Hart, and Dorothy Parker; Chico sharing his with the bookies and card-sharks who regularly mugged him without violence as they did my old man. . . .

When I calmed down I realized I had in my power what might be called The Writer's Revenge. If I could finish my article on the Marxes and slip it into *The Stockade,* our literary magazine, I could have the last salvo in my running battle with The Quid. So I expounded on the comedic art of the Marx Brothers, comparing Harpo to Chaplin and invoking the commedia dell'arte as the classic forerunner of "the Marxism of laughter." I could picture The Quid's face growing darker as he read my tribute to the comedy team he had censored so arbitrarily. A further reason for cussing out The Quid was that Maurice and I had embarked on our first filmwriting project, outlining a scenario for the Marx Brothers entitled *Bughouse Fables,* in which the Marxes inherit a lunatic asylum. Our plan was to develop the script through correspondence, each of us taking turns rewriting the other until we would have it ready for presentation to B.P., Herman Mankiewicz, and the Marxes by the following summer. Even the fact that Father had questioned the

436

soundness of the premise and Mank had laughed us off as "Hecht and MacArthur *Junior*" in no way diminished our enthusiasm. At least B.P. had promised to read our material, and so had the Marx Brothers. Twice a month our script flew back and forth across the country; as soon as a thick envelope arrived from Palo Alto I would push everything aside to add new one-liners and bits of business. We could picture ourselves marching into Paramount that summer with our risible screenplay under our arm, the youngest writing team in the history of the Studio.

That season I was something of a literary schizophrenic, trying to write funny for the Marx Brothers while trying to absorb the material on lynching that continued to arrive from the N.A.A.C.P. During the Christmas holiday, the devoted Mrs. Stanton had urged me to outline the book and write an opening chapter, in time for her appraisal when I came home for spring vacation. In bed at night, I would concentrate on the horror of a lynching. The most effective way to open the book, I decided, was to recreate the mob hysteria of lynch murder. Again, I imagined a mob stringing up and burning Oscar the Bootblack. And then I thought of an altogether different kind of black, the giant heavy-weight George Godfrey. I could see him cracking the jaw of a young redneck, and the white mob closing in on him like hyenas and tearing him apart.

One night after eating too many marmalade sandwiches swiped from the commissary, I woke in a cold sweat just in time to escape a lynch mob burning a cross on the lawn of our home on Lorraine. Obviously I was taking to heart Mrs. Stanton's advice to live myself into my material, to get as close as imagination could draw me to the actual feeling of being roped by my white enemies and dragged, battered and bleeding, to the hanging tree. They all had the face of Mr. Boyden glowering at me at Sunday morning service.

A weekend trip to New York City to visit my Uncle Sam and Aunt Milly, east on vacation, was like being sprung from Sing Sing. On the bumpy five-hour train trip to Grand Central, I started, with much underlining, *The Autobiography of Lincoln Steffens,* hailed as the book of the year. I had been curious about him ever since he first came to our house and told his fascinating stories. He had progressed from individual muckraking to a theory of the muckrake that was truly revolutionary. "Bribery is no mere felony," he learned from a St. Louis reformer. "It's treason. . . . It's systematic. . . . Bribery and corruption is a process of revolution, to make a democratic government represent, not the people, but a part, the worse part, of the people. . . . It is good businessmen who are corrupting bad politicians. . . ."

Books are time bombs that go off not once but again and again. Lincoln Steffens's clear-eyed presentation of the shame of the cities would keep on ticking and exploding in my mind for the rest of my life. The impressionable teenager was torn between emulating Steffens and exposing lynch law, going back to Hollywood to write the Marx Brothers' next comedy hit, and writing the most stirring account of a Deerfield basketball victory ever printed in the *Scroll*.

After Mr. Boyden's baleful glances and the 19th-century reproaches of my Latin, German, and math instructors, I happily gave myself up to the flattery and attention of my aunt and uncle. That weekend, word came that Mother and Father were reunited! They were having a second—or was it a twenty-second?—honeymoon at the Desert Inn in Palm Springs. From their fancy hotel suite, Sam and Milly put through a call to them and I was able to hear their reassurances: "Sometimes, I don't think you give us enough credit for being intelligent, civilized people. And try to stop taking the whole world on your shoulders. Sonya is doing fine at L.A. High. She just published her first poem there. She's following in your footsteps. And little Stuart is happy at Progressive School. Even Paramount stock is going up. I think we've got a big hit in *The Smiling Lieutenant*. By the way, Dick Arlen sends his best and wants to take you out on his boat when you get back for vacation. And Publicity wants you back this summer, with a ten-dollar raise. And every Friday night at the fights everybody asks for you, Maxie Rosenbloom, Mushy Callahan—we'll see some great fights this summer, and the Olympic Games. . . ."

Uncle Sam, still under B.P.'s protection as studio manager, assured me he would keep an eye on the situation. I returned to Deerfield refreshed, encouraged, inspired, did my Latin without a trot, practiced tennis indoors for the oncoming tennis season, finished and sent off to Mrs. Stanton my latest chapter on the lynch book, mailed off the Marx Brothers rewrite to Maurice, wrote a triumphant piece on the last-second victory of the basketball team, delivered a lecture on Russia to the history class with barely a stammer, and confided to my diary that my only worries now were that I might not make the tennis team and that the Japanese invasion of Manchuria could lead to a second world war.

At that critical moment in local and world history I received another Dear Buddy letter from Father: All bets were off. He had done his best to reconcile with Mother, but apparently that was not good enough. She seemed incapable of forgiving him for the Sidney affair, or to keep that provocative name out of the verbal attack he had to face every time he came home late from the Studio.

Father's letter was a well-written appeal for understanding. He wanted me to believe that he had done everything he could to keep his part of the bargain. The fact that he did not come home until eleven or twelve o'clock at night did not mean that he was trysting at Sylvia's house. He hardly had to tell me that these were critical days for Paramount, for the entire motion-picture industry. He had to compete with Mayer and Thalberg at MGM, with the Warner Brothers who had become a third power with their headstart in sound, and with the devious intracompany politics. Manny Cohen and his backers were waiting for him to make a mistake. And so was Walter Wanger, who was now at the Marathon Street studio in an ambiguous position since the Astoria studio had been taken away from him. So B.P. had to defend his rear while fighting a frontal action against the other majors. L. B. Mayer had become a particularly dangerous enemy. He was vindictive, vicious, egomaniacal, and my father seemed to take a perverse delight in baiting him and humiliating him intellectually at meetings of the Producers' Association. L.B., for instance, had suggested that one way to keep costs down and stop the runaway market in stars' salaries was for the studio heads to agree not to hire away each other's marquee names at the end of their contracts. "That way they won't be able to play off one studio against the other. We can keep them forever!" Mayer had declared.

"Louie, you're absolutely right," B.P. had countered. "If we could set up that system, we'd have our stars exactly where we want them. And our directors and writers. But that system was tried in this country once, and it was overthrown. It's called slavery."

B.P. got the laugh he expected from a few of his fellow-producers. But it was one more mark in L.B.'s not-so-little black book. "He has the memory of an elephant," Mank had said. "And the hide of an elephant. The only difference is that elephants are vegetarians and Mayer's favorite diet is his fellowman."

B.P. loved to repeat anti-Mayer stories all over town, from Montmartre to the Mayfair Club. Mother would caution him; it was her hope that she could still effect a reconciliation between L.B. and B.P. Irving Thalberg's weak heart made him a shaky entry in the big-studio derby. Father might be a potential replacement if he extricated himself from his

Paramount problems, and acknowledged L.B. as the leader of The Industry.

All of this led me to the brief but complex conclusion that "they are both right." They were both right not only about their emotional conflict but about Father's position in The Industry. Either because he was a rebel, as he saw himself, or because he was self-destructive, as Mother judged him, Father could never bend the knee to L.B. In his personal life he was willing to come home and try again, but he was too proud, or too pigheaded, to apologize for past transgressions. And Mother, on the other hand, was what her mother would call a *hocker,* one who hammers relentlessly at the same point until the argument becomes self-defeating. "The trouble with your mother," Ben had said—borrowing from Mank's ample quiver of one-liners—"is that she refuses to take *yes* for an answer."

Once again after lights out, I prayed for one more reconciliation. In fact, for a self-announced atheist—who occasionally softened that stand to "pantheism"—I put in my share of person-to-person calls to the Almighty that season. I not only called on Him to bring Father and Mother to their senses, but urged Him to do what He could to get me on a plane to California for Easter.

In letters to my parents I had argued that since Lindbergh's recent 14-hour flight from coast to coast, more passengers had been encouraged to take to the air, until now some 400,000 were using commercial flights. Planes stopped three or four times for refueling, and put passengers up at hotels near the airfield overnight, so I wouldn't exactly be doing a Jimmy Doolittle or a Wiley Post. The arrival of one of my appeals coincided with a fatal aircrash in Nebraska, followed a few days later by news of another 20-seater lost in a storm in the Southwest. When my parents wrote that they had decided I had too much to live for to take unnecessary risks, I was secretly relieved.

While I kept on imploring Him to help me make the tennis team, reason told me that getting my first serve in and being less tentative on the overhead smash had more to do with reaching my goal than any heavenly intercession. It was a lonely feeling. I was not really on God's side, nor was He on mine. Every Sunday morning I mocked Mr. Boyden's tight-lipped Christianity, and at the same time I felt just as cut off from the religion my grandparents had brought over from the old country. The only time I wanted to be Jewish was when Mr. Boyden ordered me to worship, as the Messiah, a controversial rabbi I could accept only as a teacher in the tradition of Isaiah.

But I did learn one thing from Frank Boyden, an important lesson: not to push people into cubbyholes and try to confine them to predetermined definitions. On the eve of my first trip to Dartmouth, where I would face my pre-admission interview before taking the train to Boston, Chicago, and home to Hollywood, The Quid intercepted me on my way from Sunday-morning chapel. "Schulberg, I'd like to talk to you for a moment."

I braced myself and waited nervously as he began, "I wanted you to know I've just read your article on the Marx Brothers in *The Stockade*." In the pause that followed, I prepared myself for "Shocking. Absolutely disgraceful! I expect our boys to live up to the high standards of Deerfield. I think you should forget Dartmouth, and apply to one of those colleges in southern California."

Instead, I was hearing him say: "I thought it was very well done. So did Mrs. Boyden. I must say, you've done very good work for the magazine. When you meet with Dean Bill in Hanover, please give him our best regards."

I walked back to the Old Dorm in a daze. Those were the first kind words I had ever heard from The Quid, and on a subject that had seemed abhorrent to him. What had turned him around so dramatically? Had he begun to have guilt feelings about cutting off the screening of *Monkey Business*? Had Mrs. Boyden, my friend at court, talked to him in my behalf? Or had my efforts to define the uniqueness of the Marx Brothers finally convinced him that they were more than vulgar Jewish cutups playing for cheap laughs? I never would know the answer. But it did me good to ponder the implications of the question.

In high spirits, I went up to Dartmouth. There was a small but enthusiastic group of us, including our Deerfield version of Superman, Mutt Ray. For me, the Dartmouth campus was love at first sight: the old New England village we drove through to reach the campus; the row of white 18th-century buildings; the inviting look of Baker Library; the coziness of its Tower Room; the sound of the chimes; the White Mountains in the background; the wide Connecticut River separating the college from the rolling green hills rising to the Green Mountains of Vermont; the impressive daily newspaper I longed to work on. The look of the student body appealed to me, checked wool shirts and windbreakers, a rugged up-country look that fulfilled our image of Dartmouth as northern New England's answer to the effeteness of Harvard or the southern-gentleman tradition of Princeton. Mutt Ray seemed perfect Dartmouth material, and I felt a little more rugged myself as I walked at his side, inspecting the sentimental landmarks, the old covered bridge and the 18th-century Daniel Webster Cottage, where perhaps the most eloquent of all New Hampshiremen had lived as an undergraduate, years before he became a senator, a presidential hopeful, a secretary of state, and the successful defender of the college in the crucial Dartmouth College Case. Every freshman memorizes Webster's summation: "Dartmouth, sirs, 'tis a small college, but there are those of us who love it."

To climax our day, Rudy Pacht, now established as one of the stalwarts of the freshman football team, introduced us to Bill Morton, Dartmouth's reigning backfield star, and one of her all-time greats. After being in his presence, I found my interview with Dean Bill a decided anticlimax.

48

HOME AND HOLLYWOOD lost a lot of their joy for me that spring. Even the usually euphoric Felix Young admitted in the privacy of his studio office that the other female stars on the lot—Claudette Colbert, Kay Francis, Nancy Carroll, the Broadway import Ruth Chatterton and the glamorous, still-Sternberg-struck Marlene—were complaining of Father's focusing a disproportionate amount of time and attention on Sylvia, to the detriment of their own careers. And, as even the carefree Feel had begun to realize, the delayed effects of the Crash and the impact of sound had made these times far more complicated. The old order was gone. It wasn't only Wall Street that had moved in on Hollywood, it was the giants of high finance, RCA and A.T.&T. Through the sound patents they controlled, they were now the true bosses of Hollywood. The Mayers, the Warners, and even Schulberg loomed big on the local scene, but they were merely junior officers in a much larger war between the Morgans and the Rockefellers for control of what was now the billion-dollar Industry.

In terms of individual owners, Hollywood had simply outgrown itself. My uncle the studio manager confirmed this ominous change. It was no longer a question of opening theater doors and letting the movie fans rush in. Now that the novelty effect of talking pictures was wearing off, and the Crash of '29 seemed to have settled under Hoover's do-nothing policies into permanent Depression, the public had become more discriminating. No matter how Father boasted of his latest hits, Paramount was losing ground to MGM, which had even bigger stars and firmer leadership. B.P. was in a spot. Mother was right. Mistakes which might have been overlooked in 1930 were examined through a magnifying glass in 1932. Warners was capitalizing on its headstart with Vitaphone. New competition was right next door, on the old FBO lot where Maurice and I used to play when we tired of Paramount's castles and Western streets. Joe Kennedy, master manipulator, had shaken up the old "B picture" studio through merging RCA and the Keith-Orpheum Circuit to form RKO. Our poor neighbor on Gower Street was now another serious competitor.

Uncle Sam Jaffe was a concerned if somewhat patronizing brother-in-law. In installing him as studio manager, Father had exposed himself to accusations of nepotism. But with his usual eloquence and self-confidence, he had stood up to his critics, insisting that Sam had shown an aptitude for "our business" from the moment that Mother had brought him out from New York, and that he was now the best damn studio manager in the business. Sam, on his part, had grown in the job, with a self-assurance tilting toward arrogance. Still loyal to Father, he was convinced that he could now stand on his own two feet if he had to. Like Ad, he had what Father described as "Jaffe push," or *chutzpah,* an eye for the main chance. B.P. had the charm and intelligence to win a thousand arguments. But there was something unprotected or naive about him as compared with Ad's or Sam's grittier instinct for survival.

In Father's office I told him what people were saying about his losing his grip on the studio because of the favoritism he lavished on Sylvia Sidney. As was to be expected, he unleased one of his brilliant defenses. Since I seemed to be so involved in studio politics—Father's sarcasm stung—I should be able to find out that none of his other actresses had protested his stewardship of their careers. Nancy Carroll was becoming a full-fledged star, and so was Kay Francis. What I had heard about this distaff mutiny at the studio obviously came from friends of Mother's. Again he urged me to concentrate on my own work and my own future; let *him* run the studio and try to work out his difficulties at home. He wanted to read my latest chapters on the lynching book. And since I was on my way to the set to interview Richard Arlen for the *Scroll,* he'd like to read that piece if I could finish it before catching the train back to Deerfield.

He kept trying to prove that he could be a good father despite the domestic triangle. He read my stories, he encouraged me, he took me to previews and fights, he was almost excessively proud of me—what more did I want? The answer was painfully obvious: What I wanted most of all was a conventional family.

In the tiled library at home, surrounded by classics I had been urged to read, I discussed with Mother her end of the drama. She looked like a beautiful leading lady—Norma Shearer or Eleanor Boardman—playing the role of the woman scorned, the elegant and dutiful wife abandoned for the studio fleshpots. Vigorously pacing up and down, smoking one cigarette after another, she sounded firmer and tougher than I had ever heard her before. She had decided it would be easier on all of us if they arranged a civilized separation, and, after the year required in California, probably divorce. "I don't know anyone in this town quite like your father," she said, determinedly lighting another cigarette. "Well, maybe Mank. They're both brilliant, and charming, and self-destructive. Only for Ben the stakes are so much higher; Mank will never be more than a twenty-five-hundred-dollar-a-week writer. [B.P. was still making his unreal $11,000 per week plus bonuses.] But if Father is no longer head of the studio—"

She paused and drew hard on her cigarette. I knew she was on the verge of tears but a fierce, mean pride made her sound angry. " —I'm sick and tired of waiting up for him, or worrying about him, or wondering where he is or—you've been through all this or I wouldn't discuss it so openly—*knowing* where he is. I've almost reached a point where I wouldn't care, as long as I thought he could keep his balance." Her voice was rasping in anger now. "If only he weren't so damn gullible. The best mind in Hollywood—if he'd only protect it. If he'd only listen to me. I'm the only one who can help him. But he'd rather listen to those hangers-on and *hoors* who 'yes' him to death and tell him only what he wants to hear. It's so frustrating to see talent like that [and *money* like that, she might have added, for she loved and respected money almost more than culture itself] slipping through his fingers. I can't sleep at night, worrying about it. I get up and pace back and forth. No wonder I smoke so much!"

I had always thought of her as tough and formidable but suddenly she looked so small and vulnerable that I had an impulse to throw my arms around her and hug her. But she had never been a hugger: She reached out to our minds, loving us vicariously through the intellectual and creative accomplishments she encouraged with the persistence of a coxswain exhorting his crew to the finish line. So I didn't put my arms around her. Instead, I watched her pause in her restless pacing to make a surprising announcement: "I've decided to hire Mendel Silverberg to work out a satisfactory settlement." Silverberg was known in Hollywood as one of the smartest, toughest lawyers in town. She caught the expression on my face and went on to explain, "I'm not doing this for myself. I have to protect the children, see that you all get a good education. Dartmouth. A good finishing school for Sonya. And maybe a good boarding school would be the best thing for little Stuart. It's all very expensive. Tuition, and travel. Your trip back on the train alone cost two hundred and sixty-five dollars, and that doesn't include meals and tips. . . ."

In Mother's head there always seemed to be a kind of double-entry bookkeeping: one emotional, the other economic. She was able to weep for the loss of her first and, as it turned out, her one true love—and the breakup of the family she over-romanticized—and, with eyes still moist with domestic rue, she could figure out to the penny what everything was costing.

"And so," I heard Mother saying, "I've decided not to depend on Father—for anything. In all these years he has practically nothing to show for the millions he's earned—a few apartment houses, some acres in Palm Springs, his Paramount stock, insurance—I don't think he's got ten thousand dollars saved—he lives in that dream world of his, with people like Felix and the Sidney woman telling him how great he is—"

More serious pacing and thoughtful inhaling. Time for decision-making.

"—So I've decided to go into the agency business."

"The agency business!" I could not have been more shocked if she had told me she was going to join the fallen ladies at Madame Frances's notorious home-away-from-home for the Hollywood famous. We knew producers and movie stars, big directors, and high-paid writers. Agents—this was forty years before they took over The Industry—were just a cut above the wantons who referred to themselves as "actresses" when they were booked for soliciting on Hollywood Boulevard. The only *agent* we knew was David Selznick's maverick brother, Myron. Foulmouthed, hard-drinking, irreverent, looking and acting more Irish than Jewish (like my mysterious Grandfather Simon), Myron would turn the business around. Until he began storming into front offices, stars were merely incredibly high-paid slaves, their three-to-five-thousand-dollars-a-week salaries not protecting them from producers who could shove them into any sort of role or picture they chose and give them an arbitrary starting date. It was standard procedure to finish one

446

picture, take a week's or ten days' rest, and plunge into the next. If they rebelled, as some of the more independent or idealistic did, put them on suspension! No more money coming in, and no competing studio allowed to touch them.

When he began to change all this, Myron Selznick was somehow accepted as the son of a pioneer getting back at The Industry for what he and his brother felt was the shafting their father L.J. had gotten. But agents in general were still at the bottom of the Hollywood barrel. And a *woman* agent! What would people think? It would be a reflection on Father, on all of us!

49

ON THE TRAIN rolling through the southwestern desert, I jotted a note in my diary to call on the overworked Being in whom I claimed not to believe: "Oh God, please don't let Mom become an agent!" And if He had time, I had a further request: "And help me finish my book on lynching."

At my last meeting with Mrs. Stanton, my patient counselor at U.S.C., she had been more impressed with my industry than with the creative future of *Judge Lynch*. Even with a feeling for the subject, and a thick file of searing N.A.A.C.P. statistics, I was like a social engineer who knew both sides of the river but didn't know how to build the bridge. In the year I gave to *Judge Lynch* (along with its loony opposite, *Bughouse Fables*) I was learning a healthy lesson: In writing there could be success in failure. I was learning to write and rewrite, and I was also learning that all the rewriting in the world won't help the poor scribe who doesn't know what he's rewriting about.

Going east, I walked the train looking for Hollywood familiars and fell in with Sol Wurtzel, a prototype of what outsiders thought a Hollywood producer should be. A burly cloak-and-suiter who had never read a book and who had his scenarios synopsized for him by more literate assistants, Sol was known in Hollywood as The Keeper of the B's, the penny-pinching minor mogul who ran the old Fox Studio on Western Avenue that specialized in oaters and mellers. The trouble with The Industry, he lectured me, was experimentation. In these difficult times, he felt that he—and not the sainted Irving Thalberg or young upstart

Dave Selznick—had the answers. "If you got a good story, stick to it. The public loves to see the same goddamn story over and over again. They feel comfortable with it. To hell with unhappy endings, offbeat material. I hear these directors bitching about what they really wanna make. Fuck 'em. What they wanna make, maybe five thousand high-brows in the whole country will pay their four bits t'see. I don't give a shit about art. It's a business—and anybody who doesn't think so oughta get out of it!"

Maybe because he knew B.P. looked down on him as an illiterate and an ignoramus, he stared at me as if challenging me either to agree with his lowbrow approach or get off at Omaha.

In those days Hollywood was such a small town that Mr. Wurtzel felt obliged to look after me in Chicago, during the long stopover to change trains from the *Chief* at the Dearborn Street Station to the La Salle Street Depot, where we caught the *20th Century* to New York. But having been locked into those Pullman cars for three days and nights with the stolid chieftain of Western Avenue, I muttered something about having friends to look up in Chicago, and slipped away.

I spent most of the day with my golden pass, taking in *The Roar of the Crowd* with Jimmy Cagney and Joan Blondell, followed by a brace of the formula movies in which Sol Wurtzel took such pride. On my way to still another movie in the Loop, I passed a burlesque theater. Glancing around as if in fear of being followed, I lowered my head and snuck in. The strippers—"specialty dancers" in my prim diary—provoked desires that had been repressed or sublimated in sports since my middle teens. One statuesque lady so demonstrated the art of titillation, to the steamy music of "Stairway to Paradise," that I suddenly realized I might miss my train.

Racing to La Salle Street, I made it to the Pullman platform on the final *All aboard!*, watched the familiar old station fall away behind me, and then realized that I had left my wallet with all my money at the newsstand where I had grabbed a *Chicago Trib* on my way to the gate. The kindness of strangers to whom I stammered out my plight provided dinner and breakfast money. Meanwhile, with another small loan, I wired Western Union to please search for my wallet and send it on to me at Deerfield. A few days later it reached my mailbox at school, my seventy-one dollars intact. In my innocence, and that of the times, I accepted this miracle of integrity with not even a cry of surprise. I didn't even consider it a news item for the *Scroll*. Times were hard, and dollars scarce, but we had a quaint attitude toward money: If it wasn't ours, we gave it back.

Spring at Deerfield should have been a happy time, but I was tortured by old ghosts. I managed to make the A list in tennis, but so far down that I lived in terror of tumbling into the humiliating B's every time my service failed. "Tomorrow is my last chance!" I suffered through an entire season of Last Chances, playing life-and-death two-hour matches in which scores like 8-10, 10-12—always on the narrow edge of winning, and always losing—punctuated my dreams.

I took out my frustrations in reading and writing, wrestling in the hallways, and heckling the dreary Sunday sermons. In what must have seemed an obviously losing cause, I continued to exhort my parents by mail and occasional long-distance calls to conform to my conception of how they should conduct their marriage.

I seemed to be living my life in a kind of righteous rage, storming against hypocrisy, from Hollywood to Scottsboro to Deerfield. I was inclined to take the positives for granted: my letter of acceptance by Dartmouth, praise for my stories and book reviews in *The Stockade,* literary encouragement from Mrs. Stanton, a growing feeling of belonging in the Old Dorm. But the hypocrisy of the more snobbish of the student body, and of The Quid himself, continued to agitate me. When B.P.'s controversy with Von Sternberg over the choice of story material for Marlene Dietrich made the New York papers, I noted: "Dad's argument with Von Sternberg has made a lot of fellows greet me who have never done so before. What hypocrites!"

Repressed violence and simplistic idealism played tug-of-war with my emotions. Headlines on the Lindbergh kidnapping prompted this outburst: "There was an extra out that the Lindbergh baby was found dead in the woods. What a lousy country this is! Those kidnappers ought to get hung up by their balls." The same week brought news of the shooting of the President of France. Retreating from a sermon in church, I was ready with one of my own: "The newspapers carry the story that the assassin of Paul Doumer was a Bolshevist. More trouble. I wonder if there will ever come a time when all nations shall scrap all armies, all armaments. Not until that time will we be fully civilized."

But my real war was still with Mr. Boyden. On his way to New York, Father requested by wire that I be permitted to come down to meet the train. "The weekend is all set!" I assured myself.

The following entry strikes a different tone: "God damn fucking bastard son-of-a-bitch! [While I had heard profanity in Hollywood, I had had to come to an eastern prep school to learn how to use it.] Jesus I'm sore tonite. Dad wired the Quid (GDHBH) to let me meet him tomorrow. Boyden refuses because it is too near finals and 'no one is having a weekend.' Now I find out that half a dozen fellows I know have permission to leave. Sons of presidents of colleges and big companies get special treatment. What a hypocrite!" The month of May was neatly summed: "Improved in tennis. Had two short stories in *The Stockade*. Acquired deep bitterness against Mr. Boyden."

I vented that bitterness by raiding the school pantry ("drowned my sorrows in orange marmalade tonight"), reading until dawn ("*Chocolate,* a new Soviet novel Mother brought me from Russia"), boycotting Mr. Boyden's beloved semipro baseball team, and checking off on my wall the days until I would be free of what had become for me a Dickensian reformatory.

I went through final exams with a chip on my shoulder, daring them to flunk me, reading novels and my own bible, the Steffens autobiography, when I should have been studying. Perhaps that attitude relaxed me, for I sailed through with high grades. Mrs. Boyden, that fine-spirited antidote to her puritanical husband, somehow had managed to brainwash me into knowing all I needed to know to get through the math final and on to Dartmouth, where I would never again have to wrestle with that wretched subject, and simply could count on my fingers for the rest of my days.

After the Latin final, a troop of rowdies, led by the first-born of the production head of Paramount, the son of the president of Wesleyan, the son of a former governor of Massachusetts, and other young eminences, gathered all their Latin books—Cicero, Caesar, the *Aeneid,* Ovid—and raucously marched with them across campus to the banks of the Connecticut. There, in a spontaneous combustion of adolescent joy, they ripped out the pages, set them on fire, and cheered as they watched the classic lines that had tortured them all semester burn to ash. The son of Ben and Ad, taught to love books and already trying to write one, applauded with the others as his Latin texts floated downriver in flames.

When Mr. Boyden called the senior class together to discuss the baccalaureate ceremonies, and emphasized the importance of our parents' attendance, I felt he was looking directly at me, as if challenging me to produce a Respectable American Family. But back in Hollywood,

Mother was getting ready to launch her agency business. And though Father was in New York, it was simply not his style to board the uncomfortable Boston & Maine, or take a six-hour motor trip along a narrow, winding road into what seemed to him an alien wilderness. If I had been in the big city, he would have squired me to George White's *Scandals*, the big fight in the Garden, and on to "21." But the Pocumtuck Valley and making polite talk with the Boydens and the Deerfield faculty were not for him. He phoned me from the Waldorf, with the charming sincerity that was his trademark, pleading the pressure of meetings with the Paramount board of directors and telling me how proud both he and Mother were of the way I had mastered a new environment— academically, on the school publications, and on the football and tennis teams. He thought I had done especially well in view of my involvement in his and Ad's squabbles. He praised Mother, as he always did, as an admirable and progressive woman. But he reminded me again that there are two sides to every argument and while he did not want to undermine my loyalty to Ad, he hoped that someday I would come to a better understanding of his position.

There was something both sad and affectionate about that strained conversation. I could see him in his lavish suite at the Waldorf, full of expensive cigar smoke and the fumes of fine scotch, possibly attended by Sylvia Sidney and a few of his studio cronies, while I stood at the pay phone in the campus post-office-store. Each of us calling out for the sympathy and understanding of the other: B.P. doing everything possible (for him) not to lose his son, while the son was trying to hang onto his father. . . .

In the graduating class, surrounded by secure young men from the best eastern families, with their proper parents in the audience in their proper dress, with their proper manners, kissing or shaking hands with their proper sons receiving diplomas from the proper Mr. Boyden, I felt like an orphan, the Hollywood outsider, the Jewish beggar at the feast of the gentiles.

Sitting next to my school paper sidekick, Mac McConaughy, I listened thoughtfully as his father, the eminent president of Wesleyan, delivered a typically New England address on the beauty of commonplace things. It was a nice talk, I noted, and yet far removed from the hard realities of the Depression that was changing the face of America. While we were sitting there in the peace and sunshine of the Connecticut River Valley, snug and smug in our isolation, dwelling on the unique beauty of the wild violet in the lovely woods surrounding the peaceful little campus (the subject of Dr. McConaughy's thoughtful little talk), Hoovervilles were spreading around every city in America, once-respectable heads of families were literally fighting for the garbage outside restaurants, and stocks like my parents' RCA, which had plunged from over 100 to around 25 in the infamous Crash, had gone down and down and now were hovering at a fraction over 2.

Thinking about all this as the kindly Dr. McConaughy talked on, I wondered what set me so apart from my classmates. I was probably as affluent as any of these rich boys and probably lived what seemed to them a far more glamorous life. Yet I worried about the shuttered factories and the foreclosed farms in a way they could never understand. I didn't delude myself that I had a kinder heart. I think my stammering, my father's teetering on the high wire between the poles of success and failure, my Hollywood Jewish background in the exclusive world of the eastern gentile all fed a sense of alienation that made it easier, maybe even inevitable, for me to identify with the underdog. Maybe the under-dog was simply me, three thousand miles from home, ashamed for having to apologize for the absence of my father and mother.

How could I explain at the oh-so-respectable reception following the graduation exercises that my father was probably at a Manhattan speakeasy, drinking bootleg whiskey with his movie-star mistress while Mother was busy in Hollywood setting up an agency business that soon would represent Claudette Colbert, Maurice Chevalier, Nancy Carroll, Fredric March, Miriam Hopkins—practically the entire list of Paramount marquee names?

Before leaving Deerfield, I took a final walk through the village cemetery. Under those weather-beaten stones lay the bones of the pioneers who had dared move on from Boston and Springfield to clear their own fields and build their strong, no-nonsense houses intended to protect them against the dual attacks of violent winters and the Indians who believed that the Earth Mother had provided this land for them alone. So much of what Deerfield had meant to me had been learned in this cemetery, and its defiant Old Testament names and its simple New Testament determination to conquer the wilderness. Here were the tiny graves of infants who could not survive terrible winters, the mother worn out in their middle thirties, an old, old man of 62 surrounded by his series of wives and the eight children he had given back to the earth. . . .

454

Still in the spirit of the place, I said goodbye to old Mrs. Sheldon, who was now waiting to die in her 17th-century house with its secret door to an escape tunnel and hiding place. My Uncle Joe had described the attacks of the Cossacks back in the years when our family had clung to its *shtetl* on the banks of the Dvina, but somehow Mrs. Sheldon's ancestors and their martyrdom had become more real to me. These ties now drew me to New England. In Hollywood even the great studios and the palatial homes of the movie stars along Sunset Boulevard were made of stucco. Glorified impermanence. Here I felt the stability of old beams that had stood against the centuries. Taking a farewell walk along the river with Eaton Tarbell, my comrade-in-stammering and in general roughhousing, I realized that almost without my knowing it I had become a part of this old world. I now felt ready for Dartmouth; the outdoor ballads of her son Richard Hovey called to me, as did the downright orneriness of Robert Frost's "Two roads diverged in a wood, and I—I took the one less traveled by."

On my first trip east I might have accepted those lines from the New Hampshireman's poem as a neat little rhyme. But now I had seen his mountains, his rocky fields, and the independent cusses who insisted on working them. I was beginning to sense what Frost meant by "And that has made all the difference." Speeding to Chicago in high style on the *Santa Fe Chief* with the lowbrow Sol Wurtzel, I had been exposed to a different kind of poetry in the drawing room, which might be paraphrased: "Who the hell wants t' follow a road nobody uses? That's a road to a box office with nobody at the window! Fuck that!" I didn't need Frost or his New England to tell me what to think of Sol Wurtzel. "You're going from bad to Wurtzel," Father had commented on one of our scenes for *Bughouse Fables*. Reading Frost had given me a new frame of reference in which to judge the Hollywood experience. It made me think about our own seekers of the road less traveled: Chaplin, King Vidor, Eisenstein, Tod Browning, the obsessed Von Stroheim, the egocentric Von Sternberg. . . . We might teach Mr. Boyden something about tolerance, but the best of New England, from Roger Williams to our own New Hampshire laureate, could teach us something about the hard choices that make for freedom.

50

WITH A CLASSMATE and his parents in their black 1930 Packard, it took three hours to drive the last sixty miles on the old road from Deerfield to New York City, but it seemed a million light-years from the isolated green campus to Father's suite in the Waldorf Towers. I was immediately enveloped in his atmosphere—the humidor of Upmanns, the Hollywood tradepapers and scripts on the coffee table, the phone calls, the telegrams from the studio, the familiar faces of Al Kaufman and Paramount lawyer Louie Swartz, and the team of writers B.P. had brought with him across the country for those obligatory nonstop story conferences.

Father may have been sitting on a shaky throne, but he knew how to hold court as if anointed for life. When his sister Val and her husband Charley arrived, I could feel the awe, the amazement that one of theirs had made it all the way to the top of the golden ladder. To the rest of his family, B.P.'s story of Rivington rags to Hollywood riches was the stuff of Yiddish fairy tales. The pauper had become a prince, and there was something truly regal in the way he received his courtiers and passed their hands with gold, for he always carried a pocketful of ten–and twenty-dollar gold pieces.

With Aunt Val and Uncle Charley, we made another million-light-year journey in a sleek Paramount limousine to Grandmother's tenement, where we walked up the narrow, creaky stairs into the world she stubbornly still refused to leave, either for a "better neighborhood" or for a bungalow of her own in the Hollywood sun. On the liberal allowance that Father provided, she had not in the slightest changed her lifelong ways. Instead, she used her monthly fortune to rebuild the synagogue she loved to watch from her window, and to support (without her son's knowledge) two poor families on the block. To spend all the money on herself seemed *goyische* waste. To eat, to sleep, to pray, to think, to talk with friends . . . what more could a person want? With a double generation-gap between us, I had never really talked to her. I had only heard the stories of how independent she was, like my own mother ahead of her time, and how she had coped with Grandfather Simon, the strapping six-footer with a red face and "the thirst for beer of an Irishman." "Your grandfather was powerful but she's the one in the family who was really strong," Aunt Val said.

A feeling of sentimentality balanced a sense of repugnance at her stale breath as I kissed her. She patted me and muttered something in Hebrew. From the stoop we looked up and waved as she watched us from her window. Our limousine and liveried chauffeur had drawn a crowd of curious men with long dark beards, women with shawls, and ghetto kids laughing and pointing. A boy a little younger than I, in a worn jacket that was obviously a hand-me-down, its sleeves rolled up at the wrist, came up to me and shouted, "Whaddya doin' down here—slummin'?"

Back in Father's sumptuous suite lay our reality. Aunt Val accused her famous brother of supporting Sylvia Sidney, at a time when his own income was in jeopardy. Father defended himself with his customary eloquence. He was not *supporting* Sylvia. Ad herself had urged him to sign her to a long-term contract. She was not even being paid as much as his other stars like Ruth Chatterton and Kay Francis, and her pictures were outgrossing theirs. At that moment, as much as I resented his illicit affair, I felt a little sorry for him. It wasn't easy having Ad and Aunt Val *and* Paramount's new bankers on his neck.

After Val and her nice but *nebbish* Charley left, Father fixed himself a stiff highball, lit another expensive cigar, and told me what he had not wanted to say in front of them. "Sometimes I get sick and tired of all the critics in this family. I wonder what your Aunt Val would say if I told her that I'm paying Charley's salary? Otherwise he'd be out of a job. I could have given the money directly to her but the poor sonofabitch is already pretty well beaten-down, and I didn't want him to lose his self-respect entirely. This way he feels he can pay me back when things get better."

How many people Father had on that secret payroll, I never knew. The way he handed money out to almost anyone who put the arm on him reminded me of openhanded prizefight champions. Was it an inability ever to say No—a weakness Mother had battled to correct over the years—or simply the flow of a generous nature, a genuine feeling for the less fortunate?

Highballing it back to Chicago on the *20th Century,* we traveled in style with a silky black porter constantly fetching ice with lots of *yassuh*ing and practiced smiles. His counterpart served our dinner—whisked with mysterious efficiency from the dining car. This was the first time I could remember traveling alone with Father. Through Europe, to Mexico, back and forth across the country, there had always been either an entourage or the rest of the family. Now we played casino and B.P. was delighted that he had found a pigeon he could beat. By the time we pulled in to Chicago, I was down seven dollars and Father was urging me to up the stakes.

After dinner that evening I asked him about the problems at the studio that Aunt Val had mentioned. He prefaced his explanation by urging me not to worry. Then he admitted that Mother's fears had been realized. Now that Jesse Lasky was gone and Zukor no longer in control, he was being pushed out of his job as vice-president-in-charge-of-production. It had—he assured me—absolutely nothing to do with Sylvia Sidney. So far his record had been just as good as in the previous year. He had been a victim of a palace revolution. Manny Cohen, who had been Lasky's assistant, would soon be taking B.P.'s place in the big sunken office from which the studio was run. But crafty, tough-minded little Manny knew nothing about running a studio. "In six months I'll lay you a hundred dollars to five they'll be begging me to come back and bail out that snake-in-the-grass!

"In the meantime," he went on with his infectious optimism, "I won't be exactly on Poverty Row. I'm getting a new contract for my own independent unit. I'll make a little less every week, but I'll have a much larger percentage of the profits. In the long run I can end up with more money, and I won't have to spread myself so thin. You know, I never really disagreed with David about the merits of independent production. But as long as I had the responsibility for the entire program, I couldn't let myself admit it." Now, Father continued in that same cheery vein, he was looking forward to making six personally produced pictures a year.

459

With the pick of the Paramount players and directors to choose from, it would be more like the good old days of Preferred Pictures back in the Mayer-Schulberg Studio era.

If Mother was a chronic worrier, Father was a congenital optimist. To put it bluntly, he had just been fired from one of the biggest jobs Hollywood had to offer. For seven years he had run a production company whose only rival was the ever-expanding MGM. Now, at the age of forty, when most executives are reaching their prime, he was being shunted aside. Somehow Father was able to herald this demotion as a personal triumph. It had been a ball to run the Stude in the silent days. But now with the Depression tightening its grip on The Industry, and A.T.&T. and RCA closing in, Father insisted he was lucky to be out from under. Now he'd be more like DeMille, with his own bungalow headquarters and his own staff.

With each scotch highball, Father's mood grew merrier. He filled the drawing room not only with expensive smoke but with an air of festivity. When I finally aroused him in the morning to tell him we'd be pulling into Chicago in an hour, he groped his way to the bathroom in his silk monogrammed pajamas and was soon singing his habitual shaving songs, "*H—A—Double R I . . .*" and "Somebody's Been Aroun' Heah (Givin' Yuh Lessons in Love)," along with a raucous rendition of "Life Is Just a Bowl of Cherries" which we had just heard Ethel Merman proclaim in George White's *Scandals.* As I listened to Father's gargled imitation of the Broadway star, I watched the ugly outskirts east of Chicago and thought about the sermon for our times he was singing so gaily.

The Hub City, once so proud of its muscle, had just reported its fortieth bank closing—a fitting setting for the Democratic Convention. There a new figure on the national scene, Franklin D. Roosevelt, inspired by a "brains trust" of Columbia professors, would call for "a New Deal" and voice his concern for "the forgotten man at the bottom of the economic pyramid."

In the three-hour layover between trains, Father bought me a new portable phonograph as a graduation present. I picked hit records from the Broadway musicals I had seen, Libby Holman torching "Something to Remember You By" and other Gershwin showstoppers from *Girl Crazy,* like "Embraceable You" and "Bidin' My Time." Just beginning to hear the difference between true jazz and the pop orchestras I listened to on the radio, I bought Red Nichols and his Orchestra (Red's sidemen were Benny Goodman, Glenn Miller, Gene Krupa, Jimmy Dorsey, and Jack Teagarden). Then, stopping at a speakeasy Ben Hecht had recommended, B.P. drew around him a group of Hecht's newspaper cronies, each one of them ready to sell him a gangster yarn that would top *Underworld*. Drinking, laughing, enjoying the attention, Father suddenly realized the *Chief* was about to leave. We jumped in a taxi and raced through traffic while the manager phoned ahead to hold the train.

Entering the oak-paneled dining car that evening for the first meal of the journey, Father was recognized by the attentive captain from previous crossings. Satisfied travelers tipped at the far end of the trip, but Father liked to hand out his gold pieces at the beginning as well. In return, the smiling maitre d' reserved Father's favorite table for him and served specially prepared dishes that were not on the menu. I don't think Father really cared that much about three-star dishes. It was simply his way of maintaining the status to which he had become accustomed.

Over his drinks before dinner (a supply of imported scotch laid on at Chicago), I would offer him for criticism descriptive paragraphs I had sketched in the observation car, invariably getting more than I bargained for. If he liked one line in half a dozen, I was encouraged. Tough criticism was helping me. The flattery I almost invariably heard from Mother was balm for the wounds. But I knew I needed the sting of the stick as a racehorse does if it is not to bear out. Already he had told me he thought I was hopelessly over my head with *Judge Lynch*. And the scenario Maurice and I had written for *Bughouse Fables* had not changed his earlier opinion that putting the Marx Brothers in charge of a lunatic asylum was a self-defeating idea. Stung, I insisted that I had just read their *Horsefeathers* screenplay and thought ours was better. Father admired my spirit, but warned me that if I were to repeat that cockiness to Mank, he'd make us the laughingstock of the town. "Cockiness is helpful *while* you're writing," he advised, "but humility is the ticket to *re*writing."

Leaving Albuquerque, that calculated tourist stop, where the squatting Navajo vendors had become familiar faces, Father made notes in the screenplay of *Madame Butterfly*, his next big production; it would star Sylvia Sidney, in kimono and clogs, as Cio-Cio-San. There had been an unspoken truce about the Sidney problem all the way out. It had been a congenial, stimulating trip in which both of us had repressed the urge to anticipate the future that waited so threateningly at the end of the journey. While Father studied and tried to cut a script he goddamned for being so long, I tried to write a short story about a young Navajo whose crude bow-and-arrow is rejected by a prosperous young passenger. "Only twenty-five cents," says the Indian boy. "I'll give you a quarter to keep the damned thing!" says the callow traveler, and flips him a coin. As the conductor calls "All aboard!" the traveler is on his way back to the comfort of his Pullman car when he feels a sharp pain between his spine and his shoulder blade. One of the rejected toy arrows has found its mark. I could feel the arrow in my own back as I wrote. I handed Father the short-short, a popular form at the time, and he pronounced it one of the better things I had done.

That night in the dining car there was a banquet suggestive of a farewell feast on a transatlantic crossing: fresh venison from the Reservation, prepared in illicit red wine, accompanied by articulate toasts from Father and other distinguished travelers.

At Needles on the Arizona-California border, the heat brought back to mind the trip a dozen years earlier: Again it was 110 in what was euphemistically called "the shade," but outside the dry, stucco houses there was no shade. The Mojave Desert was relentless: hour after hour of scorched sagebrush and sand. The drawing room was stifling. The railing on the observation car was too hot to touch. I thought of *Greed*: McTeague the simpleminded dentist and his envious rival Schouler, dying of thirst with no water within a hundred miles, as they staggered after their gasping mule loaded with gold. What would it be like to fall off the observation platform and crawl through that alkali wasteland?

And then, modestly at first, followed by an abundance of groves, came mile after mile of orange trees. A whole country of festive oranges to welcome us home. At the old station in the Mexican backwater, the entire tribe was there to greet us—Mom, Sonya, Stuart, Maurice, and Father's loyal followers from the studio. For a few minutes there was jubilation. Then my parents drove off in separate cars.

51

NSTEAD OF A joyous reunion at the Lorraine house, that night the living room was full of anger as Uncle Sam Jaffe and Felix Young clashed in heated argument as to how the studio would run without Father at the helm. Felix thought the board of directors had made a tragic mistake and that Paramount would never recover from Ben's demotion. Possibly because he was being kept on as studio manager, possibly out of loyalty to Mother, Sam blamed B.P. for losing control. "I begged him to listen to the people around him, and to learn how to delegate authority to his supervisors, like Irving. But Ben can be awfully stubborn. He wanted to be the boss."

The pros and cons of Father's new status were argued way past midnight. Sam was obviously feeling his oats. He had come up in the world from the *nebbish* brother-in-law who had had to room with his nephew at the Lorraine house. Now increasingly sure of himself, Sam began to see that he could survive without Father. Felix was more dependent, and therefore more defensive. Soon he would move on from studio supervisor to the town's leading boniface, first with the Vendôme restaurant, then the Trocadero. Of course Father would lend him money to help him get started, just as once he had bailed him out of jail. Where the elegant Felix was loyal, Sam was righteous. Mother managed to be both sad and angry. And as for me, noting in my diary that "I was up till after 2 talking with Maurice about this mess of Dad and Mom," I closed out the long day on a note of Chekhovian gloom: "I will never be really happy again."

Tension increased as little Stuart kept wanting to be with Father, and would take off on his bike to visit the rival beach establishment. Mother objected on the old-fashioned, non-Freudian grounds that it was harmful to Stuey's sense of morals to let him see his father living openly in sin "with his little *hoor*." The ten-year-old was confused because he had seen so little of his father that he kept reaching out to him. And it was more fun at Father's, where they made a great fuss over him and where our old man's booming laughter encouraged Stu to deliver his droll, precocious monologues.

Meanwhile, Mother was setting up her agency office in the Taft Building at the corner of Hollywood and Vine. She used her decorator's touch to give the suite an unusually homey atmosphere, full of antiques and fine fabrics. It looked like an extension of the Lorraine and Malibu houses, but underneath the charm it was all business. To counter the tough studio lawyers in contract disputes, Ad was the first to cast around for a lawyer of her own and make him part of the agency. With her eye for talent, she picked a winner in Charley Feldman, a tall, handsome young man with diffident charm, recently out of law school. Her idea was to pay him a mere $100 a week, but a percentage of the earnings of the clients he brought in as well. An ideal combination, Ad and Charley were an almost overnight threat to Myron Selznick's domination of the agency business. In time Charley would become an art connoisseur, a confidant of major Hollywood figures like Darryl Zanuck and David Selznick, and the producer of such films as *Red River* and *A Streetcar Named Desire*. Years later, facing a premature death in his tasteful mansion in Coldwater Canyon, surrounded by his Cézannes, Picassos and Renoirs, he would remember how much Ad had taught him. "She was really Hollywood's first lady," he said. "In different times, she would have run a major studio."

But to my innocent eyes, her new profession and way of life were still a disgrace to the family. I dreaded to watch her fill her briefcase with scripts and contracts and drive off early each morning to the Vine Street office. I debated whether or not to take a job with *The Hollywood Reporter* because, even with several in help, I worried that the children would be left unprotected. And that 14-year-old Sonya would be led astray by Adela Rogers St. John's wild daughter Elaine. And that little Stuey was going to hell on a bicycle spending so much time at that beach house with Father and Sylvia.

Actually, Mother was building a flourishing business that would in time support the family in the manner to which it had become accustomed. She had seized the reins just when B.P. was beginning to lose hold of them.

Again I tried to drown my sorrows in sports—my own, as well as the spectator track-and-field scene Maurice and I had cultivated so intensely. On our tennis court I played as if my life depended on winning.

Still virgins, still teetotalers, still babes in the holly woods, Maurice and I were increasingly concerned with the symbols of growing up. We strayed into a wicked San Francisco dance hall, and, terrified by what we saw, shyly withdrew. We assured each other that this summer we had to learn to dance. Our wallflowering had become ridiculous. Deciding to go to a "speak" we had heard about, we were rudely turned away. Still, we went to the grand St. Francis Hotel, mingled with the smart people until the late hours, and felt we were carousing.

After thirteen hours down the twisting Coast Road, running out of gas and suffering flat tires as usual, we finally reached the old homestead in the Malibu Colony, only to find a drunken party in progress, including Nancy Carroll, her hard-drinking boyfriend, and a writer I had objected to as "an old souse," who seemed to be Mother's "date." A solemn entry in the diary: "Sonya and I felt sad to think how things have changed." And the following morning, after four vicious sets of tennis and a long swim out to the raft, "That *guy* is still there this morning. God what riffraff! It seems that now I find failure and wretchedness at every corner."

These notes of despair were sounded in a lovely tower room overlooking our private beach, with those still-unspoiled meadows rising to the foothills of the Santa Monica Mountains, with Father announcing a promising program of B. P. Schulberg releases for Paramount, and Mother launched on a meteoric agency career, with my Dusenberg parked at the gate, a staunch group of friends (mostly the sons of other Hollywood producers), a good summer job on the leading Hollywood trade paper giving me entry to every studio, and matriculation at Dartmouth set for the fall.

I threw myself into the *Reporter* job, whipping my Dusenberg all the way from Universal City in the Valley to the walled fortress of Metro-Goldwyn-Mayer in Culver City, where Maurice was now working as a junior writer. Harry Rapf's Joan Crawford, having made the transition to sound that Father's Clara Bow had sadly failed, was seducing Walter Huston in *Rain,* but now Maurice and I were no longer barred from the

465

set. Now we were passing for young professionals, and instead of shyly asking for her autograph as I had half a dozen years before, I was the eager young reporter taking brisk notes on Miss Crawford's burgeoning career.

She had just surprised her critics by holding her own in *Grand Hotel* with Greta Garbo, John and Lionel Barrymore, and Wallace Beery. She was moving up from the racy but rather stereotyped jazz-baby roles of the late Twenties. Having started at the bottom, in a stag movie that had become a Hollywood collector's item, Joan had the drive that separates stars from feature players. She was mastering the art of big-studio success. It involved much more than sleeping with Harry Rapf or other MGM producers. We could see how hard she worked at stardom, in front of the camera, between takes, in her dressing room, and away from the studio. The commissary, the main studio street, the Vendôme, her limousine—these all became sets where the driven Lucille Laeseur acted out the fantasy that had become Miss Joan Crawford.

Joan Crawford may not have been the greatest actress who ever played Sadie Thompson, but no one exposed to her portrayal could ever forget that powdered, rouged, and lipsticked mask of seduction and sin. Her face was like a sensuous canvas on which were drawn come-hither eyes larger than life and a full mouth painted even fuller as if by an artist consumed by sexual hunger. As Greta Garbo represented sex repressed and subtle, Joan Crawford was sex at the ready, her dancer's figure threatening—promising—to burst from the tight silk that barely held it in. The poor Reverend Davidson had about as much chance of standing up to the onslaught of Joan's wanton Sadie Thompson as the little Pomona College eleven had to stop the Trojans of U.S.C. And yet when one talked with Joan, it was not the physical but the mental power that came through, the mind of the superachiever. *No matter where you think I came from,* her will imposed itself on you, *I recreate my life story as I live it.* She had convinced one fan-magazine writer that she had been raised in a convent and had a degree from Stephens College, where she had majored in science and studied drama. That she had been a tough little hoofer at the age of 14 had less reality for her than all the convent school-Stephens College window dressing. If movie fans escaped into their tinseled dreams, why shouldn't the movie stars who floated through those dreams? Now that the former taxi-dancer was Mrs. Douglas Fairbanks, Jr., and reigned over a castle in Brentwood, how could she be anything else but a convent-bred Stephens graduate?

An old vaudevillian turned master Broadway actor turned offbeat movie star, Walter Huston also made good copy on the set of *Rain*. I had first met Huston when he was playing bad guy to Gary Cooper's soft-spoken nice guy in *The Virginian,* one of Father's early hit talkies. Having seen Huston on the New York stage as *Dodsworth,* and having heard my old man praise him as one of the few actors he knew incapable of giving a bad performance, I approached the Reverend Davidson with considerable awe. To my surprise he wasn't interested in talking about his own career, or what choice role he was after next. Instead, he was worried about his young son Johnny. "Johnny's got talent," he said, "I know he's got talent. Trouble with Johnny is, he's got too damn many talents." John Huston first had wanted to be a fighter; even had a couple of pro fights at the Hollywood Legion. He could ride as well as any Western stuntman and had put in some time with the Mexican cavalry. He had worked in New York as an actor, he had set up a studio in Paris and decided to be a painter, had turned to short stories which he sold to *The American Mercury,* and thought he'd be a novelist, a reporter, a screenwriter, a movie actor. . . .

"He could be anything he wants to be, and what worries the hell out of me is that he could also be a bum," brooded the famous father of the future famous director. He was confiding in me because he knew my parents and was aware of their confidence—virtually amounting to a decision—that I would become a writer. There was something rather feudal about it, as if I had been apprenticed at the age of fourteen. Mr. Huston wished young Johnny would settle down to a single career. "I hope to hell it isn't acting," he said. "I think it's writing. But nothing would surprise me about Johnny—he could wind up winning the Pulitzer Prize—or robbing a bank!"

Years later, I would remember this conversation as I watched them win their historic father-son brace of Oscars for performance and direction in *The Treasure of the Sierra Madre*. Johnny would be flamboyant and unpredictable all his life. Sometimes his restlessness and versatility would affect his concentration and derail his progress as a film director. But the time when he would come into his own with *The Maltese Falcon,* and then move on to the *African Queen* and other film classics, was still years ahead of him.

On my rounds of the studios, I met what may be considered my first Hollywood date. Perhaps because I didn't think of her as a member of the opposite sex but instead as potential copy for the *Reporter,* I found myself able to talk with Sidney Fox about her career, to ask her about her role in *Strictly Dishonorable,* then being adapted from Preston Sturges's risqué Broadway hit. She was small, pert, pretty, bright, Jewish, and had given up law school for a Broadway stage career.

Since she was all of 22 and I only 18, I thought of her as an older woman, and so I was surprised when, at the end of the interview, she asked me if I would like to go to a party at the Laemmle mansion in Beverly Hills. I was afraid of parties, but the winsome Miss Fox dropped the kind of names calculated to bring me out of my social shell: It was a party honoring the All-American football team, celebrating the wrap-up of a contemporary epic entitled *All-American.*

Except for the parties my parents and the Rapfs had given—like the reception at our Lorraine house for Maurice Chevalier, at which Charlie Chaplin had gone into another room and pounded the piano to sabotage the attention being lavished on the French singer—this was the first real Hollywood party I had ever attended. It was a mob scene of gridiron celebrities, movie stars, and starlets, with saxophones blaring and bartenders serving the finest bootleg hooch. Sidney asked me to dance, but of course I refused. I had been taking desperate lessons in the box step from Sonya but wasn't ready to make my debut on the dance floor in the arms of a movie star. Instead, I did what I did best—watched and listened. And what I saw and heard horrified me. My heroes, the beloved gods of my sports pantheon, were looped in the coils of Bacchus. "Those backfield stars, all those great linemen, they were all stinko, it was a drunken orgy!" the young Puritan reported to his diary. I watched, half in jealousy, half in horror, as vivacious little Sidney Fox was bounced around the dance floor by an uninhibited blond giant from Nebraska.

I was ready to go. Sidney said she was, too—the party was getting out of hand. But instead of being driven home, she asked if I'd come with her to Paramount where "one of her beaus," as she called Jean Negulesco, the European painter now given a chance to direct, was shooting overtime on a low-budget picture. We watched a scene repeated over and over again, until Sidney said she had seen enough and suggested we move on. Again I expected to drop her off at her home, but instead she suggested a speakeasy off Sunset Boulevard. This was my first taste of Hollywood nightlife, a small, dark room full of film people who recognized us, invited us to join their tables, and seemed to take for granted that we were a new Saturday-night "item." It gave me a racy, sporty feeling to be accepted at Sidney's escort. Mickey Neilan was there, with a snootful as usual, "between pictures" after a twenty-year career that had left him shipwrecked in the rough crossing from silents to sound. Teasing Sidney about robbing the cradle, Mickey drew suggestive laughter from Jack Oakie and Eugene Palette, the gravel-voiced character actor who seemed never to stop drinking or working, averaging half a dozen features a year, a pace he would continue for years to come. When Gene wasn't on the set, the assistant director always knew where to find him: at Lucey's, the speak across from Paramount, or in one of these Hollywood late spots where an animated piano player with a midnight pallor pounded out the happy songs of hard times, "Life Is Just a Bowl of Cherries" and "Happy Days Are Here Again." . . .

1932: Tin Pan Alley, whistling in the dark, with Depression just outside the door of that Sunset Boulevard retreat, soup kitchens downtown, and in the Ventura Valley on the other side of the Hollywood Hills, embattled farmers tearing down their foreclosure notices. But in the hideaway that Sidney Fox had whisked me to, the laughter, the music, and the whiskey created a mood of timeless escape. Sidney managed to down more than her share of highballs. In the dark I sipped at mine, still loathing the taste and smell, perhaps because I associated it with Father's delinquencies, but doing my best to appear a man of the world, a Malibu Tom Sawyer trying to remember how Adolphe Menjou or Clive Brook had behaved in similar situations.

We stayed so long that not only was I getting sleepy, I was beginning to worry about an early-morning tennis date. On the way to Sidney's house she sat disturbingly close to me and chatted away about film work and movie gossip, saying she knew my father, in a way that made me wonder *how well?,* and that she admired my mother as "a real *mensch,* the only studio wife I've met who can stand up to the Mayers and the Warners." I was still too upset about my parents to talk about them, I told her; it was ruining my summer. Sympathetically, Sidney cuddled closer. Nervously, I edged away. When we reached her bungalow on a quiet Hollywood street, she turned her face to me for the expected kiss. I reached for the door handle on my side and ran around the sleek nose of the Dusenberg to open the car door for her. What I lacked in ardor I tried to make up in gallantry. She offered me her arm to walk her to her door in a way that left me no choice but to hold it, tentatively. The only girl I had ever walked with so intimately was my cousin Roz. At the door, as she fumbled for her keys, Sidney said she knew that Ad collected colored glass bells, and she had one she would like to give me for Mother's collection. A million 18-year-olds would have traded a whole month's allowance for that invitation from the little beauty whose face had graced the cover of *Silver Screen*. But my only emotion was pure panic. I muttered a thank-you-some-other-time—I had to be on the court in five hours for a big tennis match. "What a strange boy," Sidney said. "I wonder if your father was anything like you when he was your age?"

By the time I drove the long, winding road home to Malibu, where a dawn mist was rising from the ocean just beyond our gate, I was too exhilarated to sleep. Those lies I had been forced to tell at Deerfield about dating "movie queens" had become truth at last. And if I had been just a little bolder, undoubtedly I could have carried back to Green Gate Cottage a colored glass bell as a symbol of conquest. Instead, I had escaped with virtue intact, eager to share this singular experience with Maurice, my brother in innocence and self-doubt. Did anyone truly like us for ourselves? Or were we simply teenage pawns in the ceaseless Hollywood power game? Too exhausted to go into detail on my "escapade" with Sidney Fox, I settled for a single question: "I wonder why she's so nice to me?"

The "Baby Peggy syndrome," as I thought of it, rankled deep inside me. Even if Sidney Fox had fallen madly in love with me, I would have interpreted it as an insidious effort to outflank Sylvia Sidney and wind up with star roles in Father's new unit at Paramount.

That summer the sex education that my overactive Father and Freudian-minded Mother had totally neglected came to us from an unexpected source—Maurice's cousin from New York, Al Mannheimer. Although Al was only a year older, in our eyes he was already a man of the world, debonair, sophisticated, and sexually experienced. Handsome, suave, self-assured, he was our Beau Brummel, our Don Juan, our Havelock Ellis. At the Rapfs' that summer (because his mother had just committed suicide in New York), he moved in an atmosphere of what seemed to us romantic tragedy. We had become almost hardened to Hollywood suicide: "If I don't get that job I'm going to kill myself!" was more than a rhetorical exclamation in our town. Suicide, including the prolonged form of alcoholism and drugs (Wally Reid, Jack Pickford, Mabel Normand, Alma Rubens, John Gilbert . . .), was an occupational hazard. But Al's mother was different. Why would a prosperous Manhattan matron shoot herself? The details were obscure, we avoided painful questions, and Al's way of coping with it was to assume the role of young roué for whom Hollywood provided erotic escape. He had

470

studied Casanova's *Memoirs* with the devotion of a Hebrew scholar reading the Talmud. Like his 18th-century mentor, Al believed that every young creature, no matter how much she demurred, was inevitably seducible.

A full, leatherbound set of Casanova beckoned from our library, where it had been placed unobtrusively on the highest shelf. A new world began to open up to us from the printed pages. We who still had not learned to dance or to know the feel of a girl in our arms now began to fantasize about obliging French mistresses and flirtatious Italian maidens. On movie sets and in studio dressing rooms our sandy-haired, self-appointed Casanova continued our sex education. According to Al, there was "a particular look in the eyes" of those who had recently indulged in sexual intercourse. "It's a kind of a 'fucky' look—the eyes get lighter—as if they've been washed in milk," our mentor explained. So we began to look into the eyes of ingenues and leading men for signs of the Mannheimer test.

We applied this test on the set of *Divorce in the Family,* a picture I thought of as Maurice's because he had written the original story for it while working as a junior writer the summer before. The title reflected the near-divorce of Maurice's own parents after the Joan Crawford affair. In the Rapfs' case, his father suffered a heart attack, took a leave of absence from the studio, his family rallied around, and Harry and Tina were reunited—just like in the movies, indeed not unlike the movie Chuck Reisner, a holdover from silent days, was "megging" from Maurice's idea.

Conrad Nagel played the would-be stepfather wooing little Jackie Cooper from his real father, Lewis Stone; somehow the three of us, Al, Maurice, and I, found ourselves in Nagel's dressing room, where he was changing costumes for the next scene. Our junior Casanova whispered to us to be sure and look at Nagel's penis. Dutifully, we did so, trying to make it seem accidental as our eyes dropped toward the floor.

When we withdrew from Nagel's dressing room, Prof. Mannheimer gave us an improvised lecture on what might be called "penisology." Had we noticed, he quizzed, the way Nagel's seemed to be bunched up with little wrinkles and how it looked somewhat reddened at the tip? Those were the symptoms, Al explained, of recent sexual intercourse, either that morning or late the night before.

Armed with this potent insight into the carnal mysteries that both fascinated and frightened us, we continued our study in the locker room of the Hillcrest Country Club and the Paramount gym and dressing rooms. Thanks to Al, we were also beginning to study the anatomy of the opposite gender in a way we had not dared to before. In our library I read the spicy stories of Colette and also Mother's Krafft-Ebing, although that ponderous work preferred to mask the best parts in Latin. Now I wished I had learned a little more of the language that was not quite so dead as MacConaughy and I had thought at Deerfield.

As we had since we were ten, Maurice and I still took turns sleeping over at each other's houses. But now our intimate all-night talk-fests took a different turn. We were ready to take the plunge, which in our case did not go as far as Mannheimer-Casanova seduction, but merely to work up the nerve to invite a date to the Coconut Grove, or better yet—since we wouldn't have to dance but merely feel romantic under the stars—to an evening concert in the Hollywood Bowl.

Divorce in the Family featured a luscious 16-year-old being groomed for stardom, Jean Parker. No ordinary starlet, Jean was the ward of Ida Koverman, former secretary to Herbert Hoover, proudly acquired by L.B. not only as a sign of class but as a means of moving up the Republican ladder to the lofty appointments for which he panted. The ultraconservative Mrs. Koverman, who served as L.B.'s storyteller— saving him the irksome chore of reading treatments and scenarios—was determined to keep her protegée as pure as an ingenue in an Andy Hardy movie. Mrs. Koverman had to approve Jean's dates; she had to be properly chaperoned and, like Cinderella, home before midnight. This made Jean an ideal first date for Maurice, removing the pressures of the livelier Sidney Foxes. Through the musical prodigy my parents hoped to develop into a second Paderewski, Leon Becker, I met the fair Elaine Rugg, "very pretty with clean blonde hair and an unusual smile, the kind of girl that is restful to be with."

We had first met Leon at the Coaching School, where he appealed to us as a romantic figure, with his bare little knees pumping masterfully beneath the keyboard of the grand piano on which he played everything from Chopin to Beethoven. When we learned that his father had died and his mother was working as a seamstress, my parents were so moved by his plight and his talent that they virtually adopted him, paying his tuition at the Coaching School (he was there on a limited scholarship) and offering to underwrite his musical education. He had become a "third brother" we proudly showed off at parties, where he held the guests spellbound with precocious performances of études and sonatas.

472

Thanks to Leon's introduction, I was able to take Elaine to the Hollywood Bowl where, moved by the sensuous music of Ravel, we shyly held hands. Then on to the Brown Derby, the original one on Wilshire Boulevard, built Hollywood-style in the shape of an actual bowler. Elaine was lovely, gentle, sweet, passive, and over a steaming plate of tamales I wondered if the unfamiliar flush I was feeling came from the spicy Mexican dish or from my first experience of falling in love. She lived downtown in a lower-middle-class neighborhood, in a modest frame house with an old-fashioned front porch. Getting out of the Dusenberg I knew I hadn't earned, I forced myself to take Elaine's arm and walk her to the door. There was a tantalizing moment when we almost kissed. It was comforting to find someone as demure as I. In my diary is an entry suitably restrained: "Elaine is liable to become my first 'crush.'"

Early next morning I called to ask if she would go with me to the Coconut Grove. "Oh, that sounds very nice." Her voice was a gentle purring, almost a whisper. I talked so softly myself that we could barely hear one another. As I made my rounds of the studios that day, I was too distracted to take proper notes. At the end of the afternoon, the 14-year-old Sonya, with a dance style slightly this side of Adele Astaire's, put some records on the Capehart and offered last-minute instructions on my command of the box step. It seemed I only knew how to move in one direction, clockwise. Not only did that become monotonous but it tended to induce vertigo. Whenever I tried counterclockwise, my partner's feet had an annoying habit of tripping me.

It was almost time to pick up Elaine. Sonya could do no more. "I guess you'll just have to keep on doing that one step and try not to get dizzy," was her sisterly advice.

A night of triumph! Elaine was graceful, tender and helpful. By the end of the evening I even took a few tentative steps *counter*clockwise.

Parked in front of her house, I rested my arm on the backrest behind her and with studied casualness let it slip down over her shoulder. Progress. It was not quite the seductive tactics Al Mannheimer had recommended: "Guide her hand gently toward your fly. If she doesn't pull her hand away, put your hand over hers and say something romantic. You'll be surprised how many girls can't resist feeling it once you hold their hand to it. The stirring excites them even if they pretend to be shocked. If she pulls her hand away, don't get discouraged. She may want you to think she's not that kind of a girl. Wait 'til next time. But if she doesn't draw her hand away, surreptitiously begin to unbutton your fly. . . ."

Instead, while I draped my arm modestly around Elaine's shoulder, I listened sympathetically to her long, sad story: She wanted to be a classical dancer; a fortune left to her in a grandparent's will could only be claimed if she went to Sweden, a journey her parents refused her because she was too young to travel and live there alone—but unless she could claim that fortune, she felt doomed to a life of mediocrity.

The pale light of tragedy enfolding her seemed to make her more beautiful. At the door I asked her if she would like to have lunch with me at the studio next day. "Oh, that would be nice," she purred again. Of course it never occurred to me that the beautiful Elaine might be a confirmed dullard. In ecstasy I gunned the big car back toward prosperous Windsor Square, and promptly ran out of gas. In the diary the crown prince of the Schulberg fortunes had his emotions under control: "What a swell girl! Her life story would make a great yarn. Putting my arm around her is a great step forward!"

At the studio luncheon next day I innocently invited "third brother" Leon. He seemed distracted, upset, and strangely quiet. While I signed the bill—sent to Father's office—he asked if he could drive Elaine home. I was surprised, as Leon was working in the music department, writing out scores for background music, and I knew he was under pressure to get back to work. The head of the department, Nat Finston, was a demanding boss. Leaving abruptly during the middle of the day could cost Leon his job.

Later I drove down to Elaine's to discuss this serious turn of events. She admitted she had been "seeing" Leon, but in her opinion he was overdramatizing the situation. So my first tentative romance had led to dramatic complications. In the overexcitement of finally asking a girl to the Grove, I had been insensitive to Leon's feelings. In his martyrdom, Leon assured me that if Elaine and I were really serious about each other, he would step aside. But he was hurt. Underlying this drama, I knew, was his sense of inferiority. He, Maurice, and I played as equals, but there must always have been that gnawing feeling that we had been born to the Hollywood purple, while he, with all his musical culture, still came from the other side of the tracks.

52

To DISTRACT US from this unexpected romantic triangle, the 1932 Olympic Games, the event Maurice and I had been eagerly awaiting for years, came to our own Los Angeles Coliseum. Further work on *The Hollywood Reporter* was out of the question. I asked for a leave of absence, so I could give full concentration to the Games.

The entire Hollywood community seemed almost as excited as I was. A meeting of film celebrities was held to choose hosts for the various foreign teams. Maurice Chevalier volunteered to give a reception for the French team and arrange a tour of the studio. Marlene Dietrich offered to serve in a similar capacity for the German contingent, not yet appropriated by the upstart Hitler. One by one each foreign group was spoken for. Finally it came little Latvia's turn. Mother raised her hand. She, a daughter of Dvinsk in the heart of our homeland, would be proud to host the Latvian team. At the end of the meeting we were introduced to them, or rather *him,* for Latvia, we discovered, was represented by a single athlete, a marvelous-looking, ruddy-faced specimen bursting with muscles, energy, confidence, and handsome enough to be a leading man. In fact, Mother suggested half-seriously that after the Games she might get him a seven-year contract at Paramount. Of course Karl would have to learn English. He spoke and understood only his mother tongue. That gap was filled, barely, by the few words of English spoken by the small, paunchy trainer in a cheap double-breasted suit who accompanied our Latvian champion. From him we learned that Karl had become a national hero, the only athlete in the whole country who qualified for international competition. His best event was the pole vault, but he was also the best runner and jumper in Mother's motherland. Since Latvia lacked funds to field an Olympic team, sending Karl and his trainer from Riga to Los Angeles had become a national cause. Peasants had dropped their meager coins into milk cans to raise money for their "team." Thousands of Letts waving little national flags had seen him off on his two-week journey by rail and sea to our distant shores.

Overnight we became patriotic Latvians. Mother had said that she had been a babe in arms when the Jaffes were driven from their village by a pogrom, but now her memory of her Latvian childhood grew miraculously. I looked up our country's history in the encyclopaedia. From the Middle Ages we had been dominated in turn by Poland, Russia, and Sweden, and by the German land barons. We had been badly mangled in the Great War. And the Germans had struck again and occupied us as late as 1919. But our little army had fought back, and with support from a motley alliance we had won our independence in 1920. Now the 12-year-old Republic had sent us Karl. He was our houseguest at Malibu, and I was proud to run with him on the beach as he underwent his early-morning conditioning. Mother gave a luncheon for him in the studio commissary, decorated with Latvian flags and attended by dozens of Paramount stars. Even though Father had been moved to his bungalow suite, the Schulberg name had not lost its magic, and we still had the run of the lot.

In his snappy blue blazer with the Latvian crest, Karl must have thought he had died and been reborn in a Baltic heaven. The famous of Hollywood rose to applaud him when he made his charming, halting thank-you speech, which Mother proudly interpreted from a pretranslated text. He spoke of his small Latvian village and of how he had learned to pole-vault by fashioning his own pole from a slender tree and soaring over the high fences of the local farms. His mother, he said, had bought her first radio so she and her neighbors could follow his progress in the Games. Hollywood has always been sentimental about this kind of "outside" celebrity: Movie stars flocked around our Latvian standard-bearer, inviting him to their beach houses and wanting *his* autograph. At Karl's side, I basked in reflected glory.

On the day of the great event, the pole-vault competition, the Schulberg-Jaffe contingent was there to root the Latvian hope to record heights. The bar was put at 12 feet for warm-up jumps. At the head of the runway, Karl paused, took a deep breath to expand his powerful chest, struck a heroic pose, then went pounding down the path to the uprights, went up on his pole to a height of ten feet, ten-and-a-half . . . and fell clumsily into the pit *under* the bar. We looked at each other. Apparently Karl's hand had slipped on the bamboo pole, an accident that could happen to anyone. By this time he was pounding down the runway again. This time he rose to a mighty height of almost 11 feet, trembled there a moment, and then went crashing into the bar which fell humiliatingly on top of him in the pit.

Our Latvian cheering section was tense and silent as Karl went back for his final try. He expanded his chest at least four inches, ran with grim purpose down the runway, vaulted straight into the bar and fell on his back with the splintered bar draped across his mighty chest.

That was the end of Karl at the Los Angeles Olympics. For weeks we had been wining and dining an athlete who could not have made our L.A. High School track team. In fact, a boy on our B squad had cleared 12 feet! As the vaulters cleared 13 feet and on up to a record 14, Karl picked up his pole and trudged off into the tunnel on his way to the locker room and oblivion. He was too humiliated even to say goodbye.

My own connection with the Games—through my classmate at L.A. High, Cornelius Johnson— was a happier experience. He was the same skinny, barely literate Corny whose copy I had doctored in Miss Carr's journalism class.

The first day he had come out for track, in the high jump, I had advised him to try for the Class B team because we already had two six-foot jumpers on the varsity. A little later I was taking my laps when I noticed an unusual crowd around the high-jump pit. I was told that Corny had just cleared six feet on his first try, by what looked like half a foot! The bar was raised two inches, and again Corny flew over it without really seeming to try. At that point an awed Coach Chambers told Corny not to go any higher—he wanted to keep him under wraps.

Now, in the Coliseum, my Corny Johnson was up there with the greatest jumpers in the world. By some magic transformation, the L.A.H.S. letters on his chest now read U.S.A. I, who had once cleared five feet doing the old-fashioned scissors, concentrated, took a deep breath, loped down the runway toward the bar, and—secreted in Corny's body—cleared six-four without even trembling the bar. I turned and hugged my date, Maurice's cousin Polly, a very pretty girl signed as an ingenue at MGM, a warm, happy person with whom I felt safe. The bar went to 6 feet 5, and then to a fraction under 6 feet 6. The intense competition ended with Corny being edged out by a Canadian, a veteran from Southern Cal. Four years later, however, an athletically mature Cornelius Johnson would take the gold at the Berlin Games and go on to establish a world's record.

Unfortunately, after the glories of the high bar, there was nowhere for him to go but down. Lost in alcohol, he'd be carried off a merchant ship during World War II, a wreck of the genius highschool athlete who had soared like a black angel almost seven feet above the ground.

53

OMING BACK FROM the Games to *The Hollywood Reporter,* I found that my routine items—who was cast in what picture, what director had been assigned, when the next production would roll—had become boringly easy. I asked the managing editor for a chance at something bigger, like covering a sneak preview. Grumbling, Billy Wilkerson assigned me a Columbia meller sneaking in Glendale. Feeling as important as a first-night reviewer, I went alone so I could concentrate. Conscientiously, I took notes in the dark on the formula stuff I was to appraise, then raced back to the Sunset Boulevard office to bang out my review. I gave the picture no stars. Feeling righteously honest, I tore it apart sequence by sequence. Long after midnight I drove home tired but happy, congratulating myself on a hard job well done.

Next morning I couldn't wait to see my review in print, the first real chance I had had on the paper. I turned to the third-page banner over the review and read—an out-and-out rave! Socko programmer! Smart megging and first-rate cast more than make up for formula story! Here and there, toward the end, they kept a line or two of my original critique. But sometime after I had slung on my cap and hopped into my Dusenberg phaeton, little goblins had crept in and completely rewritten me to please a muscle-minded Harry Cohn who otherwise would have threatened, "No more fuckin' ads!"

Lincoln Steffens had opened a window, a whole houseful of windows, on municipal corruption. My brief career on *The Hollywood Reporter* added a local footnote: District Attorney Buron Fitts had just been caught taking bribes and at last was losing his sinecure. The dull *Los Angeles Times* and the lurid *Herald-Examiner* published nothing objectionable to the Hollywood powers. And of course the Industry "trades" religiously read at thousands of studio desks every morning carried only the news and reviews that Louie B., Jack L., and the rest of the moguls thought fit to print.

I wanted to quit. I wanted to stand up to Billy Wilkerson. But with millions out of work, and hundreds of local writers hungry for jobs, I had a strong case of the Ad Schulberg guilts. And when I dropped in at Father's new quarters, he urged me to swallow my pride, keep on working, and not alienate Wilkerson. He admired my principles, but reminded me that I was still serving my journalistic novitiate: Covering the Hollywood beat and meeting deadlines were invaluable training for the work ahead. Father's outspokenness had already alienated L.B., Sam Goldwyn, and other Hollywood rivals. But he was always ready to give sound conservative advice he was never able to follow.

That Sunday at Malibu I was bailed out of my moral dilemma by a timely visit from Dave Selznick. He and Irene—lively, loyal friends in those days—had stopped by for tennis, brunch, and local gossip. When David, ever-curious, ever-working, asked me what I was doing, I told him a story I was outlining: A Negro cook and her young son live on a Bel Air estate where her little boy and the white owner's son, of an age, become inseparable. Both sets of parents try to break up what they consider an unhealthy relationship. The cook, modeled on our own irrepressible Lucille, is as determined a segregationist as her white employers. "When us black folks mess with whites, who do you think gets the short end of the stick?" she warns her small son, then sings the old saw, "Stay in your own backyard." But the boy won't listen. When the young white master invites him to the pool and teaches him how to swim, they hold a diving contest in which the white boy is injured; the black boy tries to save him and drowns in the attempt. Of course the dead child is blamed by the white parents for challenging their son to take unnecessary risks. The mammy, obviously Hattie McDaniels, is left with her drowned son in her arms, crooning, "Stay in your own backyard."

This was not exactly Langston Hughes, or Jean Toomer, or even DuBose Heyward. But the young, enthusiastic Selznick enthused. He saw a kid's picture, a *Skippy* or *Sooky,* with a new touch of Negro pathos (or was it bathos?) thrown in. With feelers always out for new material, he was ready to buy it on the spot. My mother the agent made the deal. I was to be paid $1,500 on delivery of a ten-page outline. At that point, if David liked what he read, I would go to work at RKO for $50 a week to develop the story until I had to leave for Dartmouth.

With a flourish, I signed my first writing contract, Budd *Wilson* Schulberg (for we all had to have three names in those days), shook the mighty hand of David Oliver Selznick, and was assigned an office in the writers' wing of the studio. My immediate supervisor was an old friend from Father's staff, Benny Zeidman, whom David had brought with him to RKO. On the first day I discovered that I would not be working alone. David had decided that I should be teamed with an older, more seasoned writer. He turned out to be a published mystery writer, Stuart Palmer, a sympathetic and congenial fellow who took a rather patronizing view of my story and was more involved in the serious business of finishing his next mystery novel on company time.

Assigning two total strangers to collaborate on a film story was a bizarre but familiar Hollywood practice. It had never been clear to me why an established Broadway playwright or a published novelist could not sit down and write alone as he had done before. Hollywood believed in safety in numbers. Not just a single team but often a series of teams would be used to turn out a single screenplay. What the studio bosses failed to appreciate was the impossibility of two strangers closeting themselves in a small office and plunging into instant collaboration. First we had to break the ice.

Stuart Palmer and I talked about my father and his complex relationship to David Selznick, about mystery-writing and fiction-writing in general, about the general low I.Q. of supervisors and the specific mental deficiencies of little Benny Zeidman, and about gambling. Father's addiction was common knowledge. When I said I had developed such a loathing for the subject that I did not even know how to play poker or shoot craps, my new collaborator produced a pair of dice and rattled them against the wall of our office to begin my education.

A few days later I would enter in my ledger: "Did little work on my story. Lost $2 at craps. But we have a swell angle on the story. A *Green Pastures* touch." This was far different from being allowed to sit in on Father's conferences, indulged, flattered, and encouraged to make a suggestion now and then. I was on the other side now, waiting for conferences always late in being called. When Benny Zeidman liked our *Green Pastures* approach, our stock rose. Back to work, between crap games and bull sessions, our confidence grew. A few days later, when we heard that Zeidman—in the familiar game of Hollywood musical chairs—had been fired, and that David O. would assign a new supervisor to *Your Own Back Yard,* our stock plunged. Up and down the halls, and across at Lucey's, we found fellow-writers in the same predicament. Everybody seemed to be waiting for Selznick. And young David seemed to shuffle film projects the way Zeppo Marx shuffled cards. One of the reasons David had given for walking out on Father was B.P.'s inability or refusal to delegate authority. Now the underlings of RKO were voicing the same criticism of David. The intense D.O.S. simply wasn't geared to turn out the forty to fifty pictures a year the RKO program demanded. He wanted to concentrate on his own class production, *A Bill of Divorcement,* starring George Cukor's young Broadway discovery, Katharine Hepburn; *The Animal Kingdom; Topaze....* My little story, and low-budget pictures like it, were neglected as young David indulged ever-bigger dreams.

54

A
S THE DAYS of summer marched and then broke ranks to race us into fall, the pace of our family drama accelerated. Mother's overnight agency success was the talk of the town. Of course, as a woman wronged, a loyal Hollywood wife cruelly abandoned, she had martyrdom going for her. No matter what sexual tricks the moguls might perform behind closed doors, they were all devoted followers of Will Hays, champions of decency. While W. R. Hearst dallied with his adorable, tipsy, stuttering Marion Davies, his newspaper editorials inveighed against sin, adultery, and divorce and came out bravely for the sanctity of the home. As for Louie B., if there were adulterers in his pictures, they had to be punished for their misconduct. The threat of divorce had to be countered by domestic reconciliation neatly timed to the final fade-out. Louie truly thought of his company not just as an entertainment factory, but as a mighty pillar of society holding up the House of Rectitude that was America. In his Byzantine mind, God, Country, the GOP, and MGM had become a holy quaternity.

When Mother made her first official call on L.B., the mogul of moguls had her admitted immediately. Instead of sitting behind his enormous desk to impress visitors with the power of his authority, he had hurried across his great office to greet her as she entered. Here were two old friends who went back to the Mission Road days of a dozen years earlier, when L.B. and B.P. had shared a primitive studio for shoestring productions. What a pivotal dozen years those had been: L.B. rising from his Anita Stewart formula pictures to the pinnacle of Hollywood success, the confidant of Hoover and Hearst, the admiral of the Industry flagship; B.P. becoming a household name, at least in Hollywood households, directing MGM's major rival for more than half a dozen years, but now being pushed from his catbird seat.

As Mother came in, a smartly dressed woman of thirty-nine, looking rather like Irene Rich crossed with Eleanor Boardman, Louie threw his arms around her and began to cry. His tears, Louie explained, were for her unfortunate predicament. A disgraceful photograph of Father and Sylvia on the dance floor of the Coconut Grove had just appeared in the local paper. How Ben could do such a thing to a wonderful woman like Ad, a model wife and mother, Louie would never understand. Gallantly he led her to the couch where they wept together, two grown-up street urchins who had clawed their way to the top, he through elocution lessons, Ida Koverman lessons, and a nose for power; she through Coué, Freud, and a gift for survival. She would never have to worry about her agency business, Louie assured her, because his door would always be open to her. She could bring her clients directly to him and he would see to it that she would be treated with generosity and the respect she deserved.

It was no accident that the source of L.B.'s power was celluloid dramatics. A man of extremes, he could sob, laugh, strike out at enemies, or fall on his knees in fervent humility, on cue. Power has always been sexual. And when he wanted to exude them, L.B. could send forth waves of warmth and reassurance. On the couch he stroked Mother's shoulder consolingly, his hand slid down to her breast, and when she expressed the demurrer expected of her, "Why, Louie!" he went to his knees—a familiar position when he wasn't at one's throat—and confessed his love. He had been too much of a gentleman to express his true feelings while she had been married to Ben. But now that they had separated and she was contemplating divorce, he had to tell her that he had been smitten with her for years.

As the entreaties, and the groping, increased, Mother may have calculated what effect the rejection of this home-lover would have on her agency business. Benevolent despot to those who favored him, malevolent to those who dared cross him, L.B. could be either ardent lover or dangerous enemy. Mother admitted that she was attracted to Louie. In a scene that must have sounded like a holdover from one of Father's old Katherine MacDonald movies, she protested that they couldn't do this to Louie's wife, her dear friend Margaret. And in dialogue familiar to triangle situations, Louie countered that he and Maggie had drifted apart, that she lived in isolation from his needs and problems, and indeed that her mind had begun to wander. He needed a strong woman in his life, someone he could respect and appreciate. Ben had been a damn fool not to realize what a gem he had. Together King Louis and Queen Adeline could rule the Hollywood kingdom for years to come. It was virtually a proposal of marriage.

Mother had always been fond of Margaret, a sweet, plain-looking woman who somehow had remained the simple daughter of a struggling kosher butcher from Boston. But it would be more accurate to say that her attitude was one of patronizing sympathy. There were very few women in Hollywood on whom Mother did not look down, mostly with good reason. To her credit she tried to live with her peers and to cultivate and learn from her superiors. And she had thought of herself as a surrogate mother, having to take the Mayer daughters in hand because Margaret could not provide them the intellectual guidance and stimulation they needed. From the beginning, this Mayer-Schulberg interrelationship had been incestuous.

To give L.B. his due, Margaret had failed to keep step with him as he boldly climbed the ladder. And Mother must have seen in Louie the strength she had looked for in vain in the man she loved. At any rate, either during that first visit to Louie's office, or in subsequent visits, this tryst of middle-aged Montague and Capulet was consummated, on what was vulgarly called "the casting couch."

Of course, at the time I did not hear even the breath of a whisper of such an affair. I knew only that Mother returned from her meeting with L.B. greatly encouraged that her new list of clients would find an open door at the busiest studio in town. And that L.B. had been courtly, sympathetic, and helpful. Even this receptive attitude struck me as a vicarious slap in the face. No matter what I thought of Father's behavior—and my thoughts were still murderous—I had inherited his attitude toward L.B. as our archenemy. Obviously, Mother's turning to him for invaluable professional assistance handed him the ideal weapon with which to shoot Father down. I couldn't help feeling that she had betrayed the man she still professed to love. And yet, what was she to do? She was a free woman now, or almost, still extremely attractive, and challenged through no fault of her own to establish her identity. While she had a strong *in* at Paramount through connections inherited from

Father, and enjoyed the friendship of the Warners, the Laemmles, and the Cohns of Columbia, the stamp of approval from L. B. Mayer gave her exactly the leverage she needed to become Myron Selznick's major competitor overnight.

Her first encounter with Father's successor at Paramount, Manny Cohen, was less crucial, less traumatic for me, but in its own way almost as memorable. Because Ad's feelings toward Ben were so ambivalent, and because she found it painful to go down that familiar hall, confront a new secretary, and enter a domain so long identified with B.P., she felt herself choking up, with a large chip on the shoulder of her small, sturdy figure. She was, after all, still Mrs. B. P. Schulberg, proud of the name and of what it had represented, and she had built up a head of steam against the usurper, both for the cold-blooded way he had eased out her friend Jesse Lasky, and for the way he had weaseled himself into the good graces of the new bosses of Paramount at Father's expense. As Mother made her entrance at the top of the steps leading down to the splendid office that had been for so many years her husband's second home, she cast a withering look at the diminutive mogul squatting behind the imposing desk like a watchful toad.

"Mr. Cohen," Mother said in her *grande-dame* manner, "when a lady enters your office, I would expect you at least to have the courtesy to stand up like a gentleman."

"Madame," her adversary assured her, "I *am* standing up."

Manny Cohen was barely five feet two. But he was a calculating little giant who knew how to capitalize on Paramount's difficulties that summer. Cohen brought to mind all the small darting, predatory animals—ferrets, weasels, rats. Rats thrive and fatten on disaster, which is exactly what made Manny Cohen. Until that fateful summer of discontent, Paramount had been thought of as a family, extending from the princely Zukor to the kindly Lasky to the gracious Schulberg, with C. B. DeMille running his own show under Jesse's gentle rein. Now that the studio had fallen on hard times, it turned to hard men. Sam Katz was a business monster, and as his production chief, Manny Cohen walked—or rather ran—in his mentor's tracks.

In Father's bungalow compound there was much laughter at Cohen's expense. Writers, directors, and actors loyal to B.P. began telling Manny Cohen stories as they had told Sam Goldwyn and Harry Rapf stories. "The nice thing about having a story conference with Manny Cohen is that you don't have to see the little sonofabitch—unless you look under

486

the desk," Herman Mankiewicz would say, and everybody would roar. "I tell you, Mank, he's riding for a fall!" Father would happily prophesy. To which Mank would be ready with: "How do you fall off a six-inch footstool?" In Father's office, amidst the scotch highballs and the evening card-playing, the work went on with *Madame Butterfly,* while Father's favorite writers prepared another vehicle for Sylvia and his latest discovery, Archie Leach, soon to become a name familiar all over the world—as Cary Grant.

A cockeyed optimist, Father refused to sulk in his bungalow and give in to depression, personal depression that is. "Manny is a master of the double cross, but not the art of making pictures," he insisted.

Not long after that, Manny Cohen was on his way to Chicago on the *Santa Fe Chief* for a meeting with his Paramount-Publix masters when an angry telegram fired him out of hand. It seemed that as the contracts of various Paramount stars expired—Mae West's, Bing Crosby's, Gary Cooper's—instead of resigning them to studio contracts, the ferret-minded Manny signed them to personal contracts. These he could resell to the studio at a profit, or take with him if he left the lot. Henry Herzbrun, the conservative studio attorney and Lasky-Schulberg loyalist, had discovered this sleight of hand and reported it to his superiors. Manny Cohen was driven in disgrace from the sunken office. But Father was not invited to resume his old position. Instead, he was warned about going over budget on *Madame Butterfly,* and ordered to have some surefire low-budget pictures ready for the crucial '33 season.

Even Father's infectious laughter could not survive the chill of his reception at the Malibu Colony house when he came to see Mother for what was supposed to be "a civilized discussion of their problems." While Stuart played outside with our dog Gent, and Sonya cowered in her tower-room refuge, the meeting between my parents quickly degenerated into tense confrontation and ugly accusations.

Mother opened with a mean recital of parental neglect: "If you want to see Stuart, you should see him over here instead of letting him see you over there with that Sidney woman!"—"You're letting Sonya grow up without a father, she's at such a critical age, she could grow up with a complex of—" To which Father countered: "Now Ad, for once will you spare me your goddamn Freudian theories!"

What Father had come for, it developed, was to reduce his monthly payments to Mother on the basis of her unexpected income from the budding Ad Schulberg Agency. Hell had no fury like Mother's reaction to Father's claim of fiscal instability. All the passion she felt about losing him to Sylvia Sidney, and so publicly and humiliatingly, she poured into the subject of his financial responsibilities to his wife and children. She was not going to let him use what she would earn in the future as an excuse for failing to meet those responsibilities. He fought back: He was earning only half what he did before, and she was beginning to earn thousands a month; it was unreasonable for her to expect him to pay out the kind of money he had given her in the past. If she had her way, he charged, she would not only keep all of her money but get all of his as well.

And what would happen to the money he withheld from her? Mother demanded. Instead of going to a fund for the children's education, it would go to the gamblers, the bootleggers, and the "hoors." New expenses lay ahead. Soon Buddy would be off to college. (I had offered to pay my first year's $400 tuition and thousand-dollar room and board at Dartmouth with my check from RKO, but Mother urged me instead to buy five blue-chip stocks and gamble on the eventual end of the Depression.) With Ad now a full-time working woman, Stuart was to be sent to boarding school near Santa Barbara, Sonya to a girls' school in Paris. Ad expected Father to put us all through private schools and college and accumulate enough money to pass on to us after graduation. Besides, she had devoted twenty years to Father. He would have been nothing without her. Even a bum like *his* father. And so she and the children deserved half of everything he would ever earn.

"Ad, goddammit, don't forget I have a million-dollar insurance policy made out to you and the children. When I die, you and the kids will get this plus the money I expect us both to keep making if you don't kill me with your goddamn nagging about money. Goddammit Ad, it's not just money you want, you want to punish me—"

"—I won't kill you, you're killing yourself with your crazy life and your drinking and—"

"—If I'm drinking too much, that sonofabitch Sam Katz ought to send a case of my best Eddie Kaye scotch to every producer on the lot! Do you know that Publix theater managers are already calling Sam Katz to bring me back now that Manny is on his way out? I know you're a great expert on talent now, but did you see the piece in *Box Office* the other day? When Gary Cooper didn't want to play Pinkerton in *Butterfly*—and goddam it I made him in *Wings*—I didn't try to borrow a high-priced star from another studio, I cast Cary Grant in it. Okay, so he's just a beginner? Well, so was Coop five years ago. Take it from me, Ad, Cary Grant is going to be a big star. I'll be making new stars and I'll be making money pictures when Manny Cohen is back making newsreels."

"All right, Ben, all right! So you're a great star-maker! So great that you're not running the whole studio anymore!"

"But not for the reasons you think! It's because that sonofabitch Sam Katz—"

"Ben, you know the trouble with you, you always find excuses for yourself! I wish you spent as much time on your work as you do justifying your mistakes!"

Father went to the antique walnut bar embellished with John Held, Jr., prints. "Ad, you could drive anybody to drink! I was up until three o'clock this morning . . ."

"At the Clover Club!"

"Like hell I was! In the projection room until midnight. I worked on a script with Bud [Leighton] and Hope [Loring] until almost two. Then I read a story that might work out for George Raft next winter. You talk about 'that Sidney woman,' but at least she builds me up, she gives me confidence, you're always tearing me down! Goddamn-it-Ad! [that seemed to have become her name]—if you don't stop lecturing me I'm walking out of here!"

"Go ahead, walk out of here, ruin your life—but you're not going to ruin mine, or Buddy's and Sonya's and Stuart's."

"You know the trouble with you, Ad, you love money. Well, there are other things in life maybe even more important, like love and—"

"—You think that Sidney woman loves you! She and her mother would drop you in a minute if you weren't still so important, if you weren't able to give her parts like Madame Butterfly. . . ."

As if in open defiance of Mother's harsh judgment, Father had made himself a drink and was pacing up and down in mounting fury. "You don't know what you're talking about, Ad! If you're going to be such a great agent you should know the crying hunger for new stars in the Industry, and the bargaining power that gives them. 'That Sidney woman,' as you insist on calling her, could go out tomorrow morning and double her salary at Warners or MGM. After all, you were the first one to sing her praises when you saw her on the stage. You were the one urging me to sign her. What makes you think she's not in greater demand now than she was when she was still a minor New York actress? If she were as selfish and greedy as you say she is, wouldn't she have jumped to one of the other studios long before this? Be fair, Ad. I know that isn't easy under the circumstances, but goddamn it, be fair!"

"You talk to me about *fair*? After the way you've disgraced me and the children? At least the heads of other studios keep their mistresses quiet. But you have to be photographed with yours dancing at the Grove!" Her eyes were full of tears, her voice full of rage. "I tried to hide that paper from the children."

"Is it my fault that this town's a bunch of goddamned hypocrites?"

"I want that money, Ben. Every week. Even if I have to ask Mendel Silverberg to attach your salary."

Father poured another drink and called her terrible names. Mother gave it right back to him. Her voice was hoarse and toughened with rage. World-famous names were simply so many hard stones hurled at each other. Bow—Sidney—Cooper—Colbert—Chatterton—Grant . . .

Father stormed out of the house; the unwieldy Lincoln roadster that he drove poorly even in the best of times screeched down the dirt road out of the Colony. Mother leaned back on the couch and began to sob. I went out to our tennis court, turned on the lights and drove balls against the backboard as hard as I could. Later that night the cryptic diarist put the scene in a capsule: "Dad was over tonight. Awful row. He is getting unreasonable about money. Poor Mom has her hands full."

The next day Mother stayed in bed and didn't want to talk to anyone. She called Charley Feldman to take care of the office, and at the end of the day confided her problem to Dr. Dorothy Baruch, the child psychiatrist with whom she had founded the Hollywood Progressive School.

Next evening on his way back from the studio to the Malibu house he again shared with Sylvia, Father lost control of his car and drove off the Pacific Coast Road, over a 12-foot embankment and into the ocean. By the time the force of water stopped the forward motion of the big roadster, the waves had reached the level of the car windows. Pulled from the driver's seat by rescuers and dragged ashore, he was unscathed. Even the big Upmann cigar between his teeth was still aglow. A cat only has nine lives. Father's, at that time at least, seemed numberless. Though his power in Hollywood leached away slowly over the years, whenever B.P. and his cigar appeared at the door of the best restaurants, the maitre d' would always show him to a pretty good table.

That weekend I threw myself into the Malibu Tennis Tournament as if it were salvation from family miseries. I ran the length of the Colony beach and did pushups and knee bends until my muscles begged me to leave them alone.

To that tournament I brought an intangible advantage, undigested indignation. Every ball I drove or served or smashed was aimed at Sylvia's navel, if not lower. I destroyed Junior Laemmle, blasted Felix Young, outhit the cagey Sam Jaffe, outplayed Paul Lukas, and battled my way into the finals with our local Tilden, Irwin Gelsey. To the affable Gelsey it was only a game; to me it was life-and-death, as I played the kind of tennis I usually fantasized about: 7-5, 6-3!

"The Malibu singles cup is mine!" reports the L.A. High School and Deerfield loser. "My game was terrific and at all times I was on the offense."

Our crowd—Maurice, the Goetz boys, and Al Mannheimer—celebrated by jumping into my Dusenberg and racing to the Mexican border, where we played roulette at the Jockey Club in Tijuana, bet the horses at Agua Caliente, and, at the urging of our evil mentor, Al Mannheimer, ordered a scotch highball at the bar, followed by straight tequila. "From midnight until dawn my stomach burned." I was discovering the joys and price of alcohol.

For us this was wild adventure. "On our way back from the casino to the hotel," the diary records, "Walt [Goetz] expressed the quaint desire to get laid and wanted to get a whore to come to the hotel. He didn't."

Maurice and I were relieved. We were trying to sound like red-blooded 18-year-olds now, but sex to us was still Clara Bow in trouble, Joan Crawford as Sadie Thompson seducing Walter Huston (or Harry Rapf?), Sylvia Sidney getting pregnant and having to be dumped in the lake by Phillips Holmes (Father?).

Next morning was more our style. With the first light, we were down at the dock to find our charter boat to cruise through the Coronado Islands that rise boldly from the waters off Lower California south of San Diego, where the only inhabitants were a large, hospitable, and apparently bilingual family of seals. We fished for yellowtail and battled them like junior Hemingways. The sun smiled and baked down on us, raising blisters on the handsome nose of Al Casanova. We loved the Coronados, the seals, those yellowtail, the mysterious coastline of Baja *incognita,* far from studio headaches and Malibu misalliances.

Home to Hollywood I made my ceremonial farewell rounds of the lots, only this time the circle had widened. Goodbye to Stuart Palmer at RKO, rolling dice, writing his novel, riding high with the success of *A Bill of Divorcement* and Katharine Hepburn. Goodbye to Elaine Rugg, to whom I expressed my tender feelings with a large fish from the Coronados and a tentative kiss—with a gallant footnote in my diary: "I hope I'm not encouraging her too much." Goodbye to Teet Carle, Freddie March, Oscar the Bootblack, Dick Arlen, and all my pals at Paramount. Goodbye to the Mayer girls, Irene and Edith, and up their old man's. Goodbye to his studio, or rather Maurice's, as we liked to think of it, and to the chums on our old Culver City playground, comedian George K. Arthur, our protected starlet Jean Parker, the friendly film editor Frank Davis, serious King Vidor, and happy-go-lucky Slickum. Goodbye to my Dartmouth co-sponsors, the pipe-smoking, pretentious Walter Wanger, who tilted with Father, and Gene Markey, the free-spirited and nifty writer. Goodbye to the RKO accounting office, which kept me waiting a full month to the very last day for my $1,500. Goodbye to our loft of racing pigeons whose bloodlines had gone out of control under the careless neglect of our little brothers; goodbye to Eddie and Peggy, king and queen of our loft, whose thoroughbred squabs were never to be trained or raced again. Goodbye to Lucille the cook and Lloyd the tall black chauffeur. Goodbye to the Dusenberg. Goodbye to Windsor Square playmates, Buddy Lesser the sweet and timid son of the *Tarzan* producer and Fred Funk, already college-football material, who explained to me that two snails stuck together in our garden were doing something other than fighting. Goodbye with a half-serious little kiss from Sidney Fox, over at Universal shooting *Once in a Lifetime* with Jack Oakie. "Be a good boy, Buddy, study hard," said Sidney Fox. To which Jack Oakie added, "And maybe next year we'll send Manny Cohen to Dartmouth and put *you* in the sunken office." Goodbye to Mrs. Stanton at U.S.C., to whom I had put off admitting that I felt over my head with *Judge Lynch.* Goodbye to my Siamese twin Maurice.

In the year ahead, we solemnly assured each other, we confronted three great challenges: We would have to get laid—it was simply too embarrassing to face sophisticated Al Mannheimer's contempt any longer; we would have to make a place for ourselves on our respective campus newspapers; and we would have to earn athletic letters.

A last swim together at Malibu. A last tomcod reeled in from the end of the rickety pier. A last talk with Mother in her office full of chintz and Queen Anne furniture, and decorated with photo blowups of the $5,000-a-week stars she represented. Goodbye to Henrietta Cohn, Father's loyal, feisty secretary still there from the old New York-Paramount days. And finally, goodbye to Father in his new bungalow-office set apart from the long, yellow-brown-stucco administration building on Marathon Street. I hoped that *Madame Butterfly* with his untested Cary Grant would live up to his high expectations. (It didn't.)

A respite if not goodbye to the Sidney debate. But never goodbye to debate in general. Not much good at tennis or Ping-Pong, Father loved the volley of the mind, a happy warrior of verbal dispute. A lifelong "Al Smith Democrat," he said he hated to agree with arch-Republican L.B. but it was beginning to look as if Hoover would make it again. I despised the incumbent and liked the voice of Governor Roosevelt on the radio. "New Deal" sounded good. It promised innovations: federal power projects on the Columbia and Tennessee Rivers to give the private utilities new challenges they'd have to measure up to—government help for farmers being choked off their land by mortgage payments—old-age and unemployment insurance. . . .

Addicts of Gilbert and Sullivan, Maurice and I had sung together, "Oh every boy and every gal/Who comes into this world alive/Is either a little Liberal/Or else a little Conservative. . . ."

Duzie or no Duzie, I was a little Liberal. Heading for Hanover, my mind was about as empty a vessel as ever needed to be filled. I had yet to read Veblen's *Theory of the Leisure Class*. Hell, I *was* the leisure class. But those breadlines made me nervous. I saw the layoffs at the studio and the threat to cut company payrolls in half.

"Tell you what I'll do with you," Father said as we argued the coming election. "You like Roosevelt, I still think Hoover'll win—I'll lay you three hundred dollars to your hundred." I was afraid to gamble a hundred. "Make it a hundred to thirty-five." Even those stakes were too high for me. Father was disappointed. "After all, you can afford it, you've got your own money now. The RKO check."

"Mother's buying five stocks with it—Western Union, Westinghouse Electric, Macy's, Woolworth's, and DuPont."

"Typical, typical. Well, you worked for it, you ought to have a little fun with your money." He paced up and down, twirling his silver watch chain around his long, slender fingers. "But don't listen to me. Mother is right." He looked at me and smiled sadly. "Your mother is always right."

"I'll bet five bucks on Roosevelt," I said, "against your fifteen."

"It's a bet." Father put out his hand. "My fifteen to your five. And I hope I lose. We could all use a new deal."

The entire Schulberg-Jaffe family, complete with entourage, Father's pals, Mother's young assistant Charley Feldman, Maurice, Leon Becker and Elaine, one great happy-and-not-so-happy family, were at the old Santa Fe station to see me off. I had a suitcase full of current novels and the resolve to read two a day until I got to New York. Fearful of what lay ahead, I was already homesick for Malibu and Lorraine.

But as the train began to pull out and I leaned from the Pullman platform to wave and keep waving, I could see Mother standing to one side with Sonya and Stuart, Father standing apart, waving his cigar, and I knew that never again would there be a home in Windsor Square or a Malibu beach house where all of us would be living together. I watched the group, all thirty of them, my loving, envious, conflicted extended family, fall away, as seen through the lens of a camera slowly irising down to a small circle, a dot, to nothing.

The eastern border of the orange groves had always marked the boundary between my homeland and the outside world. When I reached it I picked up my diary and wrote, as if sending myself a telegram, "Goodbye to Home Sweet Hollywood. New page ahead. . . ."

Index

500

von Sternberg, Joseph, 220, 241-44, 265, 275-79, 291, 318, 451
von Stroheim, Erich, 51, 121, 139, 149-50, 153-54, 212, 215-21

Warner Brothers, 204
Warner, Jack, 292, 360
Wayne, John (stage name), 134, 202, 365-66
Wellman, William (Wild Bill), 265-66, 269-71
West, Mae, 487
Wilkerson, Billy (publisher), 144-45, 479-80
Wilma (governess), 44-47, 188, 281-83
Wings, 236, 265-71, 275

Wolfe, Thomas, 396
Wright, William Lord (writer), 18-19
Wurtzel, Sol, 449-50, 455

Young, Clara Kimbell, 63, 69, 100
Young, Felix (producer), 305-6, 373-74, 380, 431, 443, 463

Zanuch, Darryl, 301-2
Zeidman, Benny (writer), 481-82
Zeleznick, L. J. *See* Selznick, L. J.
Zukor, Adolph, 8, 11, 25-34, 36-40, 43, 48-50, 57-58, 60-61, 65-69, 71-75, 98, 187-88, 270-71, 350, 357, 376, 391-92, 486
Zukor, Lottie, 32, 54